DAYS OF GOLD

MALCOLM J. ROHRBOUGH

Days of Gold

The California Gold Rush
and the American Nation

UNIVERSITY OF CALIFORNIA PRESS

BERKELEY   LOS ANGELES   LONDON

University of California Press
Berkeley and Los Angeles, California

University of California Press, Ltd.
London, England

First Paperback Printing 1998

Library of Congress Cataloging-in-Publication Data

Rohrbough, Malcolm J.
    Days of gold : the California Gold Rush and the
American nation / Malcolm J. Rohrbough.
        p.   cm.
    Includes bibliographical references and index.
    ISBN 0-520-21659-8 (pbk. : alk. paper)
    1. California—Gold discoveries. I. Title.
F865.R655 1997
979.4'.01—dc20   96-34836
                                        CIP

Printed in the United States of America
9 8 7 6 5 4 3 2 1

The paper used in this publication meets the minimum
requirements of American National Standard for
Information Sciences—Permanence of Paper for Printed
Library Materials, ANSI Z39.48-1984.

This book is for
Martha Fraser Rohrbough
(1905–1993)
in memory

"And I often grieve and pine,
For the days of old,
The days of gold,
The days of forty-nine"

"The Days of Forty-nine"
California Gold Rush Song

CONTENTS

ACKNOWLEDGMENTS

This book began at the Henry E. Huntington Library and Art Gallery, where I held a Huntington–National Endowment for the Humanities Fellowship in 1986 and 1987. The Huntington is a wonderful place to begin a new book or to work on an old one. It provides, in almost unlimited quantities, rich manuscripts, varied landscapes, and a forum for the exchange of ideas. Martin Ridge, then Director of Research (now Director Emeritus), has made the Huntington a gathering place for historians of the American West and it was in these unofficial seminars that the outlines of this book took shape. In creating this medium of exchange, Martin was ably supported by Robert Middlekauff, then Director of the Library and Art Gallery. My intellectual debts begin with these two scholars and facilitators.

A vital intellectual dimension of my experience at the Huntington was the continuing counsel of the late Rodman W. Paul. The author of *California Gold*, the standard history of the Gold Rush for a generation, Rodman Paul took time from his own work to discuss my approach to the Gold Rush. As I struggled to make sense of the infinite dimensions of this extraordinary series of events, he offered constant advice and encouragement. His death in April 1987 deprived the profession of a model scholar and his friends of a wonderful man. I like to think that he would have approved of this book.

In addition to support from the Huntington Library and the National Endowment for the Humanities, I have received generous financial assistance from the University of Iowa in the form of two Developmental Assignments. The Graduate College at the University of Iowa has also provided me with research assistants, and I am grateful to the College and to the graduate students who worked on this project, namely, Peter Ellen, Jennifer J. Jacobsen, and Kathy Penningroth.

In the course of writing several drafts, I benefited from the facilities available to scholars at the National Humanities Center (Research Triangle Park, North Carolina) and the Institute for Advanced Study (Princeton, New Jersey).

Sarah Hanley and Leslie Schwalm of the University of Iowa and Stephen Aron of Princeton University read the entire manuscript; Laurie Maffly-Kipp of the University of North Carolina, Chapel Hill, and Brian Roberts of Rutgers University read substantial portions. All offered useful criticism and suggestions.

As my work on the Gold Rush spread eastward, I incurred many scholarly debts to individuals and institutions across the continent and eventually in Europe. I am indebted for professional assistance to the librarians and staff of the Alabama Department of Archives and History in Montgomery; the Bancroft Library at the University of California, Berkeley; the California State Library in Sacramento; the Coloma History Center; the California State Library in Sacramento; the Holt-Atherton Special Collections at the University of the Pacific; Special Collections at the California State Library, Chico; the Library at the University of Colorado, Boulder; the Beinecke Library at Yale University; the Library of Congress, Washington, D.C.; the Chicago Historical Society; the Margaret I. King Library at the University of Kentucky; the Massachusetts Historical Society; the Beverly Historical Society of Beverly; the Nantucket Historical Association; the Widener Library at Harvard University; Special Collections in the Clarke Library at Central Michigan University, Mount Pleasant; the Minnesota Historical Society, St. Paul; the North Carolina Department of Archives and History, Raleigh; the Perkins Library at Duke University; and Southern Historical Collection in the Library of the University of North Carolina, Chapel Hill; the Rhode Island Historical Society, Providence; the Oregon Historical Society, Portland; and the Archives Nationales and the Bibliothèque Nationale in Paris.

I have incurred other debts to friends and colleagues. I should like to mention particularly Peter Blodgett and other manuscript librarians at the Huntington Library and Jennifer Watts for assistance in finding illustrations; John N. Schacht and Robert McCown of the University of Iowa Libraries, for keeping me abreast of the bibliography of the Gold Rush; Kenneth Scheffel of the Michigan Historical Collections in the Bentley Library for help on many occasions; George Miles at the Beinecke Library in Yale University, for assistance in mining its rich collections; a valued colleague, Peter T. Harstad of the Indiana Historical Society, for his aid; Alfred L. Bush, Curator of the Rollins Collection of Western Americana in the Princeton University Library, for his encouragement; Walter Nugent, my colleague in various scholarly enterprises, for advice that was always on the mark.

I received a special measure of assistance in many forms from John Cumming of Central Michigan University. His Cumming Press printed many of the important documents of the Gold Rush in Michigan; his initiative in collecting Gold Rush manuscripts for the Clarke Library has made it a significant repository for scholars; and his generosity in opening his own personal library to me was a model of scholarly collegiality.

Alice Hutchins and Donald Kelly gave me manuscript materials for use in this book. I am indebted to them for sharing a part of their past with me.

I also owe an intellectual debt of gratitude to Richard Butsch, Eva Baron, William Deverell, Harwood P. Hinton, Robert V. Hine, Donald Kelly, and Bonnie Smith. All listened to and supported this project in many ways over several years.

Sheila Levine of the University of California Press has been patient in waiting for this manuscript and unfailingly optimistic about the final result. Scott Norton and Bud Bynack have made this a better book in many ways. I am indebted to all three.

Finally, I wish to thank Peter Rohrbough, Justin Rohrbough, Elizabeth Rohrbough, Lynn Madden, Antonius Gardeniers, Kathleen Madden Williams, Gerald Williams, Mark Hanley Madden, and Beverly Nalbandian Madden. All have listened to endless stories about the Gold Rush with patience and humor. Caitlin, Frances, Eva, Devon, Maya, Julia, Charlie, and Christina have their own stories to tell.

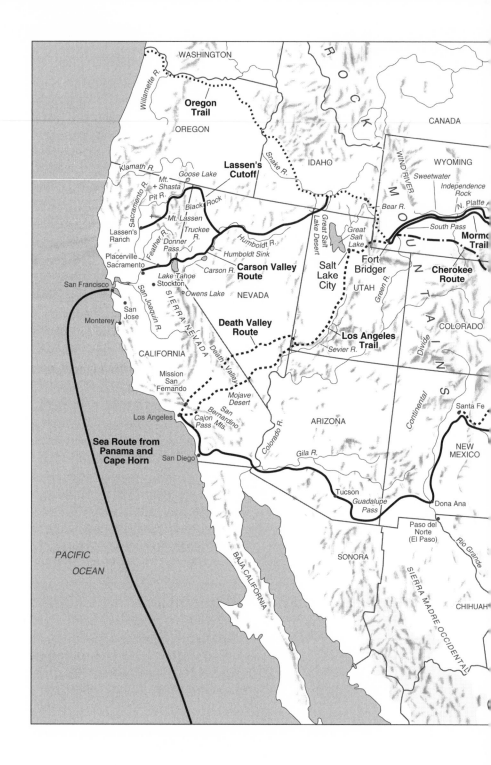

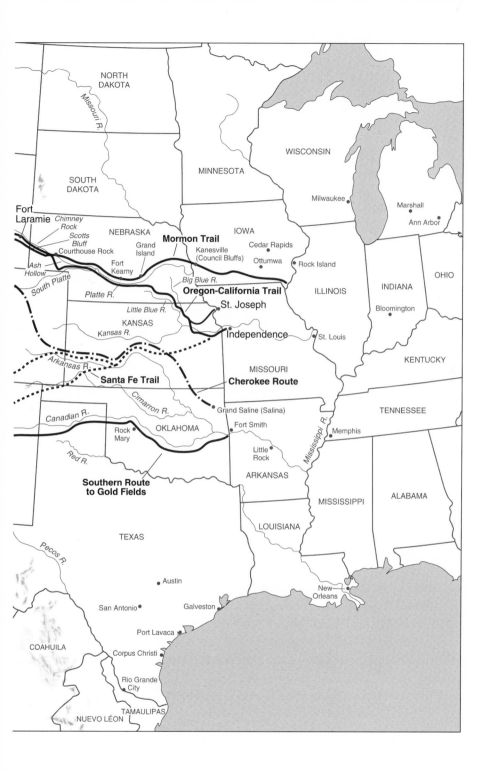

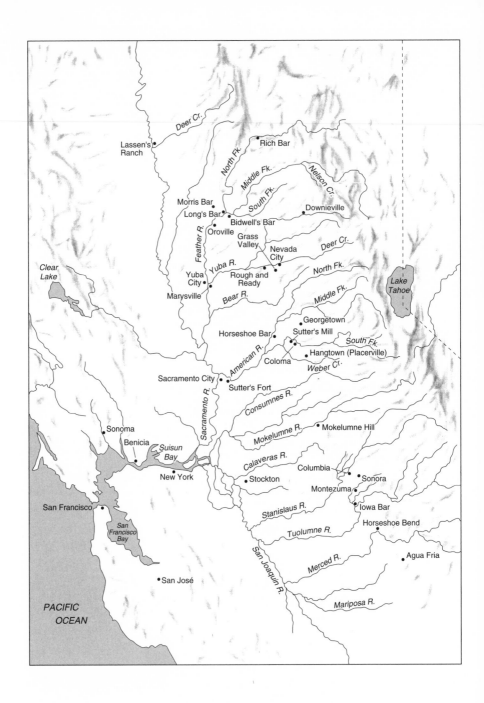

Deer Cr.

Lassen's
Ranch

Rich Bar

North Fk.

Middle Fk.

Nelson Cr.

South Fk.

Morris Bar
Long's Bar
Bidwell's Bar
Oroville

Downieville

Grass
Valley
Nevada
City

Deer Cr.

Feather R.

Yuba R.

Yuba
City
Rough and
Ready

Marysville

North Fk.

Clear
Lake

Bear R.

Middle Fk.

Lake
Tahoe

Georgetown
Horseshoe Bar
Sutter's Mill

American R.

Coloma

Hangtown (Placerville)

South Fk.

Weber Cr.

Sacramento City

Sutter's Fort

Sacramento R.

Consumnes R.

Sonoma

Benicia
Suisun
Bay

Mokelumne R.

Mokelumne Hill

New York

Calaveras R.

Columbia

San Francisco

Stockton

Montezuma

Sonora

San
Francisco
Bay

Stanislaus R.

Iowa Bar

Horseshoe Bend

Tuolumne R.

San José

Merced R.

Agua Fria

PACIFIC
OCEAN

San Joaquin R.

Mariposa R.

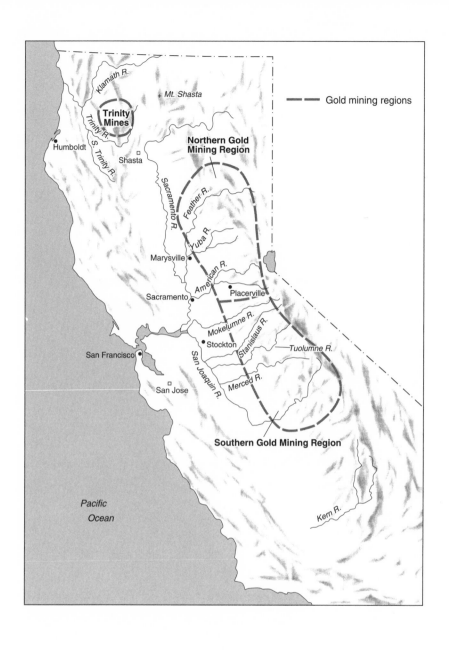

INTRODUCTION

THIS BOOK IS an introduction to the California Gold Rush.

The word "introduction" is used deliberately as a way of indicating the size and complexity of the subject. The discovery of gold in John Sutter's millrace at about ten o'clock in the morning of January 24, 1848, set in motion the people and events that we know as the California Gold Rush. The discovery and the subsequent spread of the news across the continent launched hundreds of ships and hitched up a thousand prairie schooners. The three-masted vessels departed from the ports of Boston, New York, and Philadelphia, and farther to the south, from Wilmington, Charleston, and New Orleans. The overland schooners embarked from county-seat towns and villages across the breadth of the nation, from the subsistence farms of the Ohio River valley to the great plantations of the lower Mississippi River valley. Those who joined the procession—in 1849 and annually thereafter for a dozen years—embraced every class, from the wealthy to those in straitened circumstances, from every state and territory, including slaves brought by their owners. In numbers, it represented the greatest mass migration in the history of the Republic, some eighty thousand in 1849 alone and probably three hundred thousand by 1854—an immigration largely male and generally young, but not exclusively either—by land across a continent and over thousands of miles of ocean to new and heretofore unimagined wealth.

The consequences of the California Gold Rush were vast and far-reaching. Like a stone dropped into a deep pool, the impact of the discovery of gold spread outward in ever-widening circles to touch the lives of families and communities everywhere in the Republic. For those who went to California, the decision to go raised questions about marital obligations and family responsibilities in which the opportunity for wealth was measured against prolonged absences that imposed new duties, often with reduced resources. For those who remained on the farm or in the shop, its impact was no less profound, for the absences of tens of thousands of men over a period of years led to the reshaping of a thousand communities across the breadth of the American nation.

When the impact on families and communities is totaled up, the Gold Rush emerges as a shared national experience, not simply an incident in California's history. In its repercussions, it was the most significant event in the first half of the nineteenth century, from Thomas Jefferson's purchase of Louisiana in the autumn of 1803 to South Carolina's secession from the Union in the winter of 1860. No other series of events produced so much movement among peoples; called into question so many basic values—marriage, family, work, wealth, and leisure; led to so many varied consequences; and left such vivid memories among its participants.

The opportunities associated with the search for gold in 1848 and the next dozen years lay in the context of other work that Americans regularly performed at midcentury. It was a world in which editors, elected officials, ministers, and other public figures still praised the American experience for its economic democracy, as exemplified by the continuing, widespread availability of land as a basis of economic advantage and national equality. Whatever the opportunities associated with land ownership, the work was hard. Farm families, who had assured title to 80 or 160 acres or even more, labored long hours in the fields for the return of a few hundred dollars each year. Growing numbers of working people had left the countryside and small towns for jobs in small factories and shops in emerging urban centers, where they increasingly had lost control of their work conditions in a new economic system that had begun to impose itself on this predominantly rural landscape. The California Gold Rush offered to men and women accustomed to endless hard and repetitive labor over a lifetime in the fields, shops, or small factories in pursuit of a modest freehold estate the economic opportunity that the nation was supposed to represent.

At the same time that it promised wealth, the Gold Rush assumed a form that spoke to American values at midcentury: an image of instant success available through hard work; an affirmation of democratic beliefs under which the wealth would be available to all; the discovery of gold as a logical and inevitable closure to a war that established a continental nation. The discovery of gold in 1848 and its widespread availability to Americans everywhere thus seemed to represent a reincarnation of the American dream, the promise of advantages unknown to their predecessors and of success for themselves and their posterity. The search for gold in California became the ultimate example of economic democracy: anyone with a pick, pan, and shovel could participate, at least in the early years, regardless of wealth, social standing, education, or family name.

The Argonauts—for so they were called by a nation that still knew and valued classical references—went west for something real. Among the most astounding features of the California Gold Rush was that the most outrageous stories of wealth were true. The Golden State—it would join the Union in 1850—produced a seemingly endless flood of gold. While agricultural farm laborers earned a dollar a day for twelve hours of work in the fields, and skilled artisans and craftsmen perhaps a dollar and a half for the same hours, men who were recently farmers and mechanics made sixteen dollars a day washing gravel in the streambeds of California's Sierra foothills. In the six years from 1849 to 1855, the Argonauts harvested some three hundred million dollars in gold from California.[1]

These are aggregate numbers. We might usefully here make reference to some individuals. In November 1847, Eddin Lewis, one of the most prominent farmers in Sangamon County, Illinois, with the help of hired laborers to whom he paid a dollar a day, butchered 255 hogs and shipped 6,000 pounds of barreled pork and lard south to the Mississippi River market early in 1848. From pork and lard, as well as from the sale of live hogs, several sides of beef, and 350 bushels of corn, Lewis recorded in his journal a cash income of over three hundred and fifty dollars for the year 1847.[2]

In the fall of 1850, some two thousand miles to the west, C. C. Mobley noted in his diary that in the previous week he and the members of his company had averaged thirty-five dollars a day or two hundred and five dollars each for the week, and the week before, twenty-five dollars a day, or one hundred and fifty dollars each. Mobley and his companions had, in two weeks, with a pick, pan, and shovel, each made as much cash money as one of the wealthiest citizens of Sangamon County after building his farm for a generation. Mobley wrote that his fortnight's labor "was doing a fair business. I am perfectly satisfied with it at all events."[3] He should have been. And it should not surprise us that so many attempted to emulate his example.

During the dozen years from the discovery of gold to the secession of South Carolina and the firing on Fort Sumter, the social and economic effects of the California Gold Rush prompted an examination of national standards and values. It posed issues of class and wealth in America's supposedly democratic and egalitarian society; it introduced questions about gender, with traditional roles and expectations for women juxtaposed against new and changing circumstances; and it quickly emphasized the presence of many different races and ethnic groups, for California, originally home to Native Americans and the Californios of Spanish and Mexican heritage, soon became the destination of peoples from across this hemisphere, Europe, and Asia.

Because the California Gold Rush was about wealth and its acquisition, it inevitably posed questions about the nature of wealth in America, how Americans acquired wealth, what they thought about wealth, and the relationship between wealth and family position. It delved into the deepest recesses of men's and women's expectations: their dreams for themselves and their families, their attitudes toward the present and past and visions of the future, and the relations of individuals to their families, their roles and responsibilities to siblings, parents, children, and spouses. This was a nation of outward democratic values that was already exhibiting signs of stratification. For many Americans, the discovery of gold in California offered the unheard-of opportunity to change their status and condition. The roster of Argonauts included men of wealth and position, who sought to buttress their status and realize advantage through investment, trade, and speculation; professional people, tradesmen, and merchants, many dogged by long-standing debts, who sought to clear their ledgers of failure and begin anew through the golden discoveries of a few months; as well as those from marginal economic backgrounds, who sought the economic advantage heretofore seemingly denied them, who with a few months' or years' work (and they were accustomed to hard work) might provide themselves and their children with the clothes, education, and privileges they never had enjoyed.

The 49ers ostensibly left home to seek wealth, but behind this professed motive—scarcely anyone could object to an expedition to pick up gold nuggets—lay a wide variety of unspoken motives.[4] For many participants, the voyage to California (whether by land or sea) was a declaration of independence. By their participation in this unique and distant adventure, they would establish their separate identities; the venture would distance them from the influence of their parents, especially in the case of younger sons, whose prospects at home were minimal and who perhaps could expect treatment in like proportion. At the same time, whatever their inner feelings or the circumstances of their partings, most 49ers displayed much concern for maintaining contact with their families and communities and for retaining the good opinion of both. One of the themes that runs through accounts of the Gold Rush is the anxiety among the 49ers over how their successes or failures would affect their reputations among their families, friends, and communities in the East.

The discovery of gold and the response to these accounts were closely linked to a place, in this case a range of foothills, with its canyons and streambeds, on the other side of the continent. The Gold Rush introduced the nation to California, a remote and exotic prize of the recent war against Mexico. Images of California now flowed with increasing frequency into the national consciousness as this distant place became the home (albeit temporarily) to members of the nation's families and communities. The news about California came initially from official sources, but over the next decade, spreading the word became the work of individual correspondents and small-town newspapers. Within a few years, Americans everywhere knew about California through the first-hand reports of their friends and neighbors.

From these many attempts to describe California emerged the shadowy outlines of a place that was at once familiar in its increasingly American institutions and presence and, at the same time, alien in terms of its physical landscape, its native peoples, its values, and its several varied societies. In these fleeting images, California emerged as a new world that simultaneously beckoned and threatened. The opportunities to make money, 49ers agreed, were beyond imagination. But the different values and the siren song of the life of the gentle climate mixed with the continuing search for riches also provoked fears. These same qualities might exert a powerful hold on the displaced Argonauts, and families and communities in the East found themselves forced to confront the increasing attractions of this remote place, even as the economic opportunities associated with it became gradually more uncertain.

Surrounded by opportunities to make fortunes—or so they were represented in the local press across the nation—it later became difficult for the 49ers to explain how they had squandered such golden chances. As the prospects for individuals to make substantial fortunes declined and all but disappeared with the passage of time, the search for dramatic economic advantage demanded increasing justification—to themselves, to their families, and to their communities. In the end, thousands of Argonauts soldiered on in remote gold fields in the face of repeated failures. Many returned empty-handed, others not at all. But for many, the decision to return to their families and communities became entwined with a sense of personal failure. The years that stretched out through the decade of the 1850s left the 49ers discouraged, disillusioned, embarrassed to have to admit their own shortcomings. The idea of failure and unfulfilled dreams became as much a part of the California Gold Rush as the large strikes reported in the local newspapers.

The California Gold Rush began with blazing headlines, sermons preached on the departure of companies of Argonauts, and parades to the waterfront with singing and shouting, the creak of a thousand wagons and the echoing stamp of teams of harnessed mules and oxen, all in response to a few golden flakes that emerged from the American River on a sunny and chilly January morning. It ended with a few men with long beards and brown complexions tramping down streets of towns they once knew well, with occasional accountings of money borrowed and interest paid, and finally with a deep and prolonged silence. Many never returned. They simply vanished into a California landscape once golden and now simply remote. Or the rush for gold ended with aging brothers and uncles writing from distant addresses in California, or Oregon, or Washington, sometimes with a family known only through daguerreotypes and letters, sending an annual letter to their cousins and distant kin in the East. The Gold Rush sometimes led to permanent separation and hard feelings, and almost always to a sense of loss. The older generation lamented the permanent absence of a husband or brother; the younger generation no longer recognized the names mentioned around the dining table or in the parlor on Sunday afternoons after church.

The Gold Rush survived in the varied memories of the participants. Men and women carried vivid recollections of the California Gold Rush for the next half century. For some men, it was the most significant adventure of their lives, a moment of camaraderie and companionship, of adventure and independence, before they returned to the family, marriage, farm, trade, or commerce that dominated the rest of their lives. For some families, the memories remained bittersweet. The departure of the 49ers marked the disappearance of a beloved relative or friend, or perhaps of a whole branch of the family that went West to join a 49er. It was the symbol of permanent separation, which marked the family and community with the divisions that emerged from the Gold Rush. For many, it lingered in anniversaries of departure and return, anniversaries repeated on a larger scale within communities. A final manifestation of such nostalgia was the departure in 1890 of a chartered passenger train of some twenty cars, bound from Boston to California. There, at camp after camp, the aging 49ers revisited the scenes of their youth, when they had ranged across the Sierra in a hunt for gold, and attempted to explain to their grandchildren the experiences that bound them together with memories that only had strengthened in the intervening forty years. Matching such grand occasions were the occasional notices in papers seeking word of family and friends who long since had vanished into the haze of the golden West. Whatever the memories, the search for gold in California cast a long shadow for its participants, one that mixed vivid memories of youth with the search for fabulous wealth. Whether returned, moved permanently to California, or vanished, the 49ers, along with their families, and their communities, were not the same again. Nothing was ever the same again.

1

CALIFORNIA'S GOLDEN REVOLUTION:

Enormous Wealth and Great Confusion

"It was the work of but a few weeks to bring almost the entire population
of the territory together to pick up pieces of precious metal.
The result has been, that in less than four months, a total revolution has
been effected in the prospects and fate of Alta California. Then, capital was
in the hands of a few individuals engaged in trade and speculation;
now labor has got the upper hand of capital, and the laboring men
hold the great mass of wealth in the country—the gold."

THE SAN FRANCISCO *CALIFORNIAN*, AUGUST 14, 1848

ON MONDAY, JANUARY 24, 1848, at about ten o'clock in the morning, James W. Marshall, employed by the entrepreneur John Sutter to construct a sawmill on the American River, picked some flakes of mineral out of the tailrace. Marshall immediately identified these particles as gold—"Boys, by God I believe I have found a gold mine" was his oft-quoted pronouncement—and later, primitive tests confirmed his judgment. Over the next decade, Marshall's discovery would have a powerful effect on the experiences and expectations of hundreds of thousands of individual Americans, their families, and their communities, and through them it would influence the history of California and the American nation.[1]

The peoples of California—American Indians, the Californios, and the more recently arrived Americans and Europeans—first felt its impact. The world of Mexican California and the events leading up to the discovery of gold in January 1848 are simple, straightforward, and easy to describe; those that followed are none of these things. California society in 1848 was at once decentralized, independent, and deferential. The decentralized nature of this world reflected its direct but casual ties to Mexico City as a part of the Republic of Mexico, a relationship of salutary neglect strongly reminiscent of the same kind of lingering cultural connections that had existed during three centuries of the Spanish Empire, or in the case of California, for three-quarters of a century, since the European occupation of California itself may be dated from the establishment of the mission at San Diego in 1769. Largely independent of outside control, internally, California society was both structured and deferential. Substantial landowners, church leaders, and government officials commanded respect and obedience.

With the success of Mexico's revolution and the creation of an independent nation in 1821, a score of prominent families took over the resources and leadership roles formerly exercised by the churches and soldiers through the Spanish missions. With the secularization of the missions, beginning in 1833, the influence of these families—often interconnected by marriage—and of the scattered government officials increased. The authority of the central government in Mexico City was felt only lightly by the seaboard settlements from San Diego to San Francisco. Although the great estates of these families sometimes stretched into the central valleys, the society of Mexican California lived along the sea, where lay its contacts with the outside world. Small but thriving ports of call like Monterey and San Diego provided a modest urban presence and a sense of trade and activity. The vast interior was sparsely occupied by Indian peoples and the occasional European entrepreneur, of whom the grandest in reach, style, and ambition was the Swiss emigrant John Sutter, whose fort, standing near the intersection of the American and Sacramento Rivers, was the center of Euro-American population in the interior. Sutter grazed large herds of cattle, sheep, and horses in the valleys in what would shortly become the center of the Gold Rush country.

At the time of the discoveries, the European population of Alta California, as it was known, was on the order of thirteen thousand, about evenly divided between native Californios and North Americans, with a few hundred Europeans and Hawaiian Islanders. Most of the North Americans had come within the previous decade, and many of the recent arrivals were part of the American military invasion that accompanied the outbreak and subsequent campaigns of the Mexican War. San Francisco, situated on a great harbor with perhaps eight hundred residents, was an important town, governed as were other towns by an alcalde (mayor). North Americans already dominated San Francisco trade and politics. The significant towns for native Californios were Monterey, a center of Mexican influence, and San Jose, with a population of about seven hundred.[2] Such tiny numbers spread across a range of eight hundred miles and concentrated in a few former missions and presidios further emphasized the sparseness of the European population. At the same time, the Indian peoples within California outnumbered the Europeans by some ten to one. That they were concentrated in the northwest and the foothills of the Sierra, the center of future mining activity, ensured that they would feel the brunt of the worldwide invasion over the next decade.[3]

PASTORAL

The news of Marshall's discovery of gold spread outward from the millrace on the American River, but it spread unevenly, for Sutter tried to keep the news secret, and many who heard the news doubted its veracity. In March, a trickle of immigration to the gold fields—if they may be so termed after so brief a period—began from Sutter's Fort at the location of the present city of Sacramento. The decisive impetus to the movement of people turned out to be the sight of gold itself. Walter Colton, the alcalde of Monterey, wrote in June: "My messenger sent to the mines has returned with specimens of gold; he dismounted in a sea of upturned faces."[4] People went to the gold fields from San Francisco and Sonoma in May, from Monterey and San Jose in May and June, and from Mexican communities of the south in July and August.

The first groups to hear the news and the first to respond to it in numbers were the native Californios. The summer and fall of 1848 presented an idyllic, almost pastoral view of individuals and families camped alongside streams harvesting gold through the most rudimentary techniques, a vision of Arcadian harmony set off against the occasional examples of exploitation in which large numbers of Indian peoples worked the streams for little or nothing, a promise of harsher things to come. This first season of the California Gold Rush was often a family enterprise in which men returned to their families for periodic visits or brought their families with them to the streams.

The Americans soon appeared. Thomas O. Larkin, appointed "consul" by the American government in 1844, described the living and working arrangements along the American River in his correspondence with Secretary of State James Buchanan. "At my camping place I found on a surface of two or three miles on the banks of the river some fifty tents, mostly owned by Americans," he wrote. "These had their families."[5] It was instructive that in the first year of the Gold Rush, Larkin found the growing numbers of Americans in the mines worthy of note in an area chiefly occupied by Californios. In subsequent years, American dominance in the mines in numbers and influence would come to be taken for granted.

The movement toward the gold fields gathered mass and momentum through the summer of 1848. By July, when Colonel Richard B. Mason toured the placers, the mountain watercourses of central California were a beehive of activity. Small groups dug in the streams for eighteen hours a day and then moved overnight to new discoveries. These people were unskilled, transient, and above all energetic. The strength of the movement toward the gold fields varied according to the reports from the placers, although it eventually involved every male in central California who could move or be carried, and the ease with which people could jettison their present commitments, whether professional or personal, and depart for the mines. Those with much personal independence, such as ranchers, small merchants, or day laborers, found the decision an easy one; those with ongoing institutional obligations, such as soldiers, sailors, or officials of the government at whatever level, found it far more difficult to abandon their duties. That almost all eventually did so is a tribute to the lure of gold and the growing accounts of early successes on the part of the first miners.[6]

A GAME WITHOUT RULES

Marshall's discovery found California in a political vacuum. War between the United States and Mexico had begun in the spring of 1846, and California was immediately a military objective, especially its harbors. The campaigns quickly concluded with the American occupation of strategic places, after which California lapsed into an institutional void in which one kind of institutional structure (Mexican) was in the process of being replaced by another (American), but only under guidelines that would be outlined in the treaty of peace.

The former Mexican state was still a part of a war zone in the sense that it was governed by military authority and by a military governor, Colonel Mason, who was also commander of the American military forces.[7] Under Mason's military government, the roster of individuals, offices, and cultural affiliation reflected the mixture of Mexican and American, civil and military, including (among others) Mason; Larkin, the United States consul for California; and the alcaldes of the several towns—Mexican officials of local government with varied power and authority to "maintain order, punish crimes, and redress injuries."[8]

The discovery of gold raised a range of issues about the ground rules by which gold might be mined and order preserved. Basic questions needed to be answered. To whom did the gold belong? What were the rules under which it could be found and kept? What laws of the United States and Mexico were applicable to the gold region and to what extent and in what ways should officials attempt to enforce these rules? Were the provisions of the Ordinance of 1785, which reserved for the U.S. government one-third of the gold, silver, lead, or copper found in the public domain, applicable? The entire process of laying down some kind of institutional structure had to be done quickly in order to maintain public order, and the rules had to be easily understood by all, perceived as generally fair, and rapidly and widely promulgated.

As we will see when we look at the emergence of new Gold Rush communities and societies in more detail, these goals were not all easily attained. When Colonel Mason sent back a report on the discovery of gold in California to the Adjutant General in Washington, he knew full well that the report could trigger gold fever, and he tried to give advice on how the government might cope with it:

> One plan I would suggest is to send out from the United States surveyors, with high salaries, bound to serve specific periods; a superintendent to be appointed at Sutter's Fort, with power to grant licenses to work a spot of ground say 100 yards square, for one year, at a rate of from $100 to $1000, at his discretion; the surveyors to measure the grounds and place the renter in possession.

On the other hand, he continued, "a better plan . . . would be to have the district surveyed and sold at public auction to the highest bidder, in small parcels, say from 20 to 40 acres. In either case, there will be many intruders, whom for years it will be almost impossible to exclude."[9] By the late summer of 1848, with only California itself in the grip of gold mania, so many people already had dispersed over so large an area that restraint through law or administrative proclamation was impossible except through widespread use of the United States Army. The miners in California already had adopted for their own use a long-standing principle espoused by trespassers in the East, that the land and its resources belong to those there on the spot and in physical possession of it. By the time Mason's report had reached officials in Washington, D.C., the situation was out of control, and the true Gold Rush had not yet begun.

The absence of rules was all the more significant because of the nature of the gold discoveries and the growing numbers of people that were involved. From the beginning—that is to say, from Marshall's discoveries onward—gold was readily accessible to the most inexperienced mining novice with the simplest and most inexpensive kinds of equipment. The first gold-mining techniques were simple. Gold was found in the nooks and crannies of old, dry streambeds and in the bottoms of existing watercourses, where it had been left by thousands of years' movement of water, which had carried the mineral downstream until the velocity of the water was insufficient to support the gold's weight. In turn, water was a crucial agent in early gold mining, as a force for separating the gold once again from the deposits around it. The first miners quickly mastered the primitive techniques by which moving water flowing through a tin pan would separate the lighter sand and gravel, which would be carried off by the force of the water, from the heavier gold particles, which would sink to the bottom of the pan, where they could be easily retrieved and stored in a small sack. All that was necessary to join the race for wealth was a shovel and a pan.[10] In fact, the most rudimentary Gold Rush technique simply involved digging around rocks with a knife and removing particles of gold with a spoon.

Furthermore, the search for gold was uninhibited by institutional authority. The authority of the Mexican government largely had disappeared in the aftermath of the peace treaty signed at Guadalupe Hidalgo in February 1848, which ceded California to the United States; the American government had yet to establish more than a military presence. Access to the rivers, streams, and valleys was, for all practical purposes, without limits. The issue of land ownership was in abeyance, for the land was open and largely unclaimed by Europeans, except for a few large grants, of which John Sutter's eleven square leagues was among the grandest. The California Indians were sufficiently weakened by two generations of the mission experience and the trauma associated with the destruction of the mission system after 1833 to offer little or no resistance.

Although open access to the gold in California seemed to represent the purest example of American economic democracy in the middle of the nineteenth century, from the beginning, some individuals and some groups did better than others. The distinctions were not entirely a matter of luck. They were, rather, a question of scale of operations.

These distinctions began early. Among the first miners who ascended the drainage basin of the Sierra in the spring of 1848, some were the owners of large land grants in the interior valleys, who brought with them the domesticated Indians or Mexican laborers working for them on their estates. With such labor forces, these first California mining entrepreneurs achieved a scale of production far beyond the capacity of individual miners. Others, attracted to the evident advantages of scale, employed Indians for wages paid in the form of blankets or shirts, food, or trinkets. Some Indians also mined independently for themselves, always at the sufferance of the Americans, who early adopted a proprietary attitude toward the mines, especially the best claims.

Although the first Gold Rush seemed to depend upon both luck and hard work, the American consul, Thomas O. Larkin, observed to his partners the advantages of a labor force in these terms: "I would advise you to extend your operations in every respect to obtain all the Indians on our farms or elsewhere that you can." And to a friend as early as June 3, following on the heels of his letter to the secretary of state confirming the size and impact of the gold discoveries, Larkin wrote:

> I can say to you, come to California, bring 100 Kanakas, 100 spades, shovels & picks with 100 wooden dishes and bowls—to up the Sacramento (I have 20 leagues there take a league), dig, delve and wash, turn up the bottom of the American Fork, dig down the banks of the Feather River, fill your barrels, take into your constitution the ague and fever, bury half your Kanakas, go back and make your . . . [homage] to John Jacob Astor.[11]

Charles Oliver Sterling, one of the first to mine with a large labor force, later commented to Larkin: "Altho' we have been rather unfortunate in our first attempt so far, we are all in good time yet . . . and when we get our Indians again & more than we had before we will drive things ahead." Sterling later noted that "if our Indians had not run away we would have had I think near 2000$ by this time." And Larkin himself wrote in mid-July to Secretary of State James Buchanan, "A few men who are working 30 to 40 Indians are laying up to 1000$ to 2000$ a week. One man told for this number he expected from 40 Indians $1 a minute, 10 hours in a day, 600$. None of these men had any property of consequence to commence with."[12] Thus, in a game without rules, a few entrepreneurs enriched themselves through their access to numbers of laborers.

Advances in mining techniques assisted those who did not have access to a large labor force. The new machine was the "rocker," or "cradle," used earlier in the gold mines of Georgia and North Carolina. The principle was the same as panning: to let the water do the work of separating the gold from the gravel. The difference was the economy and efficiency provided by a machine that would allow men to pool their labor into larger units. Governor Richard B. Mason found these machines in use as early as mid-June, with men working "in the full glare of the sun, washing for gold, some with tin pans, some with close-woven Indian baskets, but the greater part had a rude machine known as the cradle." He described the rudimentary machine in these terms: "This is on rockers six or eight feet long, open at the foot, and at its head has a coarse grate and sieve; the bottom is rounded with small cleets nailed across."[13]

William R. Ryan, an officer of the New York Volunteers, went to the gold fields immediately on his discharge in September 1848. He noted that the cradle "has often proved a bond of union between individuals who would otherwise have separated, for the simple reason, that one man could not work it half so profitably alone." It took four miners to operate it efficiently. The first dug the gravel from the riverbank or dry streambed; the second carried the gravel to the cradle and emptied it into the grate; the third poured water or directed water from the stream itself through the machine, and the fourth agitated a handle to produce the rocking motion that propelled the gravel through the machinery and out the lower end while it trapped the heavier gold nuggets or flakes in the cleats on the bottom. The pan and the cradle—both relying on the washing action of the water, both simple to purchase or easy to make from a few boards of lumber—provided the technology for the first two years of the California Gold Rush. The universal availability of both tools ensured that every prospective Argonaut could have access to the latest technology in the gold fields.[14]

Thus, the cradle threw men together in an economic alliance that forced cooperation among those who might have preferred solitary work. Sometimes miners would quarrel over where to mine and under what conditions, but the need to join together to use the cradle forced partnerships, however uneasy they may have been. These were the first gold companies. Larkin wrote of this presence in June: "Some have formed companies of four or five men and have a rough made machine put together in a day which works to much advantage."[15]

The early visitors to the foothills of the Sierra described a vast landscape with human occupation concentrated on a few streams emerging from the mountains. Governor Mason, who went in an official capacity, remarked on the contrast between the interior valleys ("Along the whole route mills were lying idle, fields of wheat were open to cattle and horses, houses vacant, and farms going to waste") and the lively nature of the camps themselves. Of the Mormon diggings, he noted that "the hill sides were thickly strewn with canvass tents and bush arbors. A store was erected, and several boarding shanties in operation."[16]

The first miners lived in makeshift shelters appropriate for what they thought of as a temporary residence. Peter H. Burnett, who came to California from Oregon in the summer of 1848, wrote from the camp near Long's Bar on the Yuba River in November of the "canvass tents and the cloth shanties of the miners. There was but one log-cabin in the camp. There were about eighty men, three women, and children at this place."[17] In the same vein, Ryan commented that the tents and huts of the miners on the

Stanislaus River were "all of the poorest and most wretched description." Miners expected to profit within a short time and then leave these primitive conditions and return to their homes. Ryan continued, "There were numerous tents, good, bad, and indifferent, stores and gambling booths, shanties and open encampments; and miners busy everywhere."[18]

Amid this jumble of living and working arrangements, miners worked with great intensity. Whether digging or washing, carrying dirt, or scouting out another mining site, they were constantly in motion. This frenzy reflected the random and quixotic character of the mining experience. Where was gold to be found in the largest quantities? How long would it be available to everyone? When and how might the rules be modified to limit the access of individuals? In short, these first miners acted as opportunities presented themselves, for it was not clear how long such extraordinary opportunities would last. So the response was intense, and the Sierra foothill streams were centers of activity, resounding from first light to dusk with the clang of picks and shovels against rock against a background of the roar of water and the glare of sunlight. Miners worked with a single-minded concentration, disliking the interruption of visitors, observers, and newcomers. In such a tumult of activity, miners had no time to bury the dead and barely paused in their work to assist in cases of illness or injury.

In the first Gold Rush of 1848, the entire range of gold-mining skills might be learned by instruction or observation in a few minutes, and a veteran miner was anyone who had been in the diggings for two days. Success as a miner seemed to depend less on skill in mining techniques than on a strong back and a stronger constitution. To locate the most likely places for digging and washing took a little longer, and it was here that veteran miners had a distinct advantage. This first cohort of gold miners were all amateurs, with the exception of a few experienced hands from the gold camps of North Carolina and Georgia.

Growing numbers—from five hundred miners in May 1848 to about five thousand miners by the end of the year—gradually introduced competition for space in the best mining places. The spaces between camps and individual miners diminished and then disappeared. Campsites and mining claims—heretofore available for the taking, easily acquired, worked, and discarded—gradually assumed specific boundaries. By the autumn of 1848, the definition of claims and their possession had become an important issue, and miners had begun to lay out their claims with care, establishing rules for their possession and creating procedures under which they might be vacated or sold. These arrangements were handled locally in individual camps. In mid-November 1848, E. Gould Buffum noted that on the Yuba River, where two hundred men worked on a short portion of the river, a claim was recognized when a miner "had cleared off the top soil from any portion of the bar." Claims belonged to those who worked them and occupied them physically. Upon his arrival in the mines from Oregon in the fall of 1848, Peter Burnett bought a claim, which he called "a mining location, fronting on the river about twenty feet, and reaching back to the foot of the hill about fifty feet."[19]

The last six months of gold mining in 1848 produced considerable confusion, much motion, and a large quantity of high-level energy and hard work. By its end, some of the basic outlines of mining had been established that would continue into the future. The pick, pan, and shovel were the basic tools; the cradle was the most useful machine. Mining was increasingly a cooperative enterprise. Although miners as a group were constantly in motion, mining itself involved a degree of permanence, and this condition soon led to the emergence of small towns, with stores, taverns, eateries, and boardinghouses. The best-producing (and so more permanent) camps had established rules for laying out and holding claims. Certain forms and rules finally had begun to take hold, and they would serve as guidelines for the next several months.

THE HIDALGO CLEANS HIS OWN BOOTS

The gold discoveries quickly transformed California's societies, changing the economy, social and economic relationships, and individual values, all in dramatic and fundamental ways. Thomas O. Larkin wrote in the spring of 1848, "A complete revolution in the ordinary state of affairs is taking place." Two months later, after a tour of the gold region, Governor Mason observed in the same vein, "The discovery of the vast deposits of gold has entirely changed the character of Upper California."[20]

The changes in California over a few short months were those characteristically associated with a plague or war. Larkin described the manifestations to the secretary of state, James Buchanan, in June 1848: three-quarters of the houses in San Francisco had been abandoned; every blacksmith, carpenter, and lawyer in the town had left for the mines; large numbers had deserted from the army in both San Francisco and Sonoma; crews had abandoned ships as soon as they anchored in San Francisco Bay; brickyards, sawmills, and ranches had been shut down by the absence of labor; the alcaldes of San Francisco and Sonoma had left to join the Gold Rush; newspapers had suspended publication for want of workingmen.[21] The result was the "total revolution" in society and its economic relations described by the editor of the San Francisco *Alta California*.

Before 1848, wealth in California generally had been defined by large landed estates with comfortable houses, by trade in hides and tallow through the small seaports, or by a particular trade or skill that was in demand. Gold rapidly transformed upper California into a gold-based cash economy. Goods and services were quoted in ounces of gold dust—visits to the doctor or lawyer were generally one ounce—and California rapidly changed from an economy without a circulating medium (the previous currency had been cowhides known as "California bank notes") to an economy rich in a circulating medium recognized around the world. Indeed, it was so rich that gold was sometimes discounted because it was more plentiful than goods that could be purchased. As early as August 1848, Governor Mason on a tour of the diggings reported, "Placer gold is now substituted as currency of this country; in trade it passes freely at $16 per ounce; as an article of commerce its value is not yet fixed."[22]

The prices of all goods and services rose in proportion to the new, enlarged circulating medium. E. Gould Buffum, the discharged lieutenant from the New York Volunteers, described a breakfast that he and a partner shared in a small boardinghouse near the mines. The men ate their fill of ordinary fare, and the bill for the two was forty-three dollars. The two men paid without question. Buffum apologized for the high cost and ruefully observed that the usual cost of breakfast in the mines was five dollars each. He did not mention (although he might have) that the same meal could be bought in San Francisco or Monterey or anywhere else in California for twenty-five cents six months earlier.[23]

In the mines, the flood of gold produced a new kind of economy and new relationships among people. Most miners had more money than ever before in their lives, yet they could find little or nothing to spend it on. Men who worked twelve hours a day in rushing water saw their pouches and glass vials of gold dust accumulate day by day, but for the moment, their lives remained unchanged. The high cost of provisions and tools ate into the piles of gold dust; the remainder (often substantial and sometimes astonishing) would buy nothing because there was nothing to buy. So men in the mines dressed alike because there were limited clothes to buy; they also lived in the same kinds of primitive housing, whether tents, brush cabins, or lean-tos, and they ate the same monotonous food.

These similarities and the general drabness of appearance in the mines could disguise what by the standards of the day could only be described as enormous wealth. The alcalde of Monterey, Walter Colton, described the changes in this way: "All distinctions indicative of means have vanished; the only capital required is muscle and honest purpose. I met a man today from the mines in patched buckskins rough as a badger from his hole, who had fifteen thousand dollars in yellow dust, swung on his back. Talk to him of broaches, gold headed canes, and Carpenter's coasts. Why he can unpack a lump of gold that would throw all Chestnut street into spasms."[24]

The accumulation of fortunes in the form of gold by substantial numbers of people established new ways of thinking about wealth. In this new world, gold was not slowly acquired over generations by hard work and influence. Instead, it lay on all sides, it was easily obtained and easily spent, and it seemed infinitely replenishable. Walter Colton, the alcalde, wrote about his servant, an Irishman named Bob. (It is instructive that in his account Colton did not dignify Bob with a last name; perhaps he never knew his last name.) Bob had worked many years for small wages. In the spring of 1848, he went to the mines for two months and returned to Monterey with two thousand dollars. Previously, he had saved his slim wages of a few dollars a week, except for 12-1/2 cents set aside for tobacco. In Colton's account, Bob now "took rooms and began to branch out; he had the best horses, the richest viands, and the choicest wines in the place." In questioning Bob about the changes in his spending habits, Colton alluded to the hard-earned wages that were still on account. "Oh, yes," replied Bob, "I have got that money yet; I worked hard for it; and the devil can't get it away; but the two thousand dollars came [e]asily by good luck, and has gone as [e]asily as it came."[25]

One of the immediate by-products of the discovery of gold for Californians was the disappearance of a servant class. Colton lamented his attempts, along with those of Governor Mason and a Lieutenant Lanman, to cook their own meals, for "our servants have run one after another, till we are almost in dispair . . . and this morning, for the first time, we had to take to the kitchen, and cook our own breakfast." Imagine, mused Colton, "a general of the United States Army, the commander of a man-of-war, and the Alcalde of Monterey, in a smoking kitchen, grinding coffee, toasting a herring, and peeling an onion!" He concluded of the flight of the servants to the mines: "These gold mines have upset all social and domestic arrangements in Monterey . . . the master has become his own servant, and the servant his own lord. The millionaire is obliged to groom his own horse, and roll his own wheelbarrow; and the hidalgo—in whose veins flows the blood of Cortes— to clean his own boots."[26]

To the increasing presence of wealth in the form of gold dust in the mining camps must be added the parallel absence of banks or any other kind of depository for such funds. These did not exist. So men lived in close proximity to one another, accumulating ever greater wealth, carrying their gold around on their person or leaving it in the campsite. Such arrangements demanded a high degree of mutual respect and honesty. That men lived and worked under such conditions of plentiful and open wealth was one of the unusual aspects of the first season of the Gold Rush.

In a world in which miners increasingly dressed alike and carried their gold around with them, dress disappeared as an arbiter of economic and social class. William R. Ryan described the way in which various representatives of the new California society came together on equal terms around a meal at Brannan's boardinghouse:

> We found assembled around an excellent fire a group of persons of the most opposite appearance and character, hard-fisted, unshaven, leather-coated miners, being seated side-by-side, and on terms of perfect equality, with well-dressed lawyers, surgeons, and mercantile men. The wondrous influence of gold seems to have entirely obliterated all social distinctions, and a general conversation was kept up, in which everyone, no matter how vaguely he expressed himself, had something to say, and was listened to with attention. In fact, it seemed as if a weather-beaten countenance and soiled and tattered attire formed one's chief claim to consideration. Besides, no one could judge of another's circumstance by his appearance, for it not infrequently happened that the most wretched looking and ill-clad persons were those who carried about them the largest share of this world's wealth.[27]

News of such wealth soon spread beyond California. What began with the movement of families of all stations to the placers and with their successes there, and what continued with the dislocation of the structure of traditional societies, ended with the inundation of this corner of the world by a massive immigration from the outside. The news of gold nuggets lying about the countryside and available to all, whatever their social and economic condition, rapidly set on foot an immigration that immediately numbered in the tens of thousands and eventually in the hundreds of thousands. The tremors of such activity moved invariably outward. In the autumn of 1848, the first distant gold seekers had appeared, from Oregon to the north and the Hawaiian Islands to the west, and from Mexico and Chile to the south. The following spring arrived the first immigration by sea from the eastern United States, and in the late summer and autumn, the first of the great annual overland migrations. Within a year, the small population of California—perhaps on the order of thirteen thousand at the time of Marshall's discovery—had been submerged by a foreign population eight times as large, and each successive annual immigration further inundated it.

By contrast with the mass immigrations of 1849 and subsequent years, the opening months of the Gold Rush emphasized informal arrangements in California societies oriented around extended families and small, tight-knit communities. Eventually, almost everyone in California went to the mines, from the governor and the alcaldes to draymen and servants—and there they dug, if not side by side, at least in close proximity to one another. The expulsion of the Indians and the Mexicans had not yet begun; discrimination against the French and Chileans was unknown; the hostility toward the Chinese lay in the future; and the banding together of Americans by region and ethnic group had not yet become a significant feature of living and working arrangements. This is not to say that the first short season of gold was without conflict. But the open spaces and general prosperity of the diggings seemed to work against prolonged physical confrontation, for the aggrieved party or parties could move elsewhere and achieve the same economic returns. However, tens of thousands of people were about to converge on the gold fields. The sometimes idyllic early days of California's golden revolution were about to end. When California discovered gold, the world discovered California. Willingly or not, as a consequence, Americans were about to learn some sobering and exhilarating truths about themselves.

2

GOLD FEVER:

The Beginning

*One June morning, when I was a boy, Captain Eben Latham came to our
house, and the first gossip he unloaded was that "them stories about finding
gold in Californy was all true." The report slumbered
during the summer in our village, but in the fall it
commenced kindling and by winter it was ablaze.*

PRENTICE MULFORD

THE NEWS OF THE DISCOVERY of gold in California reached Prentice Mulford's village of Sag Harbor on Long Island in the autumn months of 1848, as it came to farms, villages, and cities across the nation.[1] In cataloguing the powerful movement toward the other side of the continent that followed, Sag Harbor is a good place to start, and of the storytellers who recounted the impact of this exotic news on a familiar place, Mulford excels at conveying the sense of how it affected what had been a settled, close-knit community with its limited local opportunities for an energetic and sometimes frustrated young people. Mulford begins his account with the arrival of this unlikely intelligence, notes its gradual acceptance, and then moves on to the dramatic changes that it wrought on so many families and, eventually, in the community as a whole.

Sag Harbor had been a whaling village for a hundred years, and its life pointed toward the open sea. Its peoples fashioned themselves in response to the special circumstances imposed by its economic center: a tradition of apprenticeship at an early age, long absences at sea, and the intermarriage of families that maintained these traditions. The local economy had begun to stagnate with the decline of the price of whale oil, and prospects for young people had severely contracted by midcentury.

The prospect of economic opportunity opened by news of dazzling wealth to be found in a faraway place thus offered young people escape (if only temporarily) from the limited horizons of the village. It was not the young alone who were galvanized into action, however.

Men of all ages and conditions made plans to participate in this enterprise. Immediately, as well as gradually over time, the response to the news from the West transformed the entire village. At first, the common response and universal enthusiasm gave a unity to those who would go to California and to the families who would stay behind to protect and to nurture the values and life of the community to which the Argonauts intended to return.

The news of gold in the streams of the California Sierra first had reached the Mississippi valley and the Atlantic coastal states in August and September, but it had aroused little interest. When newspapers had bothered to notice, they were openly skeptical of the idea that real gold could have been found in California in large quantities and accessible to everyone. This lack of interest reflected the newspapers' generally skeptical attitude toward the West Coast, a recent acquisition in the Mexican War. Whigs especially dismissed the reports, for in their minds, California gold was an invention of the Democratic Party, an invention designed to justify a partisan war that produced much hostility in certain sections of the Union. Even nonpartisan observers feared that the final price for the war lay not in military casualties, or in expenditures, or even in payment for the territory acquired in the peace treaty, but rather in the reappearance of dangerous controversies about the legality of the institution of slavery in new territories. Whatever the reasons, a period of several weeks lapsed while the seaboard cities noted the various stories emerging from California without giving them much credibility or, accordingly, much publicity. What the story required was confirmation—testimonies and physical evidence of some kind to overcome the understandable distrust of rumors that gold might be picked up from the streambeds of distant California.[2]

CONFIRMATION

In mid-September 1848, Lieutenant Edward F. Beale arrived in Washington from California, bearing official written dispatches about the mines. More to the point, he also brought gold, not a large quantity, but sufficient to give some support to the written accounts. Beale's appearance generated a degree of gold excitement and led to much discussion of the discoveries, but editors generally remained doubtful, and readers were not immediately stirred to action. The citizens of the Republic seemed unmoved, and the evidence of their indifference lay in the few departures for California. The steamship *California,* on her maiden voyage to San Francisco via Cape Horn, sailed from New York harbor on October 6 with staterooms for 60 and steerage accommodations for 150, but only 60 paying travelers bought passage for California. Within three months, riots would break out over such accommodations.

At the same time, letters written by Thomas O. Larkin and Walter Colton about the California gold discoveries began to appear in print. Both Larkin, as consul, and Colton, as the alcalde of Monterey, had a degree of official status in the eyes of the press. Their communications included long, descriptive letters from Colton to the Philadelphia *North American* and the New York *Journal of Commerce,* and from Larkin to the *New York Herald.* Larkin's several letters to Secretary of State James Buchanan also quickly found their way into print.[3]

Both Larkin and Colton wrote dramatic accounts that emphasized the astonishing bonanzas that came to people who were not even skilled miners. They described "streams paved with gold" and ordinary workingmen who took from five to thirty dollars a day from the gold-bearing streams of the California Sierra. Their pronouncements on the discovery of gold and its widespread availability to all were couched in such terms of extravagance as to invite immediate skepticism. Indeed, Larkin even apologized in advance to his readers, noting that if he were in New York, he would not believe such outlandish accounts.[4]

Most editors accepted his disclaimer rather than his message, for reasons that were many and varied. The claims were indeed so extravagant that they invited disbelief. Events from the other side of the continent also were always subject to discount of distance and exotic lands. In addition, various editors immediately sprang to the defense of their own states, convinced that the activities of Larkin and Colton were simply attempts to open a new front in the ongoing war for investment and growth.

The next important step in confirming the California gold discoveries came with the arrival of Governor Richard Mason's official report, based on his tour of the gold fields and dispatched to his superiors in Washington on August 17, 1848. As a precaution against the hazards of the journey—and incidentally a comment upon them—Mason sent two messengers with similar letters. Lieutenant Lucien Losier and his companion, David Carter, arrived at New Orleans by sea on November 23. Carter, apparently aware in general terms of the contents of the letters, gave an interview to the *Daily Picayune* in which he downplayed the significance of the gold discoveries, emphasizing the hard and dangerous work and the minimal returns. A competing paper, the *Evening Mercury,* found Losier more optimistic, perhaps the result of a difference of opinion, but perhaps also a result of the newspaper rivalry in the Crescent City.[5] Whatever their views, Losier and Carter immediately left for Washington. When they got there, the second messenger, who took the more direct route through Mexico, already had arrived. The two lieutenants delivered Mason's duplicate letters to the War Department, from whence a copy was sent to President James K. Polk for possible incorporation into his forthcoming State of the Union message.

In his reports, Mason gave a detailed description of the placers, accounts of the digging operations, the daily routines, and the rich returns for the most common miners. He told it all in detail, in hard-headed soldier's language that added to its credibility, and with a professional officer's eye to its significance for the nation. Among his conclusions: that there was "more gold in the country drained by the Sacramento and San Joaquin Rivers than would pay the cost of the present war with Mexico a hundred times over."[6]

As an official communication between government agencies, Mason's letter was confidential, but rumors of its contents immediately appeared in the local press. His glowing report made striking copy for the Washington newspapers. Gold was perhaps the only subject that could draw more attention than politics in Washington. The Washington *Daily Union* quoted with enthusiastic approval other letters from California to the effect that "the riches of Peru, in the days of Pizarro, would be but a mite when compared with a mine recently opened near St. Francisco on the Sacramento River, at its junction with the Rio de los Americanos. Individuals are now getting fifty dollars a day by washing gold out of the sands." The editor concluded, " 'El Dorado' is certainly found at last."[7] Within two months, the figure of fifty dollars a day would seem conservative.

Mason's comparison of the riches to be had in California with the cost to the Mexican War was a political statement, of course, and President Polk, still justifying his costly expansionist war against Mexico on the eve of leaving office, used it to that end in his message to Congress on December 5. The news about the gold mines in California came in the middle of his message. "It was known that mines of the precious metals existed to a considerable extent in California at the time of its acquisition," he began. "Recent discoveries render it probable that these mines are more extensive and valuable than was anticipated. The accounts of the abundance of gold in that territory are of such an extraordinary character as would scarcely command belief were they not corroborated by the authentic reports of officers in the public service."[8]

What really clinched the rising response to Mason's letters and Polk's subsequent message to Congress was the gold itself. In addition to Mason's letters, Losier and Carter had carried gold, some two hundred and twenty ounces, purchased by United States Government funds. They delivered it to the War Department on December 7, the day of their arrival in Washington. Officials promptly dispatched it to the mint in Philadelphia, where experts pronounced it "Genuine," indeed, almost equal in its original form to the standard for coins. The total value came to $3,910.10. And so, some eleven months after James Marshall and others at Sutter's Fort did primitive tests on the first nuggets, government experts a continent away with the most professional tests available placed an official seal of approval on the presence of gold in California. Put on display at the War Department, the gold immediately became a magnet for visitors, officials, and newspaper reporters. Even the most skeptical journalists found their disbelief overwhelmed by the sight of the glittering rocks.[9]

MEDIA MANIA

The range of responses to the spread of news about the California Gold Rush in the eastern half of the country—from skepticism and doubt to acceptance and wild, uninhibited enthusiasm—reflected the nature of the press and of how information was transferred in the nation at midcentury. The American press, directed at a mass readership while maintaining an intensely political character that dated from the 1790s, routinely published materials that were at the far edge of sensation while at the same time criticizing their rivals for doing the same. Indian massacres, Mormon outrages of seduction and polygamy, sensational local crimes, and accounts of harems in the Ottoman Empire all formed daily fare for America's press. The bizarre and extravagant helped circulation and confirmed American readers' views about distant places and alien cultures.

The content of American newspapers was further defined by the routine exchanges between them. This was an age in which newspapers happily copied from one another, and the copying grew as one descended the ranks of the journalism scale. The small weeklies were heavily dependent upon the arrival of their larger weekly and daily exchanges for state, territorial, or national news. Under such rules of journalism, it made perfect sense to publish a detailed account of the Russo-Turkish War for readers of a country weekly in, say, North Carolina, for the story filled up the empty spaces in that week's paper. Editors tried to fill such gaps with local poetry and serialized novels, but when these materials were exhausted, they looked for exchanges to supply their needs. Rumor and sensation consequently took on a kind of homogeneous quality; they appeared and reappeared across the nation.

At the same time, editors routinely disparaged rivals who printed sensational stories by questioning their rivals' veracity and motives. Along with these neighborhood rivalries went a local and regional pride that defended the town or state against outrageous stories while emphasizing local virtues in pursuit of growth and expansion. This was the fate of the news brought by Larkin and Colton, as we have seen. In this fashion, the claims of rival territories and states were routinely discounted as exaggerations, whether they concerned crop harvests, the richness of the soil, or increases in population, all signs of progress in midcentury America.

Interest in the California gold discoveries, which had languished through the fall months after the initial reports, took on new life with the appearance of Losier and Carter in New Orleans on November 23. Their reports and gold samples were now supplemented by new letters and newspapers from California, statements of officials and private citizens in California, and the arrival of the first few Americans to return from California with gold in their pockets. In the next fortnight, as several newly formed companies began to organize for a speedy departure for California, accounts of these activities spread up the Mississippi and Ohio valleys and into the interior of the nation.

With the publication of the State of the Union message, the gold excitement was everywhere accepted as real, with one account following another in escalating tones of enthusiasm. Editors, who heretofore often had expressed reservations, scrambled to set the type for their largest headlines. They also searched for imagery to encapsulate the nature and importance of this national bonanza. Historical analogies tumbled over one another in an unending display of comparisons to the fabled riches of the past, with references to "the El Dorado of the old Spaniards," "the dreams of Cortez and Pizarro," "the Age of Gold," and Ponce de Leon.[10] That editors routinely could call upon such imagery suggested the strong hold of these figures on the American popular imagination.

In addition to disseminating the symbolic significance of western gold in the developing nation, newspapers soon became the vehicles for practical news and information about the Gold Rush and plans to participate in it. They published calls for companies to organize; they printed company rosters, officers, and constitutions with approval. They reported on arrangements for departures, and they frequently published in their entirety sermons and other public speeches on the occasion of the Argonauts' farewells.

Newspapers also published ads for the array of publications and products that appeared the winter of 1848–49 to meet the needs of so many planning to go to California. These included guide books, "goldometers," which were widely advertised devices supposed to find gold-bearing gravel and measure its richness and which were invariably found to be useless in the gold fields, and an endless array of more practical tools and equipment necessary for a trip across the continent and for work in the gold diggings when arrived.[11]

Many stories and editorials, however, bordered on fantasy.[12] Editors borrowed, exaggerated, disparaged the exaggerations of others, and then succumbed altogether to the wild enthusiasm. They scrambled to produce their own improbable stories of wealth, preferably with an equally improbable figure. Children were especially popular subjects, for the image of a child finding gold in California dramatized the claim that this opportunity was truly open to everyone. A leading North Carolina newspaper, for example, reported two such instances in language that made such discoveries unremarkable in their frequency and democratic nature. In the first case, two servants of an official went to the mines and soon returned with seventy-five thousand dollars; in the second, the gold was "*so abundant that there is not necessity for washing the earth; $700 per day is the amount by each man.*"[13]

Throughout the nation editors tended to adapt their treatment of the Gold Rush to fit local requirements. Editors in the South quickly addressed the applicability of gold mining to the institution of slavery. The question was twofold: the future status of slave labor in California and the suitability of slave labor to the nature of the work. A Georgian suggested that if three to five hundred Georgians emigrated to California, each accompanied by one to five slaves, they would force the admission of California as a slave state. A consensus gradually emerged that the status of slavery in California was uncertain, but editors and public officials urged Southerners to take their chattel labor to California, where they could perform duties as both servants and miners.[14]

The newspapers in the eastern port cities were the first to describe the Gold Rush in detail, especially its most dramatic aspects in terms of the quantities of gold available and the ease with which it might be acquired. The dailies of New Orleans, Charleston, and New York were especially noteworthy. The *New York Herald* featured daily articles on the gold discoveries, beginning in December 1848 and for several months thereafter, complete with details on the several companies departing from the port of New York. The weeklies across the eastern seaboard borrowed from their larger cousins, and by December 1848 and January 1849, these local newspapers had begun to copy the accounts of the discovery of gold in California that had originally appeared in the dailies in New Orleans, Baltimore, Charleston, and New York.

By the late winter and spring of 1849, the focus of coverage of the Gold Rush had shifted from the large city papers to the many papers published in small cities and villages, with special emphasis on those communities that had organized and dispatched companies to California. In these companies of Argonauts, local journalists, sometimes professionals associated with local papers and sometimes simply amateurs elected to the position of scribe by their companies, wrote regularly back to the local paper. Their accounts offered a running commentary on the details of the expedition to California, with special attention to dangers overcome and with the mention of individual names on a regular basis. Some directed their wives to give their family letters to a local editor for publication.[15]

This advertising of the Gold Rush experience through the newspaper publication of private letters had become so common by the winter of 1849–50 that many 49ers made specific note in their letters home that these were for the family only and not for publication. Given the candor with which individual 49ers sometimes described members of other families within the community, such discretion was understandable and wise. Throughout the succeeding years of the Gold Rush, the papers of small cities and county-seat towns, often places with many representatives in the gold fields, became the leading sources of public information on the continuing Gold Rush. They continued to note the departure and return of friends and neighbors long after news from the gold fields had faded from the newspapers of the large cities.

THE OUTBREAK OF GOLD FEVER

Ours was a whaling village. By November 1848,
California was the talk of the village, as it was all that time
of the whole country. The gold fever raged all winter.

PRENTICE MULFORD

In a nation increasingly characterized by growing sectional animosity, the epidemic of gold fever quickly spread across sectional lines. In the late fall of 1848, it seized the eastern half of the nation. The fever exhibited the intense and powerful qualities associated with any epidemic: uncontrollable deliriums, a high rate of infection, and no known remedy or inoculation except for travel to far-distant places. Prentice Mulford watched as it engulfed the whaling village of Sag Harbor. Initially, men talked in subdued voices, for this was a community of practical people. They had not wrested a living from the sea for a century to be swept off their feet by fantasies. As the most dramatic accounts of gold in California seemed confirmed by government officials and by returning Californians with gold, belief replaced doubt; an unrestrained enthusiasm soon followed. As Mulford put it, "All the old retired whaling captains wanted to go, and most of them did go. All the spruce young men of the place wanted to go. Companies were formed, and there was much serious drawing up of constitutions and by-laws for their regulation."[16] Mulford's account suggests that no one with youth, health, and ambition was spared from the ravages of gold fever.

The news and the fervent response that it provoked also ran down the Atlantic coast to the south and west, into the distant reaches of the Cotton Kingdom. Charles Harlan used the phrase "the California Mania" in describing the condition in Mississippi. Prominent citizens and yeomen farmers from Georgia and South Carolina talked of nothing else for six months. One correspondent in Missouri writing in the summer of 1849 noted that "all Creation appared to be in an uproar," and he said of the exodus to California that "the like never was known since the Israelites left old Egipt."[17]

Everywhere, the response seemed in proportion to the attractions. "CALIFORNIA THE GOLD FEVER," announced the headline in the *Star* of Corpus Christi, Texas. The most common analogy compared the "fever" to other rapidly spreading diseases: "Never did cholera, yellow fever, or any other fell disease rage with half the fury with which the gold fever is now sweeping over our land." The epidemic devastated "communities in one fell swoop, sparing neither age sex nor condition. It is the rage."[18] The nation was still celebrating its triumph over Mexico—one that would include the cession of California to the United States—and another image compared the enthusiasm for gold to the ardor displayed for war. A New Orleans paper wrote of The California Emigration:

> It has had much the effect of a war which elicits the popular sympathy. The young and ardent fly at once to arms, and the old and cautious deliberate and ponder, whether it be best to yield to natural impulse; and in the end they do yield, and go out to meet the foe. There has been a marvelous resemblance between the formation of gold seeking companies and the recruiting of a volunteer force for an aggressive war.[19]

The hundreds of accounts in the popular press identified certain themes associated with the gold fever. Among these were the universal quality of the appeal and the certainty of wealth. Newspapers in commercial centers also discussed the chances for commercial investment available for those with money to invest. Papers in port cities featured a wide range of ads offering everything from transportation to bulk commodities to membership in mining companies to "gold machines," bulky, square boxes with multiple layers of sieves to wash gravel, commercial versions of the cradle. Newspaper advertisements and notices also called attention to the number of new books and pamphlets about California, with detailed information about routes, expenses, appropriate equipment, the best digging sites, and the laws and customs of California.[20]

The topic of California gold also now spilled over from the newspapers to the other venues of the public discourse of the day. In the maelstrom of enthusiasm, gold was the subject of books, pamphlets, maps, guides, sermons, statements from civic leaders, and a wide range of entrepreneurial promotions. To this activity could be added the responses on the private level, in correspondence between and among individuals, in diaries and journals, and presumably in conversations around the table, in the store, in the barn, and along streets wherever people gathered. The new twist in these discussions was not the discoveries themselves, which were accepted as absolutely genuine, but rather what individuals and families would do to profit from this extraordinary new ingredient in American life and how these endeavors would affect families and communities. There was much to talk about.

Ministers described the potentially debilitating effect of great wealth on their flocks. Biblical and medical extracts were brought together in a sermon preached by the Reverend James Davis at the First Congregational Church of Woonsocket, Rhode Island. As the Reverend Mister Davis looked out at his congregation, he sounded a dire warning against the lure of gold as a special threat to young people and against the temptations that it offered to easy wealth. Of the national disease, he intoned:

> This excitement is become truly appalling, and reaching not our cities alone, but our villages and towns and shaking every family. There never has been any excitement equal to it within the remembrance of our oldest citizens.—War, Pestilence, Famine, the most astonishing discoveries in the arts and sciences . . . the advancement of civilization and Christianity in the subjugation of heathen lands—all these have never filled our land and the minds of our young men with such intense excitement.
> . . . the gold pestilance which is more terrific than the cholera, threatens to depopulate our land of those whom we had looked upon as the morning stars and bright hopes of future times.[21]

John Kelsey spoke for individuals in small villages and farms of newly settled lands when he tried to convey to his family his own excitement and enthusiasm. "I should like to go to California this Spring as the best men we have in this part of the Country are going and all those that wish to go now is the time," he wrote from Cedar Rapids, Iowa. And he continued, "Next Spring may be Everlastingly too late and if you hear of my being there you must not be surprised."[22] Those who caught the gold fever not only had to go to California, they had to go immediately. Seeing their opportunity as a train or steamship departing for a single trip, those who sought a new life felt they must get aboard or forever wonder how life's great chance had passed them by. One symptom of the fever for gold was this sharp contrast between the opportunities that gold promised for many Americans and the economic, social, or emotional failures that heretofore seemed to throttle the lives of those it infected. A. P. Josselyn wrote to his sister from the gold fields, "One word in regard to my family, (God Bless Them) I want to see them verry much but I cant come home yet. I must make some money before I come. I do not want to see my Children go barefooted while my neighbours Children are wearing shoes."[23]

The gold fever thus began to disrupt states and regions north and south, slave and free, and to unsettle communities and families across the nation. Discussions of whether to go, of when to go, of who would go, of who had gone, and why occupied many long evenings and evoked much emotional outpouring. Then came the partings, whether public, with parades and religious services, or private, with a small gathering at the front gate or stoop. These departures lay with a heavy hand on the families and communities from which had departed their young men for the Golden West. These adventurers, mostly young and mostly male, but far from exclusively either, left behind them spouses, fiancées, children, siblings, parents, and friends. Their absence would change forever the configurations of their families and communities.

3

"THIS IS A HARD THING, THIS BREAKING UP OF FAMILIES":

Gold and Its Personal Costs

As the winter of '48 waned the companies one after another, set sail
for the land of gold. The Sunday preceding they listened to farewell sermons
at church. I recollect seeing a score or two of the young Argonauts thus
preached to. They were admonished from the pulpit to behave temperately,
virtuously, wisely, and piously.

PRENTICE MULFORD

IN THE SPRING OF 1849, in response to the discovery of gold in California, thousands of families in hundreds of American communities were torn apart. In villages such as Sag Harbor, New York, Marshall, Michigan, and Aberdeen, Mississippi, in cities such as Boston, Detroit, and New Orleans, on the farms of rural Michigan and the plantations of the delta in Mississippi, the discovery wrenched individuals and families away from their familiar worlds and swept them toward what they hoped would be a new life. As we will see later in considerable detail, over the years that followed, the effects of this massive dislocation of traditional personal and spatial relationships profoundly changed the nature and texture of American family and community life. The first of these effects, however, began to be felt even before the original Argonauts left home.

Prentice Mulford's description of the families in the whaling community of Sag Harbor nicely captures the innocence of these two dozen or so earnest young men about to launch themselves on an adventure of which they knew only the dimmest outlines. As a prelude to their departure on this crusade, they gathered in a church to receive the benediction of their community. They stood naive and unformed on one side of a great divide that would separate them from their earlier lives, the friends and places of their youth, and even their families; on the other lay the mysteries of California, a new land with new peoples and unforeseen temptations, the prospect of wealth beyond their imaginations, and the trials of separation from the only world they had ever known. They faced this new world with the blessings of their families and with the collective support of their community. It was a defining moment in their lives and also in the lives of those they were leaving behind.

Mulford's Sunday-morning church service in Sag Harbor displays in miniature the scene and the actors of this unfolding drama. Before it took place, however, individuals and families in Sag Harbor and numerous other villages debated the advantages and disadvantages of joining the exodus to California. The nature of the debate, the participants, and the arguments reflected the nature of America's societies at that time. These discussions—intense and casual, cool and emotional, awkward and angry—brought into play issues of family authority and power; work roles, their divisions and their redistribution; relationships with parents, spouses, and siblings; family resources and the parceling out of such resources among individual family members; the family's vision of itself and its future prospects; its attitudes toward risk taking and adventures in the interests of improving family fortunes. Over the year 1849, more than eighty thousand Americans would depart by land and by sea for California, and the numbers who went represented only one response to the decision-making process. Surely an even larger number carefully considered the issue and decided to stay home.

TO GO OR TO STAY?

As the rumors of 1848 ran their course and turned into the golden promises of 1849, in families throughout the nation, tens of thousands of individuals were considering the question of whether to make the trek to California in search of golden riches.[1] The outlines of the debate over emigration were not entirely new. In previous generations, many families had weighed the economic advantages of venturing west to seek prosperity and security in the traditional manner, by settling and cultivating the land. The venture to California, however, carried a different range of risks and rewards: it was a temporary, rather than permanent, change of place; at the same time, it was extended in duration. It meant the prolonged absence of a member of the household for a period of years, rather than months. Finally, the trip involved the expenditure of family resources to finance a journey that would be undertaken for the possibility of great riches. The 49er would not lay claim to forty or eighty acres of land; instead, he would participate in a treasure hunt for instant wealth.

Two immediate influences gave a tone of urgency to the context of these deliberations. The first was the season. Voyages by sea must begin after the winter storms had passed. For those who intended to go overland, the coming of spring on the high plains marked the appearance of grass for the draft animals. At the other end of the journey, the overland Argonauts needed to reach California before the first snows closed the passes in the high Sierra. Thus, the discussions over the winter took place under pressure to act rapidly.[2]

A second circumstance that surrounded the deliberations in the winter of 1848–49 was the aggressive activity of those who already had determined to go. Local companies of friends and neighbors soon began to form. The organizational charts of such organizations could be impressive. The Wolverine Rangers from Marshall, Michigan, had a captain, a lieutenant, a secretary, a treasurer, and a steward, not to mention a board of five directors, plus three agents to purchase supplies at the point of departure. Sometimes the quasi-military organization of groups such as the Rangers carried over to the trip across the plains. A few groups wore uniforms to distinguish themselves and to proclaim their solidarity with one another. Ephriam Morse's company from the ship *Limon* went ashore in San Francisco in uniform—"red shirts, dark pants & glazed caps, belts but no knives. We actually looked well & attracted considerable attention, were mistaken in coming in for a man-of-war, &c."[3] The bustle of movement created an atmosphere suffused with the sense of a unique opportunity that was about to vanish within a few months, or a season at most. Accompanying this sense of unity and cooperation was a growing sense of competition. Here, as elsewhere, the advantage would go to aggressive and well-prepared individuals who made their decisions expeditiously and put their plans into effect soon thereafter. Gold in California was, by all accounts, plentiful, but presumably it was not inexhaustible. An implicit assumption soon developed that those first on the scene would have the greater opportunity.

The reasons that the original 49ers gave for going west remained the reasons for joining the Gold Rush throughout the decade. Charles Harlan summed up the motivation of 49ers everywhere when he wrote that he had gone to California to throw off the "distress of poverty."[4] Associated with the past were hard work, stringent living, and especially the debts that were the lot of so many families. This argument cut across class lines, for groups at all levels seemed to be burdened by debts. The lawyer William P. Daingerfield declared that his stay in California would be short, only until "I can make enough to pay all our debts and live tolerably enough for the balance of my life."[5] But many who went west in 1849 and subsequent years were not poor. Even those not in straitened circumstances, however, often needed resources to make the trip. For those with resources to invest, either in their own expedition or in speculative support of others, the voyage to California was an opportunity to profit, and profit was a motive whose legitimacy no one could deny.[6] The Gold Rush in fact did deliver on its promise: from 10 million dollars in 1849, gold production rose to 42 million dollars in 1850 and 76 million dollars in 1851. Men did not go to California solely to escape poverty or to make possible a rise in family fortunes, however. For some, it was also a coming-of-age voyage, a declaration of independence from their parents and siblings.

However elemental the motives were for heading west, the debates and discussions provoked by the risky opportunity produced a range of anxieties about the family's present situation and its hopes for a golden future. Prospective Argonauts of '49 and later years often spoke of their reluctance to make the journey, and they cast their decision to leave home and its responsibilities invariably in terms of duty to their families, a concern that echoes and re-echoes through the correspondence of 49ers and their loved ones throughout the Gold Rush. Harvey Chapman's celebration of the wonderful family that he was leaving behind was typical: "you think of me very wild for going away from my Sweet baby & affectionate wife & mild & Pleasant mother in law & Clever daddy in law but nothing but gold would take me away." Another 49er summarized both his determination to go to California and his reluctance to leave in a letter to his wife after he had set sail. He was "governed by no selfish motive," he wrote, "but that of your welfare, & that of our child is the mainspring of my exertions." He continued, "The belief that 'better days are coming,' however, cheers me up, & will I trust enable me to bear cheerfully any little hardships incident to the undertaking."[7]

Here and elsewhere, many Argonauts spoke of the hardships that they were prepared to endure for the sake of their families while at the same time naively neglecting (or perhaps dismissing) the burdens imposed on their wives and other family members by their prolonged absences. Others bartered their decision to stay for some economic advantage within the family. At least one was not above using the prospect of emigration to California as a means of enhancing his position as a suitor, forcing the reluctant subject of his affection into a favorable decision.[8]

Members of the family who opposed a voyage to California had a range of strong arguments in their turn. Those most affected by the prospect of loved ones' departure for California were well aware that it fundamentally jeopardized family life and the structure of social and economic relations in the United States at midcentury. This opposition coalesced around different members of the family, and the debate over the desirability of participating in the California Gold Rush quickly became gendered and generational. When his nephew suggested that he might join the rush to California, David Campbell summarized such views in these words: "We have been somewhat amused at your taking the California gold fever, altho only in a small degree. We have no doubt your good wife would not agree to your going upon any such undertaking—for she knows very well you are of more value to her and your fine family of children than mountains of gold."[9]

Wives often began in opposition to their spouse's proposal to join the Gold Rush to California, although they then sometimes gradually softened their stand. It was difficult for them steadfastly to oppose this unique opportunity for family advantage in a discussion conducted with gold mania raging on all sides. The situation of the 49er himself also promoted compromise: prospective Argonauts found it awkward to leave behind a disaffected wife and children outraged by his departure. In the end, the husband would offer assurances of his timely return and remission of money on a regular basis. Certainly, some Argonauts went to California over the determined opposition of their wives, but many women seem to have given their consent in exchange for the best possible terms, of which the most significant was a promise that the future 49er would return at a specified time. Women seemed to regard a commitment to return at a specific date as more important than a commitment to send home specific amounts of gold.

Occasionally, women united against emigration to the California gold fields. A group of women shoe binders in Beverly, Massachusetts, a seaport where men customarily went forth on long sea voyages, organized themselves to discourage the men of the community from leaving for California. Sarah E. Trask, who kept a diary in 1849, described an evening meeting with three of her friends as "a convention on California, All four against it so we can pull together very well." The Beverly seamstresses saw California not as an opportunity, but as a threat to their futures. Trask resented the advice freely offered to the object of her affection, Luther Woodbury, and she wrote that "other folks need not concern themselves about him, I had much rather he would be [where] he is, than at california for then I should not expect to see him again and now I do if nothing happens."[10]

The parents of prospective 49ers often opposed a trip to California, and they spoke their minds freely, as befits their seniority and their right to be heard and, by implication, to be obeyed. For most of them, dreams of gold in which men would become rich in a short period of time were the merest fantasies. In their lifetime of hard work and attention to the daily obligations of providing for family, nothing prepared them to support such a venture. Instead, the departure of one or more family members for the gold fields would, in most families, impose additional burdens on those who stayed behind. The distribution of work in such families at midcentury involved all members—including wife and children of various ages, perhaps siblings, almost certainly working or aging parents. It is not surprising, therefore, that parents argued that grown or almost-grown men had obligations at home: to wife and children for shelter and daily bread; to the elderly and the infirm for support. To the extent that parents continued to work the farm or manage the store, they needed and expected help; as they aged and became disabled, they expected care and attention. And throughout their opposition ran the heartfelt fear of parents that given the uncertainties of life expectancy in America at midcentury, they would not live to see their sons again.[11]

The hostility of mothers to such a venture was almost universal. The future 49ers responded with a mixture of love, fealty, and a determination to go anyway. One Argonaut addressed a special note to his mother with news of his decision to go to California: "Mother o Mother, why do you still resist my going my mind is made up to go. Why o why cant you let me go with a cherful heart, and with a well made up mind that i will try to do well." He then continued: "Mother i hope you will make up your mind to let me go cheerfully."[12]

Brothers and sisters sometimes were hesitant to support a sibling's voyage to California, perhaps mindful of the increased duties that would fall to them. A Kentuckian, William H. Cosby, wrote to his sister on the eve of his departure from St. Joseph, Missouri, "I am aware of your opposition & that of my very dear Mother to this course of mine But still I go I think it will be the best thing I can do & if I have luck I shall return in a year or two, if not I may stay longer. I shall try hard for fortune." A year later, he wrote from the Gold Rush town of Columbia that he was pleased to hear that his mother "submitted to my coming to Cal, as well as she did. I knew she always opposed me when I mentioned the subject."[13] That Cosby had left a young daughter with his sister probably accounted for the opposition of his sister and mother.

Some community leaders also surely helped to account for the opposition. "Every minister is preaching on the subject," wrote one observer. "Geologists are lecturing on it. It is dramatised at the theatres and it is the subject of conversation everywhere."[14] The sermon warning against the temptations of the Gold Rush preached by the Reverend James M. Davis of the Congregational Church of Woonsocket was called "The Duties of

Females in Reference to the California Gold Excitement." Preached on February 16, 1849, at the height of the Gold Rush fever, the sermon called for "woman" to mobilize against this community scourge. "Woman," although "fallen from her original high moral position, is still clothed with great power, from her vital connection with the social state," and she must use this moral authority to oppose the participation of men in this misadventure. "It is to you that we turn for help under God, in this age of excitement and revolution," he intoned to the women in the community. Beginning with small children, women must "vacinate their souls against this gold mania sooner than you do their bodies for the small pox." And they must do the same for the grown men of the family, or else fathers, brothers, and uncles would soon be on the way to "the golden tomb." He warned that women ignored such a call to action at their peril and the peril of their families.[15]

Other kinds of community voices entered into the discussions. Some anti-Democratic newspapers thought the rumors of gold a political trick by President Polk to defend his recent war. The Painesville, Ohio, lyceum debated the question "Will the discovery of gold mines in California ultimately prove beneficial to the people of the United States?" And on the campus of Oberlin College, one of the literary societies considered whether "the recent discovery of Gold in California is a curse (or blessing) to our Country."[16]

Over the winter of 1848–49, when the last appeals had been made, the last tears shed, and the last column of figures added, the sometimes embarrassed and occasionally defiant prospective 49er declared his intention. The decisions made then and over the ensuing decade—they changed little after 1849 except for the prospect of joining a relative in California—fell within four categories: first, by far the largest number seem to have made a collective decision with the participation of their family, with due attention to the views of spouse, where appropriate, and parents; second, a small and outspoken number issued a statement of intention to go to California, inviting the family to embrace the decision and support it but firm in the intention to go whatever the response; third, a small proportion of Argonauts went to California over the opposition of members of the family. And finally, of course, thousands of men decided to remain home.

Among those who decided to go to California were the brothers William and George Farnsworth of Maine, who sought and received parental permission to go to the gold fields for two years. At the end of the two years, George (who had a wife and children in Maine) returned; William (who was single) mined in California for another five years. John and Margaret Eagle from a small town in Pennsylvania made a joint decision that he would go to California for two years. John Eagle, admitting that he was bound by the agreement, later asked for an extension. Margaret agreed. James Barnes, however, went to California whatever the opinion of his family. He would go happily with his mother's permission if she would give it; he would reluctantly but still determinedly if she would not. William Swain of rural upstate New York went west against the wishes of his wife, who argued that the trip was too hazardous and that he should stay home with her and with their infant daughter.[17]

The accounts of those who stayed speak to the influence of wives and parents and obligations to families. The brothers William and Willis Dixon left Aberdeen, Mississippi, for the gold fields in the spring of 1849. Willis Dixon died in Independence, Missouri. In writing back home to offer condolences on their mutual loss to his cousin, Mary Pendleton, William Dixon in hindsight praised her for preventing her husband from joining them: "I must Congratulate you for having succeeded so well In influencing Mr Pendleton to remain."[18]

This cycle of decisions was repeated annually for the next decade, using the same arguments that the first group of Argonauts employed in the winter of 1848–49. Even as reports circulated of diminished (and later poor) prospects in the California mines, every winter brought renewed decisions across the nation, testifying to the continuing need for economic advantage in the face of declining prospects at home and, above all, to the continuing presence of the family as basic unit in making decisions.

Rufus Brown's departure in the spring of 1852 was much like those of original 49ers three years earlier. He wrote to his wife, Nellie:

> You know, dearest, I do not want to be separated from you—but we have been struggling against the advances of poverty, and if by our separation a few months we can rid ourselves of all that for the future and make ourselves, by a few months deprivation of each other's society, comfortable in money matters, how much better it will be, than to put an end to our prospects and doom ourselves, to steady and profitless storekeeping till our Creditors come in and take all, merely because it is hard and trying to be apart and at a long distance for some months.[19]

By the time that Rufus Brown went to California in 1852, it was clear that the prospects for wealth in mining had greatly diminished. Pressing debts and other impulses nevertheless continued to propel prospective Argonauts to the gold fields in search of opportunities, whatever the heavy odds.

For those who made the decision to go, the future 49ers and their families had to make two separate sets of financial arrangements. The first involved raising capital for the trip to California; the second dealt with support for those left behind. The cost of making the trip was everywhere part of the deliberations about going to California. The expense varied by time and place. The first waves to California in the winter of 1848–49 went by sea from the Atlantic coast, most of them from the port cities of New England and the Middle Atlantic states. One sea route went around the Horn and up the Pacific coast, a second to Panama, across the isthmus, and up the coast. Both voyages were relatively expensive, ranging in price from five hundred to one thousand dollars, the high figure reflecting the outrageous prices for steamer tickets on the Pacific side paid by the first waves in the winter of 1848–49. Besides cost, other disadvantages included the physical discomfort of a long voyage and uncertainty about booking passage on the Pacific side. The advantages of the ocean route were immediate departure, some degree of comfort and service, and cargo space. The capacity of vessels made them attractive for companies that intended to take quantities of tools, clothing, or foodstuffs to California for themselves and on speculation. The Argonauts who went overland in the spring of 1849 and subsequent seasons—by far the largest number—joined a company at home or attached themselves to one at St. Joseph or Independence. They left in late May and expected to arrive in the foothills of California in early autumn at a cost of as little as three hundred dollars.[20] Although it was cheaper, the overland trek was much more arduous. Because all of these routes demanded an immediate outlay of cash, the 49ers began by raising the necessary funds.

Whether they proposed to travel by sea or by land, most Argonauts first sought financial support from their families. Some asked for money as a gift; others borrowed money from family members, ranging from parents to siblings to in-laws. Of those in a position to offer assistance, parents were the most likely sources. Appeals to parents were a part of every 49er's plans, and from there the pleas for assistance might spread out to distant family members.

Young James Barnes of Washingtonville, New York, began with the cart before the horse. Fired by news of the gold discoveries, Barnes left the family farm, journeyed to New York City, and engaged passage to California "in the new and elegant steamer Ohio." Only then did he petition his family to provide funds for the journey. His appeal to his family spoke of his determination to seek his fortune and to establish himself as an adult in charge of his life, which he mixed with a plea for understanding and a request for support. "Father i need thy assistance; dont send your son emty away," he wrote. "I hope you dont think i intend to spend my substance on ritious living." To the contrary, "i intend to do the best i can let me be where i will. i dont ask you to give me the money, only lend it to me until i am able to repay you." Of course, if his father refused to assist the enterprise, then his son would land in California penniless and confront the unknown demands of the gold fields without resources. James Barnes closed his petition with an account that must have echoed in negotiations across half the continent: it was a vision of the return of the long-absent son from the Golden West, exhausted, worn-out, sunburned, and triumphant, laden down with treasure to meet all his present obligations, launch himself into the future, and reward his family for faithful support in his absence. He concluded with a promise that mixed the language of the Bible with the calculations of a rock-ribbed Yankee: "Father, i do not intend to return as the prodigal did but i hope to return and say father father here is your 200 dollars and the interest also."[21]

The needy 49ers also approached more distant members of the family. Most of them put their request on a businesslike basis; it was a loan that would be repaid with interest, secured by the Argonaut's reputation and determination to succeed. Seth Smith borrowed two hundred dollars from his Uncle Hiram.[22] Recently jilted in love, George Ormsby intended to head for California, and he wrote to his sister and her husband to solicit financial support. Companies had organized in his neighborhood, and outfits for the trip cost about one hundred and fifty dollars. Ormsby called upon his friends and relatives, "what few I have got to throw in their mites toward giving me a fit out, and when I come back, I will pay a good pr. cent. for there money." His appeal to his sister called on family ties: "now Sis show this letter to brother Fred and ask him how much he will Give to help the poor Boy off."[23]

Some prospective 49ers also entered into business arrangements with investors. Three different examples show the outlines of such dealings. Under Thomas Hill's contract with Wright's Company of Gold Diggers, the company paid his passage to California and received one-half the gold he dug and one-half his salary in the off-season.[24] Horace Ballew signed articles of agreement with John W. Boyle of Grandview, Illinois, who also was going to California. Under the arrangement, Boyle financed Ballew's trip and received, in exchange, one-half the gold and one-half the property realized. The provision for a weekly division of returns suggested that Boyle and Ballew intended to mine together, or at least near one another. John Edwards of Spring Green, Wisconsin, advanced Anthony Powers one hundred and twenty-five dollars "for overland expenses" in exchange for one-third of Powers's net proceeds, "after deducting expenses." Two investors, a New York attorney and a local man, each put up twenty-five hundred dollars to finance a company of ten from Monroe, Michigan, in exchange "for a quarter share each in the proceeds of the company" for a two-year period. That such arrangements had achieved the status of a routine investment was suggested by one man's advice that his nephew invest five hundred dollars "by fitting out some young man, on whose integrity you could rely and who had no means of going himself—and agree to divide the profits with him." The sum would support "some poor but hardy man" for two years in California with the prospect of good returns for both parties.[25]

Elisha Douglas Perkins left his pregnant wife, his failing drugstore in Marietta, Ohio, and in-laws unhappy with his prospects to seek better times in California. He joined the Harmar Company, which had two separate divisions. The first was composed of investors at home who provided funds for the venture; the second included twenty able-bodied "adventurers" who would seek the fortunes of both groups in the gold fields. The "adventurers" swore an oath, vowing "to the best of my ability" to "promote the harmony and discipline, and faithfully labor to advance the interest of the Harmar Company, and obey its rules." A part of the oath included a promise to refrain "from drinking, gambling, carousing." Adventurers in California and investors in Ohio would share equally in the profits.[26]

A second group of arrangements provided for those who would be left behind, usually a wife, and perhaps children and elderly parents. Generally, the negotiations provided for families were of two kinds: the expenditure of assets in the form of living arrangements and financial support, and the providing of less specific, but no less concrete, emotional support in the form of visitations and correspondence.

The affluent among the Argonauts of '49, professionals (doctors and lawyers), substantial merchants, and people of independent means, could depart with every confidence that their families would be provided for and the extended family suffer no inconvenience from shifting resources. These families had only to make plans that would be consistent with their economic and social standing. Such people frequently had servants and traveled extensively; they continued to do so. Yet these were also families that had sometimes suffered financial reverses that had prompted the men to head for California and a chance to recover former standing. Many of these did not intend to mine, but sought advantage through their professions or by speculations in the free-wheeling economy unfolding in connection with the rush to the mines. Sometimes they took money with them to invest in California enterprises.[27]

For most 49ers, however, money was the constant preoccupation. Many intended that relatives should help provide for their dependents, as well as help finance their adventure. Some put the burden on their wives to initiate these requests, sometimes on a regular basis, sometimes in case of need. One 49er asked his wife to apply to his father for some money: "I wish you also to say to him for me, that I shall consider it a great favor if he will furnish you with some money at some rate or other, if he has not got it to spare, ask him to borrow enough, so that you may want for nothing." He continued, "There is no kind of doubt that I can get money enough to pay all my debts, at least, at the diggings, & it would take a great load off me if I was sure you wanted for nothing."[28]

Throughout such arrangements run parallel and sometimes contradictory themes. Those left behind would "want for nothing," but the actual details of how to provide for them often were left vague. When an Argonaut left it to his spouse to petition for assistance, she was often reluctant to do so, mindful of the suggestion that her request indicated she had not been careful in husbanding the family resources. The 49ers also reiterated the theme that spouses (and to a lesser extent, parents) should have recourse to brothers or fathers to provide their materials needs, and they buttressed these arrangements with constant references to the remittances they would make promptly from California and the golden future that awaited the reunited family.

Some families lived on the edge of want, and the prospect of an expedition to California involved conflicts over allocation of scarce resources. The wife and children of a departed 49er might have to move into the house of a relative, a sibling, or a parent. Charles Tuttle sent his wife Maria to her father's home, an awkward arrangement for her that he undertook out of necessity. Tuttle admitted that his wife was very poor; he might have said that they were both very poor, and their poverty was his declared reason for his voyage to the gold fields. One 49er took his wife from Wisconsin to Ohio, where she "was to remain with her father while I got rich in the land of gold."[29] Milton Hall instructed his wife to sell some of their furniture and furnishings to raise money for the family's support. At the same time, she and the children would need to move to more inexpensive lodging.[30]

The 49ers customarily designated a family male—an older brother, brother-in-law, father, or father-in-law—to supervise financial arrangements. Arthur Thompson gave this charge to his father-in-law, Robinson, with the instructions to "watch over Miriam & Jessie as you always have." And he offered some detailed instructions about providing for his wife and infant daughter. Robinson should sell some cattle to pay debts, "for as yet I have not had an opportunity of sending any money home and it is uncertain whether I will or not."[31]

Departing 49ers with responsibilities for young children made other kinds of arrangements. William Cosby left his young daughter with his sister in Kentucky. Her letters to him over three years indicated that the sister was anxious for him to return and reassume the obligations associated with his daughter. John Eagle left two stepchildren in the household managed by his wife Margaret with their four children. All these living arrangements involved resources beyond material support.[32]

The arrangements to support spouses and children might be general or detailed. They might involve lodging, daily subsistence, and money given or borrowed for other expenses. Prior to leaving, Milo Goss took out a life-insurance policy on his life, and he paid the rent on the house where his wife and children would reside in his absence. The plans also might include surprises. William Prince wrote to his wife that he wanted her to bring Cousin Cary into the household "to make her home with you." Apparently Prince had made these arrangements with the cousin, but not with his wife, before departing.[33]

Financial arrangements for some families also involved ongoing economic enterprises. Some businesses, whether stores or farms, were solvent and doing well; others were marginal and burdened by debt. In either case, they demanded continuous attention. William Prince assumed that the income from his prosperous nursery on Long Island would cover his family's needs during his absence in California. Outstanding debts—long-term and short-term debts owed to various creditors, ranging from strangers to local merchants to family members—needed careful handling to preserve the family's local reputation in light of the departure of a wage earner for California. Many gave their wives wide latitude in addressing burdensome financial demands that were sure to arise. Wilson Day of Jerico, Vermont, left his wife, Nancy, some two hundred and fifty dollars to cover "all such debts" that might need payment and asked her to use her judgment on which ones to pay first and which ones to postpone.[34]

The emotional needs for 49er spouses, children, and parents also needed attention. To mothers and sisters went the charge to provide comfort for the spouse by making frequent visits, writing (where they were more distant), and serving as a first line of support in case of illness or death. Parents might need assistance and reassurance. Some of these arrangements worked effectively; others provoked hostility and dispute. The prolonged absence of the 49er increased the strain of such arrangements, and the absences often turned out to be long indeed.[35]

Over the first and subsequent seasons of the California Gold Rush, arrangements varied as widely as the resources and determination of the people making them. All involved a greater or lesser degree of inconvenience for family members remaining in the East. Most assumed that the Argonaut would be gone only a short time, returning wealthy and triumphant. Few were prepared for the variations that California would impose on their timetables.

ADVICE

How seriously they listened. How soberly were their narrow-brimmed, straight-up-and-down, little plug hats of that period piled one atop the other in front of them. How glistened their hair with the village barber's hair oil. How pronounced the creak of their tight boots as they marched up the aisle. How brilliant the hues of their neck ties.

PRENTICE MULFORD

With the decision made to go to California, funds secured for the journey, and arrangements made for those who would stay behind, the 49ers entered into the final stage of their preparation, offering and receiving advice. To begin with, the Argonauts offered elaborate advice on a wide range of subjects to their spouses, fiancées, children, and parents, extending sometimes to siblings and distant relatives. In return, those who stayed behind offered endless counsel on the imagined dangers of California and how to overcome them. And finally, the giving of advice on the eve of departure for this greatest adventure of the age spread from the most intimate exchanges between husbands and wives, siblings, parents and children to engage the entire community. In these wider exercises, a range of public figures—ministers, editors, elected officials, business leaders, and so forth, most of them not going to California—offered public declarations about conduct and behavior to the departing Argonauts. These representatives affirmed the values of their world and the ways in which these should be preserved, how the newly minted Argonauts should be protected from dangers and temptations and in the end returned unharmed, in body or mind, to the family and community from which they originally had set forth.

Argonauts who departed in 1849, 1850, 1851, and even subsequent years spoke the same lines, heard the same messages of love, support, and fear in return, and listened to the same official pronouncements (reduced in number and scope after 1849) about the standards and values of the community and how to preserve them in the face of temptations and hardships.

The advice that emerges from written accounts of departing husbands, sons, and brothers to families left behind falls generally into three categories. First, the essential part to be played by the wife, children, and parents in the success of the enterprise. The accounts repeatedly emphasize that those who remained at home had duties and responsibilities fully as significant as those who would dig gold in California. Second, they stress the issue of behavior and etiquette during the 49ers' absence, especially the conduct of married women with absent husbands. Finally, they frequently contain detailed suggestions with respect to the education and deportment of children.

Rufus Brown's charge to his wife was probably representative of the first kind, a mixture of affection and call to duty. On the occasion of departure, or immediately thereafter by letter, many 49ers, Brown among them, left statements about the part that each family member should play in this forthcoming enterprise. This account often began with a recapitulation of the reasons for the decisions to go to California, with the conclusion that the long-term advantages for all members of the family would far outbalance any short-term difficulties. Such an analysis helped to reconcile members of the family to an absence of at least two years and hinted that the longer the absence, the greater the rewards. These accounts reflected much about different roles and expectations of men and women at midcentury: that men would venture forth to adventure, risk, hard work, and (in this case, at least) a long absence, while women would support them from a distance, ever faithful, uncomplaining, undertaking all the usual domestic responsibilities, often with fewer resources and additional duties.

Brown followed this pattern. "And now my precious love I am going to preach you a little sermon, the day being Sunday it is all very appropriate," he began. "We have embarked on an enterprise, and the best judgment of all with whom I have consulted has approved the course—In this enterprise we have both our parts allotted, and each should try to perform to the best of their ability." In this division of labor, "yours, my love, is to guard yourself well against sickness, to resist depression of mind and spirits and to bear the separation firmly and with a resolve that all which belongs to you to do shall be done." He told her to "keep your mind from brooding on what may never happen, look at the thing firmly as a necessary evil, and be prepared to accept either good or bad results from what we have undertaken." As for himself, he declared that "my part is to go and do the best I can—It would be weakness, and even criminal, to falter now." After a canvass of their future as proprietors of their small drugstore in Detroit ("the prospect . . . is dark enough"), he continued to nerve her to what he regarded as her proper duty. "We have done right—and it only remains for us to each act our part with our best exertions, and to fear no evil." He then concluded, "So then dry up your tears, put away your sadness and determine RESOLUTELY to be a woman, and to contribute your full share to merit success in this important experiment."

Brown also gave instructions on relations with local storekeepers, admonishing his wife not to charge groceries for fear of giving the impression that the family was short of money. She should ask for credit only as a last resort. He left detailed advice about his wife's relations with her relatives, as well, suggesting the central role of the extended family in the lives of 49ers. Members of the family should each be given some attention, information, and even gossip, all of which they would regard as their due.[36]

In addition to spelling out the roles of family members, some 49ers seemed intensely concerned to set out appropriate behavior of their spouses during their prolonged absence. In the background lurked the unspoken danger of temptation and the tarnished reputation. Gregory Yale addressed these questions from shipboard on the eve of his departure. "My dearest wife," he began,

> I have already closed my general letter to you. I will add another page of a special nature. . . . I desire also to say to you that while in Boston, or elsewhere, in my absence, you cannot be too circumspect in your intercourse or company. Do not by any means expose yourself to imputations of any sort, by any conduct. Do not go out of an evening unless in female society, for you know the tone of censure in large cities toward strangers. And on no account receive male visitors in your rooms. Regularity in your deportment will be more becoming. I mean in your meals, your several habits, &c. at a public Hotel these things are observed with the greatest [?]. Take these remarks in a proper spirit. Be kind to our dear child.[37]

Some of the advice about behavior was even more pointed. Charles Tuttle's long letter to his wife Maria warned against "fiends or devils incarnate," as he called seducers of virtuous women. He continued, "Maria, I say with pain but there is a class of beings who call themselves men who move in the best society who have no confidence in female virtue and who would haul down the souls and bodies of their unsuspecting victims to the lowest depths of hell." Tuttle affirmed his faith in Maria, but he wrote to her, he explained, because "as a man he has seen more of the dark side of the world than you."[38] Throughout much advice from 49ers to their spouses and fiancées run the themes of female weakness, gullibility, and innocence, making women vulnerable to the dark schemes of unscrupulous seducers. "Women's virtue" and reputation were the shining stars by which men expected them to set their course during their absences.

As a part of this emphasis on women's weakness and innocence in their absence, men offered their spouses, mothers, fiancées, and sisters the consolation of religion. To compensate for their prolonged absences, many 49ers recommended the comforts of regular church services, Bible readings, and especially prayer. Running through this series of appeals for Heaven to support their families also was the theme of inevitable success in their ventures. In a variation of the doctrine of Manifest Destiny that so suffused the nation, the 49ers saw their voyages to California as undertaken with the blessings of Heaven, and an important part of this blessing was the assured health and happiness of their families.[39]

The Argonauts paid attention to the physical and mental health of the women they left behind, as well as to their spiritual well-being and social reputation. Men seemed to regard their wives and mothers as vulnerable to all kinds of physical maladies. Among the advice they dispensed: do not worry or "brood" over a loved one's absence, "keep your system regular," and avoid too much physical exertion. The prospect of "depression" also drew attention, and the admonition to "be cheerful" appeared frequently. This catalog of physical and emotional ills kept men writing steadily enroute to California and after they reached the gold fields.[40]

The departing 49ers also left in their wake a flood of recommendations concerning children. Men exhibited much guilt at leaving their families, and they were particularly anxious that their children should not forget them. Spouses should mention absent fathers on a regular basis, they wrote, with special emphasis on their rapid return and the great significance of the enterprise that prompted their departure for California. One man instructed his wife that their son should be taught to say "that Papa is coming home bye & bye," and he should repeat this litany on demand. Parting instructions mentioned special attention to the protection of children, whether at play or when at risk from sickness. And almost all fathers—from a wide range of economic circumstances—spoke of the desirability and even necessity of putting children in school and keeping them there. Even those scarcely literate, who recognized the labor value of children around the house and especially on the farm, displayed a powerful commitment to education for their youngsters and the differences that such instruction would make in their lives. These 49ers emphasized that school was more important than work. It was a generous gesture, albeit made by those no longer immediately responsible for seeing that the work of the farm or shop was done.[41]

Some 49ers wrote letters to each child. Fathers often promised gifts to obedient children upon their return. Such individual attention and promises were especially common in fathers writing to sons. These messages emphasized the bond between fathers and sons, in spite of the impending absence of several years, and the need for sons to obey and support their mothers. William Dressler began by noting that "little boyes get a *little* nawghty once in a while," but he went on, "Now if you *love* your Father you will try very hard to be good—You must be good to your Mother and please her now Pa is awauy all you can *and be very good to each other,* and run and help grand Ma & grand Pa do all the little chores for them you can." Several of the departed Argonauts offered special gifts as rewards for good behavior. Of those who made such promises, the most creative incentive was offered by William Elder, who promised parrots to his well-behaved children.[42] With such sound counsel, supported by bribes where appropriate, the 49ers probably considered that they had discharged necessary responsibilities to both spouses and sons.

A second level of advice was addressed at large to the departing Argonauts. In sermons, public addresses, and private exhortations to individuals and groups, the advice affirmed the God-given virtues of American Protestant democracy and civilization, established in a revolution and most recently confirmed in a successful war against Catholic Mexico. Distant from their families and communities, the 49ers would see exotic peoples and places and be exposed to great temptations. Speakers exhorted them to stand by one another and by the values of their home, church, and community. They should conduct themselves in ways that would make their families and communities proud, they were told. And they should not neglect to work hard and earn the riches that would surely be theirs (if only a small proportion of the stories from California could be believed) and return promptly and in triumph to their homes.

Politicians, ministers, and editors across the eastern half of the newly realized continental nation contributed their public wisdom to these gatherings. The secular counsel emphasized the conduct of the 49ers toward one another and toward others they would meet with a view to preserving their own standards of honor. On the occasion of the departure of the "Mississippi Rangers," the Honorable S. Adams addressed the group: "You are leaving us with the reputation of the most moral, elevated company of gentlemen that ever left this State on an expedition of this kind; this high character you must, you will sustain, wherever you go."[43] Here, as elsewhere, the spirit of enterprise received high praise. The energy and ambition of the 49ers blended with assumptions that the wealth would be put to good uses overcame any sense of the naked lust for gold that sent men surging to the distant West.

In ports, the sailing of the California vessels brought forth crowds to witness the departures, which were often occasions for communal statements involving both those departing and those staying behind. In Boston, several ministers preached farewell sermons. The Reverend E. N. Kirk spoke for an hour to the assembled company of the *Edward Everett.* "In leaving your mothers, wives, and sisters," he reminded the Argonauts, "you are leaving behind you an indispensable element of civilization." He called upon the 49ers to remember their early training and to carry these elements of "civilization" to California with them.[44]

Sometimes the departures involved ceremonies that stretched over several days. The Reverend Doctor Edward Beecher addressed the entire company of the "New England and California Trading and Mining Association" at an evening meeting in the Tremont Temple on January 25, 1849, a week before the company's departure. Beecher saw the company as a future outpost of American civilization on the West Coast: "An object, therefore, rises before you higher than the attainment of wealth; it is the work of affecting, for evil or for good, the character of future generations of California. And certainly, no subject is more sublime, or of deeper interest, than the beginning and progress of a great community." He concluded: "Never forget that it is in your power to have the eternal honor of carrying from New England to California, that which is of infinitely more value than anything in California is now able to send back in return. She can send gold and silver; but you can carry the examples, and principles, and virtues of your pilgrim fathers."[45]

The departure of the seagoing Argonauts also drew forth the wrath of some who deplored the endless search for Mammon. The Reverend Doctor Putnam compared the settlement of Pilgrims at Plymouth Bay in 1620 with the emigration to the Bay of San Francisco in 1849. He excoriated the universal interest in gold that would lead directly to the decline of civilization. Spain's decline dated from the "tide of American gold flowing over her," he reminded his audience. Gold would lead to lawlessness, "deadly affrays," robbery, and "many will part with their gold, and leave their bodies to the vultures, somewhere in the wilderness on the road to San Francisco." He concluded that "those who have ties and obligations at home, and other avocations alien from those of such adventure, and the means through industry of a frugal and comfortable livelihood" should stay.[46] Religious exercises were a common feature of departure ceremonies across the nation, although such sermons (or at least reports of them) were most common in New England.

In these messages, California and its gold were seen to be as remote and exotic as the Hawaiian Islands or Australia, and the opportunities for wealth were balanced against the dangers and temptations. That the 49ers would return with gold was taken for granted; what was also necessary was that they return with their beliefs unimpaired. For those who gathered in churches to receive the blessings of their religious and community leaders, whether in Boston Harbor or Sag Harbor, the emphasis was on the Argonauts in California as harbingers of a superior civilization. That these men absented themselves from their families and communities for years in order to get rich was a necessary price to pay in this great venture. If, while spreading the values of Protestantism, political democracy, and economic opportunity through hard work some also found quantities of gold, it was assumed that this would be appropriate. They would then return to the bosom of their families and put their new riches to the best possible uses.[47]

PARTINGS

How patiently and resignedly they listened to the sad discourses of the minister, knowing it would be the very last they would hear for many months. How eager the glances they cast up to the church choir, where sat the girls they were to marry on their return. How few returned. How few married the girl of that period's choice.

PRENTICE MULFORD

Finally came the day of departure. The good-byes echoed across the Republic, from the doors of individual homes and the public squares of villages to the docks and wharves of busy harbors and rivers. The emotional outpourings on the occasion of the final separation, in words and in last letters, expressed introspection about marriage, family, children, and parents, mixed with outbursts of guilt, anger, despondency, longing, and intimacy.

By their own admissions, the 49ers found themselves powerfully affected. In a world in which men characteristically eschewed emotional display as a quality associated with women, the partings of the 49ers often broke down this division of feelings. Many men wept openly.[48] Robert Beeching had an emotional parting from his "Dearest Harriett." William Parker's bride of five months accompanied him to Cincinnati, where the two separated with much anguish. Margaret DeWitt captured the poignancy of the moment when she wrote, "This is a hard thing, this breaking up of families."[49]

Even those who retained their outward composure spoke of how much they had been moved. "I observe that there generally has to be 2 or 3 times set for leaving before the emigrant can get familiarized somewhat with the idea of separating from home, friends, and family," William Rothwell of Fulton, Missouri, wrote in his journal. "Parting with near relatives & friends on such an occasion is a tender affair." Rothwell's friends and companions also felt the impact of departure from their families. The individual most deeply affected was his brother-in-law, Pemberton Gibbs, recently married to Rothwell's sister Polly. "It was harder for him to get over parting with you than any of the rest of us. He stood it manfully enough," he wrote of Gibbs.[50] Rothwell's account emphasized that it was the duty of a departing 49er to act out the part of the strong and self-sufficient man who could regret, but who soon could put the departure behind him in the interests of the challenges ahead and his responsibility to the traveling companions to whom he had given his allegiance.

Others were less clinical and more deeply affected. Joshua Sullivan wrote openly of his feelings: "Dear wife, my heart bleeds within me to think of starting on the west plains to be gone so long from you but I will do the best I can and serve the Lord. My daily prayer is that the Lord will bless your soul and body and prosper you and spare your lives, and that we may all meet again." And James Lyne of Henderson, Kentucky, confided, "And yet I have found it no easy task to expatriate myself from my childhood's home & tare myself from Friends I love. Nor am I so weak as not to confess tears flowed freely when I thus left all I loved on earth behind."[51] These and other diaries and letters suggest that men wrote of deeper feelings than they could bring themselves to express in person.

In their farewells, the Argonauts continued to speak of the burdens imposed upon them by the decision to go to California, a prolonged absence undertaken solely in the interest of the family. Their future financial independence would make all sacrifices worthwhile. William Pierce wrote to his wife Georgiana of his desolation at parting from "my best friend on earth & that *Darling blue eyed boy.*" He went only from a sense of duty, for to succeed "may place us where we will be slaves to none, independent of want, able to go through life with plenty & cultivate Social feeling, virtue & peace without being Compelled to struggle for Daily bread." Harvey Chapman asked the forgiveness of his parents "for leaving Caroline to take this wild goose chase." James Alexander wrote, "Remember how you looked and how I felt when I was parted from you. I shall never forget the secret kiss I had from the lips of little William." The sorrow at parting further confirmed for him that only a powerful sense of duty to his family had forced him into such a separation, and he concluded, "I some time think I have committed a Great Crime by leaving you and our dear Willie boy." After the departure, the imprint of smiles, tears, and kisses remained over many miles and even days. Some 49ers opened little presents and ate carefully prepared and packed meals as final reminders of the care and affection they had given up to pursue a higher duty.[52]

The parting of 49ers from parents had a different quality to it. Here, the unspoken words were simply that they might never see one another again. Vast distances, the frailties of aging in mid-nineteenth-century America, and the sudden onset of disease made a prolonged separation possibly a permanent one. Yet in a culture in which parents directed so many aspects of the child's and adolescent's worlds, the departure for an independent voyage might also be a cause for rejoicing on the part of some young men. Not all 49ers so expressed their views of the past and their hopes for the future, but such considerations surely lay in the background.

Like so much else, parting had a public as well as private dimension. As communities sent forth to the California gold fields the best of their young people, they gave these departures a celebratory quality. At piers, on board ship, in public squares, those who left and those who stayed joined in a public observance, commemorating the beginning of a new national adventure that would benefit participants, families, and nation alike.

In New York City, "the docks are crowded with fathers and mothers, brothers and sisters and sweethearts, and such embracing and waving of handkerchiefs." One departing Argonaut threw his last five-dollar piece toward shore, shouting, "I'm going where there is plenty more." As the ship moved away from the wharf, the 49ers on board and the crowd on shore exchanged cheer after cheer. Never in the history of the Republic had departing Americans—whether headed for the fur trade, rich lands, or military glory—left with higher expectations.[53]

On the crowded wharves of Boston, ministers conducted solemn services; in Philadelphia, singing throngs along a parade route serenaded the 49ers to their ships. And people gathered to pay tribute to strangers who had come from distant places to join this national adventure. One 49er left Danville, Pennsylvania, for the gold fields in March 1849. As his company passed through Philadelphia, he wrote, "we were greeted with Cheers from different crowds who stood on the wharves to witness our departure, to which we responded with cheers and the California gold diggers song." In the village of Marshall, Michigan, the Wolverine Rangers paraded on the occasion of their departure. The whaling port of Sag Harbor held a special church service to bless the undertaking, and in honor of the occasion, the young

Argonauts were permitted to stay up late with their girls. Everywhere, the departing 49ers received the ministrations and honor of their communities.[54]

One of the largest public celebrations took place in Bloomington, Indiana, where some two thousand people assembled to mark the occasion. The 49ers initially gathered at the Methodist Church for religious exercises and the presentation of a Bible to each member of the company. The assembled crowd sang missionary hymns to the departing company. Then, "at about noon the wagons rolled off toward the Pacific Ocean, bearing away our beloved friends, some of whom will doubtless fall in that far distant land, and we shall see them no more on earth." The following day, the remainder of the company departed, led out of town by the Masons in full-dress "Regalia," who had come to honor one of their members on the occasion of his departure for California.[55]

In terms of the hopes and fears expressed both privately and publicly, the first great surge of emigration in the winter and spring of 1849 was remarkable for the high expectations it excited, for the public display of the emotions it aroused, and for the power of those emotions on all sides. For later waves of emigrants, these partings were more private and less public, and less highly wrought, even if they did repeat what the initial emigrants had endured. As the thrill of the first season of Argonaut activity passed, editors no longer pontificated; ministers no longer saw the Gold Rush as God's work in the extension of "civilization" to California, or if they did, they were more subdued in their public expressions. By 1851 and certainly by 1852, almost every community had one or more residents who were returned 49ers. The decision to go now took place in the atmosphere of experience. Some of those who initially had declined to go now changed their minds, caught up in the vivid descriptions that emerged from the letters sent from the gold fields by those who had "seen the elephant," a phrase that represented the unknown and the adventure that 49ers associated with California.[56] Sometimes younger siblings went out to California to join their brothers; or wives and families left for a reunion with their husbands; occasionally, fathers joined sons. That so many continued to do so was a commentary on their present condition and the continued hopes associated with the vision of California and its golden opportunities.

4

JOURNEY AND ARRIVAL:

Coming to California, Coming to Terms

ANNUALLY, BEGINNING in the winter of 1848–49 and for the next decade, Americans journeyed to California by sea and by land. The journey by sea could be begun at any season, anywhere along the Atlantic coast, and could follow either the long route around Cape Horn or the shorter route across Panama. The trek overland began in mid-May from the edge of the prairies outside St. Joseph or Independence, Missouri, and concluded in Placerville, in the foothills of the Sierra, after a journey of twenty-two hundred miles.

Even as they moved in response to economic opportunity, Americans remained a local people, accustomed to the supportive surroundings of their families, friends, and communities. This encounter with exotic peoples on a long ocean voyage or with the western half of the continent by travel overland was something they always remembered. Many kept journals and diaries to mark the occasion; others wrote voluminous letters to their relatives and friends, filled with minute descriptions of the dangers and wonders of the trip.[1] Their accounts, whether to family members, friends, or editors, and whether private or public, conveyed astonishment at a series of new worlds encountered and a sense of wonder that was often mixed with uneasiness and sometimes hostility. The new people, customs, and values that awaited them in California were equally striking and disturbing. They were also part of a new and different world with which they all had to come to terms.

SEAGOING ARGONAUTS

For many Americans—especially New Englanders, but also for others on the Atlantic coast, from New York and Pennsylvania through the Carolinas to New Orleans—a voyage by sea was the sensible way to go to California. The voyage itself began with weeks of preparation, and as we have seen, the myriad duties for planning and departure found scores of willing hands to carry them out. Young men who had recently been clerks or apprenticed tradesmen, farm laborers, or students found themselves officers in a company bound for California. Company officers and company committees crisscrossed port cities in search of a ship, then laid in provisions for the voyage and supplies and equipment for the mines, and finally tended to the thousand details that led to a prompt departure. The prospective 49ers found a sense of independence and importance in their tasks that signaled a transition from their families to a new community of like-minded Argonauts.

The departed Argonauts now encountered for the first time their diverse companions. Lafayette Fish left his home in Jackson, Michigan, and went down the Mississippi River to New Orleans, where he took a steamer to Panama. Of the other travelers, he wrote, "We have 200 passengers which puts us pretty close together they comprise every grade and condition in life, and nearly if not all the States are represented." The vessels from Boston and New York were largely filled with New Englanders and New Yorkers, but one 49er who sailed from Boston in May 1849 described his companions as "Yankees from Cape Cod, Western men, New Yorkers, an old man of sixty, all alone, a one-eyed Baptist preacher about forty-five, who is the butt of all, more especial on account of his having brought a formidable looking revolver with him, but forgot to bring any powder."[2]

Some 49ers expressed unhappiness about their companions on the voyage. One wrote of the voyage up the Pacific coast in 1850 that he had been thrown together with several Southerners, "nearly all of whom were excessively addicted to swearing and many of them, to gambling." Among the passengers were two "fine men" from Michigan who also had left families behind, and with whom the Argonaut passed his time. William P. Daingerfield sketched the origins of his fellow passengers in these terms: "Virginia sends four representatives, Baltimore four, Ohio one, and where the rest hail from the Lord only knows and I don't care." He observed of his companions, "Our party is composed of very ordinary materials, there are more good clothes than brains in it, more affectation than politeness, more cowardice than courage, more deceipt than good feeling."[3] Many felt this sense of superiority on meeting 49ers from other states and distant sections of the nation.

The length of the voyage and the ensuing idleness associated with it soon generated internal conflicts as companies of 49ers split into factions and bickered among themselves. "Nothing can be more dull and monotonous than a calm at sea," observed one Argonaut. "A kind of uneasy restlessness creeps over a person which he has not the power to repress. So much of his time seems lost and thrown away." Enoch Jacobs, a 49er who took passage on the *Edward Everett,* wrote six weeks out of Boston, "I observe Cliques forming which seem to bode anything but good." His apprehensions were well founded, and the listless wind that delayed the passage increased internal acrimony. "God Grant us a breeze soon for these long Calms are fruitful in producing dissension and disaffections," he continued. And later, he commented of his company, "this is truly a jealous people, Strangely given to fault finding."[4]

Variations in accommodations and services increased the divisions. Those who could afford to do so sometimes brought along special food and drink for themselves and their friends. Edward P. Abbe, a Bostonian with aristocratic airs, sailed on the *Edward Everett,* along with 150 members of the New England Mining and Trading Company. On board, he dined with his friends. They ate well, supplementing the ship's dining arrangements, or "mess,"with their own "picknicks" of delicacies. Others referred to them as "the aristocratic mess," a term that Abbe embraced with satisfaction because, he wrote, "we have generally speaking the most gentlemanly & polished & educated men in our mess."[5]

As a way of reducing the tension and boredom, many companies organized activities of an entertaining and practical nature. The entertainments included amateur theatricals, military drills on the deck, and improvised music performances. Some companies sponsored lectures ranging from the geology of California to customs of the peoples in the ports of call. And from the beginning, companies laid plans for what they would do on arrival, establishing a command structure (would the elected officers continue to exercise authority once the party reached California?), organizing the company into squads of miners, and making plans to distribute equipment and to parcel out the resources of the company. These projects testified to their leisure and boredom, their images of the gold country, and the serious nature of their enterprise.

The idleness associated with a long sea voyage soon led to other recreational outlets, notably gambling and card playing. Both these exercises were among the vices that ministers, editors, officials, relatives, and friends had held up to scorn in public and private partings, and now they quickly became the most popular recreations. John J. Craven wrote after a scant five weeks at sea, "I am out of all patience and never was so heartily sick of cards in my life for it is nothing else from morning til night." Another 49er commented,

> All kinds of amusements have become stale except that of gambling, which is carried to the greatest excess. I counted today, no less than seven companies on the deck, of from four to six persons each, with a pile of coin before him which is lessening or increasing every moment. . . . Several of those who have learned to play since leaving New York have rushed into it with the greatest rashness.[6]

Cards and gambling not only drew veteran players, but also rapidly seduced those heretofore innocent of such vices.

Into the boredom and routine of shipboard activity intruded at irregular intervals an astonishing array of new sights, sounds, tastes, and smells that alternately astonished, confused, and dismayed. The voyage to California provided most seagoing 49ers with their first contact with the tropics, new cultures, and new values. The revelations included flying fish, swarms of birds, strange aromas, and brilliant sunsets and sunrises. Rinaldo Taylor from Boston wrote to his wife of his ship's passing Savannah, "The night was bright & clear, and as warm as we could wish, while the air came from off shore absolutely loaded with perfume. It was like nothing I ever experienced at the north." Neither was the slave sale that he visited in New Orleans. Like many Northerners on the way to California, Taylor had his first direct contact with the institution of slavery, and he had strongly negative reactions.[7]

The largest group of seagoing 49ers sailed down the coast—sometimes calling at Charleston or New Orleans—to Panama, where passengers disembarked for a trip across the peninsula to the Pacific. The stopover in Panama—sometimes extended to several weeks by bad weather and the scarcity of vessels on the Pacific side—gave the 49ers a look at a new tropical world that simultaneously captivated and appalled them. It was the first experience for most with a Spanish and Catholic culture. The transient Americans called the tropical landscape exciting beyond words and the native peoples heathen (which for them was synonymous with Catholic) and lazy. "It appears to me as fine a country as one could wish, but it is cursed with the most lazy indolent population that breathes," ran a characteristic observation. "They cultivate nothing whatever. The finest land in the world lies just as nature made it, at the very gates of Panama."[8]

Most of the 49ers sharply criticized Panamanian customs. J. E. Clayton called a "fandango" dance "the most vulgar thing I ever saw. They seem to have no sense of shame about them." James Barnes from upstate New York expressed shock at the vigorous social activity on the Sabbath, with music and dancing, and he wrote of it, "Sunday is no more respected here than any other day gambling and drinking is carried on here to a great extent I have seen thousands of dollars piled on gaming tables all in gold and silver." Like other 49ers, Barnes did not know whether to be shocked at the desecration of the Sabbath or impressed by the large quantities of hard currency in plain view. Milo Goss shared this low opinion of Panamanians, and he wrote, "Rioting, debauchery in all its different form, prevails here, in all its deformity. The Sabbath day is a day of revelry among the Spanish and of drinking and gambling with the Americans, and all kinds of sin is committed with more boldness than one performs a good act." He was also astonished to see Spanish ladies smoking. Once again, what seemed disturbing was the degree to which Americans were vulnerable to such blandishments. Of their experiences, one wrote, "Many an American who never thought of such a thing at home, gets carried away by the general excitement & gets his pockets emptied 'presto.' "[9]

Many Americans found the Catholic churches old and impressive, the services ranging from "very solemn and imposing" to "pompous." Christian Miller wrote of Rio de Janeiro, "the riches and beauty of the interiors of these churches I cant describe."[10] The 49ers, especially Yankees from New England, showed no inclination to join the services, but their reactions suggested a sense of awe and respect, if not sympathy for this alien church.

The trip across the isthmus by canoe and mule took three days, and the jungle landscape evoked wonder and admiration. J. E. Clayton summed up the river trip inland with the comment, "For me to attempt to describe the scenery on this river would be to overrate my powers of description. It is so different from anything I ever saw that I am lost in admiration and wonder." S. Schufelt loved the "howling of the monkeys & chattering of parrots" that formed a chorus for the 49ers across the isthmus. The capacity of Panamanians to carry heavy loads and maneuver the loaded canoes evoked much admiration. The tropical downpours on the trails and on the rivers produced resignation and humor. One 49er wrote to his wife, "If you could have looked upon me then, groping through the forest, with my red shirt, straw hat & linen pants, the only clothing I had on, covered with mud, with the rain pouring down on me, you would have thought I was the most miserable being imaginable."[11]

The pungent smells and rich foods were also reminders of a different world. Jacob Townsend, who shipped as a member of the crew from Nantucket for fifteen dollars a month in order to get to the gold fields, loved the oranges of the tropics, "some of them sweet as my wife's kisses." William A. Brown of Toledo, Ohio, was fascinated by the variety of foods served in Panama, and he wrote his parents elaborate descriptions of the meals.[12]

A second group of seagoing 49ers sailed down the coast, around the Horn, and up the Pacific side, calling at ports along the way. For these Argonauts, being certain of the accommodations, costs, and traveling conditions they would encounter more than compensated for greater distance and a longer time at sea. The ports of call for these 49ers had their own surprises, however. William F. Denniston expressed shock that men and women bathed together on Grenada. John Stone considered Rio de Janeiro "a disgusting filthy city." He thought only slightly better of Callao and Lima, Peru. Enoch Jacobs found the character of Chileans wanting ("a very indolent and idle class of People possessing but little enterprise"), while at the same time he was enormously impressed by the natural beauty of Valparaiso harbor. "The dawn of this morning disclosed one of the most splendid views I ever beheld. The Towering Andes extended north and south as far as I could see," he confided to his journal.[13]

The long periods of idleness that were a dominant feature of the voyages by sea, and that followed the hectic physical activity of preparation and the emotional stress of parting, led frequently to intensive introspection. As the Argonauts stared out at the wide expanses of water, they had time to consider their ties to their families and their motives for making the voyage to California. Some tried to come to terms with the sense of selfishness that seemed to lie at the root of the search for gold. William DeCosta was more frank and introspective than most in his analysis of his motives. His companions, he confided to his journal, were "bound by bands of gold," slaves to the search for the precious metal. As for himself, "I will not say that gold is not my god, for it is, and further that it is the god of almost every man, though there are few that will acknowledge it." But DeCosta was ultimately persuaded of the uprightness of the enterprise, and he continued, "I look upon it as a good god and a great operator in human affairs. Gold is charity and makes love, it produces smiling faces, relieves the sick and afflicted, and, in fact, does everything great and good." Therefore, he was engaged in a search for an instrument that would do enormous good in the world. Indeed, he concluded, "Let us call it good, looking for no evil, and leave it, the mighty engine, to revolve around everything save the great wheel of time." His Biblical allusions echoed American values and language at midcentury. Perhaps such arguments provided the Argonauts with an armor against the shocks of California and the gold fields and their continued sense of guilt at leaving home and family.[14]

Interspersed with the leisure and boredom of the long voyages were experiences of otherness that many of the voyagers found disturbing. The 49ers were struck by how rapidly they were cast into a new world. William Elder wrote to his wife, "Although it is less than six weeks since we parted it seems to be more than so many months; so many new and strange scenes have continually passed before. Scenes so unlike anything I have before seen that it all most seems like a dream." He was delighted when the voyage was at last over. Aside from boredom and monotonous food and cramped quarters, he loved the "American" character of San Francisco, where "I seemed to feel quite at home among the good honest Saxon countenances are everywhere to be seen contrasting favorably with the sallow narrow visaged Spaniards."[15] The sense of relief on reaching California extended beyond the gold of their dreams and the boredom of the voyage to a comfort in finding a familiar culture and familiar ways of doing things. In many respects, the voyage to California by sea might be thought of as a dress rehearsal for the placers in California. Men jostled one another in close quarters, competed for space, for sustenance, and for services, paid a high price for everything, and above all, focused on the same objective.

The voyages of the 49ers to California placed in sharp relief the wide range of individuals and groups set in motion to the gold fields. More than other routes to the California gold fields, the sea voyages confirmed social and economic distinctions within the passengers. Some could afford superior accommodations and food; others had to settle for primitive quarters and plain subsistence. Some went to San Francisco with the leisure and resources to speculate and to spy out the main chance; others had to trek to the mines immediately to support themselves and to make good on the promises to their families and relatives. These distinctions might enlarge over time in California, but they were already clear and sharp on the voyage there, as explicit as the traditional American reaction to new cultures and values in foreign lands.

OVERLAND ARGONAUTS

The overland 49ers faced a formidable journey across half the continent. Some voyagers from Atlantic ports were accustomed to long sea journeys, but almost no one among the Argonauts who chose the overland route had made such a journey before. A few thousand pioneers already had made the transcontinental migration to Oregon, but these had been farm families headed west in search of land. Never in the history of the Republic had there been a mass migration of tens of thousands overland to the West Coast. The voyage of the overland Argonauts was all the more striking because these pilgrims included city dwellers, along with people from small towns and farms, who now found themselves caught up in the greatest pioneering challenge of the day. The great distances and monotonous character of the landscape, together with towering mountain ranges and deserts, posed dramatic obstacles. Added to these physical challenges were fears of the Plains Indian tribes to heighten apprehensions.

Like their seagoing counterparts, these 49ers also joined together for purposes of travel. From the earliest creation of companies in home communities to the great campouts in Independence and St. Joseph, groups of men sought out others with similar origins and values. Beginning with family groups, these associations extended out to include those from the immediate community, nearby villages, and regions or sections, as New Englanders and Southerners sought their own kind for traveling companions. Those with special concerns formed their own companies. The Sabbath keepers joined in groups that would observe a Sunday of rest, and temperance men often banded together.[16] There were also exercises in the random selection of traveling companions. A St. Louis company, the "Pioneer Line," offered freight wagons, wagonmasters, teamsters, and guides to transport 49ers to California at a cost of two hundred dollars each; the Argonauts would furnish their own tents, cooking gear, and rations. For many, joining a traveling company involved coming to terms, at least temporarily, with new kinds of people—new kinds of Americans to be sure, but still different peoples.[17]

The Argonauts soon came to view the overland expedition as a competition, as well as an exercise in cooperation. Tens of thousands of men were on the same trail to California, narrowly intent on the same objective. The sense of rivalry was the stronger because the Argonauts could literally see the competitors everywhere around them, ahead, behind, and even alongside. "There are thousands of men going along the road; in fact, it looks like the wagons hauling cotton to Macon just after a rise in the staple," wrote John Milner of Alabama to his family. "I believe there are wagons stretched in sight of one another for 500 miles."[18]

Of the notable differences from the sea voyage, the most significant was the enormous amount of work on the trip itself. Whereas seagoing 49ers suffered from boredom once underway, those on the California Trail coped with endless daily chores. Henry Packer's observation on the daily duties on the trail was repeated in a hundred letters to family and friends:

> When traveling, we are up at day break; and by the time the horses are fed, curried and harnessed, the breakfast is ready; as soon as that is dispatched, we hitch up and away. At noon—heretofore we have spent no longer time than is just necessary for the horses and ourselves to eat; but when we got to feeding them on grass, a little longer time will be required. In the evening, after stopping, the horses are to offgear, tie up, currey, and feed and water; the tent is to put up—bed clothes to arrange, supper to prepare and eat—which last is not hard to do—by this time it is bed time, and we "turn in." Then again, each member of the company comes upon guard duty once every fourth or fifth night.[19]

These were familiar routines for men from rural areas, but other kinds of tasks emerged for which the 49ers had little or no preparation. Thousands of men had their first experiences with sewing, washing, and cooking, and in company with the other duties on the trail, they found these burdensome. Little did the overland travelers realize that domestic work on the overland trail was only the beginning of a new range of chores that would confront 49ers in the gold fields.

Along with the combination of exhilaration and danger in the West went encounters with new people and new places on a more familiar scale. Like those who went to California by sea, the overland 49ers admired the scenery and generally disliked the new peoples they encountered. Indeed, their experiences seemed to confirm the provincial views of Americans at midcentury. Southerners despised Northerners as reformist fanatics and grasping merchants, interested only in cheating their fellow travelers. Men from Massachusetts clustered together in self-admiration; others disdained emigrants from the Bay State as coming from a place "where the majority are in favor of amalgamation."[20] Everyone castigated the Missourians as crude, a miserable, impoverished group of pioneers "on the extreme border of civilization." One 49er characterized them as "nasty, dirty looking whelps and all Hogs or most of them." The new state of Iowa, by contrast, drew praise for its rich lands and industrious population, but widespread condemnation for its terrible roads and gouging prices.[21]

The overland route west was more than a test of physical strength and endurance. Those who went to California in the summer of '49 and in subsequent annual migrations saw the challenges of an overland journey as a test of their character and of their capacity to maintain their standards of conduct surrounded by strangers and a new landscape. The trip across the plains was the first test of their traditional standards of behavior and conduct in a world without institutional force to ensure compliance. This struggle to preserve individual character appeared on two different levels throughout the journey: in setting and fulfilling the contractual arrangements to which so many men had agreed prior to setting forth and in coming to terms with the question of identity.

Almost everyone going overland to California joined a company. The company's arrangements were democratic in the sense that participants signed a document (generally referred to as a constitution) that spelled out rules of conduct, especially with respect to participation and sharing of duties. Deviations from these agreements began with the first turn of the road beyond the farm or the village, for no sooner had the trip begun than some men left to return to their farms, their parents, their wives, and their children. The situation was sometimes awkward. These men were now returning to the very farms and villages from which they had departed only a few days or weeks earlier with so much emotional outpouring. The term "backed-out Californians," always spoken with contempt, quickly came into use to describe those who turned back. Continuing 49ers were sometimes at pains to assure those at home that the Argonauts continuing to California held no hard feelings against the returning individual and that he should be welcomed back into the family as a member in good standing. William Rothwell saw the defection of his brother-in-law, Pemberton Gibbs, with regret, but he assured his father that all had parted on most amicable terms.[22]

The overland Argonauts also confronted the question of the identity of their fellow travelers, an issue that would carry over into the placers in California. From the intimate world of family, relatives, and friends, the 49ers entered increasingly into an anonymous condition in which one's identity might with little effort be hidden or changed. A striking quality of the mining camps in California was the anonymity of the individuals who lived there. Part of the unsettling experience of meeting new people, and in the gold fields, of having to place trust in strangers on short acquaintance, lay in confronting a world in which people were not always what they seemed. Except for a circle of close friends, in the case of those who had gone together, these were gatherings of strangers. Those so inclined could create an entirely new identity. The only connections with the past were friends, who were easily evaded, and mail from home, which could be left unclaimed or ignored. Some women complained that men along the trail and in California hid the fact that they were married. In this transient world, where men had come temporarily in pursuit of wealth in a separate chapter of their lives, no one cared to inquire too closely into the past. This anonymity became more faceless as men moved west.[23]

One of the astonishing features of the overland trail to California was the enormous waste of goods. Argonauts who went to California by sea took more of everything, but ships carried the weight effortlessly. Draft animals demanded more personal attention, and parties of 49ers shared a common characteristic in casting aside supplies and possessions to lighten the load. The 49ers littered the California Trail with discarded food supplies and heavy gold-mining equipment, often fancy gold-washing machines. They began to throw things away at the beginning of the journey, littering the trail for a thousand miles to and past Fort Laramie. Commenting on this array of discarded supplies, one Argonaut noted, "there has been enough thrown away on this trip to make a man rich." At the beginning of the final stage on the Humboldt River, many 49ers left their wagons and proceeded on foot, using as pack animals the stock horses they had brought for breeding. Horace Ballew described his astonishment at the sight of hundreds of abandoned wagons in the Humboldt River valley.[24]

Almost all the overland Argonauts wrote of their journey as characterized by hard work and danger, an odyssey to the farthest reaches of the new American Empire in which they triumphantly reached California against great odds. John Gish of Logan County, Ohio, compared crossing the plains to the hardest physical labor of his own work experience when he wrote, "I would rather tend a threshing machine than take a trip a cross the plains." And Joshua Sullivan commented that "nothing but poverty would induce me to go any further."[25]

The 49ers who went overland celebrated their participation in a triumphal march, a voyage whose successful completion welcomed them to membership in the club of American pioneers. It was not an exclusive club, certainly not by the early 1850s, but still, to cross the plains at midcentury was the great American pioneering experience. In their eyes, it forever conferred on those who made the journey a special status, different from those who went by sea at the start of the Gold Rush or by the railroad in the next generation. This journey by land with draft animals was a final large-scale reenactment of America's pioneering pattern, which had been largely unchanged for a century. It brought them into contact with what would become the fabled icons of the American West: the huge herds of buffalo, the dangerous Plains Indian tribes (sensed rather than seen), the towering peaks of the Rockies and the deserts of Nevada, and the great monuments of American expansion—Chimney Rock, Fort Laramie, the Great Salt Lake, and the desert reaching to the eastern foothills of the Sierra.[26] These varied peoples, geography, and experiences seemed to provide a suitable introduction to the infinite varieties of California.

COMING TO CALIFORNIA, COMING TO TERMS

Experiences on shipboard or on the California Trail that sometimes called on the 49ers to come to terms with their values and standards of behavior and conduct were only a prelude to the range of choices and temptations that began at the docks in San Francisco, on the streets in Placerville (or Hangtown, as it was called in those days), and in the diggings along the Feather or American Rivers. From the moment of their arrival, the 49ers acknowledged that California was different. It was different in its opportunities; it was different in its standards of doing business and of personal behavior; it was different in its wide range of attractions. The most dramatic introduction to these differences lay in San Francisco itself. Here, the dynamic town that was turning into a city met the ambitions of the 49ers who had traveled so far and who now landed with such high hopes. "The land of promise," wrote Charles Buckingham as he sailed into the great harbor: "Every heart beats high as we near the Golden Shore. All is speculation, expectation & anticipation."[27]

Gold brought together people from the distant reaches of the Western Hemisphere, and by the fall of 1849, San Francisco was booming. In December 1849, Rinaldo Taylor of Boston wrote of the City on the Bay, "It is now a great place, such a one as the world never produced before. Crowded with people from all parts of the world, the Yankees & the Chinaman jostling each other in the streets, while French, Germans, Sandwich Islands, Chillians, Malays, Mexicans, &c &c in all their varieties of costume and language go to form a 'congrommoration' of humanity, such as the world never saw before."[28] Here, the arriving Americans, a provincial and local people whose tolerance level was further limited by the sense of the search for gold as a competition, came face to face with one another and with peoples whose varieties they could not have imagined.

John C. Collbreath wrote in the summer of 1849, "The city of San Francisco presents the strangest state of society I ever saw or heard of."[29] This sense of differentness began in the harbor, where the Argonauts saw for the first time the masts of hundreds of idle craft, deserted by their crews stampeding to the gold fields. Arriving 49ers had not been ashore for ten minutes or gone more than ten feet from their landing site before they experienced a flood of powerful impressions.

For the newly arrived 49er, more impressive than the varieties of peoples and cultures were the opportunities to make money. From the streets at the edge of the harbor to the crests of the distant Sierra, California was a new economic experience. Even more than the display of goods, the ostentatious flaunting of money jolted the new arrivals. What had begun as incomparable riches in the imaginations of men in small towns and on farms seemed to receive the most dramatic kind of confirmation in California. Forty-niners from all places and of whatever previous economic condition again and again expressed astonishment at the quantities of hard money visible, passing from hand to hand. William Daingerfield wrote on his arrival in California, "Gold is measured here by bushels and shovel full."[30]

The large quantity of money in circulation dramatically inflated prices and wages. Gold, the standard currency, was plentiful, the property of everyone. Albert Osbun reflected his astonishment at the widespread holding of wealth when he wrote that gold was as common as sands in the seas. He concluded: "Money here seems to be of little value, & every person has plenty."[31]

The 49ers could not help but observe that gold was most visible in connection with activities of questionable morality. The gambling houses that lined the streets of San Francisco were its most prominent and opulent buildings. They paid the highest rents; they were, from all accounts, the most profitable; they were the first structures rebuilt after a fire. The widespread presence of gambling and other leisure time activities—from prostitution to billiards and bowls—shocked the newly arrived Argonauts. "If any persons wants to convince himself that money is the root of evil let them come here," wrote John Craven to his wife. "Nearly every other house is a gambling hole many that come down in the money from the *placer*—independent & rich are forced to lie down at night in the open air for want of means to pay their lodging."[32] That hard-earned money should be risked and so spent provoked astonishment—and the more so after the 49ers worked in the mines and realized first hand how dearly bought by labor were such sums.

The range of the entertainment industry—gambling, drinking, prostitution, music, and variety shows—and its universal presence and success, even on the Sabbath, testified to new kinds of beliefs and spending habits. In the gambling halls of San Francisco, "you may see a dozen tables in a room on which are displayed thousands of dollars in gold, and silver surrounded by a crowd of eager victims, betting from 25 cts to many doubloons or ounces as they are called," wrote Lafayette Fish. Rinaldo Taylor commented of the gambling houses with reference to images from home: "I could not help thinking today (Sunday) what our staid New Englanders would think could they have stood with me, about the time of church opening at home, in the door of one of these places in the most public street in the city, & cast their eyes over the scene." Taylor's comments capture the sense of displacement from family, community, and a lifetime of accepted patterns and standards of behavior. In California, from one end of the gold camps to the other, these values seemed turned upside down. "Here are to be found two extremes, good and bad, and here it is that vice predominates," Milo Goss told his wife.[33]

The riches of San Francisco extended beyond its displays of gold to its streets, where goods of every description lay discarded and rotting. The city—if so it might be called in the summer of 1849—was a hodgepodge of tents and wooden shacks where "millions of dollars worth of goods of every description from Canton silks & toys to Yankee 'nick-nacks' lie stacked up in the streets or strewn about the vacant lots, for want of buildings to store them in."[34] Lafayette Fish commented in early 1849, "The destruction and loss of property is astonishing...thousands upon thousands of dollars worth of every kind rotting in the streets. This arises partly from the unsaleableness of some kinds, and the difficulty of getting storage when the rainy season first commenced."[35] This profligacy of resources testified to the city's central position in outfitting and trading, in which the arrival of a few shiploads of goods would drive down the price of woolen shirts or pans and make stocks of these goods worth only a fraction of their original value.

This treatment of trade goods as expendable extended to the treatment of the landscape in the mining camps of the Sierra. California's mining areas were rapidly transformed into a vast public dump. Transient miners filled the placers with unused, unneeded, or depleted goods. Men bought clothes, wore them until they literally disintegrated, and then threw them away and bought others. The devastated landscape of the California Sierra was soon littered with the debris of tens of thousands of miners who considered time more important than possessions and surplus clothing or food of insufficient value to save. This expenditure of raw materials seemed justified by the high rewards awaiting them and by the temporary nature of their stay.

How did the new arrivals from New England and upstate New York and Pennsylvania, from the Middle West and the South, react to the presence of these different values, so strange and contrary to their beliefs, and yet seemingly accepted by all? Some simply could not resolve the strife between the conflicting standards of value. Immediately on arriving, they looked around, did not like what they saw, and took the next boat back. (Most of the return travel was by sea.) Those who stayed were a self-selected group who were willing to adapt to the new moral climate they found. They wished to pursue wealth in California and were willing to make the concessions of principle necessary in order to succeed. To succeed in this world, they realized, they must be prepared to deal with it on terms and under conditions already set by others.

They did not have to accept the gambling of San Francisco, the drinking of the camps, or loose spending habits so visible around them, but they did have to adjust to the extent of putting moral differences behind them in the interest of profiting from economic opportunity. To this end, they bought what was necessary to mine at the inflated prices demanded for these goods. Most 49ers also accepted the new habits associated with Sunday, a day into which was crowded the miner's errands, leisure, business, and recreation. The degree of adaptation varied, of course, from individual to individual and group to group. It was simply easier to do business on Sunday, and in a world of intense work and competition, to make things easier was an important consideration. Isaac Owen, a missionary, observed that a man who considered himself "a good Methodist" routinely sold goods on Sunday, to Owen's great distress and presumably to the other man's profit. The longer someone stayed in California and worked in the placers, probably the more complete was the change. Indeed, one of the striking qualities associated with the Gold Rush was the degree to which each arriving annual wave of 49ers adapted to this new world.[36]

The presence of gold and its widespread availability forced the 49ers to modify their views about a wide range of subjects. Among the first they had to confront was the issue of new patterns of earning and spending, investment and return. The newly arrived Argonauts soon discovered that the prices of goods and services were high beyond anything imaginable for people coming from the East, such as a dinner at a San Francisco hotel for two gentlemen, two ladies, and four children for which the bill was ninety dollars.[37]

The 49ers also found that before washing the first pan of dirt in the streams of the Sierra, they had to invest capital in tools for mining and equipment and supplies for daily subsistence and shelter. Those who arrived in California with the right equipment (as opposed to one of the useless goldometers and gold-digging machines advertised in the East) had to land it and move it a hundred miles overland. Those who bought the proper tools and supplies in California itself—shovel, pan, pick, tent, blankets, cradle— also had to purchase food and transport everything to the placers. Procuring supplies for the mines—salt pork, flour, sugar, tea, and coffee—might involve the outlay of one hundred dollars per miner, plus transportation costs of another one hundred. It was appropriate to the expense involved that when Argonauts later described their financial condition to interested parties back home, they listed foodstuffs as among their assets. Allan Varner wrote to his brother from the diggings in late 1849, "I have got one thousand dollars in gold dust and three hundred pounds of provisions which are worth five hundred dollars here."[38]

For the 49ers, the California Gold Rush also raised the larger question of what something was worth. This issue first emerged in the decision of what to take to California, in most stark terms for those who went overland and who found what they could take severely limited. Money had no value on the overland trail to California, for there was nothing to buy. James Wilkins noted the question of value after only four weeks on the trail when he wrote, "Money does not here represent the value of property. If one man has a thing that another wants he will give twenty times its value in something he does not want. There is a great deal of trading done in this way at this point."[39] The issue of value soon became more concentrated on a few items as the journey stretched on toward the West. Livestock, food, and water were necessary and irreplaceable items. All else was expendable.

In the mines, the necessary tools for work were the items of greatest value. A grand piano was useless in the diggings, whereas a half-dozen shovels were immensely valuable. The list of items valued for providing comfort and well-being was precise and short: a sack of flour, tools, newspapers from home, and especially mail. These took precedence and commanded the highest possible price, or were literally beyond price. As prospective miners moved farther into the diggings, money was worth less and vital goods and services more. The 49ers newly arrived in the gold camps were astonished that bearded men would emerge from tents and offer them fifty dollars, say three ounces of gold, for the pair of boots they were wearing, for which they had paid three dollars in St. Louis. What they would come to realize quickly is that in the isolation of the gold camps, items necessary to wear, to eat, and to work with were much more valuable than gold dust.

Another major adjustment to the conceptions of value that the 49ers brought with them was in the range of work that men were willing to perform. Thousands mined, but others flocked into the mining camps and the towns and took the other available jobs. Farmers from Illinois did day labor on the streets and in construction; lawyers from Philadelphia unloaded ships and transported goods around the city; doctors from St. Louis waited table in restaurants and dealt cards in gambling houses. California society had a dramatic openness about it. It was an unformed world in which men took new work identities, just as they might well take new personal identities. Richard Cowley of New York City noted that "a man can Work at anything here and need not be ashamed." William Daingerfield knew a Philadelphia lawyer who worked in a circus and lawyers and editors with jobs as auctioneers. Daingerfield himself had mined, auctioneered, clerked, and practiced law since his arrival in California, and he concluded that "all classes engage in anything that may present itself."[40]

What the 49ers would not do was work as a servant class. In a world outwardly characterized by independence, by movement from place to place and from occupation to occupation, even the most marginal of laborers valued a sense of his own work. One 49er noted on his arrival in San Francisco, "One hates to ask even a servant to do any service much less an equal as it is so reluctantly performed." He concluded, "It seems as if the usual habits & actions of men were subverted."[41] These attitudes represented one of the many differences found in the land of gold.

These adaptations to varying standards of value began on the dock and extended to the most distant camps. Coming to California, and coming to terms with the emerging values and allegiances it offered, now placed the 49ers in a new and different world, a world with new values that demanded that they form new bonds and allegiances with those around them, even as they struggled in the name of their duties to the world they had left behind.

5

OLD BONDS AND NEW ALLEGIANCES:

"Me and John Stick Together Like Wood Ticks"

"THIS IS A TERRIBLE CITY to live in, one is in a continual state of excitement," Milo Goss wrote to his wife from San Francisco. "It is in a community like this that man feels his own weakness and insignificance." Most Argonauts would have extended Goss's comments from the City on the Bay to cover the most remote mining camps of the gold country, where there was more space and fewer people, but the same degree of impersonality. The 49ers, parting from the support and intimacy associated with families and communities, after long sea voyages and expeditions overland, suddenly found themselves cast into a rootless, chaotic, and impersonal world driven entirely by the search for money. "There is no sympathy for the living or the dead everyone for himself—little Confidence between people & no truth told to strangers about the mines when here," observed one recently arrived Argonaut. It was a another shock, another part of the new ways of California. Thomas Forbes summed up the cold-hearted nature of the California Gold Rush with the comment: "It is every man for himself and the devil for them all." He concluded: "I am looking out for number one."[1]

This was a condition radically different from the sense of close-knit social relations they knew back home. It was an uncomfortable condition, and it could not last.

The 49ers did their best to take those who loved and supported them with them. As soon as they made the decision to go to California, they sought to persuade relatives, friends, and neighbors to join them. The written accounts refer frequently to brothers, uncles, cousins, in-laws, and even fathers as companions in this great adventure. William Rothwell left his home in Fulton, Missouri, with two uncles and a brother-in-law. In the Applegate family of Howard County, Missouri, the father and two older sons went to California; the mother and two younger sons remained at home. The presence of relatives ensured continuing support on the trail or ship and in the diggings. Family members later joined other Argonauts who went to California alone.[2]

Among those who went joined together by family and community ties, perhaps the largest and closest knit group were the 705 residents who left the island of Nantucket in 1849. The community of Nantucket represented an unusual example of the closeness and family ties of seagoing Argonauts. Of this group of emigrants alone, 35 bore the surname Coffin; 28, Folger; 25, Swain.[3]

Membership in companies of Argonauts also offered an assurance of support; it was a response to the fear of surviving alone in a strange land. When Mr. Foster addressed a company on the eve of its departure, he told its members that "men in California were different from what they was at home." He asked the members "if we did not Calculate to stand by each other in sickness and in health when we should be in foreign climes far away from home and friends." When he asked for a show of support, men raised their hands in a gesture of solidarity with one another. In California, Foster hinted, traditional values of loyalty eroded or vanished in the headlong rush for gold. In a California full of injury, disease, and misfortune, he reminded them, establishing a support system to enclose and protect individuals was a vital step.[4]

Other groups put declarations of mutual support on a more formal basis. John Gish of Logan County, Ohio, signed "Articles of Agreement" with four men "who mutually agree to stand by and sustain each other in sickness and in health." Gish and his four colleagues each put up two hundred dollars to support their collective commitment.[5] Thousands of other 49ers undertook such a responsibility in the stages of their expeditions to California: in their villages, across the county, or in St. Joseph or Independence, where they joined such groups prior to departure across the plains.

For those who chose the land route to California, the journey was also the first test of the agreements they had made and the commitments they had given in order to preserve the supportive social cohesion they had known back home. The first stages of the trail west offered a time for trying out the new groups of family members, friends, and neighbors in familiar surroundings and with minimal stress. It was also the period of the first defections, as we already have seen. Circumstances and feelings changed, even after a short period on the trail. James Lyne of Henderson, Kentucky, spoke in supportive terms of the departure of a member of the company who was also a neighbor. "I regret very much Ben Floyd's leaving us," he wrote. "He is not only a good fellow & one to whome I have become very much attached from his excellent qualities, he is truly a loss to us all as he has acted a brother's part to all."[6]

At the beginning of the overland trails in Independence and St. Joseph, the issue of organization took on a more serious tone. Those who set out alone from home, or with small numbers of relatives or friends, needed to join larger companies at the points of departure at the edge of the plains. Most groups that organized to cross the plains did so in companies of about forty. It was the most efficient number in terms of the organization of men and the demands of draft animals for grass and water. Thus, Independence and St. Joseph in the spring of 1849 and annually during the spring for the next decade were scenes of serious matchmaking in which groups of different numbers, origins, and interests (except the intention to dig gold in California) searched for alliance with others of generally similar interests and values for purposes of crossing the plains.[7]

These male courtships often began by matching individuals from the same town or the same state, or those sharing a common interest, such as temperance, as we have seen. Sometimes an Argonaut simply tried to find "honest men" with whom to throw in his lot, favoring judgment of character over geographic origin. George Applegate and his companions from Kestesville, Missouri, "had the good fortune to get in company with a very intelligent Company from Iowa" and joined forces with it. With a degree of common ground established, representatives could canvass the practical questions of the kind of draft animals (mules or oxen), the loads permitted in each wagon (and by division, the amount of load allotted to each individual), the daily pace of progress to the west, and the anticipated cost. These negotiations might conclude by veering off into issues such as guides, experience, and so forth. They bought or traded whatever skills might be useful in exchange for membership. One woman agreed to perform duties as a nurse and teach nursing skills in exchange for her membership in a company.[8]

Once on the trail, the strains and tensions of the trip tested these travel arrangements, as well. Some 49ers soon reflected great dissatisfaction with their traveling companions and even the rules under which they marched west, but once departed from Independence or St. Joseph, it was difficult if not impossible simply to leave a wagon-train company without having another group to join. James Lyne's was one of several companies to split up at Fort Laramie.[9] Other disaffected Argonauts left their companies at Fort Bridger or Salt Lake City, outfitting points where travelers might wait while in search of new arrangements.

The real hazards of the overland trail were not the attacks of the Plains Indian tribes, as Hollywood has made us believe. Rather, they came in the form of injury and disease. When these inevitably struck, the 49ers found themselves without medical attention and dependent upon their new companions. J. E. Clayton wrote about the death of a man from Vermont: "He was strong, fine looking and died, no doubt, for want of proper attention, notwithstanding his uncle and several friends are along with him, but going to California is like going to sea—no one goes to nurse, so if one gets sick he must get well as he can." When Clayton himself became sick, he was nursed by his friend Traylor, of whom he wrote, "I shall feel under special obligation. No mother could be more kind and attentive to her children than he was to me."[10]

Such tests of the social bonds the Argonauts brought with them still awaited those who went by sea. The arrangements of the seagoing Argonauts generally lasted to California, except for those who divided the journey in Panama, where individuals went up the Pacific side on their own or in small groups with passage on steamers and sailers that plied the route from Panama to San Francisco.

IN CALIFORNIA

The best and tightest arrangements—whether by sea or on land—often collapsed within a few days or even hours of arriving in California. The dangers of the trip had ended and so, too, had the need for individuals to do things in concert for the good of a group. In California, the newly arrived 49ers immediately encountered a multitude of options that attracted each individual differently. One recently arrived Argonaut wrote that his company "has all smashed up....I believe that every company that came out here has broke up." J. E. Clayton offered a more general comment on the changed circumstances. "We have not done much in the way of gold digging, but a great deal in the way of contention," he wrote; several members "are dissatisfied and...seem determined to split the company; they have become inveterate enemies."[11]

Individuals, small family groups, and the residue of former companies all were now on their own. They had yearned for the end of their voyage since the ship first weighed anchor or the wagon had first rolled west. Now confronted with the reality of California and its impersonal chaos, many were uneasy. One 49er summed up the condition on the occasion of his arrival in San Francisco Bay in these words: "Notwithstanding all our discomforts, it cost me a pang to leave the steamer. It seemed like cutting loose the last tie that bound me to home & friends, & found myself indeed alone & entirely dependent upon myself for everything."[12]

Those bound for the gold camps immediately began the search for companions with whom to make the trip. Often they joined with friends from the voyage to California; sometimes they sought companions elsewhere. On the beaches and the crowded streets of San Francisco, in the meadows around Placerville, and in between, the 49ers spent much time and emotional energy in finding what they hoped would be trustworthy and loyal comrades with whom to share the dangers and potential wealth of the mines. The choice was a very personal one. Not surprisingly, the 49ers once again tended to seek companions from the same town or county or, if necessary, the same state. Rinaldo Taylor from Boston wrote that he was going to the mines with two young men from Massachusetts. "I know I can depend on them," he confided to his wife. Rodney P. Odall chose fellow New Yorkers, "all tough and smart as crickets. All Married but Willy and myself." Their occupations—schoolteacher, cabinetmaker, farmer—and family commitments marked them as reputable men likely to make good companions in the diggings. The need to find honest and dependable partners extended beyond the mines to include the cities and towns. When Milo Goss moved from the mines to San Francisco and opened a store, he described his business partner, a man by the name of Johnson, as "a worthy and pious man," and on another occasion as "a sound substantial man," fifty years of age, with a family in Mishawaka, Indiana.[13]

Through his new partners, the 49er established a new set of social bonds and allegiances. As early as the summer and fall of 1848, the first observers in the gold fields commented on the advantage of working in groups of at least three or four.[14] The same divisions appropriate to mining, with its unending hard physical labor, long hours, and collective work, also helped to define new living arrangements. For the 49ers, it was cheaper and more practical to live in groups. As few as three men, but more generally from six to eight, would occupy a large tent or cabin (for the winter months), where they would take turns cooking, cleaning, and making trips to town for food and mail.

The mining company as a unit of work and living offered support in case of sickness and even in case of death. Here were the companions who would sit up with the ill miner, fetch the doctor, and make the soup. In the world they had left behind, sitting up with the sick was a part of the service offered by the family and almost always by women. In the gold fields, the messmates of the sick man would perform this service for one another. Here, also, were the partners who would close the eyes of the dead man, dress the body and bury it, and handle the estate. And, in a final act, they would communicate with the dead man's family and carry out his last wishes.[15]

As the experiences of those who came overland had shown them, among the reasons to join together in the gold fields, illness was one of the most forceful. Harvey Chapman described his illness as a nightmare that was every 49er's worst fear. "I had no one to stay with me in the tent and could hire no one," he wrote to his wife. In his desperation, he hit upon an unusual strategy: "I then enquired if there were a Mason in the crowd at the eating house...and to my great satisfaction, a young man from Ohio came to me and said he was a Mason, and he felt like a brother, indeed, for he nursed me untill breakfast next morning."[16] Occasional accounts of Good Samaritan strangers emerged from the hustle and movement of the Gold Rush, but most 49ers preferred to rely on carefully chosen companions and relatives. Support for the sick rested on the values that became generally accepted within the mines. That the sick should be cared for was part of the unwritten contract associated with shared living and working.[17]

But the obligations of members of the company had limits, and various questions soon emerged about the limitations of care and the liability of the sick miner to his caregivers. Among these were, first, the issue of whether the ill partner was entitled to a share in the returns of the claim during his illness. Responses to this question varied. Some companies accepted the principle of a kind of collective social insurance against physical illness or disability. Others did not. Such questions were often spelled out at the time the company was formed. A second variable was the issue of cost. When the charges for a doctor and medication exceeded the savings of the ill miner, should his messmates meet such costs as part of their commitment to one another? And, as an extension of this condition, should the messmates forward a statement for payment to the surviving relatives in the old neighborhood? James Barnes passed on such a duty to his father:

> Father i shall send you the account i have against Thomas Collins which i have paid towards his doctor bill when he died he had 64$ in city scrip and 3$ in cash and the ballance i have paid his bill was 170$ i paid 103$ what close and tools he had when he died would hardly bring what he owed me i wish you could go to washingtonville and collect it of Henry Still and give me Cr for the same.

That the arrangements among messmates might extend from the gold country to the surviving family in the states testified to the serious and continuous nature of the commitment.[18]

Another question related to compensation for extending nursing. To the extent that a sick man required someone to tend him, the gold harvest of a claim would be reduced by the absence of two able-bodied men, and the other members of the mess penalized accordingly. Friends who had served faithfully in illness and in the death watch sometimes presented claims against the estate for their services in nursing the now deceased companion. The business of settling an estate after an extended illness could prove long and difficult. Joshua Sullivan asked his wife to collect "a bill against the Widow Young."[19] The 49ers were very practical, especially on issues that had to do with money. They were prepared to stand by members of their company; they were not prepared to accept great personal financial loss.

Comrades in a company living situation also provided companionship. The impersonality of the gold fields was in part associated with the temporary nature of the exercise, the fear that partners who slept in the next bed and shared work and leisure might be gone next week—gone home, to better diggings, or to the towns or the city in search of alternative work. Part lay in the sense of competition that permeated the Gold Rush. It was present on the ships bound for the gold fields and in the wagon trains. It appeared in the competition over claims, grew with the passage of time as miners increased in numbers and with the jostling for position, and became more acute as the returns lessened. Within these rootless, ruthless societies, the company offered a basis for companionship. This was a consideration not only as support in case of personal illness or disaster, but also as trust and companionship, providing someone with whom to talk and confide in, a messmate with whom to spend an idle Sunday in a trip to town or a hike in the mountains.

The 49ers spent much time thinking about a good friend or good friends—how to find them, how to keep them, and especially how to identify at least one person to trust. The desire to have a single individual upon whom a man could rely in all circumstances was a powerful one. When the Argonaut made such a commitment to someone, he wrote of it in the strongest terms. One 49er described such a relationship with the comment, "me and John stick together like wood ticks." Joshua Sullivan worked in a company of seventeen men to dam and drain a portion of the Yuba River, but he had a special relationship with one man. "I have a partner," Sullivan wrote his wife, "a good, industrious young man that I mess and work with."[20]

The commitment and cohesion of a company involved as many as a half-dozen men in close proximity to one another. If a pledge of support in work and illness was one side of this arrangement, irritation and disappointed expectations were the other. Men did not always agree about working habits or the personal style of living accommodations. C. C. Mobley confided in his diary that one member of his company was "lazy," and he characterized a man who left the company in the middle of the mining season as "whimsical and old woman like, and as miserly as any other man I know of."[21] Throughout accounts of mining partnerships ran an impatience with those who were perceived not to carry their weight. In a world of the hardest kind of work, with the proceeds evenly split, the style and standards of labor became an important issue within companies.

The nature of mining companies also reflected the cyclical nature of mining and other economic enterprises in California. Washing gravel, the technique that characterized the first two years of mining in California, rested on a dependable supply of water. When the water failed, or when the rivers were too high in winter, mining ceased. Just as mining was seasonal, so mess arrangements tended to be seasonal. When a mining cycle ended, mess agreements often ended with it. A separate range of decisions now confronted miners: they might settle in and ride out the winter in a cabin; they might leave the mountains for towns or the city in search of temporary employment; they might return home. These decisions often determined whether friendships would continue or partners would detach themselves and go their own ways. Thus, for those who remained in the gold fields for several seasons, the business of searching for close relationships was often a continuing one that had to be repeated at the close of each mining season.

When these arrangements ended, whether through seasonal adjustment, the return of one party to the states, or desertion, miners could be sad at the departure or outraged by a sense of betrayal. Their parting was sometimes as traumatic and emotional as the original separation from family and community. Indeed, it was the breakup of the 49er's new community. Obadiah Motley wrote of the change, "I am in pretty good health, but I am low spirited, not because I am not making money, for in that part of the matter I am doing pretty well, but it is because I am in a measure all alone, having lost all of my best friends." C. C. Mobley wrote that he was "troubled much on account of the departure from among us of an old man whom I love as a father. I was very sorry for him to go, but I could not help it. He left with the intention of going to the Southern Mines." Another 49er reacted bitterly to the departure of his best friend. "So I bade him good bye &c., & he went on his way," he wrote. "Thus ended all the professions of friendship, the promises of sticking together, of taking care of one another &c wich were so profusely made before we left Boston. All vanished into 'thin air' at the moment of trial."[22]

A final dimension of this close relationship between 49ers was the visit of the friend to the family in the states. When a partnership broke up, the remaining 49ers sometimes weighed down the returning pilgrim with money, letters, or gifts for delivery to loved ones in the East. Sometimes, one or more companions would exact a promise that the returning 49er would visit their families. It was an important symbol: the original family would meet the new friend. William Brown wrote to his family—in addition to collective letters, he also often wrote separate letters to his mother, father and sister—that friends from the gold fields would call on them and "muddy up your carpets with the golden earth from Cal." On such occasions, it must have been difficult for the 49er's family to understand the close relationship of the son or brother or uncle with these ordinary, sunburned men who came to call in their ill-fitting clothes. These were ties formed in the gold camps not in the drawing rooms, and as such, they were inexplicable to those without the first-hand experiences that bound such men together.[23]

NEW FAMILIES

The search for support by 49ers had one obvious final step: the reestablishment of the family in California. This reconstitution of families in California included family groups who initially came to California together and relatives and friends who emigrated to California to join the original adventurer. In some cases, these arrangements had been agreed to prior to departure, perhaps as a condition of support for the enterprise. In others, reports of the opportunities to make money were so glowing that various members of the family clamored to join the rush to the golden West.

Brothers Henry and Elizah Spiegel of Bennington, Vermont, went to-gether to California and worked as partners for two years. They shared everything equally except the burden of correspondence, which was handled by Henry alone. Henry wrote of their collective work, "We ought to be satisfied for we have done better than most of the Burlington boys." His tone suggested the ongoing sense of competition with others from the home neighborhood. Eventually the brothers established a "public house" and took turns serving their customers and digging in the ravines. Later, in part-nership they opened a carpenter shop on Horseshoe Bar. After two years, Elizah left to return home, much to Henry's distress. The latter wrote that his brother's decision "is the hardest thing that has come acrost me yet." But Elizah's health had begun to fail. Henry wrote to his mother: "I could not ask him to stay as he thought that he would not be able to stand the work as he thinks of staying with you if not able to work and take my place if he does as well by you as he has by me you will have no reason to complain for he has been more than a Brother to me."[24]

Family partnerships provided the best possible mutual support and assur-ance in the confusion and chaos of the Gold Rush. David Hewes went to California in 1850 and became the sponsor and guardian of his younger cousins, who arrived later that year. The boys soon were settled on a promis-ing claim. "Cousin Joshua . . . is in good spirits and ready to make his for-tune in the old Yankee way (Quick)," Hewes wrote, and he left them in partnership to open a claim himself nearby.[25]

A variation on this pattern emerged in the activities of John Collbreath from Buffalo. Collbreath organized a company known as Collbreath Hite and Company. When he had established himself, he sent for James and Joseph Huntington. "James must stay in San Francisco and open a shop," he wrote. "I will give him all the capital he will want to carry on the carpenters business and next season I will have him with me in the mines." California, he admitted, was a frightening place, with its confusions and temptations, but it was a great opportunity for young men "of steady habits James and Charles Craft must come together I will assist them both."[26]

James Barnes tried to entice his brother William to California: "I should like to see you very much i am quite lonesome i have not seen a person i was acquainted with in the states for six months." He admitted that William had responsibilities to their parents: "i suppose they need you to help them in there old days but there are enough left besides you," he wrote. Barnes also tried to attract his brother Jeremiah: "This is the first time that i have held out any inducements for you to come out here i like the country very much so much so that I think i shall make this my future home."[27]

Wilson Day crossed the plains to California in the summer of 1852. A year later, he welcomed his father and younger brother. The father bought a small house and soon found employment running a sawmill at five dollars a day. The brother found work as a packer at seventy-five dollars a month, while Wilson continued to manage his hay yard and livery stable. Younger brother Alvin worked as a carpenter. Robert found a job on a nearby ranch.[28]

Sometimes the 49er went to California as a scout for younger male members of the family. It was his duty to spy out the opportunities for the others and prepare for their arrival. This exercise betrayed a sense of tension as well as of family unity, for it carried the image of younger brothers or cousins anxious to escape the drudgery and responsibilities of the family farm or the local store, waiting for news that could liberate them and send them on their way to the Golden Land. The new family communities in California worked differently for different members. Some thrived on the new opportunities; others sat around idle. The arrangements were not always happy ones. Relations between siblings in California could be fully as awkward as those in the same villages in Michigan or farms in Kentucky.

Or 49ers might be burdened by the arrival of unwanted relatives. Perhaps someone shifted the responsibility for younger brothers out to them. Charles Randall exhibited little enthusiasm upon the arrival of his younger brother James. "He had better staid at home at least until he heard something from me," he wrote. If Charles could find something for James to do, he would keep him; if not, he would send him home.[29]

The ties that bound the Argonauts together through what they regarded as a unique experience extended throughout the breadth of California and, eventually, to the states. When they returned—and 49ers came home from California on a continuing basis from the beginning of the Gold Rush— many kept contact with their friends from the placers. Connections between and among former miners spread across the states and from the several communities in the states to California. One of the characteristics of these contacts was that 49ers sometimes wrote to returned miners rather than to their families or other neighbors. These were, after all, individuals with whom they had shared physical hardships and financial risks, and who ultimately understood the peculiar combination of opportunity and luck associated with the mining experience in California between 1849 and the opening of the Civil War. Only those who had burrowed into the sides of hills, risked their stakes on damming a river only to see the investment carried away by a sudden storm with its wall of water, or confronted the decision of whether to stay another season in the gold fields or return could understand the anguish and euphoria that were so close to one another. So in the end, the communities that were reconstituted in California stretched across the continent in two strands: one connected Argonauts with their families and communities in the states; a second connected miners in California with former miners scattered across the breadth of the nation. Both added to the complexity of reconstituting support systems and communities in this decade.

NEW COMMUNITIES, EAST AND WEST

The departure of tens of thousands—and eventually hundreds of thousands—for the gold fields in California reconfigured the sense of community in many localities in America. The new unit was the local company of adventurers that had gone west. The families and friends of these individuals now had a common interest that drew them together: news from California. That companies frequently split up on their arrival in California did not lessen the identification of those left behind with their friends and relatives. Indeed, this splintering meant that those left behind were more than ever eager for news.

In planning the voyage to California, the 49er often found his ties to his community reinforced, as we already have seen. Others probably joined him—friends, neighbors, members of the same church. Many 49ers borrowed money to support their expeditions from local entrepreneurs, arrangements that were both businesslike and an expression of community solidarity. Local capitalists of various kinds supported them as a community service but also as an economic venture.[30]

With the arrival of the Argonauts in California, this network of interests took on a new dimension. It was concerned with what was going on in the placers, with particular reference to the health and economic well-being of the miner. To his immediate family, the issue of health was a significant one. To the extended family and certain members of the community, economic support and potential return loomed large. And finally, for the community of the family and friends of 49ers generally, every letter from California might contain information about other local Argonauts.

As a result, correspondence took place at several levels. In messages from the immediate family, there were personal expressions of love and support, mixed with requests for information about economic prospects and the expected time of returning home. The latter two issues were often closely interconnected; that is to say, presumably the better the prospects, the higher the expectation that the 49er would be satisfied and return, and on his return, repay those to whom he was indebted. Within the family, a letter from the gold fields might be regarded as private—intended solely for the addressee—or public, in the sense that it should be shared among all. Henry Spiegel of Bennington, Vermont, conveyed to his brother the news of immediate family and friends: "[Brother] Elizah says he shall git Gold and will have it he sends his love to you & Mother and his Brothers & Sisters . . . say to Margaret & Henry I hope to be Home in the Fall and that I think of them every day. White wishes you to say to his wife that he is well tell Seymour to get words to George Whitten's wife that he is well."[31]

Within the community in the East, a letter to an individual might also take on the status of a public resource. The individual Argonaut as a public asset reflected the fact that the voluminous correspondence that connected families and communities to the gold fields was the work of a relatively small number of men. Many Argonauts wrote occasionally—on arrival, on holidays, family birthdays and anniversaries—but only a select group wrote regularly and in detail. These 49ers became community scribes, whose reach transcended their own camp to include all Argonauts from the home community.

George Applegate of Kestesville, Missouri, was one of these public figures. His letters were quite literally community bulletin boards. On one occasion, he began by telling his brother that "Mr. Ousley" had started for home. He continued:

> I saw Clarkston here yesterday who you recollect taught school on the Muscle Fort. Dr. Brooks was well a few days ago and thinks he has a fair prospect this winter. Coleman and Jabine are in company with him. They are at Coloma. The Dempsey boys I have not seen for some time but hear from them very often. The Owens boys are at Houghton mining. . . . Felix and John Redding I have not seen.

Applegate then went on to mention eight men and one woman ("Mrs. Halley and family reside about a mile below this place") in the next half page. His other letters were equally filled with news of the whole Chariton County, Missouri, community.[32]

Often, correspondents in the East made specific requests for information. "I took tea with Mrs Ormsby & her mother a few days since," wrote Jane Blackwood to her husband Thomas, "they wished me to say to you that if you know any thing of the fate of Dr. Ormsby or could learn any intelligence of him to mention it in your next."[33]

This search for specific information was increased not only by the intermittent correspondence habits of the Argonauts, but by the transient nature of the camps, where men were often on the move. The seasonal relocation of Argonauts in response to the arrival of winter in the diggings further dispersed camps and local mining companies. That men circulated from one camp to another, and sometimes in the winter into the growing villages and cities of the gold country, including San Francisco, created random encounters with other members of the home community. These chance meetings led to letters of collective information.

Correspondence that ran from the East to the West also took on a collective character. G. K. Hill of Logan County, Ohio, wrote to his former neighbor, John Gish, now in the gold fields: "John Gish your family is well The Cacer [canker] on Marys leg is Entirely well. She is very well Contented as far as I know your little Louisa Jane has grood fine Since you left Nancy is a teaching this summer and your little girl wen once day and she was well pleased." Hill also had news for other 49ers from the neighborhood: "John S. Hodge your Family is all well at this time . . . your little Girls has been well since you left and they grow lots," and "Joseph all your folks is well." He closed with a listing of recent marriages.[34]

No eastern community had more internal cohesion than the whaling settlement of Nantucket. Henry Worth's letters from California to his wife Ann were filled with news of other Nantucketers. Some of the news was general; other portions were quite specific, including details about wages: "J. C. Swain has gone up with a party of 15 or 20 with John Greenwood a son of 'old Greenwood'. . . . I heard from J. W. Clapp today, I know he made last week digging over $100 & only working 5 days in the week." One of his friends, P. F. Ewer, used to drop by the shop where Worth worked and read selections from his wife's letters. Other Nantucketers were also good correspondents. Worth heard of his wife's giving birth to a son from Charles Wood before he heard from her. The Nantucket people kept careful track of one another.[35]

James Lyne from Henderson, Kentucky, did the same for the members of his company. He wrote his brother from San Francisco with what must have been a complete account of those who came across the plains. The listing is of interest in identifying the wide range of places and occupations of a group that originally went west together with the intention of mining:

> I saw Tom Ford on yesterday who gave me the first news of the Boys. Tom himself looks well, & has not been sick for a moment. He has not been successful & is in the same mood as are the rest of us. His report is: Tun Eastin who was for some time sick in the Sacramento Hospatal, has recovered, & procured a situation in runing a circular sawmill there, which

augers that he will do well. . . . Ed Hall clearks for him. David Hearnson who arrived soon after I did, drives an ox team. Jim Wilson has been sick since his arrival, has made nothing, stay with Tom & Ed; he speaks of returning home soon. Gazlay & Hart are at the mines, Posey on Yubu River getting timber, Foulks sick, W. & B. Dixon not far from Sacramento, both well & Buchanan dead. John Burbank, Ross & Light doing nothing at Sacramento; the two former very sick. So you can see the fate of those who were tenderley nurtured & so it is with nearly all who visit the mines, 1 probably in 100 being successful in good health & in procuring 2 or 3 thousand in gold after great toil.[36]

Lyne's account identifies the salient questions that concerned all those in the home community: health, wealth, and location, probably in that order. That one of his friends' fathers wrote to ask for news of his son indicates that the network of information about the Argonauts of this particular community, as well, was probably the work of a relatively few correspondents.[37]

The exchange of news from the West to the East actively reconnected large numbers of 49ers to their home communities. Their anonymity had vanished (or had been diluted), and they found themselves once again under the influence of community standards. To some degree, their actions in the distant gold fields were monitored and reported to members of the home community. In addition to information about health, economic condition, and place of residence, reports might also note drinking, gambling, and other forms of immoral behavior. Some 49er correspondents noted with a mixture of relish and sorrow the questionable behavior in California of Argonauts of impeccable reputation in their home communities. This new community connecting the East with the West ensured that the behavior of 49ers might be scrutinized, with new reputations established and old ones confirmed or denied.[38]

NEW COMMUNITIES: CALIFORNIA

During the first two seasons of the Gold Rush, the 49ers had to find a common ground among the polyglot adventurers who came west to pursue the search for gold. Henry Packer described his company in the placers as a wildly diverse group, with representatives from across the eastern half of the continent. "My companions are a mixture of all sorts," he wrote, "a regular Yankee" whaleman; a Portuguese native, also a veteran of the sea; a Briton "who nevertheless claims to have been born and raised in N. or S. Carolina"; a man from Buffalo, New York; and, finally, "a dutch boy, who according to his own account, is from every place but this." Packer indicated that he got along well with this group.[39] Others suggested that contact did not increase their liking for Yankees or Southerners or people of a particular class or place, but they could work alongside these fellow 49ers—at least in prosperous times.

As we have already briefly noted, in order to give a degree of organization and structure to a world without institutional force—California became a state in 1850 and its county governments began to function in 1851—the miners established their own forms to give some necessary structure to what looked like unorganized and disorderly societies. The reason was the assumption that all profited more in a world characterized by order rather than chaos. So miners organized themselves to lay down ground rules for mining and standards of behavior. Generally they did so by camps and bars, terms that were used interchangeably to describe their several settlements, although strictly speaking, the latter referred to the place where mining took place, rather than to where the miners lived.

These informal governments—the term may be too strong—dealt with two separate issues. The first, the question of claims, we have already examined. As mining space became scarce and the struggle for places to dig and wash became subject to dispute, each camp or bar established its own local rules under which claims might be staked out, worked, and retained in absentia. They also created machinery to adjudicate disputes between miners.

These informal governments also dealt with criminal matters: violence, claim jumping, and the most reprehensible of all, theft. The miners' world was one in which men worked all day, leaving their belongings usually unattended. They had to leave everything but the clothes on their backs in camp. Cabins, tents, and lean-tos lay open, with their bedding, cookware, and personal effects strewn about. The most damaging of all theft involved gold. As miners accumulated gold dust, they had to carry it around with them or hide it somewhere. Most of the time, they buried it in or near the campsite. The theft of gold represented the loss of months of work and often meant changes in plans to return home or to move to other kinds of ventures. The crime of theft aroused a camp to a fever pitch of indignation. Those caught were tried in a people's court of their peers, and where found guilty, they were flogged and expelled from the camp. Punishments, in the style of other early settlement experiences, were quick and brutal.[40]

This form of government reflected the needs of the 49ers. They were generally unarmed, for they quickly discarded the pistols, rifles, and swords of the voyage overland as too heavy for the mobile existence of a miner. Most property was portable, especially gold. Authority during the Gold Rush lay in collective, rather than individual, action, and the forms for regulating behavior that developed in the camps and bars sought to reduce individual confrontation and the possibility of violence by interposing the authority of the group. This strategy generally worked, and within a few months of the arrival of the first great annual migration, California's placers had a substantial degree of order, and a consensus about how the mining world was to be regulated had emerged. Of course, it was an order that worked against those who were different from the group whose authority provided that order or who did not speak English.[41]

One of the best observers of these early forms was the missionary Israel Lord, who traveled widely through the gold-mining region in 1849 and 1850. Lord spoke to a wide range of issues, as befits a man trying to change the values of his constituents. He also mined seriously, and he brought to his observations the perspective of a dedicated miner. His account of a meeting about a disputed claim identified the local law (or custom) and the way it might be applied:

> He [Lord] was called up to the Oregon Bar, three quarters of a mile, to sit as a juror in a claim dispute, where there had been *assault and battery*. After a short investigation, and hearing all witnesses and parties, who wished to speak, the jury brought in for the original claimants. They were somewhat at fault, and did not strictly comply with the letter of the law, by putting up notice every ten days or occupying the premises. But they lived only 30 or 40 rods above their claim and the jumpers knew before hand that they claimed and intended to work it as soon as the water would permit.—In equity they should hold the claim, but governed by the common, absurd, legal technicalities, those who had no right what ever would have held it.[42]

Lord and others in the diggings constantly criticized lawyers. He wrote upon one occasion that justice was done because "there were no lawyers to delay—no petty technicalities to obstruct the course of justice." And on another he called law "one of the mightiest humbugs of the age." Justice needed to have a quick and inexpensive air about it, for the business of mining camps was washing for gold, not arguing about legal forms. The camps had no provision for confinement; jails would appear later. For these reasons, lawyers with their technicalities were not welcomed. At the same time, those charged had a right to be tried before a jury of their peers. Americans felt strongly about the right of trial by jury. They carried this form over into proceedings against other nationalities, so French, Chileans, or Mexicans would be tried by American forms of law. The adoption of these forms apparently salved American consciences in seizing the claims of foreign nationals.

Amid the chaos and confusion of the first two seasons of gold mining, numerous observers testified to a high degree of honesty and sense of order. Israel Lord wrote in the fall of 1849, "Judgment and sentences and justice are too speedily executed here to make stealing profitable."[43] The 49ers wrote home in wonder and amazement at the openness and the honesty of the gold camps. They wrote of lost gold returned, missing baggage restored, mining claims marked by tools casually left in them, and mail redirected to the rightful addressees. Everywhere, they contrasted this honesty with the high quantities of gold and other property involved. Even Israel Lord, who had a low opinion in general of the moral standards of the gold fields and the intense self-interest in individual gain, wrote of them, "With all this latitude, there is still a species of honesty, and a semblance of good faith, at least, in all business transactions, which prevents violence and outrage." He went on to analyze the reasons with this result: "I suppose that a common interest, here, answers to the legal restraints which the Laws of the States impose on their citizens. We have here, at least, much less difficulty in business, everyway, than there. If one refuses to pay, another might refuse to pay him. ...As a rule, all pay as soon as possible."[44]

For the first two years or so, this sense of community was one of the wonders of the Gold Rush. The contrast between confusion and order produced one of the many paradoxes about California. The 49ers often viewed the standards and values of others with a jaundiced eye and took for granted the selfish nature of their comrades in the Gold Rush. This view emerged from their many encounters with strangers from other sections and nations, from their sense of how many succumbed to the manifold temptations available in California, and from a sense of their own uprightness in the face of those same temptations. At the same time, they praised the general sense of order and security that these informal institutions gave to society.

This strong sense of the rights of individual property—while it lasted—should not be confused with tolerance toward different kinds of people. Mining camps and bars—the basic unit of work, living, and as it turned out, government—were designed to promote the search for gold, not to create understanding among different groups. In addition to exhibiting a long-standing hostility against the California Indians, by 1850, groups of miners also had moved against the Mexicans, the Chileans, and thereafter, the French. Israel Lord noted in the spring of 1850 that "petitions were in circulation yesterday, and again to-day, to exclude foreigners from the mines."[45]

What began as petitions would gradually evolve into violence under the guise of legal proceedings, with local groups organized as sovereign bodies to take whatever action was necessary, as we will see. The extreme tolerance of the first year gradually faded with the arrival of larger numbers, including larger numbers of different ethnic and racial groups, and with the increased sense of competition.

The 49ers brought racism and intolerance with them, along with everything else. Racial, cultural, and linguistic differences provoked criticism. Asides about "niggers . . . their infernal rattle" and "swindle hearted jews expose their wares for sale" reflected the routine hostility toward distinctive groups.[46] The sense of a larger community in the Gold Rush was not commodious enough to wipe out distinctions of race, religion, and origin. In this sense, California and the Gold Rush were already very American.

6

THE SCARCITY OF WOMEN:

"I Have Not Spoken to a Lady for Five Months"

IN ADDITION TO THE OTHER social and economic dislocations brought about by the news of the discovery of gold and the subsequent decisions of tens of thousands of American men to go to California, the Gold Rush plunged the Argonauts into a society that was almost entirely without women. The communities that the Argonauts began to build in the West were as a result defined in many ways by their absence.

The Gold Rush was a search for a scarce and valuable commodity, but the presence of women in California turned out to be, initially at least, even rarer than gold. Indeed, the scarcity of women was one of the most significant shocks that California imposed upon the 49ers. From the bustling streets of San Francisco to the most remote mining camps, the Argonauts commented constantly on the rarity of women. They came from a world in which they had taken for granted the presence of women in their lives, and with their presence, a wide range of services performed for them by the women. A functioning society without women was unthinkable to them. In the gold country, however, men joined into small companies for living and working. When in so doing the 49ers recreated communities and reforged a number of social bonds, these turned out to be largely all-male.

The lack of female society—as the 49ers referred to the condition—became the object of comment in several contexts. From the beginning of organized companies or chartered ships, the Argonauts remarked on the absence of women in this migration west. They continued to do so across the ocean or across the plains, and their observations extended to the most remote camps of the Sierra. Indeed, the more distant the camp and the scarcer female society, the more it became a central topic of conversation. For some, the absence of women in California became something of an obsession, whether driven by the need for sexual gratification, for intellectual companionship, for domestic services, or for "civilizing" influences. In their private and public thoughts, in their letters home, and in their diaries and journals, the 49ers used the presence or absence of women to measure the transformation of California into what they called a genteel society, and they commented on the many economic opportunities available to women in the context of the Gold Rush. Sometimes they had to deal with requests from women in the East to be allowed to share in this great enterprise.

ON THE VOYAGES

When the Argonauts of 1849 and subsequent years formed themselves into companies, in the heady business of drawing up constitutions, electing officers, creating committees, and the flurry of activity surrounding departures, they seemed to accept the all-male composition of these groups without question. A few wives accompanied their husbands to California, but in general, only men gathered together to prepare for the greatest adventure of their lifetimes. Thoughts of families and personal attachments were set aside in favor of the pragmatic issues at hand.

Once the Argonauts were embarked on the journey west, whether by land or by sea, the recognition that they had become members of all-male societies evolved in separate stages, marked by time and distance. Married men immediately missed their wives; single men felt the absence of a warm hearth and a mother's presence. Those Argonauts who went to California by sea had little to do except gaze at the horizon and contemplate the growing distance from home. Sometimes new experiences made the absences especially poignant. As he and his companions inhaled the intoxicating scents of the tropics, Rinaldo Taylor of Boston wrote to his wife and infant daughter: "One of our Californians remarked to his friend, while we were all gazing silently upon the scene, 'John, wouldn't this be nice if our wives were only here?'" Taylor continued, "This was in exact unison with the feelings of us all, I venture to say, although the observation created 'something of a smile' all around. It was the only thing lacking in this intoxication of the sense. By the way I will remark here that almost all of our California passengers have left wives & families at home, & most of them are young men too."[1]

In response to this loss, many of the seagoing Argonauts wrote long letters describing at great length the details of the sea voyage, the great storms and high winds, the fish and sea birds, the sights, sounds, and smells of the new worlds of tropical lands and exotic peoples. They wrote as if the sheer detail and length of the letters could reestablish an intimacy with the women they had left behind.[2]

The overland Argonauts experienced the same sense of loss in a different context. In their journals and in long, detailed letters to be sent to their families when they reached California, they wrote of the vast herds of buffalo, the signs of dangerous Indians on the trail, the majesty of the trek westward across the landscape of the expanding American Empire. Other, more practical, considerations, however, soon intruded. From the moment of their departure from home, the 49ers found themselves responsible for all those domestic labors customarily performed for them by wives, sisters, and mothers. One Argonaut from Kentucky confessed to his sister, "I have always been enclined to deride the vocation of ladies until now but must confess it by far the more irksome I have tried & by way of taking lessons in sewing have often examined your stitches in my work bag."[3] Many diarists and letter writers celebrated their first successful home-baked loaf of bread or the first successfully attached button. By the time they reached California, the 49ers who journeyed overland had come to recognize that their new all-male societies had undertaken what previously had been considered women's duties, and indirectly at least, they recognized the skills they had always taken for granted demanded time and competence.

After an initial period of loneliness and longing, 49ers moved on to a second stage: celebration of new adventures and the good fellowship associated with newly adopted companions. When he ventured across the isthmus with his 49er colleagues, Rinaldo Taylor wrote of the trip through Panama's mud and rain as a kind of adolescent frolic, concluding "I assure you I enjoyed the whole affair mightily. The excitement and novelty of the trip kept my spirits up to the highest point, & I could laugh at the mishaps of the rest, with a relish."[4] However much Taylor and others might lament the absences of their wives, they displayed much enthusiasm for confronting the physical obstacles of the Panamanian jungle and other physical challenges, whether by land or sea.

What emerged were two parallel responses to an increasingly all-male world: the Argonauts of 1849 and subsequent years missed their wives and their families, but they rejoiced in their new adventures and the independence associated with it, far from the mundane duties of farm, shop, and family. Gradually there developed a sense that these expeditions to California were initiation ceremonies for members of a new kind of all-male club. Wrote one 49er, "Altogether we have a jolly set of fellows who are bound to take things easy whatever may turn up."[5] To the extent that they considered the women of their families as future 49ers, they generally preferred them to stay at home for the time being, far from the hardships of the trail or the heat and disease of Panama. The suspicion lingers that while they saw such an expedition as inappropriate for a lady, they also wished to preserve the all-male aspect of the club.

IN CALIFORNIA

Arrival in California and coming to terms with the mines and the camps brought many 49ers to a different view of a society without women. On the trail or at sea, the 49ers lamented the absence of women as companions and friends, and married men especially missed their wives and families—as they thought they should and did. However long they were, these travels were but a prelude to the business that had sent them west. In California, the Argonauts confronted for the first time the prospect of living without women for many months and perhaps years.

At the close of 1849, even 49ers in the gold towns of San Francisco, Sacramento, and Stockton lived in largely male worlds. William Prince wrote in the fall of 1849 that Stockton had so "few females that I never yet have seen one in the streets." And a year later, William Brown wrote from the same place, "In fact a woman is a curiosity in this country!"[6]

As the Argonauts pressed through the towns into the mining country along the ridges of the Sierra, they entered into a thoroughly all-male world. One 49er reflected a common experience when he wrote that he had talked to only two women in his first year in the mines, and another commented in August 1849 that the visit of a Mexican woman to his camp had "created a general sensation."[7] Indeed, many camps and bars were entirely male; the towns and villages only slightly less so. The federal census of 1850 reflected that in California, the male proportion of the entire population was 92.5 percent; for several mining counties, the proportion of women was less than three in a hundred. These figures indicate that the mining camps of the California Sierra were among the most male places in the nation, and for that matter, in the world.[8]

The Argonauts now quickly discovered that the search for gold was not a romantic vision but an intensely hard and competitive business, heightened by the strong sense of obligation to those they had left behind with such golden visions. In this context of physical labor and aggressive competition, the "feminine" duties of cooking, laundry, sewing, housecleaning, and other such domestic chores were indeed burdensome. Miners did the hardest kind of physical labor, often working in cold, rushing water up to their knees for ten hours a day. To then return to a dirty cabin and prepare an evening meal became one of the hardships with which they saw themselves afflicted.

As they had among the overland Argonauts, in the gold fields these endless chores (which were often costly, as well, for those who hired them done) gave rise to new expressions of respect for women's domestic roles. Men who had rushed to the gold fields and left wives, sisters, and mothers with all the responsibilities men were expected to shoulder wrote to express admiration for their loved ones' domestic abilities.[9] Men had to cook on a continuing basis, and they had to lay in provisions for what they would prepare. They had little choice. With single meals at boardinghouses or roadside eateries at a dollar to a dollar and a half each, cost was a powerful incentive.

Because domestic service occupations commanded high profits, men hastened to take advantage of occupations formerly exercised by women alone. Epaphroditus Wells wrote to his wife that he and two other men had formed a partnership "to keep an eating house—one of our firm to be Maid of all work." He noted the incongruity of an eating place with a male cook: "I suppose you will think it a singular Tavern where there are none but men to do cooking but I assure you there are scarcely any other Taverns here."[10] He made clear that where money could be made, men would do women's work. If this work involved cooking for other men, then with meals at twenty-five dollars a week, men would cook.

The absence of women to perform the customary domestic services and the high cost of hiring these services performed by others thus increased the value of women in the eyes of the 49ers. For most of the 49ers, the need for women was eminently practical, and they tended to speak of the value of women in the unabashed idiom of a society where everything had a price. When William Daingerfield wrote his mother that California was the greatest place in the world to make money, he added that in order to make it a perfect place to live one needed "a woman on the place to keep things neat about the house." And after two years in the gold fields, James Barnes wrote to his brother, "If you send me any thing send me a woman and then i never will come home wimman command a very good prise out here." Just as their initial scarcity made them immensely valuable, as they increased in numbers, their value was somewhat diminished. Horace Ballew wrote along these lines in early 1851, "Tell the girls that women is not so valuable here as they used to be, because there is too many here now."[11]

Yet the men who came to California in search of gold were not entirely selfish in their wish for a female to assist in domestic duties or crass in their sense of women's value; some of them simply longed for the physical presence of women. "My heart was gladdened this evening, by hearing the voice of a pretty girl raised in song—a thing I have not heard before for months," wrote C. C. Mobley in his diary. "O! how pleasant it sounded! My heart leaped with joy! and in its fullness I could scarcely refrain from tears."[12] The 49ers also missed children, and they sometimes wrote of their happy surprise in encountering a young child in the remote gold camps.

As they settled into California in all its varied aspects, the Argonauts saw women as absolutely necessary to the transformation of California from a series of transient, mercenary societies (and recently Mexican and Catholic, at that) into something like the orderly communities from which they came. George Raymond wrote his sister: "I like the country much better than formerly and were it not for the want of society (I mean ladies) the Sabbath and the faces of my friends at home, should be content to stay here. There are no women except a few spanish."[13]

The more forward-looking 49ers saw the eventual arrival of large numbers of women and the rise of a society based on families as an important future benchmark, a sign of California's maturity. "As for the history of California...I believe it is the finest country in the world Women is all that is wanted to make it habitable," wrote Seth Smith in 1851. And William Brown added that California needed a particular kind of female society: "Refined, intelligent & amiable Female Society.... We Californians get very little of that kind of Society." It was a distinction with implicit implications about race, ethnicity, and class. What Brown referred to was the influence of educated and refined Euro-American white women. Perhaps it was, by implication, a statement of their sense of membership in a society superior in its refinements and social standing to that of most other Argonauts. Underneath the outward manifestations of egalitarian camaraderie, the 49ers often displayed a well-developed sense of social class. Their observations about women were a form of drawing these distinctions.[14]

The 49ers had an almost mystical attachment to the idea of women as civilizers.[15] Yet they also gave the strong impression that however much they sought women to transform California into a moral society, they did not propose to volunteer their wives, fiancées, sisters, female relatives, and friends for the task. As some women made subdued and genteel but persistent entreaties that they be allowed to come to California to join their men, the 49ers responded with horror at the thought. They replied with a continuous litany that they did not want their female companions and relatives to come to California.[16] They preferred to leave them in the states, a perpetual monument to the civilized, orderly, and familiar communities they had left. In part, they saw it as a tribute to their sacrifices for their families and communities that they would endure a lack of female presence and all it implied for months and even years. In part, this was also a declaration of their protective posture in defending the sensibilities of their women against the grossness of this new world. Perhaps also they did not want women to come to California and spoil the campout with their male friends. Whatever the hardships of cooking and sewing, some men clearly enjoyed the conviviality of a male social club of like-minded comrades. Of course, they enjoyed it even more if they were making money.

"LADIES" AND OTHER WOMEN

When E. D. Perkins wrote, "I have not spoken to a lady for 5 months," he made reference not only to the scarcity of women in California, but also to distinctions that men made among them.[17] That the 49ers carried the values of their families and communities with them was nowhere truer than in their attitudes toward women. These values led them to offer constant judgments about the conduct and behavior of the women they met, judgments that were sometimes based on minimal evidence. What they found en route and in California were diverse groups of women in many different settings. Among the varied groups the 49ers encountered were women from the tropical way stations of Panama or Cuba or the coastal cities of South America; women from the indigenous peoples of California, a category that would include women of Mexican origin and Native American women; and the women who came across the plains or by sea with them who were married and accorded the designation "lady."

Forty-niners began to distinguish among women as soon as they set sail or began to journey overland to California. One Argonaut expressed his suspicions about a woman and her reputation as soon as his vessel left the harbor when he wrote, "We had on board Lucy Allen a bad woman, two young men with her, who were very bad characters from New York City, called by some Bowery boys." Others seemed to share his suspicions, for "one of the passengers threw some soft grease on the woman and the two young men, which made them still more mad." He and his companions assumed that any woman traveling with "very bad characters" must herself be of questionable character or worse.[18]

On the expedition overland, Henry Packer wrote his fiancée of two gentlemen from Bloomfield, Iowa, who joined the company with a woman of uncertain origin. Packer decided not to speak to the woman until he knew more about her. His response was indicative of the suspicion with which 49ers tended to treat any unmarried woman traveling with male companions or even traveling alone. Like other Argonauts, he assigned one standard of conduct to women, another to men. He spoke in strong terms about the identity of the woman, her antecedents, and her behavior; he said nothing about her male companions.[19]

Once arrived in California, the Argonauts had encounters with other kinds of women in the port cities and larger towns of the interior, such as Sacramento and Stockton. They quickly established distinctions among "ladies" of standing in society (generally married, with servants), working women from the bars, camps, and towns in various occupations, and finally, prostitutes and others in the entertainment businesses. The wives of professional men generally (although not exclusively) lived in the cities of San Francisco, Stockton, and Sacramento and in the larger mining camps in the Sierra. These were entitled to respect and deference by their married condition and their scant numbers. In a sense, these women were oddities in the overwhelmingly male world. They were also unapproachable, on a pedestal, with those qualities of gentility that characterized the women the Argonauts remembered in the East. Louise A. K. S. ("Annie") Clapp, who signed herself "Dame Shirley" in a series of published letters from California, was perhaps the most famous woman observer of the 49er mining camps. Dame Shirley noted that when "lady gold washers" went to the "diggings" in "pleasure parties," veteran miners preceded them and carefully mixed gold dust with the gravel, so the lady "mineresses" invariably returned with at least twenty dollars in gold.[20]

Among those not designated "ladies," the Argonauts found a wide range. Many women in California worked; they sought the same range of economic advantages from the Gold Rush as their male counterparts. The men around them, unsettled in a new place and determined to retain some of the standards they had been admonished to uphold even as others eroded, often were uneasy about women who were not clearly wives and mothers in the traditional sense. The recent arrival who wrote to his mother that the greatest drawback of California was "the absence of women" went on to report, "I have not seen half a dozen since I came here, and they were of a class whose acquaintance I would not wish to cultivate." His letter both reassured his mother that he was on his guard against suspicious women and betrayed his own uncertainty about how to deal with the women, albeit in small numbers, who were found intermixed in what had seemed to be at first glance an all-male world.[21]

The 49ers had only contempt for women in the entertainment industry, or so they said in their private comments to their friends and families. Charles Tuttle wrote to his wife Maria concerning her desire to join him in California: "We have but few females in this country. There are none within many miles of here. The cities are however filled up with prostitutes. I almost dread to have you walk their polluted streets.... Whenever one calls me where I can see them I turn away in disgust. What sets so lovely on a woman as virtue." At the same time, the Argonauts apparently did not bother to make distinctions among women who worked in various entertainment occupations. In addition to prostitutes, women worked in saloons as hostesses; they sang and danced; they also had public roles in the great gambling establishments in San Francisco. The 49ers did not, for the most part, see these women as laborers in service industries, but rather as women who had deserted the values and places that set them apart as women.[22]

However they might adjust to doing business on Sunday, most 49ers clearly did not propose to change their values about women.[23] Nor did they sense any ambivalence about judging the women they did encounter. Henry Packer wrote to his fiancée from the mines, "Ladies society is rather scarce here; but not all unknown. Those who are entitled to respect, receive it to the outmost extent; while those who are not, receive much marked attention from some of the gentry." Packer had no doubts about the distinctions between those two categories.[24]

NOSTALGIA AND COURTSHIP

Once settled at work and in their living arrangements, the Argonauts often thought of the local social scene back home, parties and sleigh rides, church socials and dances, visiting and calling. They had left all that behind physically, but they still recalled their friends and their good times together with great fondness. Indeed, the attractions of the social world they left behind took on an added glow in the light shed by a California sunset across the continent.[25]

Sundays, in particular, were occasions for revisiting these memories. For many, it was a day of introspection. They read, wrote home, and walked in the mountain fastness that was also their work site. It was during these weekly breaks in the routine that miners might ask themselves what they were doing so far removed from the women who formed such an important element in their lives, to what gain and what end, and how long they proposed to continue pursuing the same end. Their letters on such occasions conveyed not only their sense of the absence of women from their lives, but their resolve to do something about it. On Sundays, nostalgia for home often led to courtship of the girl back home.

A letter from John Cowden summarized the common view among 49ers that eligible women were to be found only in the communities they had left. Of a woman from his home town, he wrote:

> The Young Lady at Elmira who expressed a desire to see John Cowden, can be gratified only by coming out to Californy, and by enquiring at the upper hole close to the hills on the upper bar of the Mukelenmes diggings, she will find him there or at least his tent during all hours of the day, if she is handsome, accomplished, with a good disposition and reasonably rich, I shall be glad to see her. Though you say my friend Kate Baldy is still in the market, I may yet be in time for her, if she will only wait till I return.[26]

That the "Young Lady" should be "handsome, accomplished, with a good disposition and reasonably rich" represented a catalogue of the qualities that must have formed a staple of conversation among the young 49ers. Cowden then abruptly moved on from humor and fantasy to the reality of "Kate Baldy," a young woman "still in the market," who would apparently do very nicely.

In contrast to such affirmations of their ties to the social world they remembered back home, the Argonauts who arrived in 1849 and over the next dozen years constantly denigrated the attractions of women in California in their correspondence with their families and friends. Eli Mossman wrote with unusual candor from the mining camps, "I should like to know how you and your miss Emley Bearde is getting along miss Drury and all the rest of you we do not knoe whare to go see girls here without we go to see some feamail indian squaw and I would just as leave go to see one of dads horses."[27]

Perhaps this hostility had to do with uneasiness when confronted with different kinds of peoples and values, or with the absence of what the 49ers considered suitable "ladies." It may also have reflected the lack of a normal social life, of opportunities to meet eligible people, and the absence of the usual opportunities for courtship. For whatever the reason, from their first hour away from their homes and communities, most of the Argonauts thought about the girls they knew and had left behind, or others they simply had heard about. These variations made for another of the paradoxes that seemed everywhere in California. In a new world, surrounded by widely varied peoples and ways of doing things, in the context of new choices and new economic opportunities beyond their wildest dreams, the 49ers doggedly clung to the family in their contact with women. After describing their daily routine, they would write in ordinary and reassuring terms (reassuring for themselves, as well as for the objects of their affection) to the women they left behind, expressing longing for the people and places they had abandoned, rather than enthusiasm for the new world that lay around them. The more they moved into the unknown, whether geographically, economically, or socially, the more they sought to hold on to familiar ways of doing things in their courtship rituals. They discussed the same issues and raised the same questions with the ladies to whom they wrote as they would have voiced to them at home.

Those 49ers not engaged and not actively courting a special lady continued to look eastward for eligible ladies in general. They filled their letters with constant reference to dear friends and suitable women of their own age. They wrote only rarely to these women themselves, preferring instead to let their brothers and sisters, even parents, convey their interest and report responses. This shadowy flirting had a youthful and awkward quality about it. The style of their letters was remarkably similar in tone. William Scott closed his letters to brothers and sisters by sending "my respects" to six young ladies that he identified by name. John Milner wrote to his sister, "All I want is to come home . . . to see the folks, more especially the Geogin Girls. Tell the young ladies in Pike & adjoining counties I am ready when I get home." One 49er sent "my love to the ladies in particular," without specifying any particular lady, while another was very specific about the object of his interest. He sent instructions to his sister, Sarah Hardy: "She must not take unto herself a partner until I return. . . . To hear from her would be a pleasure, the greatest I can or could in reality wish."[28]

Behind these light and casual references ran a deeper concern. These young men who went to California had been removed from the courting cycles of farm and village and community. To the extent that they were part of a distinct group defined by age and long connection from childhood, their prolonged absences changed the expectations that they would marry into this group and join the community as a couple. Many 49ers seem to have been conscious of this gap in time and space, and with it, the loss of an expected and anticipated opportunity, or at the very least, the loss of a kind of assurance that things would be done in a familiar way. J. C. Collbreath reflected this concern when he wrote, "Society will be greatly changed when I return I am afraid few familiar faces will greet me the Girls will all be married and the young ones that fill their places will grow out of my Knowledge." And

Charles Dulany wrote to his sister, "Molly is telling me of several marriages that have taken place in Ky, say that I must return soon, or all the girls will be married."[29] As Argonauts found different voices and subject matter for their separate family correspondents, this particular issue seems to have been reserved for sisters, and to a lesser extent, mothers.

George Raymond arrived in California in 1849 at the age of 23, single and anxious. He used his correspondence with his sister Sarah to maintain contact with eligible women, mentioning, among other things, his attachment to several ladies of mutual acquaintance. "Give my love to all the girls and my best respects to all friends," was a characteristic closing. When Raymond returned to Utica, New York, in 1852, his friends still in the gold fields, who were using the new technique of quartz mining for extracting gold, wrote to him in familiar and boisterous tones. "George I suppose you are haveing a good old time with the Girls. Well, go to it while you are young for when you are old you can't," wrote B. L. Rick from Angels Camp.

> I see that all the girls that I knew at home are married off. I shall have to go up the River about seven miles to find one just suited to my kind. I know you have lots of Pretty Girls left in your city so just speak a good word for Bob and me. You can represent us to the Girls as Two good looking young QUARTZ MINERS with the ROCK!!!

He concluded in a burst of male jocularity, "All the boys are well and send their respects. I wish you a long life, a good wife and plenty of babies."[30] Raymond's Gold Rush friends rejoiced that one of their own was at last returned home and living out their own dreams.

The worry that the cycle of flirting, courtship, and marriage had passed the 49ers by cut across sectional and class lines. Men from Massachusetts and Alabama wrote the same kinds of nostalgic notes as did 49ers from New York and Michigan. Those in marginal economic circumstances expressed the same kinds of concerns as the wealthy and presumably socially accomplished. The language was different, but the message was the same. Robert La Mott, from a wealthy family in Philadelphia, divulged his social concerns to his sister and mother in separate letters. To his sister, he noted an engagement of a woman and expressed the hope "that all the girls won't follow her example before I return, but that some good, clever souls will wait till our return." To his mother, La Mott confessed himself smitten by a Miss Lola. News of her charms "makes me feel quite dissatisfied with California & makes me wish myself among you all again to enjoy some of the pleasant society." He charged his mother to keep Miss Lola from becoming engaged "till I come home again for I dont know what I'll do if the girls don't stop." Nor did these expressions change much over time. The Argonauts who wrote about the women in their villages and communities in 1855 sounded very much like those who wrote in 1849. For both groups, their stay in California was a nomadic and a monastic pursuit of wealth; their families and communities represented warm friends, home-cooked meals, and "ladies." John Nagy summarized the differences in these terms: "you are where you can injoy good society and have the pleasure of running around with the girls for if you come here you hav to fite fleas."[31]

Some of the gold seekers courted the girl back home on the voyage, or rather, finished courtships they had begun before departures. On one side, the exchange of news and views must have become increasingly difficult as the men moved into ever more distant and strange landscapes and as encounters with new peoples replaced the familiar with the exotic. Added to these alien experiences was the necessity of defending an absence that stretched from months into years, in many cases, and of persuading the woman that this distant figure at the end of a thin line of communication by letter was worthy of a commitment to and then the long wait that followed.

The task of maintaining continuous contact as a basis for the discussion of a common future was one often talked about, but it was achieved only with difficulty. As the 49er disappeared into the remote camps of the Sierra, the lapse of time in delivery of letters grew, and along with it, the likelihood that letters could become lost or misplaced. Of course, there was another side: the sense of the familiar and comfortable that formed the basis of the original attraction and beginning of courtships. The bond of family, neighborhood, and communication formed a departure point for discussions of a life to be shared by the courting couple.

The 49ers would woo their chosen mates by mail, by proxy, or rapidly in person if necessary. Aaron Hyde licensed his mother to act for him in a letter that was playful but not without its serious side: "Dear Mother please look out some nice bit of a gal get Father to court her, and send her out to me, or else save her till I come home, but I reckon you had better send her out as I think some of going into farming next summer if I can find a suitable place, and then I shall want a housekeeper." Hyde wrote in jest, but only half in jest.[32] William H. Cosby wooed a well-to-do Kentucky widow for three years entirely via letters to his sister. There is no evidence that in this time he wrote directly to the subject of his interest, and perhaps he should not have been surprised that she married someone else.[33] John Milner's Uncle Edward returned from California in 1850, married Jane Hill, and left his bride of a few days to go back to the gold fields for two years.[34]

An engagement won by means of transcontinental correspondence was an assured way to confirm future marriage prospects within the community. Perhaps it also offered various Argonauts a chance to articulate intimate feelings that they found awkward to bring up in person. Henry Packer used his three years in California to court Mary Judkins, the subject of his affection. That Henry and Mary had known one another for a long period did not appear to speed the process or to make the language of their correspondence more specific. On the way to the gold fields, Henry wrote, "In regards to the peculiar relation in which we stand to each other I have nothing to say at present, only that it is a source of much gratification and pleasure to me to know that it is so." He repeatedly declared that he did not need to write of his love, respect, fidelity, and so forth, because their relationship had passed that stage and such assurances "are certainly useless when no longer required."

Imagine his shock when she replied almost a year later that she had not promised herself to anyone! Given the vague convolutions of the language of their courtship, nothing specific had been declared or promised, but a final exchange cleared up misunderstandings. The confusions were consistent with their restraint. After all, as Henry confirmed in his analysis of their happy engagement, he had "loved you more than I could tell, you returned that love more than you thought prudent to express." And, he went on, such prudence was necessary, "for if you had all the confidence and at once thrown off all reserve, you would at once have proven yourself not what I conceived you to be, and hence have ceased to be the object of my affection." Thus, Packer apparently sought the kind of woman whose purity and circumspection was of such a high level that she could not lower her reserve to accept him without losing his good regard. Fortunately, in Mary he found exactly the right woman.[35]

Not all courtships by mail were so convoluted. Within six months of his arrival in California, Asa Thompson wrote to Abby Hobbs, "I will answer your question in that Yankee style by asking another when do you wish to be married?" Abby's acceptance was as forthright as his question. Thompson happily recounted their earliest times together "when I first began to stop with you." And he concluded, "it is now almost ten months since we had our first interview and I can truly say there has been no time during the ten months when I would have wished to retrace my steps."[36]

Those who thus courted from afar the women absent from their lives had a vision of recreating amid the gold camps and boom towns the comforts and assurances of the lives they had left behind. Seth Smith wrote to his father in Baltimore, "I wish you were out here with all the family We could do first rate 4 of us working together & Ma & Margaret to do the cooking & washing for that is all it wants to make any man contented in this country Women to do the house work for after a person has been at work in the hot sun all day it goes against the grain to come home at night & go to work & cook for the next day."[37] But if life in a world without women posed many difficulties for the 49ers, life was also difficult for those who remained in the world they had abandoned to look for gold. The departure of the Argonauts for the California gold fields in extraordinary numbers—some eighty thousand in the winter and spring of 1849 and annual migrations of substantial numbers in the next half a dozen years—meant significant adjustments for many families and communities in the eastern part of the nation, as well. In addition to a society without women in the West, the Gold Rush created a society without husbands, brothers, and lovers in the East.

7

"I COULD SELL SOME OF THE FURNITURE":

Adjustments in the East

By spring most of the Argonauts had departed. With them went the flower of the village. Their absence made a big social gap, and that for many a day.

PRENTICE MULFORD

THE STRAINS IMPOSED on the social fabric of the nation by the Gold Rush registered in the East in a different form than they were experienced among the gold fields. The absence of the men who went west in 1849 and throughout the next decade was felt at several levels: the loss of love, affection, and companionship within families by women whose spouses, fiancées, sons, and brothers were among the Argonaut companies; the loss of physical support for children and elderly parents; the loss of economic base within communities through the absence of wage earners and farm laborers. Within both family and community, these losses required adjustments in the practices of everday life and in the social rituals that help structure them. As the years of the Gold Rush wore on, the necessity to make such adjustments was one of the great constants in the lives of those the 49ers left behind them. As we will see, only as the nation began to turn its attention to the great sectional conflict looming before it did the overall effect of these many adaptations to the strains imposed by the Gold Rush become apparent.

Within families, the changes began immediately with the departure of the 49ers. Those who went to docks, piers, the end of country lanes, and even railroad stations still had to return home. How well would the arrangements for the support of the family work, pending the return of the vanished Argonaut? As we've seen, the voyage to California was financed by means of an interlocking series of financial arrangements that involved the costs of the trip, support for the family, and small sums borrowed at interest or good will. These arrangements invariably produced confusion and tension in family relations, disputes over money and authority that were heightened by the passage of time. The plans and obligations made in haste and the golden glow of optimism now had to be carried out over months and years of hard work and inconvenience. Along with obligations and reduced resources went a shift of roles and status for the family members left behind. Some people took on additional burdens and with them, perhaps, additional influence within the family.

Communities also had to accommodate. Prentice Mulford remarked upon the changes in Sag Harbor with the departure of the 49ers. They would surely have been flattered to be called "the flower of the village," but whatever their social qualities, their farewell meant a change in the community's social life. When this cohort of young men vanished from Sag Harbor and a hundred villages like it, the marriage prospects and plans of young women of the village had to be recalculated. The courting rituals continued, conducted now by mail from afar, but absent faces and silenced voices changed responses and promises. Asked and unasked questions intruded into calculations. When would the 49ers return? How would personal, social, and economic relationships survive a prolonged absence measured in years? How long should eligible women wait? For countless individuals, families, and communities, the prospect of great riches blended with lengthening absences to pose a wide range of pressing questions.

ECONOMIC ADJUSTMENTS

Because the Gold Rush drew participants from across the economic spectrum, it left in its wake great differences in the economic condition and resources of individuals and families. When families with financial resources lamented the absence of their fathers, fiancées, and sons, they tended to stress personal reasons for their distress. Individuals and families in straitened economic circumstances, however, found their lives increasingly focused on obtaining lodging and food.

It was one of the many contradictions of the California Gold Rush that it aroused a powerful response among those in vulnerable financial circumstances, so that scarce resources had to be stretched ever further to raise funds for the journey to the gold fields. This lack of economic resources in the absence of the departed 49ers and the accompanying adjustments imposed on families occupied a major part of the correspondence that passed from the East to the West and to a lesser extent in the other direction. Henry Worth, a clerk who left Nantucket to do clerical work in merchant houses of California, summed up the concern about daily bread in a poem written to his wife:

> You say you'll leave us all, John
> To Providence alone
> You'll trust to fill our mouths, John
> With bread, when you're gone.
> Be it so.—I'll trust him, too, John
> And turn my tears to laughter:
> Who'll leave his wife for Gold, John
> Is not worth crying after.[1]

The individuals and families left behind might be divided into two major groups: those in possession of an ongoing economic enterprise such as farms or stores or shops, and those dependent on continuing wage labor, everyone from farm laborers and clerks to doctors and lawyers. For those who ran farms or plantations, the loss of ongoing labor, particularly heavy labor in the fields, was significant, and others had to step forward to assume the additional burdens left by departures for California. Yet these families had a source of support.

The spouses of 49ers who came from farms usually continued to live there. Sometimes, the wife would rent the farm and live on the proceeds; sometimes, she and the children (if there were children) would operate the farm themselves. Whatever detailed advice she had received, for the first six months or so, she did so independently, for her husband was out of contact. The wives on farms knew the annual cycles of plowing, planting, cultivating, harvesting, and marketing because they had participated in them for years. Now they supervised them. In addition to questions of cultivation and marketing, farm management involved clearing new lands, making improvements, constructing outbuildings, and breeding livestock, the cash crop of many farm families. The decision to sell livestock was always a serious one, involving as it did a portion of the permanent capital of the enterprise. In the shop or across the counter, the issues were less clear-cut. Here, women simply exercised their best judgment, sometimes advised by male relatives.[2]

Jonathan Heywood, for example, left his wife, Jane Heywood, in charge of their farm in Belvedere, Boon County, Illinois. He wrote her in 1851 not with advice, but with praise for what she had done. "I am glad to hear of the enjoyment of your good health and good succes in carrying on the farm," he commented. "You must have a hard task to manage the farm and take care of the children, and built so much as you have. I am almost afraid you are making more improvements and more money on the farm than I could if I were there." He concluded: "Live well and keep the babies warm, and be careful not to work too hard." Jane Heywood probably did live comparatively well, but with family and farm, she must have worked very hard indeed.[3]

Those wives who took over the family business often came to their duties, whether those of running a farm or managing a store, already burdened by debts, obligations that had formed a backdrop for the decision to seek an immediate remedy in the gold fields of California in the first place. The departure of the 49er for California was often an alarm bell for creditors, a signal that the signatory was no longer around to be held responsible for his obligations. So a wife often spent the first months after her husband's departure reassuring creditors that their often tardy notes were indeed secure and encouraging them to delay in presenting notes for collection. The sense of uneasiness over these debts radiated out to members of the extended family, who might be security signatories on the notes. The two influences most immediately noted within a community on the departure of its Argonauts were the scarcity of labor at harvest time and the difficulty of local merchants in collecting debts from those gone to California. In a world where so much economic exchange revolved around debts and labor exchanges of various kinds, the disappearance of a man whose signature was on several notes and who might also be obligated in other, more informal arrangements could send shock waves through the community. The spouse left behind assumed responsibility for quieting that concern and moving ahead with the family's economic base.

For those without the assurance of a farm or a property that could provide maintenance during the spouse's absence, the issue of support was immediate and often involved moving to a less desirable place to live. Spouses sometimes had to live with parents or in-laws. Sometimes they might board with friends. "I have already expressed my wish in my former letters for you to go to boarding with some of your friends (when you make all your visits out) where you can best suit yourself, and find it convenient with them to board you & the children," wrote one 49er. Should this arrangment not be possible, he advised, "find a place, as near to them as you can, to board."[4]

Spouses and families sometimes boarded with strangers. Rinaldo Taylor left his wife and baby daughter in a boarding house in East Boston. It was, he admitted, a most unsatisfactory arrangement. "With regard to your position," he wrote from California, "I am far from wishing you to remain enslaved in a boarding house, & I know the place is not congenial to you, & yet know of no other course." Within a few months, he wrote in a similar vein: "I hope you will be as patient as you can in your new situation. I know you cannot feel quite contented, & I am sorry you are so situated as to be obliged to have so much care devolving upon you. But you must get along as easy as you can & not work hard."[5]

Some spouses took in boarders. John Fitch's wife did so in spite of fragile health. "From what I learn of the state of my wife's health it is requisite that she should avoid excitement or over exertion," Fitch confided to his brother, "and I have repeatedly advised her not to take over one or two Boarders which with the proper care of her children is as much as she ought to attend to."[6] Fitch's letters confirmed that like the wives of other 49ers, his wife took in boarders strictly from economic necessity.

The mixture of emotional and economic factors in this prolonged separation surfaced in the contrasts between financial penury in the East and new vistas and opportunities in the West. The result might be a series of communications at cross purposes. One would write of love and longing, mixed with wonder at a new landscape; the other would talk of shoes and bread. The early exchange of letters between Maria and Charles Tuttle represented these different perspectives. Charles Tuttle wrote of his love as soon as his horse turned the corner at the end of the lane in Milwaukee, Wisconsin. By the time he arrived in Independence, Missouri, he wrote, "Maria love strengthens with the distance that separates me from you. I believe no man ever loved as I love you." As he prepared to set forth on the overland trail, he continued in the same vein: "Maria does your bosom still burn with love. Amid the gay world do you think of me. Yes I know you do. The flame which burns in my bosom is one extremity of an electric wire extended to your own. I cannot express the strength of my attachment, you must therefore take my cold language as a poor index of my heart."[7]

In addition to his abiding love, Charles referred to his poverty. "I took you an artless girl from the home of your parents to live in poverty," he wrote. "Your great ambition was wealth. I saw it but could not gratify it." Indeed, it was to escape this impoverished condition that he had launched himself on the California journey whence he would return only when "my purse is filled with gold."[8]

From Milwaukee, where she lived during his absence, Maria returned his love with equal fervor. She was reconciled to six months without hearing from him, yet "six months seem quite too long for me for Charles I am not strong." And at the end of the six months, when she had still not heard from him, she could write, "I long to clasp you in my arms to imprint a thousand kisses on your lips and tell you again how dear you are to me. How true my heart has ever been, how to feed the flame of love, it must revel in the scenes of the past, where you alone are the hero, and look forward to a reunion to keep it from breaking."[9]

Maria Tuttle, far from being caught up in a "gay world," was preoccupied with her precarious financial condition. At the same moment that she could write of her undying love, she could add, "If I do not get some assistance from you soon I must earn some money for my wardrobe will need replenishing." And as if ashamed of her weakness, she continued, "But my dear do not rob yourself to help me, for I can get along some way."[10] Within a week, she returned to her deteriorating financial circumstances. "I must begin to look to earn some money for my wardrobe is getting quite shabby. My shoe bill counts up more than any others I would take a school if my health would allow," she continued. "I can do enough to keep me in pin money. I could sell some of the furniture, but do not like to." Amid these confessions of her financial circumstances, she continued to reaffirm her care and economy in the management of money. "Charles I have not run into debt one penny since you left, neither have I disposed of the furniture I brought home, which is worth more than a hundred dollars. Don't you think I have been economical?"[11] The two had decided before his departure that if the financial circumstances became desperate, she would in fact sell the furniture. Yet this was clearly a step that she was reluctant to take. The furniture that she brought to their household reminded her of their lives together in the past; it would form the basis of their commitment to one another in the future.

CHANGES IN WOMEN'S ROLES

The families of 49ers at midcentury tended to be close-knit groups—a necessary defense against a highly competitive and sometimes hostile world. Within this larger context, gender helped to define duties and relationships. Women of several ages were responsible for the domestic affairs of the family. They worked within the home, where their most important charge was training the children. The adjustments to their family roles that women had to make following the departure of the 49ers for the gold fields included taking on new obligations and responsibilities. They also involved, in some cases, more independence and greater authority in decisions that affected their own lives and their families. For example, John Eagle left his wife Margaret to operate the family store, leaving detailed instructions about inventories and credit risks. The store was heavily burdened with debts. "I wish you to say to *all* those who may inquire for me, and to whom I am indebted, that I still hope and expect to be able, by next fall, to send home means to settle their accounts, and they will oblige me by being as patient as the nature of the case will allow," he wrote. Margaret Eagle's business responsibilities were extensive, and John left all the decisions about the business to her judgment.[12]

Milo Goss gave to his wife Catherine the task of conducting their business affairs. He also urged her to consult with various male advisers. Distance, personality, and family interaction often made close consultation impossible on a permanent basis. Thus, women such as Catherine Goss gradually increased their independence of action over the years of their husbands' absences, perhaps through their own design, perhaps simply through their husbands' neglect. Goss added another declaration that also characterized the protective instinct of 49ers. "There are many things of a business character I wish to write you but I can not call them to mind," he wrote, "but there is one thing of the greatest importance. I wish you never allow business matters at home to trouble or annoy you."[13] Considering that their house and store were about to be sold for debts, his concern for her mental health was admirable.

Catherine Goss had every reason to be anxious. Left to manage the family affairs in Kalamazoo, Michigan, she soon discovered that her husband's facile explanations of their affairs had disguised the precarious condition of the business. Four months after his departure, she reproached him for not being more forthright with her about the family's financial difficulties. Her letter began with reference to the traditional male determination to keep their wives separated from the sordid world of practical business affairs and then moved on to the new authority that she had in directing their business. She wrote:

> Now husband, I must censure you a little for the mistaken kindness you have always shown. Why couldn't you have had moral courage enough to have told me the actual state of your affairs; I have ever shared your joys, and wish to in your trials. I insist upon it, No woman can properly discharge her duties as a wife who is ignorant of the state of her husband's affairs; she will be liable to expenses which would be perfectly right if her husband was unembarrassed, but incurs the censure of the upright under the circumstances, which are the reverse. Now from this time *henceforth and forever,* please be communicative when we are equally concerned. You do not yet know your wife (that is if she knows herself) if she is only fitted for the *smooth path of life,* and cannot endure its trials. Nothing is more essential for my happiness than to know we are living within our means.

Now my dear husband, I do not like to write you in this strain, but do it especially for your good, and that of our family.[14]

While numerous women took over new duties and responsibilities in managing family affairs, it is less clear whether such alterations changed their status within the family. Did they then become an equal voice in family affairs, an equality to which their new duties in the economic sphere gave them title? Only faint echoes of divisions over issues in family decision making come down to us. Certainly these were among the myriad new questions faced by families in the wake of the mass departure of men for the gold fields in 1849 and for the next half-dozen years thereafter.

TWO WOMEN'S ADJUSTMENTS

The departure of 49ers produced a void of months extending into years in the lives of individuals and families, and beyond them, in whole communities. Of the many adjustments, the greatest fell to those women most directly affected by absence, a combination of emotional and economic changes within the context of shifts within the extended family.

These adjustments might be said to fall into three periods. The adjustments of the initial period of nine to twelve months dealt with the void before the 49ers arrived in California and regular communication could be established. The second period brought an acceptance that financial returns from the gold camps, whatever the promises that energized the initial decision to go, would in most cases be rare and small. Finally, the women left behind arrived at the recognition that 49ers would be gone longer than anyone imagined and that their extended absence stretched forward without a specific terminal date. The experiences of two women from different places and with different resources indicate the range of problems faced and solutions found (or not found) during the first two years of absence, from the effort to deal with the initial loss of contact well into the recognition that the Gold Rush would not mean immediate relief from pressing financial difficulties and that the loved ones' return lay far in the future.

Jane Blackwood

Jane Blackwood and her husband, Thomas, a medical doctor, lived in Ann Arbor, Michigan. The Blackwoods were well-to-do, although their financial standing recently had undergone a series of reverses. Among Thomas

Blackwood's several problems were debts and a trial over a paternity suit, in which he had been found innocent. In February 1849, Thomas Blackwood departed from Ann Arbor for New York, from whence he sailed to California. He left behind his wife, four children, and a range of personal and financial problems. On the occasion of his departure, Thomas Blackwood smothered these obligations in detailed advice. He wrote to his older son in Ann Arbor—a second son was at sea—of his responsibilities to his mother and his two younger sisters. He also left plentiful advice to his wife Jane about all sorts of personal and public matters.

Jane Blackwood found herself the center of a close-knit but dispersed family, with three children in Ann Arbor and her son at sea, long unheard from, other relatives in Chicago, and numerous groups of cousins. She had to adjust to the absence of her husband, to added responsibilities within the family, and to the handling of innumerable business transactions left her by her husband. The continuing correspondence from her to brothers, sisters, in-laws, and friends at a distance was a reminder of the ways that the personal effect of the Gold Rush spread out in ever-widening concentric circles. Writing, she found, was "a profitable pasttime in my 'hours of idleness' which since I saw my Macon friends, have crowded themselves unaccounted."[15]

Jane Blackwood's main family responsibilities were the children. The first to be consoled were the young daughters, Mary and Alice. "When Mary showed Alice your likeness and asked her who it was she said father at once after looking at it a while she said, father don't speak," she wrote. In her emotional account of the evenings with the two girls, Jane concluded, "Oh that I could hear from you daily and know that you are well and happy I do hope that you will grant me this one favour, to write, *write* me once a fortnight as long as you have an opportunity." When son Richard returned from his sea voyage, she had to counsel with him about his future. Thomas Blackwood's advice was ambivalent. Of course "our Dear Dick" should stay at home and go to school, but if he should decide to join his father in California, he would be welcomed with open arms.[16]

Business matters also assumed a major role in Jane Blackwood's life. She had to supervise numerous financial transactions, for which Thomas offered endless advice. He also recognized her difficulties. "I know I have left you all comparatively without an earthly protector left a good business & increasing public favor, which would insure a competence with good management," he wrote. "These I know were certainties when compared with what I now can offer. But the die is cast I cannot return back, and I pray God will help you all & success me & if it is best for us all in the future, crown my enterprise with success."[17]

From Jane's friend Mary Ann Nelson in Chicago came a declaration of her surprise that Thomas had gone to California and an unspoken criticism of his departure from his family and financial responsibilities in Michigan.[18] In this case and others, Jane Blackwood found herself in the role of defending her husband's decision to seek their fortune in California. But, caught in the middle, she was also one of those who kept track for the rest of the community of the men who had vanished into the placers, writing her husband to inquire "the fate of Dr. Ormsby," as we have seen.[19]

As the head of the family, Jane Blackwood also found herself heir to the role of arbiter and financial resource. Relatives had a claim on family ties, and it now fell to "Cousin Jane" to deal with such requests. A "Cousin Thomas" wrote on the eve of his departure for California—a common tie with her husband—for assistance in solving "one Trouble." Cousin Thomas had borrowed money for his ticket and outfit. Now, as he was about to embark, his sponsors had asked for some of the funds, and if Cousin Jane or her friends could "help me out," he told her, it would be most pleasant. As he explained the financial awkwardness, "I promised Mr. Herrick to send his family some of the money advanced me, as they will be in need of it before they can get returns from him in C. I then supposed I could have done so, but circumstances connected with my New York affairs, have entirely put it out of my power to do so & had I not purchased my outfit and Ticket before I ascertained this fact, I should have remained behind & sent his family back the money I borrowed. But for this tis now too late." Cousin Thomas then went right to the financial heart of the matter:

> The favor I am going to ask of my Cousin Jane is this: that you borrow for me a 150 Dollars & send to Mrs. Smith Herrick at Pontiac & as soon as I reach my destination I will remit you the money & Interest. I would like to have it sent by the first or middle of April. This my dear cousin may seem a strange request for me to make of you who I already owe so much for the kindness you have ever shown me. Yet I make it from a necessity which heaven knows is not my own fault, but the fault of my unlucky stars. When I see you again, I will tell you all. I cannot see a helpless family suffer by even my misfortunes.[20]

He did not mention that the innocent family that might suffer if he couldn't repay her was that headed by Jane Blackwood.

This exchange offers a useful insight into what made possible this woman's and this family's adjustments to the absence of Thomas Blackwood in California. The Blackwood family had achieved a comfortable economic position in the world. Jane Blackwood directed some complicated financial dealings with debtors and creditors at various levels, but the family always had sufficient resources. She traveled when she wished; the children were comfortably provided for. Unlike many 49ers, Thomas Blackwood had not left his family in straitened financial circumstances, and Jane Blackwood's skills, together with the family's resources, meant that financial pressures played little or no part in the stresses and anxieties associated with Thomas's departure for and his extended sojourn in California.

Margaret H. Eagle

John Eagle went to California in January 1852, leaving his wife Margaret with an insurance policy on his life, four children (plus two stepchildren), and a store. John left in January; his first letter home from California was dated from San Francisco on April 10, and the first from the mines, from Auburn Ravine, was dated June 13, 1852. Over the first year or so of his absence, John and Margaret each came to terms with new tasks. His involved learning to mine in the Sierra with his brothers, Joe and Jim. Hers included tending the children (illness and school), running the store (endless business decisions), and juggling the debts (who should be paid and how much). There were many debts, for this was the reason that John decided (with her full support and permission) to go to California in the first place. John sent back regular drafts, generally in the sum of one or two hundred dollars, marked for debts, and the two made collective decisions about who was to be paid and how much.

After the first months of separation, the outlines of her adjustment had been set. She often consulted John, and the contact between the two continued regular and strong. Between 1852 and 1857, they exchanged some ninety letters. They were secure and openly affectionate in their relationship with one another, but it was clear that all the duties of home now devolved upon her. Among her personal responsibilities were the four children, including a baby; in addition, there were the two children of John's by an earlier marriage, who at first lived with grandparents but later moved in with Margaret. Margaret's degree of responsibility for the stepchildren and parents became the subject of much discussion. The management of the family store also meant hard choices. Margaret worried about the inventory; John was troubled by unreliable credit risks. And the couple's substantial debts overshadowed all financial plans. He wrote, "I wish you would say to all those who may inquire for me, and to whom I am indebted, that I still hope to expect to be able, by next fall, to send home means to settle their accounts, and they will oblige me by being as patient as the nature of the case will allow." He was unhappy away from his wife and family, and he stayed in order to make money to pay their debts. If things go well, he wrote, "We will, in the space of two years, be able to square accounts with the world, which we could not have done at home for ten or fifteen years to come."

Margaret also took responsibility for the eastern branch of the extended family. John's two brothers in California mined within a hundred yards of his claim. The three Eagle brothers were all married, and their wives also lived in proximity to one another. John's extensive correspondence informed all three women. Brother Jim worked hard and industriously, but he never wrote home, except an occasional postscript to one of John's regular letters, so Margaret conveyed the news. Yet Jim had saved his money and intended to return home when he made his "raise." This term represented a sum that the 49er reckoned would satisfy both his expectations and those of the family that had sent him forth with such high hopes, although most Argonauts declined to specify a number.[21]

Jim's wife Net was a great favorite in the brothers' camp because she sent supplies of snuff for the three men. Brother Joe, on the other hand, acquired a number of bad California habits. He drank and gambled. He had made a substantial sum in the placers, but he had spent it all and constantly sought loans from John to buy bread and bacon and pay his debts. Margaret and John discussed whether Joe's wife Mat should be informed of his irresponsible behavior toward himself and his family by wasting common resources. They weighed the responsibilities of each with reference to their kin. John eventually returned home to his beloved Margaret, his mining ventures having been successful—so successful that he soon returned to California for another two years. On his second trip, he was accompanied by Joe's long-suffering wife, who undertook the long voyage to the mines to straighten up the slackard husband. What Joe and his messmates said when John and Mat walked into camp was not recorded, but a year later, Mat and Joe had a new baby.

Margaret and John Eagle also confronted the issue of physical changes over the long separations. Baldness and gray hair were prominent topics. John Eagle, who wrote directly and intimately to his wife, mentioned with some embarrassment that he had lost two teeth. A further exchange of letters revealed that at almost the same time, two thousand miles away, she had lost three teeth. Eagle was relieved. In assessing their aging, he wrote playfully that the two of them must put on what he called "new feathers." He promised that both of them would get new teeth, whatever the expense. "Make yourself feel as contented as possible, and that will improve your looks still more," he continued. "As your cousin said, you are a fine looking woman. So I say again I want you to look spruce."[22]

Such adjustments continued over the years of absence, and their outlines seem to have been remarkably similar. The Argonauts who went to California in 1852 like John Eagle dealt with the same issues as men like Charles Tuttle who went in 1849. The basic questions of emotional deprivation and economic problems remained central to changes in families and communities in the East. Men began by offering detailed instructions; they ended up letting women, in large part, manage the family's affairs. The demands imposed by absence were continuous, and women—whether wives, sisters, or mothers—were most often called upon to meet them.

8

OCCUPATIONS:

The 49ers Begin Work

The time is now approaching when there will be a chance
to make something in the mines.

JOHN J. CRAVEN

THE ARGONAUTS WHO CAME to California beginning in 1849 held two powerful beliefs. The first was an abiding optimism that this venture and their participation in it would produce a substantial sum and possibly a fortune and that these riches would profoundly alter their lives. Ephriam W. Morse, who arrived in San Francisco from Boston in July 1849, wrote in his diary, "This is the ever memorable day on which I left for the mines expecting soon to become rich enough to return home a wealthy man."[1] The second conviction that united this cohort of arriving 49ers was the firm belief that the experience in which they would participate was a continuation of the American dream that rewarded hard work and honest endeavor. One Argonaut who landed in San Francisco in early June 1849 expressed to his parents this creed with the observation that whatever the varied tales from the diggings, "the story that appears most reasonable is that steady, industrious, persevering fellows seldom fail of making a handsome fortune in a few months."[2] The idea that hard work and perseverance would be suitably rewarded was a catechism that most 49ers had been taught from youth. They now expected to work hard and to profit as never before by their labors.

Whether they arrived in San Francisco by sea or in Placerville by land, the Argonauts had to move themselves and their supplies to the places where gold was found. This movement produced immediate encounters with two of California's most striking features. The first was the high wages and costs of supplies and equipment covered by the term "Gold Rush prices." The second was the land itself.

Everything in California—whether labor or goods or services—cost more, and some things were so expensive as to be beyond belief. Ordinary laborers commanded twelve dollars a day, and the prices to unload or move baggage to the mines reflected this scale. So the 49ers, divided and subdivided into small groups, organized to travel as lightly as possible to the mines and to be free to move at will in search of better sites once they got there. The basic equipment for a company of four to six would include, for example, "a tent, camp kettle, bake pan, shovels, picks, hoes, pails, pans, a lamp, an ax, a hatchet, beef (boiled), pork beans, bread, sugar, spices, tea & coffee." Some groups carried one or more of the many varieties of gold-washing machines that had flooded the market by the time the overland Argonauts departed in the spring.[3]

The 49ers who came by sea proceeded to the mines by two routes: by riverboat to Sacramento and thence overland to the diggings; by land from San Francisco to the mines. The riverboat was slow and expensive until competition drove prices down in late 1849 and 1850; overland, the 49ers moved at the pace set by loaded mules or oxen. The cost of transporting goods to the mines averaged fifty dollars per hundredweight, depending on the distance. Teamsters charged three hundred dollars to transport three barrels of flour, one barrel of pork, and another two hundred pounds of foodstuffs a distance of fifty miles. Under such a price structure, the cost of transportation was more expensive than the original cost of the supplies themselves.[4]

Although they had come from everywhere, drawn by the prospect of literally picking wealth up off the ground in California, when they arrived, the 49ers discovered that the land of gold was not always welcoming and hospitable. Through the hot, dry, California summer and fall, the Argonauts struggled both eastward, from the coast, and westward, at the final stage of their journey across the continent, toward the distant line of green that marked the foothills of the Sierra, their company uniforms or new clothes stained with sweat and dust. At night, they camped out or stayed at one of the many shanties that had sprung up to provide shelter and meals for this first wave of 49ers. Alexander Spear called it "the most tedious jerney that i ever had." His party of twenty-three, traveling with two four-horse teams, was lost part of the time. He concluded, "i like to have given out on the road, for my feet ware bad by blisters and very sore i never sufered so mutch in my life."[5] It was an appropriate introduction to the hard and repetitious labor, done in the heat of the day, supported by very expensive services, that many would come to associate with gold mining. By the time they reached the first gold-bearing streams, most Argonauts agreed that if they had not yet seen "the elephant," they certainly had spied it in outline.

The perspiring 49ers now confronted the landscape that would be their new home for the next several months and even years. Depending on whether the gold fields on the western slope of the Sierra were approached from the east or the west, the journey to the placers presented the Argonauts with strikingly different experiences of the landscape. Those coming overland had to cross the high passes of the Sierra, and as they finally moved down the western slope, the heavy forests gave way to scrub pine and finally a series of sterile valleys, dry and cracked, a forbidding and unattractive introduction to the land of gold.

Those who came to the mines from the seaboard first had to pass through the interior valleys, one of the flattest landscapes in the nation. Here, the 49ers saw only a level expanse, broken by dry watercourses and the Sacramento River, a landscape that would later become a center for corporate agriculture based on irrigation and machinery. As they toiled toward the distant foothills, the level interior valleys gradually rose in elevation, giving way to narrower, mountainous slopes. Primitive tracks across this dry landscape (tracks reduced to dust in the summer and mud in the winter rainy season) guided the 49ers to breathtaking mountain vistas and valley slopes garlanded with flowers that, in spring, drew admiration from even the most prosaic and businesslike of adventurers and left those of a poetic nature grasping for words. One 49er celebrated his arrival in these words:

> The face of the country has changed from a level to a rolling prairie, and to add beauty to the scene, the plains were completely strewn with flowers of various colours, most yellow, blue or purple; some white, and a few red, making the whole a carpet of rare beauty, there being a thick coat of grass and clover for the ground colours, the flowers peeping above in irregular bunches.

And a practical miner of limited education from Maine still took time out to describe his surroundings: "O how butiful it seems in the morning to git up and hear the birds of Spring and to look around on the distant hill and see them covered with flowers it is a site worth seeing there is not a spear of grass without there is a flower on it."[6]

Poetry aside, the land imposed difficulties on those who would exploit it. Sandy bars, where the slowing of the water flow dropped gold in several forms, were among the first important mining sites. The access roads were poor and laid out in random fashion, not by planning, but by usage. Isaac Barker marched toward Big Bar over "the most horrible road I ever saw," and of the landscape that awaited the 49ers he wrote, "Never saw finer scenery and steeper hills." Some of the richest gold-bearing land was virtually inaccessible, lying in valleys surrounded by almost sheer walls. One 49er described the diggings and the countryside around Placerville as "hilly, mountainous & barren of vegetation, except trees.... The hills...are high & steep in many places, & some very deep ravines in which there has been large quantities of gold found. The rivers appear to a person standing on the bank almost sunk out of sight, & in places very difficult to descend and ascend on foot."[7]

From the side of a mountain, the Argonauts, burdened by tools and tents and barrels of provisions, would creep down sheer hillsides to these distant streambeds in the canyons. Joseph Wood's first claims lay at the bottom of such a descent, and he clambered down two thousand feet at a forty-five-degree angle to reach the rushing stream, to a site where the sun never shone—not even in the middle of the day. One 49er wrote this account to his family:

> The gold region, many portions of it, is comprised of *little* hills varying from one to seven miles from bottom to top, and so steep that it is futile for a man to attempt to set on the back of a mule—many of them it is out of the question to take a pack mule—you ascend for hundreds of feet so steep that we must hold to the brush to keep from falling—and if he makes one misstep and loses his hold he goes down down and still he goes down, perhaps he may catch some friendly brush or bring up on a projecting ledge of rocks—if he does not his case is hopeless. Such is the country we are living in and hope to make a fortune.[8]

To move to a different claim, the 49ers had to scale the walls that they had come down with such difficulty. Another 49er wrote that a ladder placed against the side of a hill would fall backwards. Benjamin Baxter wrote of his exit from one mining site: "I shall never forget my feelings when about half way up I could not go back for fear of falling I had to crawl forward on all fours when I got to the top I was completely used up."[9]

After their arrival in large numbers in the summer and fall of 1849, the 49ers began to make significant modifications in this landscape. To improve accessibility (often at a profit to themselves), they leveled roads (in the most rudimentary fashion) and built bridges. They also began to cut timber for dwellings and firewood, and they hunted the game of the forests. Added to these significant but modest changes were the large-scale engineering projects begun late in 1849, which changed the course of rivers and dredged up large tracts of terrain. Euro-American pioneers had changed the eastern landscape for two centuries, and in California, they made remarkable changes within two years, whether by endless digging in watercourses or by the construction of dams and flumes to change the direction and flow of the water.

The endless mining and movement of thousands and tens of thousands of Argonauts that changed large portions of the California landscape with great rapidity brought the miners into immediate conflict with the Native Americans and planted the seeds of future conflict with agriculturists over natural resources.[10] The California landscape soon came to present a striking contrast, with vast open spaces of semi-arid grazing land edged by mountains and great untouched green forests juxtaposed against selected streambeds and watercourses that had been changed beyond recognition. The banks and bars of these watercourses seemed to have been repeatedly excavated by giant moles—"rich places are dug out, every little hollow & ravine is torn up."[11]

IN THE DIGGINGS

Most of the Argonauts of '49 and their subsequent annual reinforcements came to the gold fields knowing little or nothing of mining. The exceptions were a few experienced miners from the North Carolina and Georgia gold fields.[12] Fortunately, in the fall of 1849 at the time of the first mass immigration to the gold fields, the mining techniques then in use were still those of the previous year—washing gravel using the pick, pan, shovel, and the newest technical innovation, the rocker or cradle.

The 49ers learned how to pan for gold by watching and imitating. Occasionally, someone might instruct them, perhaps a relative or friend who had reached the placers earlier, or even a stranger. One Argonaut found a friend who "went with me two miles down the stream to enable me to see the operations of the miners—showed me how to wash the black sand &c was very attentive."[13] He was fortunate. Most future miners had less formal instruction. "We pitched our tents, shouldered our picks & shovels & with pan in hand sallied forth to try our fortunes at gold diggings," wrote one 49er. "We did not have very good success being green at mining, but by practice & observation we soon improved & found a little of the shining metal."[14] The most profitable economic enterprise for individual citizens of the Republic in the nation's history up to that time was almost entirely self-taught, and the rudiments of the exercise could be acquired in ten minutes.

One of the striking features of the Gold Rush was the universally shared nature of the technology of mining. Unlike many other economic enterprises, there was little suggestion that superior techniques produced better results. Almost every miner in the diggings did the same things. Although experienced miners were better at spying out the likeliest sites and organizing the work—one 49er claimed that the "old hands" knew better how to exploit a claim, that is to say, where to begin work and then how to proceed—the tasks of dredging up the dirt and washing it rapidly achieved a universal quality in which the newest greenhorns apparently did as well as the veterans.

In this first stage, which preceded more complex mining techniques, the emphasis was on the common nature of the enterprise. For the most part, men talked endlessly, as they had from the early months of 1849, about claims and locations; they spoke little about their superior technical and mining skills or those of any other group. The Methodist missionary Israel Lord caught this focus in an entry in his journal for spring 1850: "The finding of gold is the common topic of conversation, at all times, on all occasions, under all circumstances, and among all classes and professions, with very few exceptions to any of these items." In short, he concluded, "The great, moving, impelling power here is money."[15]

A dominant feature of mining for gold was that the end product was immediately visible to the eye. Americans who went to California in search of gold always remembered the sight of buffalo on the plains or sailing into San Francisco Bay, depending on the route; the initial encounter with miners in the placers—the noise, the sense of activity, and the single-minded intensity of those at work; and, finally, the first bucket full of dirt and the way the gold sparkled in the bottom of the pan.

The initial reaction to work, and especially to the sight of gold, was excitement. Gold fever flared up again at the sight of gold dust or nuggets, even if it had been cooled by the long journey. The visual image of gold, whether in the bottom of the rocker or in the sacks of veteran miners, fired the determination of the new arrivals. Faced with actual gold, the new arrivals in the gold fields responded with redoubled efforts. "I saw some of the Gold today," wrote William Pease. "It made my eyes sparkle. I shall not be satisfied untill I can get some money and send it home to you."[16] And A. C. Sweetser continued in this vein: "it is the prettiest kind of Labour that I ever had to do, about 10 days since I dug a small hole, about 3 feet deep and 4 feet square, and I was less than two hours digging it. I sat down and picked out with my knife eight lumps...or a little more than one dollar."[17]

Mining in groups had begun in 1848, and by the time of the arrival of large numbers of new immigrants in the diggings in the summer of 1849, the usefulness of group endeavor was universally recognized. "I have learned by experience that a single man cannot make as much as he can if he is with 2 or 3 others," wrote William Brown after a month in the gold fields.[18] The actual numbers varied: as few as three or four friends, neighbors, or relations, bound by a high degree of personal trust, or as many as a dozen or fifteen, united by a wider interest in efficiency. Mining in groups not only matched the labor demands of the cradles, it meant that miners could rotate through various tasks during the day, minimizing the drudgery of work in cold, rushing water and the boredom of repetitive work. As we have seen, living and working together in a small group, with common housing and meals, also offered an indispensable element of support to the lone 49er in a remote and impersonal world.

Among the few variations tried or considered was the use of others to work a claim. Some of the most successful entrepreneurs of 1848 had hired groups of Native Americans, and beginning in 1849, Southerners who reached the mines sometimes used slave labor, as we already have seen. Editorials and statements by public officials in the South confirmed Southerners in the belief that they should be entitled by law to take slave property into any portion of the empire seized in the war against Mexico, and the nature of mining in California, with its repetitive digging, carrying, and washing, seemed to encourage the use of slave labor. John Milner from Alabama quickly saw mining as work suitable for slave labor, and he wrote to his father, "with twenty good negroes & the power of managing them as at home I could make from ten to fifteen thousand dollars pr month, but a fellow has to knock it out here with his own fist or not at all."[19] Yet custom worked against the use of slave labor—perhaps because of a preponderance of 49ers from the North, or perhaps because few Southerners were willing to risk bringing large numbers of slaves to California. Milner himself brought three slaves to the gold fields.

As a first step, the new mining company had to establish rights to a claim. Because mining for the three years after the summer of 1848 was generally associated with streambeds, claims were rights to places on the banks of a watercourse. They had a specific frontage on the stream or river and would extend back to a specified depth. In the first year of mining, relatively small numbers of miners had scattered out over the vast landscape of interior California—the best guess is about five thousand miners in the placers by the end of 1848. These miners originally cared little about ownership of specific sites in what seemed like a wide-open landscape. They generally mined where they chose and moved on when instinct or rumor told them to go elsewhere. By the spring of 1849, however, the numbers in the gold fields had expanded considerably; by autumn, they grew exponentially, to some forty thousand by the end of the year, and by the autumn of the following year, to fifty thousand.[20]

As we have seen, the idea of a claim already had been established by the time of the arrival of the great migration of 1849 as a result of conflicts over what were viewed as especially desirable sites on a few watercourses. When Peter Burnett and his partners arrived at Long's Bar on the Yuba River from Oregon in November 1848 and bought the rights to a place to work, they paid three hundred dollars in gold dust for about a thousand square feet, including twenty feet of river frontage.[21] By the autumn of 1849, the pressure of numbers had expanded the range of claims up and down all the streams of the northern and southern mines over some one hundred miles, and the same force of numbers had reduced the size of claims. By the middle of the 1850 season, some claims were only fifteen square feet per man. Of course, a company of four would pool their allotments. Some claims were more expansive. Israel Lord's company of seven purchased a claim—for which it paid one thousand dollars—that extended upriver twenty-five rods and downriver sixteen rods, covering approximately six hundred and sixty feet of river frontage.[22]

The procedures in laying off a claim, working the claim, and retaining possession were well nigh universal across the Mother Lode after 1849 and rested on wide acceptance, not law. An individual or company laid off or purchased rights to a claim (presumably of the size allowed by the local rules), registered the claim with a local recorder, and then kept their rights by the customary method of leaving tools in the spot and working the claim on a regular basis. "Prospected around, found a claim, Drop'd our pick in it, and then came back to our camp," wrote one 49er. The next day, "cleared claim down 6' in AM. Washed dirt in PM." As late as the season of 1850, William Parker's company laid off a claim in Cold Spring and "left our tools there to keep our claim alive."[23] The presence of a pick or shovel retained rights while the owner went to the nearby camps for supplies and mail or had to be absent for other reasons, presumably for brief periods, but under the regulations generally accepted in most camps, claims had to be worked on a regular basis to maintain the right of ownership. Just as rights to claims could be established in systematic fashion, so they could also be leased or sold.

As the numbers of miners increased in late 1849 and throughout the 1850 season, claims—especially on the most attractive watercourses—increased in value. New mining companies found it necessary to buy claims before beginning work. As the cost of claims rose, so did the original investment required of the 49ers, and often the size of their debts. By the summer of 1850, one 49er noted that those intending to mine must buy someone else's claim "and pay all it is worth." Alexander Barrington's company paid four hundred and fifty dollars for a sixty-foot claim on the Little Deer. Claims might be sold under a contingent scheme: if the buyers took out, say, two hundred dollars, they paid one hundred to the owner, if they realized five hundred dollars, then they paid two hundred, and so forth. Claims sold on credit generally brought a higher figure than those sold for cash. Sometimes sellers took equipment or supplies in exchange. Occasionally, the purchasers also bought the cabin, lean-to, or living quarters of the sellers. Like other such transactions in the gold fields, credit arrangements were sometimes difficult to collect on—as they were for merchants and tradesmen.[24]

As competition for claims became more severe and the stakes higher, so-called claim jumping became more common. Men faced off against one another in a show of force to defend their interests. Lafayette Fish wrote in June of 1850 that on the Feather River, "it is difficult to get claims and there is considerable dispute in consequence." The mining associations organized in each unit of the watercourses worked to solve such confrontations peacefully. Conflicting claims went to local tribunals for adjudication. Richard Cowley, who had an altercation over a claim, had recourse to influential friends to protect his interests. "I had a little difficulty in securing this claim, but being acquainted with the Alcade or Justice of the Peace and having a few friends I had the preference," he observed. "I marked off my claim put up my stakes & put my name on a board in the center of my claim."[25]

Most of the 49ers, who brought with them the broad range of other occupations common in midcentury America, from farmer to clerk to artisan, thus soon mastered the trade of finding, opening, and working a claim, with its routine of digging, carrying, and washing. For all the work was hard, and for many, initially profitable. For others, however, the avenue to wealth in California lay elsewhere.

THE VARIETIES OF ECONOMIC ENTERPRISE

Although the common denominator in California over the first decade of the Gold Rush was the abiding interest in mining for gold, both for the miners and for their families and communities in the East, this was only the first of a long chain of economic activities that came to encompass a wide range of occupations. The repetitive nature of mining meant that the miners in the placers needed the same limited number of goods and services: tools, food, clothes, and boots, transportation and packing to move their baggage to the mines, and so forth. But as the 49ers made money, they extended their demands into a broad assortment of services, creating new and profitable occupations ranging from personalized mail services to cooked meals and an expanding entertainment industry that ran from prostitution and selling liquor to gambling, billiards, and ten-pin bowling. Henry Kent arrived in California in late 1852, and based on a year's observation, he decided that the best way to maximize advantage in the Gold Rush was to mine long enough to make a stake, and then move into some other occupation. "I find that all shrew calculating men, if they can git one or two thousand dollars either go home, or git into other business besides mining either trade or farming."[26] The accounts show that numerous Argonauts followed his advice.

The first professionals to arrive in California often found wonderful opportunities. In the booming economy of California, which was practically growing overnight in size and wealth, doctors, dentists, and especially lawyers prospered. The money generated in the gold fields inflated the value of real estate and immediately produced the litigation that accompanied wealth. William Daingerfield wrote his parents from Sacramento that the real wealth in California lay in the law. He made thirty-three hundred dollars in his first ten days of practice, and he continued, "There is nothing more certain than if we have health we will make a fortune in a few years. You have no idea of the extent of litigation in this city or the size of fees." And another young lawyer who came with the first wave of 49ers wrote from San Francisco that he charged one hundred dollars for a consultation and fifteen hundred for pleading a case.[27]

From its initial appearance on the national scene onward, the Gold Rush also offered an unparalleled opportunity for speculation in goods and commodities of various kinds. Many of those who went to California by sea chose that route in order to transport goods to the gold fields or to the market where they would reach miners. These articles ranged from lumber and house frames to meet the rising demand for shelters in San Francisco and other California towns farther inland to purses and mining oddities such as goldometers. Entrepreneurs of all kinds hurried to join the boom. William Prince from Long Island was one of the most energetic. He took some suits from New York and bought others in Havana to sell in San Francisco. As soon as he had canvassed the markets on arriving, he sold the suits and sent an order to his wife for magnets, gold scales, and extra sets of weights, to be forwarded "by fast steamer."

Prince noted that the hardships and scarcities of the first winter of 1849–50 returned profits of more than 50 percent on his goods. When a major fire devastated a large portion of Stockton, his inventories, spared through good luck, rose substantially in value, a development that he noted with a modest celebration.[28] Other Argonauts went west in order to sell a single item suited to the demands of the Gold Rush. Offered a one-half interest by the inventor, Rufus Brown went to the gold fields in 1852 to make a fortune on a new "Elector-Magnetic Separator" machine that rapidly separated gold dust from sand. The machine did not attract much interest, and Brown found himself far from home and increasingly discouraged with his prospects.[29]

Other 49ers took to California small quantities of goods they intended to sell quickly at a high profit. William Elder's stock of pants sold well, but his cigars, waterlogged by a dip in the Chagres River in Panama, did poorly.[30] Added to those with goods of various kinds were 49ers with capital, perhaps the most attractive of all commodities. Money in California could be lent or invested to return as high as 60 percent a month in late 1849. Risks lay on every hand, of course, and accounted for the high rate of interest, but the opportunity to double money every two months was a compelling one.[31]

Edward Abbe of Boston was a good example of the large-scale speculator who went to California in search of opportunities for investment and profit. Abbe was a member of the original New England Company that departed Boston on the *Edward Everett* and arrived in San Francisco in June 1849. He immediately set out for the gold fields but stopped in Sacramento to exploit the opportunities for profit with his medical training and to trade with the mines. By fall 1849, he was waiting for the arrival of barrelled pork and speculating on the price. Even as he laid plans to profit from those wintering in the Sierra, he inquired into prospects of trade with the Sandwich Islands, where he proposed to buy quantities of potatoes, onions, yams, poultry, pigs, oranges, and other citrus products for shipment to San Francisco. For this enterprise, his father would furnish much of the capital. In the interim, he occupied himself with speculating in commodities in Sacramento. He noted in his diary that the "hard winds" on the river prevented travel, "and consequently there is nothing in the market to speculate upon."[32]

Many speculators worked on a smaller scale, mixing occasional mining with trade opportunities. Among these was John Fitch, who left New York City for the gold fields in February 1849. While he mined successfully—he was one of the rare 49ers who made good on his promise to remit funds to his family on a regular basis—Fitch also sold purses sent to him by his brother. At seventy-five cents each, the purses sold well, according to Fitch, and fully paid the costs of shipping them. Many 49ers had relatives in the East who attempted to launch speculative schemes designed to merchandise some scarce items to captive consumers at high prices. In the economic climate of California as described in the eastern newspapers, it was inconceivable that any item shipped to California could lose money. The 49ers in the camps knew better; they were hesitant to assume responsibility for a relative's speculative fantasy. Still, relatives had a claim, and the claim might be especially strong if they had advanced funds for the voyage to the gold fields. John Fitch was under obligation to his brother for managing financial affairs for his wife, Theodosia, and perhaps he found it difficult to refuse to serve as retailer for his brother's purses in the gold camp of Rocky Chucky. For whatever reason, Fitch continued to oblige his brother, albeit with a notable lack of enthusiasm.[33]

The flood of arrivals generated a demand for a wide range of services, beginning with the basics: transportation and food. Because 49ers were constantly on the move, the demand for horses and mules rose in like proportion, and several 49ers went into the business of supplying them. One Argonaut owned a ranch where he dealt in "horses mules Cattle wagons and harness." Another family bought a half interest in the Shasta Corral and Hay Yard, where they rented mules and horses for eight dollars a day, including saddle. William Dresser failed at raising cabbages and broke even on sales of wild strawberries in San Francisco, but he pronounced the hay business a continually profitable one. Every wagon that departed for the mines, he wrote, took one or more bales. As more and more people and animals moved across the California landscape, travelers had to carry feed for the animals.[34] The demand for transportation that began with hay, horses, and buggies eventually extended to stagecoaches, and there were 49ers eager to supply them all. The need to offer lodging and meals to those on the way to the gold fields and in the camps led many into the business of supplying produce and daily products for the table, and a cadre of 49ers supported themselves as professional hunters who provided meat for the restaurants in the cities of the Gold Rush.

Their first encounter with the suppliers of such services came as they laid plans to move to the gold fields in the Sierra. The distances involved ranged from fifty to one hundred miles, and the baggage to be transported included supplies and equipment for an extended period. Since they had transported a good part of it across the plains or around the horn or through Panama, they were not inclined to leave it in San Francisco. The business of carrying miners' baggage and supplies into the diggings—from San Francisco or Sacramento/Stockton for those who took water transportation inland—expanded with the arrival of overland immigrants, beginning in the spring of 1849 and reaching a high point in the fall, with subsequent annual immigrations subject to the same cycles. Numerous observers testified that the business of transporting 49ers, equipment, and supplies to the mining camps could be enormously profitable, and a team of horses could pay for itself very quickly.[35]

Economic ventures appeared literally overnight in response to demand. Thousands of the 49ers who landed in San Francisco took passage up the river to Sacramento, and their presence quickly created a large fleet of vessels that made the journey. Upon his arrival in Sacramento, one 49er purchased a sailing vessel and observed, "My business will be carrying freight & passengers, and buying and selling produce." Another Argonaut purchased a boat, loaded it with "chili flour, mess pork," and sugar and started up the Sacramento River toward the distant camps to look "for a market."[36] In the first few seasons of the Gold Rush, such economic ventures were highly informal. Men simply launched boats or loaded up pack animals and headed toward the mines. They expected to find a market for their commodities, either wholesale or retail.

Some ventured into distant mining country, with its greater risks and profits. One Argonaut went into partnership with two others to open a trading venture in the distant Trinity mines in the mountains near the Oregon border. Each partner invested five hundred dollars for a wagon and four mules. Their wagons would march two hundred miles north, up the valley, where the partners would transfer the goods to mules for the last twenty miles across the coastal range. One of the three would run the tavern they planned, he continued. "The store will be attended by myself—one will be constantly employed in hauling our goods from the city." To work their mining claims, the partners hired recent arrivals from the states, "as labor can be had much cheaper than heretofore as there is to many coming from the States this season." He was convinced that trade was much more profitable than mining, and if their venture went well, they would never have to dig again themselves. He completed his array of new arrangements by purchasing an interest in a ferry on the Trinity River. His services now included transportation, supplies, and meals.[37]

Such economic opportunities lay everywhere, and they attracted innumerable 49ers who saw the chance for profit in selling rather than digging. The business of selling supplies to miners began on the streets of San Francisco and Sacramento and extended into the most remote gold camps, and as distances increased, inventories diminished and prices rose. San Francisco itself was a catalogue of economic enterprises, all directed to serving the miners and their needs, its streets from the docks to the outskirts of town strewn with the cargoes of late-arriving vessels. Added to the merchants and vendors of San Francisco and its booming entertainment industry were the small-scale entrepreneurs who poured off the arriving ships in the harbor. Many Argonauts who mined, noting the high prices they paid for the most necessary supplies, saw the transition from digging and washing to selling something as providing both relief for their bodies and opportunities for larger profits.

Closer to the gold camps lay numerous opportunities for those who would provide services, especially in the areas of housing and food. Miners on the move demanded lodging and meals, and those who camped out and prepared their own food had to purchase supplies. After two years in the diggings, Richard Cowley and his two partners sold their mining claims, and in the spring of 1851, he wrote, "We have opened our Store, got a very assortment, sell cheap, and do well, as well as we can expect." Over several months, they did a continuous business, or as he put it, "mining dull Trade brisk." Whatever their returns from their claims, miners had to eat the same amount every day. What Cowley and others gradually came to understand was that eventually, when mining declined, commercial enterprises could remain afloat only so long before they, too, began to slide.[38]

Among other miners who made the transition, John Crawford built what he called "a *public House*" on the road between Georgetown and Big Bar. The building was 36 feet by 18 feet, with a dining room extending the entire length in the back. Cloth covered the front of the structure. "There is now and will be during the summer and fall an immense site of travel by this place," he wrote, "and I am almost certain of doing well." Another success-ful miner, Isaac Perkins, invested his profits from the diggings in lumber and a share in a toll bridge. He also made plans to build a mill.[39]

The small stores on the roads to the mines and within the mining camps themselves offered a variety of goods and services. They also served as restau-rants and saloons, providing the hungry, thirsty, sleepy traveler with all the services that he might require, including care and fodder for his horse—all at a price. One 49er wrote with some envy of a small store in the mining country whose main regular business was serving meals. The owner had "from 12 to 20 boarders at $16 per week and the provisions do not cost more than $5, this is connected with the store; the man that kept it before made $7,000 since last spring."[40]

Stores in the mining country were makeshift affairs. Like much of the housing in the mines, they usually were constructed of canvas. Seldon Goff described his "Store" as "made of canvas 22 X 32 and one story high." He went on: "We keep all kinds of Liquors and Groceries provisions & Sell Goods real estate &c at Auction this latter trade I am sorry to inform you is generally done by Sunday in this country." Stores that also were eateries made excellent family enterprises, and Goff wrote to his wife, "If I had you here to assist me I should open an Eating house or something of that sort I could make money I find what few are here with their families do first rate." And Solomon Gorgas offered this picture "from behind what I call my own counter in this place, where you may imagine me, most of the time, busily engaged waiting on my customers, whom I serve with pies & cakes & beer & brandy & everything that is good to eat & to drink—all prepared by our own hands with the assistance of a cook, & all nice and clean of course."[41]

On a larger scale were what their owners described as "hotels." In the first couple of years of the Gold Rush, these could be enormously profitable. John Milner wrote his father that "we have a hotel that cant clear less than 100 dollars pr day." Milner later moved to San Jose—"the finest & most civilized town in California"—where he bought a house and divided it into ten sleeping rooms, which he rented for one hundred and fifty dollars a month each. The extended Milner family had prospered in California. John and Uncle Ben departed for home in late 1849 with some fifteen thousand dollars. Even allowing for exaggeration, few miners had done as well.[42]

Lafayette Fish provided goods and services on a smaller scale. After a year mining on the Feather River and its tributaries, he opened a store at the mouth of Nelson's Creek. On weekdays, he sold about fifty dollars' worth of goods a day; on Sunday, more than five hundred dollars. He also cooked meals and found "plenty of eating customers." He was especially proud of his fresh-baked biscuits, which he served with fresh pork, and he baked pies and cookies, all of which found a ravenous market. He also tailored on the side. In December, he closed the store and returned to the mines, leaving the food service in the hands of an African-American, whom he hired to cook over the winter. By February 1851, he was himself cooking again, serving an average of ten each meal, two or three times daily. At the usual charge of one dollar a meal, the profit reached the standard marker of an ounce of gold a day. With experience in both camps, Fish could testify that the work in the kitchen was easier than digging in the streambeds.[43]

Most of the so-called stores found in the mining country offered a variety of services and products, including overnight accommodation. In a world in which men worked hard and begrudged time spent attending to routine but necessary matters, the convenience of one store with many services was clear. John Eagle wrote of these businesses to his wife, "The majority of stores in this country are boarding houses, drinking houses, gambling houses &c all under one, so you can form some idea of how matters are done here. All stores have regular bars in them."[44]

The intense physical demands of mining, played out from sunrise to sunset in the most isolated locations, created a demand for less orthodox services than those connected with shelter, transportation, and food. William Brown, a younger son in a prominent Toledo family who arrived in the mines in the fall of 1849, mined with only modest success for four months and then sought a "situation" (as he told his parents) at between one hundred and fifty and two hundred dollars a month. He considered the entertainment business, reporting that running a "public house" with five or six dance-hall girls was an excellent business opportunity. The entertainment business was of course one of the largest and, by all accounts, most profitable in California. Like other enterprises, in the diggings it became less elaborate than in the cities but presumably was no less profitable. San Francisco's entertainment business was continuous, and new arrivals were sent to the diggings with the cry, "Don't forget us, Mr. Barrington, when you come down from the mines."[45]

Before the end of the year, however, Brown had gone into the "express business," instead. He picked up letters in the San Francisco post office and delivered them to his list of subscribing miners in the small camps at a dollar per letter. Most of his business was on the weekend, when he carried between five and six hundred letters to the camps, finding places to deposit about four hundred of these. While in the camps, he took orders for goods on commission, and by 1851, he had begun to buy about five hundred dollars' worth of gold dust from the miners each week. His profit on the price of gold dust in the mines and in San Francisco was about 7 percent. He also took four hundred newspapers to the camps, which he sold for a dollar each. Brown originally worried that his parents, especially his mother, would find the express business beneath his talents, although they probably would not have been pleased if he had chosen to run a "public house," either, and he expressed relief at receiving his father's blessing. By the opening of 1853, he could write home of his rising reputation as a businessman, and his friends referred to him as "a monied man." He wrote that with an investment of five thousand dollars he might go into banking.

Brown had found a perfect niche in the labor-intense economy of the gold fields; he filled the needs of miners who could pay well for his deliveries. When the streams began to give out, the river dams failed, or the autumn rains came early, Brown's business suffered. Along with the decline in the conditions in small camps came an expansion of some of the services he offered, especially mail delivery. Within two years, the conditions that gave him his opportunity had changed. Yet his enterprising approach to the Gold Rush exemplifies the varieties of economic activity open to entrepreneurs, and even to a single enterprising individual, in the gold fields after 1849.[46]

9

"THE REAL ARGONAUTS OF '49":
Life and Leisure in the Gold Fields

*What an innocent, unsophisticated, inexperienced lot were those forty
odd young Argonauts who sat in these pews. Not one of them then could
bake his own bread, turn a flap jack, re-seat his trousers, or wash his shirt.
Not one of them had dug even a post-hole.*

PRENTICE MULFORD

PRENTICE MULFORD'S OBSERVATIONS are a reminder that the newly arrived 49ers—fresh from a triumphant journey and filled with anticipation—
now confronted a wide range of work of the most onerous and unexpected
kind. At the height of the first full season of 1849, E. Gould Buffum toured the
gold region. Having been in the placers as early as October 1848, he could give
a degree of perspective on the expansion and intensity of mining. The common characteristics that he remarked upon for the entire region were growth
in numbers and area, especially the camps that had turned into towns, and the
intensity of the work. "The labour of gold-digging is unparalleled by any
other in the world in severity," he wrote. "It combines, within itself, the various arts of canal-digging, ditching, laying stone-walls, ploughing, and hoeing
potatoes."[1] Most readers at midcentury would have recognized a listing of the
hard and dreary physical labor assigned individually to hired men on the farm
and collectively to new immigrant groups. The Irish especially were already
known as a work force that dug the canals, and German immigrants had done
their share of ploughing, ditching, and walling. The 49ers undertook similar
labor for what they assumed would be substantially greater rewards. What is
more, they did so under living conditions that were new to most of them.

To gain access to the gold-bearing streams, the 49ers penetrated into the foothills, canyons, and ravines, and in some cases, into the mountains. These remote locations—ranging from dry and barren in the southern mines to steep, timber-covered hillsides in the northern mines—forced the Argonauts to take up residence (if that is the term) in remote and sometimes difficult locations.

The first living arrangements were simple campsites—a familiar way of doing things for the 49ers who had come overland over the summer of 1849 and would continue to do so in subsequent annual migrations. The seagoing Argonauts packed tents or purchased them in the cities, towns, or numerous general merchandise stores that, as we've seen, quickly sprang up enroute to the diggings. The 49ers established a camp in the closest proximity to their claims to work and protect them most advantageously. A campsite for five to eight men who mined together might be set up in a matter of hours and taken down in even less time. Such a consideration was important for a people constantly on the move. Finally, living in a campsite was inexpensive, and it offered the cheapest way to live while mining.[2]

THE ROUTINE

Work began on the streams at daylight, and miners rose in the dark to dress and prepare themselves. The designated cook prepared what passed for breakfast. Standing outside the tents or seated inside on logs or homemade chairs, the miners would eat and smoke, silently preparing themselves for another day of hard labor and high expectations. Within the canyons and ravines of the watercourses, the sun appeared late. As the sky began to lighten, the miners put away their tin cups and tin plates, and with their picks and shovels, pans and buckets, advanced on the holes or dams that would provide their daily work. The walk might be brief and direct, down to a nearby watercourse, or long and difficult, to a distant spot at the bottom of a steep canyon.

Once arrived at the claim, the 49ers began a routine of digging, shoveling, carrying, and washing that continued unabated and with little variation throughout the day until sunset. In 1849, most companies operated one or more "cradles." In a pattern that stretched from one end of the Mother Lode to the other, one man loosened the "dirt," whether by digging or shoveling; a second carried it to the site of the machine, generally a cradle; there, a third washed the materials. Men rotated the jobs to equalize the work. Fourth or fifth members of the mess might dig or carry. When mining groups reached six or so, they would operate two cradles.

By the following season of 1850, the "long tom" had become the preferred machine. Although it functioned very much like the cradle, it was larger, some eight to nine feet long, eighteen inches wide, and some six inches high. The box had an iron sieve at one end, with holes one-half inch in diameter, with water brought to it through a hose. "The dirt, stone, clay & all is then thrown in and stirred with a shovel until the water runs clear," ran one account. "The gold & fine gravel goes through the sieve and falls in under the box and lodges in the ripples." With it, "three men can wash all day without taking this out as the water washed the loose gravel over and the gold settles to the bottom. One man will wash as fast as two or three can pick & shovel it in, or as fast as three rockers or cradles."[3]

Such machines aside, whatever the greater technical efficiencies in the retrieval of gold, the basic unit of work in the gold mines was the human body. Everywhere across the Mother Lode, in these first years of mining, the dirt had to be loosened and carried to the machine, and the miners performed this labor over and over again, often under unpleasant conditions. Several members of the company (or everyone) might work up to their knees and sometimes higher in swift, ice-cold, moving water. In spite of their determination to present a stoic face to the members of their company and their families, 49ers often complained in diaries and letters about the cold and wet. F. T. Sherman wrote to his parents, "You will have to work in water & mud Morning until night it is no boys play."[4]

Contrasting with the icy waters of the snowmelt watercourses was the heat of the California summer. The summer months were crucial for mining because the dry season meant a drop in the water level and, accordingly, exposed bars and riffles that could be dug. So hot were the days that even in the context of the hectic pace of the miners, the company often rested during the heat of the day. For many mining companies, summer hours were from 6:00 to 11:00 in the morning and again from 3:00 to sunset. Or the miners might be idle from 11:00 in the morning to 5:00 in the evening. Of course, with more daylight hours, the workday was still a long one. Mining was so repetitive in its routines that 49ers sometimes lost track of the days. William Parker once remarked that "we have lost our reckoning of time & no one in our little colony of 4 can set us right but it is somewhere in the early part of November."[5] One 49er observed of the routine, "They say all days are like here."[6]

The work was exhausting. One 49er summarized the labors of mining in these terms: "Digging for gold is the hardest work a man can get at—I have dug holes 20 feet deep and about 6 feet square—and I have seen holes dug 100 feet deep." And William Rothwell reflected on the physical challenges,

"Mining is the hardest work imaginable and an occupation which very much endangers health." He concluded, "A weakly man might about as well go to digging his grave as to dig gold." Even the strongest of the 49ers felt the strain; their less vigorous companions had to leave the diggings for less stressful occupations.[7]

The 49ers often were asked whether conditions in California favored immigration. That California was a place to make money, all agreed; they were also virtually unanimous that such economic advantage would be bought at a high price. John Eagle offered this summary of the range of physical challenges that awaited the future Argonauts on a daily basis:

> A person thinking of coming to California ought to consider whether he can stand to work all day, under a hot sun, up to the knees in water and mud, shoveling or pumping as the case may be; cook his breakfast, and be at work a little after sun rise; then cook his dinner at noon, and his supper at night, chop wood, bake bread, wash and mend clothes, &c. If he is content to do all these things and run the risks of the journey, then he can come to California. If not, he is better at home.[8]

Added to the severity and the continuing nature of the enterprise was the sense that the wholehearted participation of each man was necessary to the maximum accomplishments of the group. The working and living unit of the company required mutual commitment. The parts of the mining operation were interchangeable insofar as duties were concerned, but each member had to do his duty throughout each day. The failure of one member of the company reduced its efficiency and shifted additional work to the others. Allegiance was strong; expectation was part of the allegiance. The presence of a partner who did not do the expected work—whether from lack of will or lack of strength made no difference—was a constant source of irritation in a mutually reinforcing group based on equality. C. C. Mobley wrote of his company, "I am glad to see them work so willingly. It makes it much more pleasant for all. Then there are no hard feelings but when a portion of them lag back and don't do their duty, as is sometimes the case, it produces hard feelings on the part of others.—Nor is that all, it causes the others to have to labour harder than if all done their duty." Mobley later noted that one member of his company was "Lazy," and he wrote of several loud evening arguments about work responsibilities.[9]

Although a mining company of four to eight was common, the working unit was sometimes a family. William Parker encountered a family of four from Oregon—a husband, wife, and two teenaged daughters—mining in the fall of 1850. All mined, he wrote, including the girls, aged sixteen and fourteen, whom he described as "naturally smart & industrious, but entire uncultivated. Their language is as rough & boisterous as that of other mountaineers." Single miners were also found in numbers. John Fletcher could not find a suitable partner, so he hired himself out to other miners.[10]

During the long workday, a combination of restless energy, hope, self-interest, and group loyalty sustained the labor at a high level. Men drove themselves forward in their routine tasks by the visions of future wealth, encouraged by present small returns and pressed by the need to dig and wash something every day on a continuing basis. Over the first two years of the Gold Rush, the returns of a claim could be calculated by a mathematical formula. A bucket of dirt on an "average" claim in 1849 would produce gold worth about ten cents. Miners needed to wash an average of one hundred and sixty or so buckets of dirt a day each—or eight hundred buckets for five men—in order to generate the anticipated one ounce (or sixteen dollars) for each working man.[11]

An hour before sunset, with the returns quickly calculated from another day of hard labor, the miners trudged back to their tent. The cook must now prepare dinner for all (although he might have been dismissed an hour or so before quitting time in order to begin the meal). Exhausted though they might be by their labors, the Argonauts now entered into that period of time when they might do what they wished, consistent with the light left and their duties within the company itself. A few men would build a fire, and with the companionable heat and light, they would relax in anticipation of an evening meal, relishing the twist of the schedule that had made someone else responsible on this occasion, although their turns had come before and would come again. John Hovey wrote in his diary that a full day of washing had netted ten dollars a man: "Went to camp—eat our supper, and turned in, and thought to ourselves this is a confound hard way to make a fortune."[12]

The intangible compensations—if such existed—lay in the sense of male camaraderie over the evening meal and around the fire as the shadows lengthened. Then, with the day's work behind them and the next one not yet in sight, men relaxed, smoked, and talked. In this male company, the most common topics of conversation were courtships and stories of happy youthful adventures and pranks. Robert Butterfield wrote to his brother this account of how he and his three "chums" relaxed after a long day:

> Thus we lived contently and happy. We worked as usual hard all day and sit around the fire-place with our boots off at night telling stories about what we heard and see, reading papers, re-reading old letters, reading

books of whatever kind comes our way. Around the cheerful blaze too as we sit drying our feet at night we enjoy the wholesome pipe—occasionally indulging in a cigar.

Lengthening silences and increased fatigue soon led to bed. The next day's work would be upon them soon enough.[13]

Even the most cynical miner spoke with affection and later nostalgia of the period after the evening meal. As the landscape darkened and the continuing background noise of rushing water, which called them to labor and provided the source and discomfort of their work, now also lulled them to sleep, the Argonauts collapsed in various postures, measuring the contentment of the passing moments of leisure and unity against the need to be early to bed and well rested for another increment of work the following day. Richard Cowley wrote in his diary after a typical work day: "We miners indulge in smoking sometimes, and after having a good Smoke by our large fire place, and talking of our relocation and friends at home. finally I retired to the night thinking of my friends at home also Thinking I might be soon on my way home."[14]

Still, this was a world in which most men in most occupations did hard physical labor of various kinds. The miners' work of digging, carrying, and washing was probably no greater than for many other menial tasks that were less well paid. Robert Sweetser put the level of work in perspective in a letter to his wife.

> Hundreds come here with the expectation of picking up the gold without any trouble, but they have to *pick it in reality with spade and pick axe* and that kind of Picking does not suit their fancy they complain of the hardness of the work, it is no harder than any other kind of labour a person can fatigue himself by picking up pins as well as by gold diggings, it is not half so hard work as pitching or mowing hay, but admitting that the work is hard, there is an excitement about it which counteracts the hardness of it.[15]

In the uncertain world of the mines, where a rich "raise" and a worked-out claim were equally close at hand, and where the mining season was limited, some miners preferred to work on Sunday, although they often had difficulty in explaining this blasphemy to their families. Many miners worked with a single-minded determination that turned them into working machines, a pattern broken only by illness, injury, death, or return. Initially, they worked with the intensity of men who believed firmly, perhaps even devoutly, that hard work would be rewarded by success, and they worked in the knowledge confirmed by experience that the random nature of returns from the Gold Rush rewarded those constantly in motion turning over new claims and tunneling in new bars.

DOMESTIC CHORES

John Eagle's description of the domestic arrangements within a small company of miners who lived and worked together did not perhaps reassure the people back home that life in the gold fields proceeded with the same tidiness of domestic economy that they were accustomed to in the East. Eagle wrote:

> You would think it was Bachelor's Hall, were you to have seen us this morning, a table covered with dirty dishes, a rock by the side of it with dirty knives, spoons &c, on another a sack of onions, on another, a frying-pan, with a little meat that had been left from breakfast, a barrel of potatoes, coffee-pot camp kettle &c; lying under a Chapperel bush . . . in the rear of our tent is a cooking stove, which we use for a wash stand; we have a shelf nailed against the old tree, containing our eatables generally, with here and there, scattered around our premises, books, pants, shirts, and old clothes generally.[16]

When Charles Bush's mother wrote to inquire about his domestic arrangements, this 49er responded from a camp on the Middle Fork of the Feather River with a detailed, though less graphic, accounting of life in mining camps. His summary described the basic necessities and even a few comforts.

> Mother wants to know what we eat, drink and wear, and who does our washing. First we eat bread, meat, rice, molassis, our drink is water, tea, coffee, and some times a snort of Brandy. We wear cloaths here the same as we did in the States, such as pantaloons, but no peticotes. We do our washing; we wash our own cloths and our own faces and when we dont choos to we go with dirty cloths and dirty faces too. Last winter we got a woman to wash our cloths but now there is not a woman within 19 miles of us.[17]

Bush's account suggested both plain living and an uncertainty on the part of his parents about his world. It seemed to confirm the remoteness of California in the minds of Americans at midcentury—even after the emigration of tens of thousands of Argonauts to dig in its streams.

The question of food and meals engaged the 49ers from the beginning of their expeditions, whether overland or by sea. In the mines themselves, this question had two aspects. The first involved the duties of cook, which required men to attempt to master the practical arts of meal preparation and practice a degree of sanitation in their personal habits; the second involved the range of food and the dishes available.

The task of cooking, serving, and cleaning up was customarily rotated on a weekly basis among all members of a company. That some individuals had more skill than others might vary the assignment of chores, or it might not. A particular skill at baking bread or making a stew did not make a 49er liable to more than his share of work in the kitchen, any more than a clear lack of talent in these areas excused another. Some men obviously liked the duties of cook; others were indifferent or hostile. All served. Most living units were reluctant to accept incompetence or failure as a reason for avoiding the cooking duty. One effect of the system was to produce standardized meals that varied only marginally from one end of the Mother Lode to the other.

Meal preparation and consumption were significant social occasions. The most important moment of the day, aside from counting the gold dust at the end of the work session, was the evening meal. Miners had large appetites as befitted their daily labors. They spent much time in the twilight discussing the prospects for the evening meals and teasing the cook of record. Even though bad cooks were not excused from cooking, cooking skills were valued; poor cooks were criticized and sometimes harassed. The group expected that each individual would put forth a full effort in all work, including cooking and housekeeping, as well as in the collective effort of the day's work on the stream. Those who shirked their duties or who gave the impression of giving less than their all could expect to hear in detail about their derelictions. At the same time, the failures of a cook also could provoke good-natured teasing, provided they represented a full-faith effort and the disaster left something substantial for the evening meal.

The cycle of meals began with breakfast. The cook was the first riser. By the time his messmates returned from washing (if they did so), he had prepared coffee. With the steaming cups, he also distributed bread, which he had baked. The main course was often the heated remains of last night's main course, whether a stew, meat pie, or just a slab of meat. One miner noted he "fried some fritters for breakfast." The miners were headed for a heavy morning's work, and most of them ate a big breakfast. From all accounts, the 49ers did not do much talking at breakfast. Men ate and drank silhouetted against the dawn sky and candles, which were constant companions at breakfast and the evening meal.[18] With the meal ended, the miners trooped to the claim. Sometimes the cook stayed behind to clean up and perhaps bake; more often, he simply shouldered his tools and marched with his companions.

Miners learned how to bake. It was one of the universal skills associated with the mining camps. Bread was the staple of every meal. It could be fashioned from flour that was bought by the barrel. It was often baked on a weekly basis, although sometimes miners baked at night after the day's work. Isaac Barker captured the two strands of work in his notation: "Carried dirt all day on a bad road, was tired. Made some bread after dark and baked it, the first I ever made—succeeded quite well." Most miners remembered their first loaf of bread as vividly as the first sight of buffalo on the plains and of gold flakes at the bottom of their pans. Variations in meals— the result of local food suppliers—might include game, fish, or sometimes fresh vegetables. The basic diet seems to have been the same everywhere: meat (fresh or preserved), bread or biscuits, and coffee or tea with plenty of sugar.[19]

With each succeeding season, miners had more options in their meals. What started out in the fall of 1849 as bread and meat prepared from barrels of flour and pork (with occasional supplements of venison) expanded to include varieties of meats and even fresh vegetables by 1850 and 1851. Many miners hunted—for sport and to put fresh meat on the menu. Jacob Engle wrote that he and his companions had killed twenty deer in the winter of 1849–50 to supplement their diet. Richard Cowley described the diverse diet in the fall of 1851 in these terms: "At the present time we live as well as miners can live, Bread, Butter, Ham, Potatoes, Pickles of all kinds. Sardines. Coffee Fresh meat twice a week and preserves of all kinds. In fact we get all Miners can get. I live as well as men possibly can live occasionally we get a fresh Salmon."[20] When James Clarke toured the mines in the spring of 1852, he traveled everywhere by stagecoach over bumpy and rutted roads that connected the remote camps and towns he found execrable. His compensation was the meals, which he praised in high terms. The menus included beefsteak, fried fresh salmon, pork steak, fried potatoes, biscuits, pancakes, and the universal tea and coffee.[21]

The constant demand for meals and the inexperience of almost all 49ers in preparing food produced the boardinghouse, which met the needs of miners without close companions or who preferred to live alone. The boardinghouses that quickly appeared in 1849 served miners and transients alike, and almost every dwelling on the roads connecting the mines to the coast offered meals to casual travelers. Some miners went into the business of meal preparation, opening a restaurant or tavern, as we have seen. Lafayette Fish thought that whatever the demands of his customers, a restaurant and "frying doughnuts" was a lot more profitable and certainly more comfortable than mining twelve hours a day in snowmelt mountain waters.[22]

SEASONAL VARIATIONS

The guidebooks and travel accounts described in much detail the California that the Argonauts would encounter in spring, summer, and autumn; they said little or nothing about winter in the mines. The mining season began in the Sierra of the central mines in July or August and ended in late November or early December. The first date represented the time when the streams had fallen sufficiently to permit active mining in their richest sites, that is, those subject to rushing water for most of the year and now uncovered for the dry season. The closing date identified the beginning of winter, or the rainy season, when the cold and wet of California's winter (including snow at the higher elevations) descended on the Argonauts and ended their mining activities for the year.

When the rains began in the mountains, the watercourses rose quickly, and the Argonauts found themselves unable to dig or wash dirt. Thus, the onset of the winter in 1849 revealed to the new arrivals that the cycle of mining was as seasonal as the daily cycle of working and relaxing in the diggings. The 49ers now confronted a range of choices that fell into one of four groups. They could move to the southern mines (or "dry diggings") and dig out dirt to be washed in the spring. Or they might retreat to the cities and towns of California for the winter months, where they could seek jobs as laborers to support themselves during the winter. This alternative offered more pleasant winter conditions; it also placed them in competition for work and, in so doing, drove down wages. Or, they might return to their homes in the states. Each of these three options involved the breakup of the mess. The fourth choice was to pass the winter in the mines. To stay in the mines meant to incur expenses for more substantial housing at precisely the time that actual mining was impossible. Joseph Wood described this condition as "on expense." He continued, "Of the 400 dollars we made on Deer Creek, we have not more than 100 left, besides our winter provisions tent &c."[23]

By late November 1849, the tens of thousands of 49ers who had poured into the placers in the previous six months confronted the special qualities associated with California's winter. The daylight hours, which defined the working day, had shrunk in the late fall. Nighttime temperatures—mining was often at higher elevations—fell toward freezing. Campsites with their tents and lean-tos no longer provided sufficient protection against the natural elements, and the Argonauts needed more permanent shelter. Some two thousand Argonauts retired from the High Sierra to Happy Valley, a huge campsite, where they enjoyed a degree of comfort while pondering a decision about the upcoming winter.[24]

The 49ers who proposed to stay in the mountains for the winter had to prepare. They had to purchase supplies and build, buy, or take over suitable quarters in the form of a cabin or house. By the opening of the winter season, all varieties of shelters had appeared in the placers, from the simple to the complex, from single dwellings to large houses for groups of miners. Daniel Woods referred to the range in these terms:

> The houses are of every possible variety, according to the taste or means of the miner. Most of these, even in winter, are tents. Some throw up logs a few feet high, filling up with clay between the logs. The tent is then stretched above, forming a roof. When a large company are to be accommodated with room, or a trading depot is to be erected, a large frame is made, and canvas is spread over this. Those who have more regard to their own comfort or health, erect log or stone houses, covering them with thatch or shingles. . . . Some comfortable wigwams are made of pine boughs thrown up in a conical form, and are quite dry. Many only spread a piece of canvas, or a blanket, over some stakes above them, while not a few make holes in the ground, where they burrow like foxes.[25]

In addition to its costs, a winter in the mines imposed an unwanted idleness on the Argonauts. From a condition of continuous work during waking hours, sometimes including Sunday, the 49ers abruptly entered a period of prolonged inactivity for several months that always exhausted their supplies of reading material and often their topics of conversation. At the opening of the new year in 1850, Charles Ross Parke described the routine in these terms: "Prospecting, hunting game, cooking, eating, reading, sleeping, and wishing for letters from the 'dear ones at home' has been the order of the day for the last month."[26]

These periods of enforced idleness, intensified by the severity of the first winter, raise intriguing questions about periods of introspection in which men might confide in one another about their hopes and expectations and the families they left behind. These periods of idleness were times of frustration for most 49ers, living for weeks or sometimes even months at high cost without income. What were they doing in California, and at what price? Sometimes the miners shared these months of self-doubt with their families in the East; sometimes they did not.[27] In a world of reticence among men, did miners share these thoughts with their messmates? The winter of 1849–50 in California represented a remarkable example of men from different places and classes thrown together for a prolonged period in the middle of the nineteenth century. Some had dealt with the same questions of idleness and friends on the long voyage to California, but then most men traveled in companies that had been organized among those of similar interests, resources, and locale. Three or four months of mining had partially mixed these homogeneous groupings. Many companies had dispersed. Men had sought and found messmates among their original friends but also had made new ones.[28]

Diarists often wrote extensively in the wintertime, expanding on the laconic entries of weather and gold-dust returns that characterized entries during the work season. Men sometimes wrote home more often, perhaps because they wished to hear more frequently. Still, comparing the volume of correspondence within seasonal patterns remains a matter of guesswork. Certainly the isolation of the mountains in the winter made it more difficult to receive and to send mail.

LEISURE

Observers of the Gold Rush and many miners themselves acknowledged that the 49ers often drove themselves relentlessly in their work, propelled forward by optimism and ambition, guilt and fear. Aside from a few brief hours of leisure at the end of the workday—the leisure of exhaustion—the one period of real leisure was Sunday. Of course, some miners worked their claims on Sunday with the same intensity as during the week. For most 49ers, however, Sunday offered a respite.

In the day-to-day life of the 49er, Sunday was like a separate existence, so much so that the mining experience for most 49ers emerged in two related and yet entirely distinct forms: the repetition of work and living from Monday morning through Saturday evening, then the completely new schedule and duties associated with Sunday, from early morning until late evening. Sunday made accessible a new range of services and occupations designed for the miners; it shifted the focus of the miners from the claim and the cabin to the camp and the town; it stood in stark contrast to the prescribed and inescapable duties of the week. On Sunday, miners left the placers in trickles and then streams and finally rivers of humanity that headed for the nearest center of leisure and companionship.

Sundays in Gold Rush towns tended to be crowded, loud, sometimes rowdy affairs. Henry Packer wrote of noise generated by the ten-pin bowling alley nearby: "incessant rumble of balls and rattle of pins from nearly breakfast until 12 or 10," and in the three blacksmith shops the "tink tink of the hammer ceaseth not the entire day."[29] After six days of the most arduous labor, the miners needed to enjoy themselves, and in so doing, they encountered a variety of temptations. In a nation that was beginning to experience the power of a temperance movement—the well-known "Maine Law" would be passed in 1855—the question of drinking already was an issue of concern. Many men came west strongly committed to the principles of abstinence. Some 49er company constitutions prohibited drinking alcoholic beverages, and failure to abide by this principle was grounds for expulsion.[30] The temptations against which so many Argonauts had been warned at length had begun for the seagoing 49ers in the seaports of call on the long voyage out. The attractions increased in California, where institutional religion and reform movements were still in their infancy, and reached a high point in towns in the Gold Rush country. Miners of every persuasion generally refrained from drinking during the week; the work was too arduous and the hours too long.

Sunday was a different matter. Israel Lord, the Methodist missionary, found the reincarnation of Sodom and Gomorrah in what he called "a California Sunday in full blast." His description continued:

> Four tables surrounded by gamblers, and a Bar by Drunkards, the whole swearing out of all time and measure, so that one might readily imagine himself in the "purlus" of hell. . . . The utter recklessness, the perfect "Abandon" with which they drink, gamble and swear is altogether astounding. You know nothing about it in the States; never did; never will, I trust. This eating is physically their worst fault. They gorge themselves on beef & bread and stale butter and peppered pickles & stimulating sauces, like wolves or anacondas, and the last thing before going to bed, must have sardines at 3–5$ a box or pie at 1 dollar, or its equivalent.[31]

Most observers were less horrified and more understanding. After a week of the hardest labor imaginable, it was not surprising that on Sunday saloons did a heavy business at outrageous prices. The mining-camp saloons bore little resemblance to the grand palaces of San Francisco or even the more modest halls of Sacramento and Stockton. Instead, they were generally a series of plank tables under a canvas to provide protection from the sun. Sometimes saloons served meals; often they did not. Frequently combined with pool rooms, bowling alleys, and saloons, the focal point of the entertainment industry was the gambling hall. Every crossroads village within walking distance of mining operations had at least one. John Eagle wrote to his wife of the gambling houses in Gold Hill:

> A gambling house in this country is just like our hotels at home.... These houses are what might be called public houses, for it is the first place a stranger goes to see if he can find any of his friends, or to hear the music, for they have good music at these places; some go to gamble, some to drink, some to hunt up old acquaintances, some to hear the music. These are the only public places we have, and *hard* places they are, but all classes can be seen there occasionally. We go down of an evening, sometimes once or twice a week, to hear a few tunes played. We seldom go to a neighbor's tent, we never go out of an evening, only to the store or to the gambling house.[32]

Whatever their habits of alcohol consumption, the 49ers were unanimous about one aspect of the business of leisure: the sale of liquor in all its forms was enormously profitable. Many individuals hitherto strongly in favor of abstinence wrestled with the demon of profits in the liquor trade. After all, these men were far distant from their families and communities, desirous of making money rapidly and in substantial amounts in order to return to them as soon as possible. Confronted by the temptations of large profits and the competition of other establishments that sold whatever customers wanted, many succumbed. Others kept the faith and trumpeted their strong principles in their diaries and letters.[33]

The gambling establishments might bring on other temptations, and the attractions of women were even more compelling and less easy to explain than the occasional glass or game. The 49ers were lonely men in a world with few women, and many had to struggle to curb their sexual appetites and remain faithful to their wives and fiancées. The stolid Henry Packer described the nature of these enticements to his fiancée in a burst of candor. Commenting on the fall from grace of one of his acquaintances, he wrote, "Well men do some strange things! When relieved from the watchfull eye of his wife he 'cuts up such phyfastic tricks before high Heaven as make the very angel weep.'" And he then continued in a very personal vein:

> Sometimes I only wish you were here to watch and guard me, for I am horably beset with temptations, and though my virtue is of the most stubern kind—yet, unaided and unsustained by kindred virtue it might—I say might fall. You know the human heart and I believe you will sympa-

thize with me when I tell you that those temptations however weak they might be in the eyes of true virtue are fully sufficient to overcome the consciencious scruples of the two thirds of all the men married or single, in California.

Packer then went on to describe these temptations in more detail. He began the scene with the emergence of a woman from the rear door of a gambling saloon. She was

> a fairy form—by Heaven a woman stands in the door—she is richly dressed. In her ears and on her fingers are massive gold rings displayed around her neck is a chain of the same. Glossy curls play over her full neck and shoulders. On her countenance plays a smile that would bewitch if not be guile a miniester—Hist she speaks. "Come in you fellow with the mud on your hat, I like a miner." And the hombre minor or major is very apt to walk in accordingly. Do you blame him: I think you would. Now if thus invited, I was to walk in just to see the fashions and go no further would you forgive me? I hope nothing more than a curtain lecture would be the penalty of the crime. I must confess. . . . I did go in just once—only once, and then but for a few minutes.[34]

Packer's awkward and at the same time revealing description and confession (however mild the sin) was a rare admission. The related issues of sexuality and the temptations produced by the presence of women in the enormously profitable and well-patronized Gold Rush entertainment industry were subjects to be canvassed at night around the campfire, not in letters to wives and fiancées. The prompt and unyielding response of his fiancée, Mary Elizabeth Judkins, suggests why.

The presence of so many drinking, gambling, and prostitution establishments, the relaxed air of a Sunday after a hard week's work, pressure from friends, and the anonymity of the world of the mines accustomed many young miners to new forms of leisure. On a Sunday afternoon, the 49er could attend a bullfight (in the southern mines), a circus, an auction, or a bear fight, drink in one of several saloons, pursue various games of chance in a gambling hall, and in the evening, attend a dance or a fandango (once again in the southern mines). These leisure activities (all at a price) offered a range of choices beyond anything they had known, and they were at liberty to indulge in them without fear of criticism by their families and communities. Adding to this new panorama of leisure activities were new contacts with women, also far removed from anything they had known in their villages or towns.[35] Did the 49ers change in California? Did they fall willing victim to the dangers they had been warned about in the editorials, sermons, and parental advice that accompanied their departures? Did they go to the land of gold with one set of values and standards and gradually succumb to another when caught up in the heady specter of wealth on every hand, whether in the streams or on the gambling tables? Did men accept drink and the widespread violation of the Sabbath and even come to profit from them? Certainly some did. Many accounts note how California changed 49ers in a variety of ways. William Brown concluded, "Such is life in California; every man changes his appearance manners & habbits after he has been here six months."[36]

Leisure time was not all given over to wine, women, and song, Hollywood again to the contrary. Some 49ers read a lot in their leisure moments. Of course, the written records to which we have access are work of a group both literate and verbal. Whether they were representative of 49ers in California in the first years of the Gold Rush is impossible to know. Their favorite reading materials were letters from home. But on Sunday, Argonauts also read other things, beginning with newspapers. Selling newspapers in the mining camps on Sunday for a dollar each was what helped put William Brown on the road to wealth. Many 49ers subscribed to their home newspapers. Families mailed clippings and whole copies regularly. Friends in the placers from the same community passed local newspapers around among former neighbors. Newspapers in the mines were read and reread until they literally fell apart.[37]

Reading was one of the most popular pastimes, although the winter imposed darkness and continuing discomfort. "Read a little and passed the rest of the time shivering over the fire," noted one 49er. He was reading Shakespeare's *Hamlet*.[38] Many men read the Bible, often a gift from the family in leaving home. Urged to do so by their correspondents, they would write of specific passages to give evidence of their regular reading habits. Others read Shakespeare's plays, and poetry by Byron and Pope. Among the novels read were Harriet Beecher Stowe's *Uncle Tom's Cabin* and James Fenimore Cooper's *Last of the Mohicans*.[39] Some reported reading the travel books for the West Coast, such as Edwin Bryant's *What I Saw in California* or Lieutenant Ruxton's *A Life in the Far West*.[40]

Miners also used the leisure of Sunday for personal chores. They took baths and washed clothes; they sewed and mended. Miners wrote of washing on Sunday as among the most dreary of chores. It reminded them of home, of their wives, mothers, and sisters, who used to do these duties for them. For those unmarried, it brought forth "the need for an affectionate wife away with old bachism." Alexander Spear summarized a Sunday's chores in these terms: "i dun my Duty this afternoon I washed my shirt and mended my trousers and scratched this [letter] with a pine stick."[41]

The most universally celebrated of the leisure occasions in the gold camps were holidays, which fell into three distinct groupings: the Fourth of July, a general holiday (no miner worked on Independence Day) with food, drink, and sometimes orations; Thanksgiving and Christmas, with their memories of and connections to home; and New Year's Day, the close of one year and the start of another.[42] The holidays had many variables. To begin with, some groups worked on the holidays. The largest number of those so employed were in the entertainment and service business, that is to say, they intended to profit from serving others.

Others continued to mine, pursuing the same schedule on holidays as they did on other days. That they did so testified to the drive and ambition associated with mining for gold in California, and their determination, whether from avarice or guilt, to ignore no opportunity for gain. Joseph Wood confided to his diary on Christmas Day, 1849: "We this day worked our machine. Oh Christmas! where are the joys and festivities? not in California surely."[43]

From the perspective of the placers as a whole, on holidays, "joys and festivities" were everywhere. Many Argonauts anticipated the holidays, prepared for them, and celebrated with wholehearted enthusiasm. Festivities differed by place, whether celebrated in the camps or the towns. All combined festivities with nostalgia in various degrees. Inevitably, the celebration of a holiday reminded the Argonauts of previous celebrations at home. Ephriam Morse of Boston wrote on Thanksgiving Day at length about the comforts and warm relationships he had left behind "for sordid gold, & have I been successful? far from it, I am just as rich now & as when we left Boston worth 300.00 not a real cent more. I expect I am remembered in two families at least."[44] On holidays, memories were more valuable than money. On such occasions, the 49ers could speak in casual and even deprecating terms about their financial accounts for the year; this tone contrasted with the intense seriousness with which they discussed such affairs with their families and friends, when they confided in their friends.

The holidays that marked the close of one year and the start of another tended to be a special time of introspection for Argonauts, reminding them of what they had done over the past year and calling forth resolutions about what they intended to do in the course of the next. On the occasion of Christmas, E. D. Perkins wrote of his wish to be back in Ohio, of the noise created by powder and pistols fired in honor of the day in the mining camp, and of the rude cabin and warmth of the fire. That "some have passed the time drinking & gambling" made Christmas just another day of leisure.[45]

A common denominator that united the holidays was special food. Whether on the Fourth of July or Christmas, whether in the most remote bars or the thriving camps, the Argonauts who made their own holiday meals prepared food for several days before in anticipation of the day itself. "This day being Christmas we did not work," confided Lafayette Fish. "We had a present of a mince pie, we have fresh oysters, & parsnips bought." Argonauts without funds or supplies made do with what they had. On New Year's Day in 1850, one 49er wrote, "We have not the spare ribs, Mince Pies &c but instead things we bought made Some corn Pancakes & eat sugars on them."[46]

Restaurants and other public facilities did a huge business at high prices on holidays. William Denniston wrote of Independence Day in 1850: "This day work was suspended at Aqua Frio, and dinners were prepared in several different bowers, the prices of which varied from 2 to 8 dollars. Thinking the prices of public dinner too high for me I dined at the private table of Mr and Mrs Erickson, which was well furnished, for which I paid 12 shillings."[47] Far from towns in the remote camps, the memories were the same but the materials available more limited.

"THE REAL ARGONAUTS OF '49"

Cast in the role of free spirits—at least in the eyes of their friends and communities in the states—the 49ers exhibited a high degree of conformity among themselves, nowhere more so than in their dress. Their heavy boots, sturdy trousers, checked shirt, large belt, slouch hat, and gloves formed a uniform worn by miners up and down the range of the Sierra that made them indistinguishable from one another. The sameness of clothing available at the stores forced a degree of conformity. So, too, did the similar tasks at hand for miners. But considerations other than dress also came into play to make the 49ers look alike. Miners lost their identities in the collective and similar nature of work, leisure, and diet. Faces covered by heavy beards were hidden from even close friends. The conformity in appearance became more complete over the months and years the 49ers spent in the mines. Injuries, illness, and hard physical labor under difficult conditions aged many men. With a similarity of appearance came a growing degree of anonymity, especially as their friends returned home or headed to distant strikes in search of richer diggings.

Miners wore their uniforms with the same practical air as soldiers. In a world where clothing was expensive but laundry services were more expensive, where men carried their outfits on their backs and would transport no spare clothing except a pair of stockings, most Argonauts wore clothes until they literally fell off. They also wore their uniforms with pride. Their dress was a badge of membership in a large fraternity, and it established their status as workers rather than idlers such as lawyers, storekeepers, merchants, hotel operators, and gamblers.

The conformity in their dress thus expressed a powerful sense of identification as a group for the 49ers in the diggings. The winter of 1849–50 was instrumental in provoking this feeling. It was an exceptionally hard winter, with heavy snows even at the lower elevations and extremely high prices for basic foodstuffs like flour and pork. Many of the wintering Argonauts suffered severely from the prolonged cold, for which their quarters were inadequate, and all were indignant at the high prices charged by merchants. The hard times and high prices did much to foster hostility of miners toward merchants and to create the separate sense of identity that miners celebrated.[48]

The miners saw themselves as the true workers in the Gold Rush. Their interests were separate and distinct from those who supplied support services: merchants, muleskinners, teamsters, stagecoach operators, tavern keepers, boardinghouse operators, and the professionals, especially doctors and lawyers. The latter especially drew the scorn of true miners as the scavengers and bloodsuckers of the diggings. Although the 49ers hated lawyers and avoided them on every hand, many needed doctors. Medical men of various competencies uniformly charged one ounce of gold for a visit. The many cases of sickness and injury ensured that their services would be much in demand. On the occasion of their patient's death, doctors often demanded fees out of the estate before other claims on it were settled. As California filled up in 1851 and 1852, the professions became crowded. Miners shed no tears for the reduced fees that resulted. Twelve hours of hard labor in freezing water seemed a high price to pay for a ten-minute visit from a doctor dressed in a tie.[49]

Hostility toward service groups and professionals had a kind of class solidarity about it, grounded in what miners saw as price gouging. At the same time, the 49ers as a whole celebrated the democratic nature of the gold mining exercise and the societies that emerged in the diggings and the camps. Their attitudes reflected, among other things, the structured sense of the world they left east of the Mississippi River. Allen Varner wrote of his initial reactions to the placers in November 1849 that anyone who would "work hard and live rough (For there is no Aristocracy to contend with here) for 10 or 12 dollars a day let him come for he can generally make that and sometimes much more." And John Magruder wrote to his brother in late 1851 that "Our Mule drivers & teamsters &c are just as much respected as if they were Members of Congress or any other prominent position."[50]

Of the various occupations in the mines, the lowest status belonged to gamblers and other entertainers such as ten-pin alley proprietors, who made a living from the hard labor of working men while standing by idle themselves. It is probably no accident that gambling and entertainment were also among the most profitable occupations in the mines and mining camps. So William Brown wrote in derision of the idlers who came to the mines and stood around to watch the frantic work underway. They were "nice young men that never have done any thing like work at home who come here only to blister their hands. They then *stick their tails* between their legs & run home as fast as they can. I expect you will hear some hard stories from them."[51] By contrast, the miners thought of themselves as the "real Argonauts of '49," the vanguard of the American civilization that would transform California. Their dress of working clothes was a badge of productive labor, not an emblem of the social graces. That it was almost always blended with dirt, perspiration, and stains gave it further legitimacy. It served to separate those who wore it with pride from the broadcloth of the California towns and cities and from the traditional dress of their communities in the East.

"Miners in the Sierras," Christian Nahl, ca. 1851. From Stevens, *Artist of the Gold Rush*. Courtesy National Museum of American Art, Smithsonian Institution, gift of the Fred Heilbron Collection.

"Saturday Night in the Mines," Christian Nahl, ca. 1856. Courtesy Stanford
University Museum of Art, gift of Jane Lathrop Stanford. Frank Wing
Photography.

"Miner's Cabin: Result of the Day," Christian Nahl, ca. 1852. Courtesy the
Bancroft Library, University of California, Berkeley.

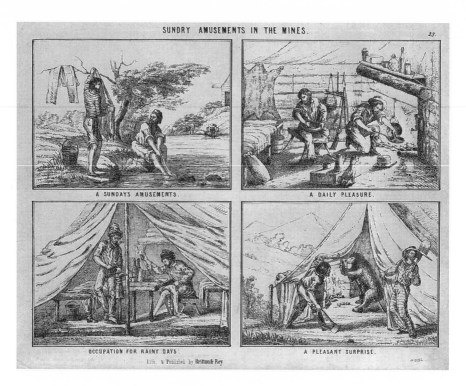

"Sundry Amusements in the Mines," from California Letter Sheets. Courtesy Huntington Library.

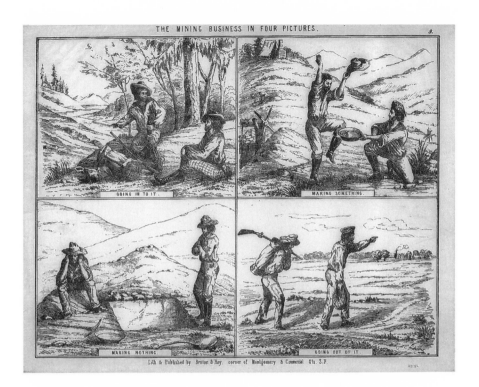

"The Mining Business in Four Pictures," from California Letter Sheets. Courtesy Huntington Library.

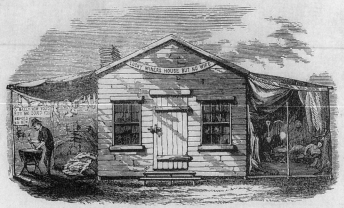

THE MINERS' LAMENTATIONS.

[Copy-Right Secured.]

Published at NOISY CARRIER'S, 77 Long Wharf, San Francisco.

"The Miner's Lamentations," from California Letter Sheets. Courtesy Huntington Library. Excerpts from the accompanying "list of grievances" entitled "We Miss Thee, Ladies":

We miss thee, too, at early morn,
When we our meals prepare;
No words of true affection speak,
To soothe domestic care.
We miss thee when at eventide,
The sun sinks o'er the hill,
When the nightingale's sweet notes pour forth,
And the moonbeams gild the rill.

. . . .

We miss thee at the washing tub,
When our sore and blistered digits,
Hath been compelled to weekly rub,
Giving us blues, hysterics, figits;
'Tis then we miss thy timely aids—
Oh, do have pity gentle maids!
We miss thee when our Sunday shirts
Are sadly rent and buttonless,
With not a thimble, button, thread
To help us in our dire distress:
'Tis then we miss thy timely aids—
Oh, do have pity gentle maids.

DO THEY MISS ME AT HOME.

Do they miss me at home — do they miss me?
　'T would be an assurance most dear,
To know that this moment some loved one,
　Were saying I wish he were here ;
To feel that the group at the fireside
　Were thinking of me as I roam,
Oh yes, 't would be joy beyond measure
　To know that they miss'd me at home.

When twilight approaches, the season
　That ever is sacred to song,
Does some one repeat my name over,
　And sigh that I tarry so long ?
And is there a chord in the music
　That's missed when my voice is away,
And a chord in each heart that awaketh
　Regret at my wearisome stay?

Do they set me a chair near the table
　When ev'ning's home pleasures are nigh,
When the candles are lit in the parlor,
　And the stars in the calm azure sky ?
And when the " good nights" are repeated,
　And all lay them down to their sleep,
Do they think of the absent, and waft me
　A whispered " good night" while they weep ?

Do they miss me at home—do they miss me,
　At morning, at noon, or at night ?
And lingers one gloomy shade round them
　That only my presence can light ?
Are joys less invitingly welcome,
　And pleasures less hale than before,
Because one is missed from the circle,
　Because I am with them no more ?

Published by JAMES M. HUTCHINGS, 201 Clay street, Plaza, San Francisco.

"Do They Miss Me at Home," from California Letter Sheets. Courtesy Huntington Library.

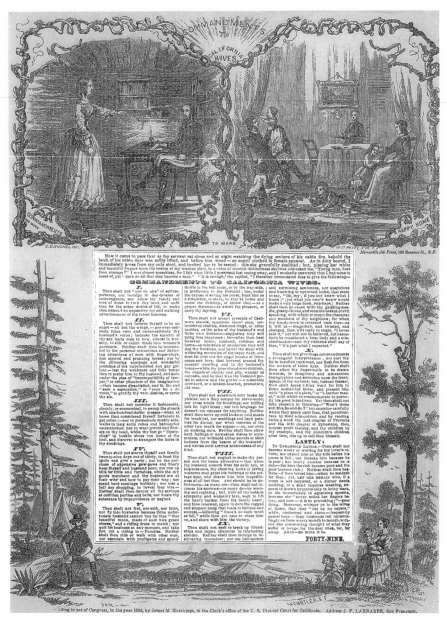

"Ten Commandments to California Wives," from California Letter Sheets.
Courtesy Huntington Library.

No. V.   SUN PRINT.

"The Miner's Ten Commandments: V." "Thou shalt not think more of all thy gold, and how canst make it fastest, than how thou will enjoy it, after thou hast ridden, rough shod, over thy good old parents' precepts and examples, that thou mayest have nothing to reproach and sting thee, when thou art left ALONE in the land where thy father's blessing and thy mother's love hath sent thee."

No. X.

"The Miner's Ten Commandments: X." "A new Commandment give I unto thee—if thou hast a wife and little ones, that thou lovest dearer than thy life—that thou keep them continually before thee, to cheer and urge thee onward until thou canst say, 'I have enough—God bless them—I will return.' Then as thou journiest toward thy much loved home, with open arms shall they come forth to welcome thee, and falling upon thy neck, weep tears of unutterable joy that thou art come. . . ."

"Seeing 'the Elephant,' " from "The Miner's Ten Commandments."

"The Miner's Ten Commandments."

The Idle Miner.

"The Idle Miner," Christian Nahl. Courtesy the California History Room, the California State Library, Sacramento.

The Industrious Miner.]

"The Industrious Miner," Christian Nahl. Courtesy the California History Room, the California State Library, Sacramento.

Return of the Industrious Miner.

"Return of the Industrious Miner," Christian Nahl. Courtesy the California History Room, the California State Library, Sacramento.

10

THE URBAN 49ERS:

"A Very Good Chance to Make Money in This City"

ALTHOUGH AMERICA AT MIDCENTURY was still predominantly a rural nation, it had growing cities, and the gradual movement of population into urban areas in response to new economic opportunities ensured the continuing expansion of the urban dimension of American life. The 49ers who went to California saw economic opportunity in many forms and many places. That they responded to the discovery of gold was not always a declaration of their intention to dig in the rushing streams of the Sierra; rather, it was their sense that gold mining on a large scale would produce economic opportunity throughout California. Many Argonauts lived and worked in California's cities and towns, some permanently, others seasonally. Whatever the length of their stay, their continuing presence promoted the growth of urban places. Like the 49ers themselves, some cities, towns, and camps would do better than others, but even the fortunes of the most favored would rise and fall. Through these variations and over the first decade of the Gold Rush, the urban dimension of California life would expand and diversify.

San Francisco, the great city of the Gold Rush, began life as a harbor. It was its potential as a sheltered anchorage for a great fleet that caught the eye of Spanish explorers in 1776 and marked it as the site of a future mission settlement. It is one of those implausible symmetries of American history that Europeans noted San Francisco harbor at almost the same moment that the signing of the Declaration of Independence in Philadelphia signaled the establishment of an American nation. The mission on the site of the harbor grew slowly, eclipsed in importance by Monterey, the center of Mexican government after the revolution of 1821, and other ports through which ran the trade in hides and tallow to the outside world.

James Marshall's discovery of gold in January 1848 changed the life of this small village of eight hundred in the most dramatic kind of way. Almost overnight, San Francisco's harbor became the destination of a hundred ships carrying 49ers and their annual reinforcements toward the gold fields. Later, as rapid and more affordable ship transportation developed from San Francisco to the East Coast ports by way of Panama, the Argonauts returned to the city to take passage home. Thus, an enterprise that was in many ways remote and isolated—as gold-bearing streams tended to be—quickly came to include a striking urban experience as well. Whether approached by land or by sea, entering or departing, the young city made a powerful impression. "The city of San Francisco presents the strangest state of society I ever saw or heard of," observed John C. Collbreath in 1849, and most of the Argonauts who went to the diggings by way of San Francisco harbor would have agreed.[1]

With its swelling population, San Francisco in 1849 was in transition from temporary tents and byways to permanent brick buildings and regular streets. One 49er left a description of the sounds of enterprise and growth: "The city is humming with business & industry, the Carpenter's hatchet & saw constantly fills the ear from the first dawn of day till dark & reminds me of an immense copper & tin manufactory."[2] Under the impetus of the rush to the gold fields, San Francisco grew so rapidly as to defy description and even numerical representation. Bayard Taylor, an observant traveler, noted on landing that "every newcomer in San Francisco is overtaken with a sense of complete bewilderment." He continued, "Never have I had so much difficulty in establishing, satisfactorily to my own sense, the reality of what I saw and heard." Taylor concluded his astonishing array of superlatives with the observation that San Francisco had telescoped a half-century's growth into four months in the summer of 1849.[3] Its population rose to twenty thousand in 1850, thirty-six thousand in 1852, and fifty thousand in 1860. By the middle of the 1850s, San Francisco was an important financial and commercial center, noticed by New York and Boston. It also had developed a social and cultural life commensurate with its wealth, and if the wealth was unevenly distributed—and so it was—the same was true in other American cities.

But San Francisco's astonishing physical growth and rise in population are an incomplete guide to its variety and significance in the Gold Rush. We already have examined the catalogue of its expanding occupations, including merchants and wholesalers; professionals, such as doctors, dentists, and lawyers, the latter influential in the resolution of California land claims that became so significant; entrepreneurs with a wide range of interests, from city lots and buildings to financing mining enterprises; the entertainment industry, which encompassed, among others, prostitutes, gamblers, and musicians; the wide range of skilled tradesmen, from carpenters and builders, who formed the backbone of the building industry, to day laborers who dug, carried, and cleared; and the expanding services demanded by the arriving Argonauts, all of which demanded construction, maintenance, and supervision.

This growth in numbers, area, and range of services and institutions took place in spite of a series of continuing physical disasters. Most of the city burned in December 1849 and in May 1850, and although it was immediately rebuilt, fire again destroyed large parts a year later. In addition to the resulting fear of arson and of widespread robbery and violence, a pall of corruption and political intimidation hung over the city. The response to these dangers was the rise of one of the most powerful and long-lasting vigilante movements in the history of the Republic. The Committee on Vigilance appeared in 1851 and was revived five years later, when its private army ruled the city for three months. Throughout, the Committee had the support of large portions of the commercial and professional groups in the city.[4]

Some of the patterns in the emergence of San Francisco's urban population may be examined in the activities of the DeWitt family. Alfred DeWitt and his brothers sailed from New York for San Francisco in April 1848 before the discovery of gold was known in the East. The DeWitts—Alfred, his wife, his brothers, and his brother-in-law—intended to pursue a mercantile venture. In late July 1848, the DeWitts landed in San Francisco, to find this small port and all of California in a turmoil. James Marshall had discovered gold, and the American River had become the destination of all Californians. The DeWitt family found itself in an ideal place to pursue their commercial venture, and their personal activities over the next five years coincided with the emergence of San Francisco as a city.

The DeWitt brothers had brought a stock of goods to San Francisco, and they opened a store under the name DeWitt & Harrison just in time to benefit from the initial gold excitement. By September 1848, the firm was in operation, but San Francisco was "nearly deserted" because "all who have not any particular occupations to bind them to the town are now on the hills some 30 or 40 miles back to gather gold dust." Nowhere was the change greater than in the new position of laboring men. Alfred DeWitt commented on the changed relationship: "Laboring men are now very independent in fact we are obliged to accept their services as a favor, and if their dignity is anywise tested, they will immediately discharge their employers throw their Blankets over their shoulders and quit the service." It was a tribute to their commercial nature that none of the DeWitt brothers ventured to the gold fields for any length of time, even at the height of the gold mania in the summer of 1849.[5]

For the next five years, Alfred DeWitt presided over the family's mercantile house, and his business (with ups and downs) prospered. The expansion of a town turning into a city meant more competitors; on the other side of the ledger, the annual immigrations to the gold fields created continuing demand for his goods. The city had fires, epidemics, floods, and throughout, streets fouled with trash, but his profits continued unabated.

What was remarkable about the story that emerges from the correspondence of the DeWitts is that they gave little thought to San Francisco as a new urban center associated with the Gold Rush. It was simply another town turning into a city, and the DeWitts were there to benefit. The initial surge to the gold fields had made servants scarce and had provoked a degree of hardship, but in many ways, Alfred and his brothers lived lives scarcely different from those of affluent merchant families in other emerging American cities. As for his wife's life in California, the only aspect that marked San Francisco as different was its distance from her family in the East. Plans to return to New York to see their two families were complicated and expensive, pressed forward chiefly by the death of family members, Margaret's sister in 1850 and Alfred's father in 1851. By 1853, Alfred had begun regular trips between San Francisco and New York, sometimes with his wife Margaret, and sometimes without, testimony to the growing routine of travel between eastern and western cities.

San Francisco was quickly home to a large number of small commercial businesses. One of the new merchants to appear in 1850 was Milo Goss. As we've seen, Goss had run a store in Kalamazoo, Michigan, with indifferent success before heading for California in the spring of 1850, leaving behind his wife Catherine and small children. After a season in the mines, Goss settled in San Francisco, where he opened a small store "selling groceries and provisions." He wrote to his wife that he and his partner "were doing exceedingly well." By March 1851, he was increasing his "pile" at the rate of about one hundred dollars a week, information that he shared with his family with much pride for his accomplishments and concern that the numbers be kept confidential. Perhaps Goss was afraid that if his new prosperity in San Francisco became public knowledge, his creditors in Kalamazoo would present their notes for immediate payment. He was torn between sending money home to save the store and house and his need for capital in San Francisco. Eventually, he sent her funds to purchase the house. She handled the real-estate transactions; he provided the money.

Goss characterized the business climate in San Francisco as uneven but inviting to the active, aggressive entrepreneur who "will soon retrieve himself and here much sooner than anywhere else." When the city burned in May 1851, Goss and his partner lost about three thousand dollars, and he immediately joined another firm. Of the chaos produced in the city by a fire and then an earthquake, he wrote, "This is a *great country*. Nothing too marvelous or improbable to be enacted here."[6] He found such natural disasters only a temporary interruption in his own growing prosperity and the progress of his adopted city.

Goss's letters moved beyond the endless commercial activity of the city to comment upon its moral tone. For him, as we've seen, San Francisco embodied the extremes of virtue and evil. "I thought before I came to this country that I had seen wickedness in its worst forms," he told his wife, "but I must confess that I had seen but little of the wickedness of the human heart.... vice shows itself in this country in such disgusting forms." The spectacle made him a vigorous defender of the Vigilance Committee. Composed of "merchants, doctors, and the most respectable men in the city," the Committee set out to clean up those vices that Goss so deplored.[7]

Even with the losses of the fire, Goss continued to profit. He bought a ship of five hundred tons in the fall of 1851 for the coastal trade. Within the year, he found himself faced by a quandary that affected few 49ers: he wanted to return home, but the store was so prosperous he could not afford to be absent from it, even for three months. He wrote to his wife, "My business prospects are so good, that I sometimes think it perfect folly for me to return this spring. There will probably never occur such opportunities for accumulating money as the present year."[8] San Francisco was a bubbling stewpot of economic opportunity, and Goss was a symbol of its success.

San Francisco quickly became a city of contrasts. On the one side were the chaos and confusion of crowded streets, discarded goods rotting in the mud and dust, hurrying men and women who represented a cross section of the Western world, a mixture of professionals on the make and hard-handed miners down from the diggings to take passage home. One recent arrival described the scenes on the streets in these terms: "crates of crockery, barrels of ship bread, hams, beans, boxes of pipes &c are washing about the beach buried in the sand, or fill up the mud holes of the streets."[9] The entertainment industry that lay in wait for the departing Argonauts and those simply down from the diggings for a spree merely typified the mixture of many choices and repellent immorality that many like Milo Goss found so perplexing about the city. And as the city grew, spreading out toward the hills and the bay, the chaos and confusion increased. Efforts to bring order and cultural maturity were stumbling and confused, and the whole was shot through with corruption and vice.

However, the unmistakable scent of respectability also was in the air. Through the mud and stink and immorality of the city, another San Francisco was emerging. This was the city of lawyers and bankers, large houses with servants, men's clubs, blocks of commercial buildings, and growing economic distinctions that increasingly separated the respectable elements from the underside of city life. It was this group that formed the Vigilance Committee to serve as the stern parent that would administer the corporal punishment necessary to give the order and stability required for a city already becoming the most important urban place in the American West.[10]

John McCracken was a representative of the cosmopolitan, urban elite of San Francisco. McCracken was a lawyer who left New York City for California in the spring of 1849. A thorough "gentleman," he found his companions on the voyage noisy and crude, and he excoriated the bad manners of the stewards, "who did not know their place, became impudent, & one thing led to another." From the moment of his arrival, McCracken had "no intention of going to the mines." Instead, he set out to practice law in San Francisco, where already, he wrote in the summer of 1849, "lawyers are doing by far the best business here now." He thought San Francisco a place of great opportunity, but he discouraged others from emigrating because only "smart men can succeed here." He clearly saw himself as one of those "smart men" who could and would succeed.[11]

McCracken's life quickly assumed an urban pattern. He went to the office at midmorning, left at four every afternoon, walked in the park, dined with friends, and returned to his lodging house. Over the course of two years in an extensive correspondence with his family, he said little about San Francisco and nothing about the Gold Rush. He was concerned with his business, which was growing and prospering, and his social life, which was awkward and confused. He and his sisters corresponded about personalities, character, social distinctions, and proper manners. Should he accept or decline invitations? What did guests discuss at the latest dinner party? His observations, acute in their limited way, could have been those of a professional man writing to his affectionate family from any major city in the nation at midcentury. He concluded with a declaration to his sister of social standards that for him were of universal applicability: "I would not surrender my refinement, for all the gold that unborn millions yet will handle, neither would you, nor any of us." His activities in San Francisco over his four years of residence there were perfectly consistent with these views. However new and unformed it was in some ways, the City on the Bay could comfortably accommodate 49ers like John McCracken.[12] When McCracken returned to New York City in January 1854, he probably had little sense of having participated in the California Gold Rush. He simply had practiced law and lived in another city.

Part of San Francisco's distinctiveness lay in its urban lifestyle. This was the city that not only offered great opportunities to make money, but at the same time, to spend it in all sorts of leisurely ways. During the week, for example, William Brown enjoyed the life of leisure in San Francisco after profitable weekends in the mines, handing out letters and newspapers, taking orders for goods, and collecting gold dust. Brown boarded at the Revere House. His daily routine included three or four games of billiards at one dollar a game. He also attended the theater regularly, where, he wrote, "I have been in the habit of throwing away a good deal of money by going to a poor theater at $3." In addition, he played cards and chess. He also rode his horse every day. His express business and related economic enterprises cleared three hundred dollars a month (he employed a clerk to whom he paid one hundred dollars a month and expenses), and Brown invested much of it on his comfort. He described San Francisco to his father as a wonderful place "to spend money in."[13]

What set San Francisco apart from other rapidly growing urban areas of California—and there were many, thanks to the influx of one hundred thousand people in twelve months—were its cosmopolitan style and sense of itself as a city. Other towns in California had pretensions to city status in the 1850s. About San Francisco, from the middle of 1849 forward, there was never a doubt. This assurance separated it from the others, and nothing in its upward trajectory through the decade of the 1850s gave it any reason to look back.

Although San Francisco was the great city of California and the Gold Rush, other substantial urban places also emerged in the aftermath of the discovery of gold. Sacramento and Stockton were twin centers of enterprise that stood astride the entrances to the northern and southern mines, destinations for steamers and later for stagecoaches from San Francisco. They were also outfitting places for the diggings and locations for transportation facilities. They offered many of the same facilities and services as San Francisco on a smaller scale. They were more fragile as urban creations, more vulnerable to economic change and to natural disasters.

Sacramento especially was buffeted by the cycles of immigration and mining. It sprang to life each July with the arrival of advance elements of the annual overland migration. At about the same time of year, waters in the streams in the Sierra had dropped enough to begin the annual mining cycle. The hurry to and from the mines would last until late autumn, when rain, snow at the higher elevations, and the rising watercourses would put an end to the mining season, and miners from across the reach of the Mother Lode would pour into Sacramento and Stockton in search of seasonal work to fill the winter months.[14]

In 1849, everything about Sacramento was new and temporary, "a city built almost entirely on cloth spread upon light frames." It was also growing rapidly, "& almost any thing can be had & seen in this city of 6 months growth as in an eastern city. Lynch law is the only law known & yet though there are in the population of 7 or 8000 20 or 30 large gambling houses & liquor bars—there has been no cases of riot or bloodshed." It was a strategic point for the immigrants to purchase supplies to arrange for transportation to the gold fields. E. T. Sherman called it "the place where all parties fit out for the mines & consequently a very heavy trade is carried on here." Already the main business of Sacramento was "buying & selling."[15]

With few permanent structures, Sacramento merchants piled their goods in the streets, and the onset of the rainy season took them by surprise. The great flood of that winter turned the town into a vast lake, and by January 1850, its citizens had retreated to the second stories of their dwellings—those who had them—and watched as the barrels and boxes stored on the streets floated out of sight. Disastrous as the high waters seemed, within a few short months, Sacramento was back in business. By the summer of 1850, one man described the place as a town with a population of fifteen thousand with a temperature over a thousand degrees, a figure that could convey the intensity of commercial activity, as well as of the valley heat in summer. The seemingly endless output from the mines and the thousands anxious to go there provided an insatiable market for its commercial transactions.[16]

At the same time that the larger towns offered steady wages, fifty to one hundred dollars a month in 1851, instead of the long odds of a big "raise" in the diggings, they also held out the inducement of a more pleasant place to live. They were maturing; a growing group thought about churches and schools. Wrote one 49er, "We are not deprived of all the good things of life we have church and good preaching we have good living."[17] With this "good living," however, also came the annual influx of miners at the opening of the winter season, a continuous transient population that was looking for work or looking for a stake to return to the mines. This group continued to give an unsettled look to towns like Sacramento.

There was also a more or less permanent population of what looked to the 49ers like idlers. Not all of these were people getting on by their wits, rather than by the sweat of their bodies. Some were down from the mines for a rest, perhaps even on their way home. Others could not find work. Still others had mastered the art of survival in urban places. These picked up casual labor at the prevailing rate when necessary, and such opportunities were almost always available at some wage, supplementing their work by scavenging discarded goods—some of which the owners had not yet realized they had "discarded"—in the streets.

Compared with the urban settings of San Francisco, Sacramento, and even Stockton, the camps and the bars near to the mining sites were distant, temporary, and crude. Still, these settlements scattered on and near the watercourses of the Sierra sometimes grew and assumed the role of urban places. Tent sites and a few cabins would multiply in numbers of occupants, and the presence of the miners would attract a store, where goods might be displayed on planks, and almost immediately, a tavern, where benches of raw wood would provide a resting place for customers consuming drinks at fifty cents for a shot of whiskey. Eventually (and perhaps in a remarkably short time), a more mature town might emerge, with boardinghouses, wooden stores, opportunities for recreation on Sunday, and eventually perhaps a post office, a courthouse, and even a jail. John Eagle's account of the growth of Auburn Ravine reflected this rapid pace. "It is astonishing with what rapidity towns spring into existence in this country," he began. "When we came here, about six weeks ago, there were only one or two tents in sight, and in one short week, our tent is in the center of town, with six stores, two blacksmith shops, Drug Stores, Taverns, Bakery, Circus, &c. Verily, California is a go-ahead country."[18]

Israel Lord, the Methodist missionary, traveled across the length of the gold country in his first year in California, and his journal identified the range of urban places that had begun to grow in response to the demands of the 49ers. Of the small settlement of Fremont, he observed, "Almost every house is open for boarding," and Yuba City "is 4 or 5 weeks old, and has about a dozen houses."[19] Even some of the larger settlements had a temporary air about them. He wrote of Long's Bar: "I reached a hill above Long's, just in time to see 200 or more tents and canvas roofs, shining like skulls among the trees, 300 feet below." The next day, he described two hundred people washing for gold, with a return to each of at least an ounce a day.[20]

The next stage in movement toward permanence was the appearance of wooden structures, of which a large number were boardinghouses. Stringtown made this transition by February 1850, when Lord commented that the "town" consisted of "40 buildings strung along water course, gardens, and a young woman." When he returned, several months later, he tried out one of the new boardinghouses: "Slept in a long low attic or lodging room of the boarding house. Thirty or forty persons are lodged in the one room, and that not one of the neatest. One half lay on the floor, the other in berths of no comfortable construction."[21] Some of these small towns grew to substantial size over this year. Lord was alive to strong growth, equating size and permanence with a greater interest in religion and religious institutions. Marysville, one of the villages that grew rapidly, "which had 2 houses last fall now has 3000 besides a number of tents. Buildings are irregular. Most contain hotels, stores, shops, bakeries, &c."[22]

The jumbled nature and newness of these towns disguised variations among them that Lord was quick to pick up. Some were far more developed in terms of the range of stores and services, and in a few, the citizens had made a determined effort to achieve a degree of physical order and attractiveness. Take, for example, Park's or Sugar's Bar, of which he wrote, "There are a number of taverns or eating places and stores, and a great deal of taste is displayed in setting them off to the best advantage. The whole street as I passed up in the twilight, and darkness, the candles just lit up, had the appearance of a long street in the suburbs of a great city. The inhabitants are mostly from the eastern states."[23]

The variations included the quality and quantity of meals, conditions not controlled by size so much as by the presence of an attentive cook. On dinner at a boardinghouse in Boone's Bar kept by a widow, Lord was extravagant in his praise: "It was 'sliced-up' in as good style . . . as at a *first rate* boarding house in Chicago. We had sweet potatoes, *fresh lobsters,* and large, green, marrow fat pease, as fresh and fine flavored as if just picked from the vines."[24]

More mature towns provided an opportunity for professionals to practice their trade, presumably for much greater remuneration. John Baker left his

wife and three children in Meridian, New Hampshire, and went to California
to practice dentistry. He settled in Mokelumne Hill, a small but thriving mining camp. In "the Hill," as the town was often referred to, he entered into partnership with a Dr. Holbrook and bought Dr. Teall's half of the practice and his
half share in the building used for an office, its furniture, and merchandise.
The total investment was fifteen hundred dollars, and he paid 3 percent per
month ("considered a very reasonable rate of interest here") on the debt. He
expected to make this sum in his first four months of practice. In that interval, his wife Julia Ann would have to "get along for the next 4 or 5 months
with the means I left you," he told her, "or if you come short, I want you to
get father to assist you in obtaining money or such things as you need."[25]

Baker was a constant critic of California society, especially in small mining camps, with "the noise and confusion of drunken men and women and
the unseemly sights of all kinds which occur in our street constantly," but he
admitted that such settings were alluring places to make money. He did
much of his work on Sunday, when miners came to town from their diggings. His standard charges were five dollars for filling a cavity and five dollars for cleaning. On his first day at work, he took in forty-eight dollars, and
on one Sunday he made forty dollars and an additional eighteen dollars for
filling three cavities. The last patient, a miner, "went out 3 times and drank
a glass of Brandy each time and by the time he was through he was quite
drunk." Such cases were not uncommon, he wrote, "so you see we are
bound to make money."[26]

Baker boarded at the Eagle Hotel, where he paid ten dollars "per week for
a seat at the table." It was the best place in town, distinguished for the variety and abundance of its well-cooked food, "which is an uncommon thing
in this fast country." In spite of these attractions, Baker insisted that his wife
remain in New Hampshire. It was cheaper to support her there ("less than
half the cost of our support here"), and he was adamant that she not be exposed to "the immorality that is constantly before the eyes of the young."
He regretted that they would be deprived of each other's society, but he was
convinced that the absence would work to their mutual benefit. As he
wrote, "I think California is the place to accumulate a fortune and N. England the place to enjoy one." The departure of Dr. Teall for the states with
the six to ten thousand dollars that he made in three years was the model
that Baker hoped to emulate.[27]

As Baker struggled to pay his debt and began to accumulate money, he tried
to explain to his wife the opportunities that California offered. "I think of the
severe labor I was obliged to undergo from week to week and month to month
and in the end the meagre pittance I received, and that only sufficient to

sustain us together in times of prosperity," he wrote. She should understand their separation in such a context. After fifty-two letters and three years in California, John Baker returned to New Hampshire. He brought back two thousand dollars. With an additional eight hundred dollars that he had sent home in the interval, the California earnings would buy them a house. Practicing dentistry in a small town had paid handsome dividends, but only at the price of a prolonged absence. Still, Baker had done something dramatic to better the condition of his family.[28]

Some urban 49ers settled in a town and pursued economic advantage in that one setting. Others moved from place to place, as opportunities offered. Samuel A. Morrison was one of the latter. He started with a store in the mines—at Smith's Bar. He used profits from this venture to start another store farther up the American River. Next, he sold the two stores for six thousand dollars in gold and bought a lot on which he established another store in Sacramento City. He then expanded his economic activities to three stores, a hospital, a bakery, and a butcher shop. By the close of 1849, he calculated his profits at about seven hundred dollars a week. In the coming year, he expected to take over operation of a ranch and invest heavily in agriculture.[29]

Small towns, even those growing into bigger towns, were not a route to unending prosperity. As the claims gave out along the watercourses and the sudden freshets of early fall overwhelmed the dams that held so many hopes, the impact of these changes spread out into urban areas of all sizes and shapes. Merchants found themselves with uncollectable debts, dunned on the other side by their suppliers in Sacramento and San Francisco. Profitable enterprises in prospering camps and towns drew others that wished to emulate them, and soon suppliers, groceries, grog shops, bakeries, and blacksmith shops (to mention only a few) lined the streets. Other competitors were to be found at every crossroad and as close to the diggings as a 49er could build a lean-to to shelter his goods. Thus, the economic viability of these small urban places varied greatly and changed over time. Placerville was one of the first mining towns in California, and its growth in 1849 was astonishing. By the beginning of 1851, observers called the town "on the decline," with its population "discouraged and many are leaving."[30] Like the best mining claims, Gold Rush towns might eventually give out. When such places went into decline, their people simply moved to another urban setting.

THE LA MOTTS OF PENNSYLVANIA

Sometime in the middle of the 1850s, the main chance to achieve something important in California passed from the mining camps to the towns and cities. It was a significant transition, however imperfect, and it marked the close of one phase of the California Gold Rush. In the end, that is to say by the end of the decade, urban places had come to symbolize the continuing opportunities associated with the Gold Rush. Nothing illustrates this change better than the speculations of Robert and Harry La Mott, two sons from a family of economic and social standing in Delaware County, Pennsylvania, who went to California in late 1849. They carried a shipment of powder for the Du Ponts of Delaware and capital for investment in the many opportunities associated with the Gold Rush. After landing and settling in, Robert, the elder of the two brothers, wrote to his father about the astonishing profits generated by men of capital, "not by risky speculations but by regular business transactions." San Francisco was the center of these schemes and their high profits, and the La Motts established themselves there.[31]

Robert La Mott immediately took a job as a surveyor grading San Francisco's streets while he speculated in trade on the side. He made about three hundred dollars on the stock of pants he had brought with him to sell, he reported, the nails sold well, but white shirts moved slowly. Clothing was a good investment "& will continue to do so for a long time to come, provided the articles be heavy, well made, and dark colors." Mr. Pepper's chronometer "is bad stock," and firearms were worth less in San Francisco than in Philadelphia. Merchants in San Francisco, he declared, expected to make a profit of 50 percent on everything they sold. Within a few months, Robert La Mott had accumulated seventy-six ounces of gold.

Brother Harry, in search of more adventure, found himself disappointed with San Francisco. It was too much like the urban places he already knew. He sensed immediately that "the Elephant has not taken up his quarters in San Francisco neither can he be seen here at any time." Instead, those who desired to see this fabled Gold Rush figure must go to the mines.[32] It was a commentary on how much, even in 1849, San Francisco could remind Harry of Philadelphia, his frame of reference for a larger city.

Their father had provided the capital for the venture in California, and Robert sent regular reports to him. The goods they brought with them realized a profit of several hundred dollars, and Robert had lent out five hundred dollars at 4 percent a month. He and Harry built a house on speculation. The surveying and engineering business was profitable in a steady but slow way, and Robert soon searched for other investments with more spectacular returns. Building new towns seemed to offer the best opportunity for an immediate fortune.[33]

The surge of people into California, the demand for services, and the simultaneous appearance of entrepreneurs and investors with capital meant the opportunity to launch a series of new urban ventures. Location was the key, of course. The approach to the mines up the Sacramento River led to the promotion of Benicia and New York as thriving port cities as early as the summer of 1849. The 49ers who took the inland ships up river to Sacramento commented with wonder on these paper towns projected for the mosquito-infested lowlands. Neither town ever emerged to threaten the sovereignty of San Francisco or Sacramento.[34]

Among the proposed urban centers that caught the eye of entrepreneurs was the village of Humboldt, a port city on the northern shore of the Pacific, some one hundred miles north of San Francisco. Humboldt was an ambitious project, even among the dozen planned future cities, for its promoters proposed to establish a second port of entry from the Pacific Ocean. It would service the northern extension of the mines now expanding beyond Mount Shasta into the far northern counties of California. With suitable facilities for docking and storage, the town's founding entrepreneurs could construct a road across the mountains, only thirty-five miles to the Trinity diggings, and reach the northern mines directly from the sea, rather than through the laborious route inland by water to Sacramento, and thence north up the Sacramento River. It was a prospect to delight the ambitions of any 49er whose interests ran to commercial ventures rather than mining enterprises, to selling town lots rather than excavating them, to the enormous profits that would accrue to the successful town builder.

"A fair prospect of making a moderately large fortune for us," Robert La Mott wrote to his mother of his plans for Humboldt. Under his energetic direction, he continued, Humboldt was destined to become the second largest city on the West Coast, or so he thought in June 1850. Robert La Mott owned four hundred lots in the town. When he became personally involved in the future of Humboldt, the lots were worth about twenty-five dollars each, or ten thousand dollars. If the place grew as he intended, he would indeed make a substantial fortune.[35]

To his brother Daniel, Robert wrote of the complexities of creating a city in California. "Hunting a place to put a town" was only the first step. Then, "surveying said location, building cabins, dividing lots, & just as I got through making out the various deeds &c" came the call to build the road. Humboldt's rosy future (in Robert's eyes) rested on the access route across the mountains, and he continued, "I am requested to go with three others to make explorations in the interior among the mountains to ascertain the feasibility of making a road to the Trinity mines." More specifically, the end of the road would be Big Bar on the Trinity. The term "road" was a loose one, and so honored throughout road construction in the West from the beginning of the seventeenth century onward. In California, the difficult terrain made standards for what could be called a "road" even more flexible. "A good mule road in California is what you would call a villainously bad path," Robert wrote to his brother in Delaware County, Pennsylvania. "The worst bushes, fallen logs, stones &c removed sufficiently to let a mule walk by them, & in most only recognizable by the blazes on the trees." Whatever the acknowledged difficulties, Robert's plans for Humboldt would fail without a road to transport supplies from the town to the mines.[36]

Robert's position made him a leader in road construction. He headed the group of investors who laid out the route. Each member of the town company had to work ten days on the road or pay one hundred dollars, "& so nearly every member here shouldered his axe or pick and started to work out his road tax." The call to road work drew forth a roster of investors not accustomed to the physical labor of the Gold Rush. The eighteen in the party, complete with mules and horses, included "Lawyers, MDs, Merchants and gentlemen all dressed in their strongest clothes."[37]

As Robert led his construction crew of future wealthy investors into the hills, he had to come to terms with several pressures. To begin with, Robert's father needed to be reassured about his investment in the brothers' expedition to California. Robert wrote in encouraging terms about the family's prospects in mining wealth represented by the urban places in the Gold Rush country. It was true, he admitted, that he had been carried away by the opportunities in California: "I should not be so regardless of your feelings & the object for which I came to California, as to allow the 'spirit of adventure' to carry me away from a good business & the means of constant & regular communication with home." He had transferred the family's interest to Humboldt because of the generally depressed economic conditions in San Francisco. The house he put up in San Francisco was "a poor speculation," with materials costing eight hundred dollars and construction two hundred and fifty dollars, but the rent was only fifty dollars a month. Humboldt offered the best prospect for investment, but he would proceed with care and restraint. He needed to, for his father was impatient at his sons' inability to realize a windfall in a place where eastern newspapers reported new fortunes every day.[38]

Robert also required some project for his younger brother, Harry, and his immediate plan was to open a store in Humboldt. Harry would manage the store, which would profit from the influx of people into the future city, sure to be rapid and dense. Harry would also be nearby under Robert's close supervision. Harry played a minor role in the family's entrepreneurial activities, but he had to be treated as a partner in these affairs. Among his duties was that of the faithful correspondent who kept the family in Pennsylvania apprised of Robert's many ventures.[39]

Harry reported with obvious delight mixed with curiosity the arrival of new settlers in Humboldt, "bringing stock of all kinds as well as their families." Here were the professionals who flocked to new towns, merchants who hoped to supply the mines across the mountains, and a few of the pioneer families who settled everywhere. Harry noted the presence of one such group: "A few days ago I saw an old Mountaineer & Hunter... bringing his 'women and children' to Humboldt. The old man rode ahead dressed in a full suit of buckskins with a long rifle across his knees, next came his cattle & horses driven by his eldest son dressed in the same manner then came his wife on horseback in company with her daughter and little son." This family parade through Humboldt was similar to those moving along the trail to Boonesborough in 1775 or toward Santa Fe in 1830. They would not purchase town lots, but they would settle the surrounding countryside and give the future city a degree of permanence beyond its reliance on mining and miners.[40]

In the end, Robert was unable to meet Humboldt's continuing demands for capital investment. He even lacked the capital to start up a store in the town. Pressured on one side by his father's demands that he return to more stable investment opportunities in San Francisco and on the other by his inability to collect debts due him, he gave up his large stake in Humboldt.[41] Once he was relocated in the financial respectability of San Francisco, Robert's first duty was to find something for Harry. He sent Harry on a commercial trip to Honolulu, and when he returned, found a place for him with trusted companions in the mines. There Harry worked for a steady forty dollars a week, safely out of the way and in no danger.[42]

As opportunities for a quick profit faded, Robert La Mott attempted to explain to his family why urban life in California was different. It seemed to offer the opportunity for immense fortunes, but it did so within rules that were really anarchy. "No one who has done business in the East can have an idea how things are managed here," he wrote by way of justification. Not only was personal honor almost unknown and "unblushing rascality" the order of the day, the cycles of profit and loss were short. Speculation in anything from city lots to shovels might be affected overnight by unforeseen circumstances—a flood that put the lots under water or the arrival of a vessel filled with shovels—and the anticipated gains might never appear.[43]

Robert and Harry La Mott stayed in California another two years. In this time, Harry worked at several different claims in the diggings, and after a year of hard labor he returned to the city and went into the business of raising chickens. Robert succumbed briefly to the craze for investment in the new quartz-mining claims, but he worked steadily in the general commission and brokerage business. Throughout these many months, he attempted to reduce his father's rising criticism of his activities in California—including "a quiet rap over the knuckles" for a risky draft. With a wry gesture, he could write to his mother, "Father says that though I have some application (mil gracias) I do not possess the necessary go-ahead ativeness." In spite of his light treatment of the issue, he was hurt that he could never explain sufficiently to his father why to expect more modest returns from investments in California. Harry praised his brother constantly, apparently in an effort to deflect his father's continuing criticism. All parties ended up disappointed.[44]

Nevertheless, California's growing urban centers could reward the high expectations that many brought to them as often as they disappointed them, and by the middle of the 1850s they certainly presented better prospects than the diggings. One 49er, who had spent two years in mining and trade—he also owned a ranch—wrote to his brother of prospects in California, "I would not advise you to come to work in the mines although there is plenty of gold to be dug there yet there is a very good chance to make money in this city at a great many different things."[45] As cities and towns changed, they offered a greater range of opportunities to make money. A broad range of chances was no more a guarantee of success than a small range. Still, the cities of San Francisco, Sacramento, Stockton, and Marysville continued to grow steadily amid the growing uncertainty of the mining economy.

11

WOMEN IN THE CALIFORNIA GOLD RUSH:

Duty, Adventure, and Opportunity

I think that I may without vanity affirm that I have "seen the elephant."

LOUISE A. K. S. CLAPP, "DAME SHIRLEY"

THE GOLD RUSH HAD BEGUN as a predominantly male phenomenon, with its economic and psychological center located in the remote camps in the Sierra. During the first two full years, however, the emergence and growth of cities and towns set the stage for the participation of women in the Gold Rush. Women participated in the California Gold Rush for the same reasons men did: out of a sense of duty to their families, because they, too, wanted to pursue California's golden opportunities, and because they sought adventure.

Economic and social conditions helped to define women's place in California, as they did elsewhere. As women began to appear in greater numbers in towns and cities, they usually either managed households or worked at occupations based in such places. In California, as in the East, there was a broad-based division in women's roles between gentility and labor. From the cities and towns, the participation of women in the Gold Rush extended out across California—to the farms and ranches in the countryside, to the camps and bars, and to the gold fields themselves. As early as the autumn of 1849 and in the years thereafter, women began to appear in California in a widening range of new and old occupations.

MOTIVES

Duty came first. The question was, of course, whose duty to whom. Most women accepted the idea of duty to their husbands and families, but many of these also voiced their own opinions about what represented an appropriate duty and under what circumstances it was appropriate. Markedly different ideas of duty soon emerged. On one side, many family members thought it was the duty of spouses and mothers and sisters to prevent men from going to California, as we have seen. Their trust was a sacred one, they were told; they must preserve the family and remind men of their solemn obligations at home.

This view of a woman's duty to her family was enforced by the community at large and its institutions. In his sermon "The Duties of Females in Reference to the California Gold Excitement," the Reverend James H. Davis warned that the "duty" of a woman to persuade men everywhere, especially within her own family, to remain at home followed from the nature of the gold mania itself as "the emblem of human depravity." The enterprise was immoral, for it elevated the specter of Mammon and gold above spiritual things. This made women responsible, for "if any of these young men should die in their exile, you could never forgive yourself for having consented to their departure." The whole gold scheme was also illegal, and he called it "a system of public robbery." And even were it legal, "it is not one that can develop manly virtues." Finally, the Reverend Davis concluded that should "your male relations succeed in finding immense wealth, it will prove their ruin." In the great scheme of values, "the New England Primer is worth more than all the gold mines of California, and would weigh more in the balances of the Almighty than all the gold-diggers on the banks of the Sacramento."[1] The image was a striking one, using as it did scales that would become a standard implement for the 49ers.

Viewed in these terms, and in terms of the accepted role of women in America at midcentury, the Gold Rush seemed to be exactly the sort of enterprise in which women should not participate, either. Whatever they might be told was women's duty in relation to the Gold Rush and however they acted upon it in the deliberations over the prudence of the journey, however, once preparations for departure were actively underway, some women began to consider whether they themselves should not also go to California.

They had strong arguments to back them up. They emphasized duty to their husbands: a wife belonged at her husband's side. They also cast their requests in forms that stressed their potential contributions to the economic advantages that would accrue from the trip. With the support of a woman, a man could devote himself exclusively to the amassing of gold that was the reason for the voyage to California. "Oh Charles I wish you would send for me or come after me," wrote Maria Tuttle to her husband. "How much I would like to go to California. My ambition does not in the least abate. I would be willing to share with you almost any difficulties I could become independent and live in easy but plain circumstances."[2]

Most men resisted these calls for their spouses to accompany them. Their counterarguments were equally strong, equally rooted in American values at midcentury: it was a dangerous and expensive journey to a distant place whose reputation ranged from unknown to uncivilized (that is, Mexican and Catholic), with no physical amenities and little society. A woman's responsibility was to remain within the family and do the myriad chores of domestic service, nurturing children and caring for the elderly, that demanded regular attention, chores broadened and heightened by the departures of men for the gold fields.

Even as many men and women struggled to come to terms with the idea of duty, others already had begun to think in terms of opportunity. The interest in the presence of women in California—by which the 49ers meant Euro-American women—began with the first plans to go to the gold fields. The character of early arrangements quickly suggested that the emigrations would be not only large, but also almost entirely male. The scarcity of women would make them a valuable addition to such parties, opening opportunities for them and for the entrepreneurs who were already hatching schemes to benefit from the migration west.

Finally, although it was judged to be unseemly for a woman to pursue adventure, some noted its appeal, especially when they were actually on the trail west. The idea of leaving the limitations of the past and confronting the opportunities of the future in a new physical and social setting affected women as well as men. Emeline Day, who went west to join her husband in 1853, wrote one month after leaving home, "I do not regret my course. I am happy & contented. If I could return I would not."[3] What is more, the issue of whether women should go to California tended to raise questions about the presumed propriety or impropriety of such pursuits for women, and the Gold Rush experience helped call their conventional roles into question and redefine them. After all, for two hundred years, women had participated in the great adventure that was the emigration toward new lands in the West, and sometimes these departures had carried them long distances and into new kinds of country, across the mountains into Kentucky, for example, or down the Ohio River into the Northwest Territory. No one had seemed especially alarmed by this, or by the departure of women with their families for Oregon in the 1840s.

Indeed, not everyone was alarmed at the idea now. Some of the first notices that offered ship accommodation to those heading for the gold fields also tendered similar arrangements to women at the same price. A North Carolina company organized in Raleigh "for gathering gold" sought one hundred "sober, moral, respectable citizens." The cost was two hundred dollars for each member, including wives and children, "payable into the common fund by the first of March." "Respectable single ladies will be admitted into the Company on the same Terms," the company notice continued. "Separate accommodations will be allotted to the females." The organizers emphasized the scarcity of women in California and added the comment, "a few of the stout hearted and lovely girls and widows, of the Old North State, would assuredly find the enterprise a princely speculation—in immediately getting rich husbands in this fine country." The people most needed in California, the notice continued, were "wives, sempstresses, house-keepers, milliners, tailors." But "wives stand at the head of those most wanted, Just think of that!" Respectable single women "would go off like hot cakes—not for husbands and tobacco, but for husbands and gold!"[4]

The most widely publicized of the efforts to bring a group of women to California and the Gold Rush were those of Mrs. Eliza Farnham of New York. Mrs. Farnham's husband had died in San Francisco in September 1848. Based on her experiences with him in California, she now proposed to organize a company of 100 to 130 unmarried women to go from New York City to California. Those who joined should be "not under twenty-five years of age, who can bring undoubted testimonials as to character, education, &c." The cost to each member would be two hundred and fifty dollars. Mrs. Farnham would purchase a vessel for the trip, pay all expenses, and "take care of them till they can find suitable 'occupation' in their new home." The party also would include six or eight "respectable married women and their families." She declared her purpose "that the gold diggers of California are likely to have helpmates to share the fruits of their labor." Editors across the eastern seaboard praised her efforts and declared that the members of her company "will be valued higher than gold."[5]

The plans of Mrs. Farnham to colonize California "with intelligent females" gave rise to a wide range of comments on the roles of women in populating such a remote and presumedly uncivilized place. "An intelligent woman will carry three books with her—the spelling book, the New Testament, and the Constitution of the United States," noted one commentator. "With these assistants she will educate her children, teaching them the A, B, C's, the pure principles of the gospel, and the fundamental principles of self government. Armed with these, the children of such women will be capable of holding any station in civilized society."[6] The powers of women as civilizers and educators were such as to make them independent of institutions such as schools and churches. Indeed, on such distant outposts, each woman might constitute her own church and school. The Farnham Plan, as it was called, failed. The company that departed New York consisted of Mrs. Farnham, two other widows, and one "solitary maiden lady." Editors and other observers mourned its passing and the opportunities to influence the future shape of California.[7]

Although their accommodations may have been marginally better—especially on shipboard—women do not seem to have experienced special difficulties in making the trip to California. To the women as well as the men, the voyages in ships seemed long and tedious, but they had the usual degree of service and safety. Women passengers included the wives of ships' captains, the wives of company officers, and the wives of military officers stationed in California. Because the greater cost of a sea voyage created a clear distinction between those who could afford such accommodations and those who could not, the latter group had to go by land.

The overland expedition across half the continent, beginning with the infinite spaces of the Great Plains and ending with high passes in the Sierra Nevada, seemed to many totally unlike anything that women were prepared to endure and certainly not something that they would enjoy. When elaborate ceremonies marked the departure of a large company for the gold fields from Bloomington, Indiana, a local observer commented, "We noticed in one wagon in which there were some three ladies, Mrs. Lundeman, Mrs. Knighten, and her sister Miss Matilda Chord. And we observed that they parted with their friends cheerfully, without shedding a tear. Such heroism, we believe is not common among women."[8] Arkansas newspapers followed in detail the journey of Miss Mary E. Conway, who went to California with her father. Reports from the Little Rock company treated her experiences separately from those of the men. Noted the correspondent to the Little Rock papers, "there are many here who will be happy to learn that she stands the trip bravely, and is still sparkling and bright through all the dangers and privations of such a journey." Miss Conway apparently had surmounted the dangers of the continent without infringing on those ladylike qualities that were appropriate to her qualities as a woman.[9]

WOMEN IN CALIFORNIA

Up to a point, women's experiences in California seemed much like men's, many and varied. Like many of the male 49ers, women often settled in cities and towns, in their roles as wives, when married, and in search of the economic advantages that urban places offered, when single. Some, like their husbands, lived in an interchangeably urban world.

Margaret DeWitt was married in April 1848 and left at once for California with her husband Alfred. Once arrived in San Francisco, Margaret became responsible for managing the household of an extended family of her husband's male relatives that sometimes reached twelve persons. She immediately sought to hire a servant to assist her. Alfred had preferred a man, but Margaret wanted a woman "and a nice American servant." She soon employed "a nice Irish woman." The Irish woman, Margaret wrote, "has been 10 years in America and came out with her husband who is going to the mines—and she wanted a good home was willing to come for Sixty dollars a month." She considered herself fortunate. In other households, servants demanded and received one hundred dollars a month. Furthermore, she wrote, "This woman is a good washer and ironer which is a great thing." Margaret spent much time dealing with the problem of servants and their conditions of employment.[10]

Margaret DeWitt saw her continued presence in California as part of the duty she owed her husband. She missed her mother, father, sister, and friends, and she wrote constantly of her adjustments to the new world of San Francisco, especially those necessary to keep house for Alfred and his bachelor brothers. She regretted her inexperience as a wife and constantly expressed her determination to make Alfred happy. Lodged in and responsible for a household of bachelors, she seemed acutely conscious of her married status and her duty to make all male members of the extended family content. When Alfred wrote to her parents critical things about her household management, she apologized, not for herself, but for him, with the comment, "he was like all new married people...I doubt (now he knows me better) if he would write in the same way—Alfred's so kind and good—he deserves a good wife—and I sincerely hope he may not be disappointed." After a long day in the store, the brothers sat around the fire in the evening, smoking cigars and "talking over ventures and things." When they did, Margaret tried to please and thought about the family she had left behind.[11]

Margaret DeWitt was an acute and interested observer of other housekeeping establishments among the new arrivals in San Francisco, as well as of her own. By the fall of 1849, she noted, many of the first families to arrive in response to the Gold Rush had begun to break up. The men moved to the towns or to the diggings in the gold country, and the women returned to the East. The reason was cost, Margaret continued, for "it was so very expensive and difficult to get along without several servants and that besides the high wages cost a great deal." At the end of 1849, she wrote, "a great number of ladies have left in the last two months—and society is entirely broken up—

A number have arrived lately—but they are ladies I do not care to be acquainted with."[12]

In addition to household management, Margaret also took on the universal occupation of women in families—that of nurse. Alfred was often ill, and whenever he was confined to his bed, Margaret became a full-time caretaker. The two even took a trip to Oregon for his health.[13] The collective responsibility of the brothers for the store imposed intense pressure on Alfred to support his part of the arrangement, whether in the house or in the business. That his wife had become responsible for the maintenance of the brothers did not seem to occasion comment, presumably because all the men took it for granted that she would perform such duties. Certainly California and the Gold Rush made little difference to Margaret's sense of her domestic world, except for the initial scarcity and high cost of servants.

For those women who sought active employment, urban Gold Rush California offered a wide range of opportunities. The employment chances exemplified by Margaret DeWitt's Irish woman highlight one dimension of the rising demand for services. As the new waves of 49ers prospered in the cities, towns, and even the diggings, they sought to use a portion of their new-found wealth to hire servants, who were both scarce and expensive. The wives of arriving 49ers provided one source of domestic service, as in the case of Margaret DeWitt and her Irish servant. As Margaret DeWitt noted, the presence or absence of a servant class and the cost of such services helped to define family patterns in the major urban areas. Those families that could not afford servants sometimes dispersed, with the spouse and children returning to the East.

The demands for domestic services in a world of growing prosperity—especially among the commercial and professional classes in the cities and towns—continued for some years. Henry Packer wrote from Sacramento in the fall of 1850 describing the continuing employment opportunities for women: "Women's time is much more valuable than men's. A woman can get $150.00 per month for house work, while hundreds of men are now employed upon the levee, which is being constructed to prevent another overflow of the city, at $75.00 per month." Two years later, Milton Hall, pursuing his trade as a carpenter, canvassed the employment possibilities for a woman. His wife, Sarah, could find work as tailor, cook, or "chamber maid in some publick house which she would never want to do," he wrote. She would be paid at least $150 a month for such employment. And even "such a girl as Hannah that lived with us" would get the same wage "verry quick."[14]

For women with capital to invest and for those who sought employment with a greater degree of independence, the most profitable option was owning or running a boardinghouse. Emeline Day crossed the plains to California in 1853. After her husband returned to Ohio, she managed a rooming house in Sacramento "in partnership with a Mr. Ward." For three months' work, she received one hundred and eighty-four dollars, plus room and board. Of the work she wrote, "I have enjoyed the labor, am content and happy. I have done all the work for from twelve to fifteen and sometimes as high as thirty persons."[15]

Day's generally optimistic views about her work disguised the long, varied, and continuous demands associated with providing lodging and meals for miners and transients. Mary Ballou's account of her boardinghouse, dated from the fall of 1852, suggests the range of activities and the primitive conditions under which she worked. "Now I will try to tell you what my work is in this Boarding House," she began.

> Well somtimes I am washing and Ironing somtimes I am making mince pie and Apple pie and squash pies. Sometimes frying mince turnovers and Donuts. I make Buiscuit and now and then Indian jonny cake and then again I am making minute puding filled with rasons and Indian Bake pudings and then again a nice Plum Puding and then again I am Stuffing a Ham of pork that cost forty cents a pound. Somtimes I am . . . making gruel for the sick now and then cooking oisters sometimes making coffee for the French people strong enough for a man to walk on that has Faith as Peter had. Three times a day I set my Table which is about thirty feet in length and do all the little fixings about it such as filling pepper boxes and vinegar cruits and mustard pots and butter cups. Somtimes I am feeding my chickens and then again I am scareing the Hogs out of my kitchen and Driving the mules out of my Dining room. . . . Sometimes I take my fan and try to fan myself but I work so hard that my Arms pain me so severely that I kneed someone to fan me so I do not find much comfort anywhere.

Mary Ballou had other work, too. She took care of children (including nursing them), made soap, and sewed. Amid the wide range of economic opportunities for women, she wrote, "I would not advise any Lady to come out here and suffer the toil and fatigue that I have suffered for the sake of a little gold neither do I advise any one to come."[16] Yet the experiences of both Day and Ballou into the 1850s suggest that employment for women in the service sectors of the cities and towns probably lasted longer than the chances for individual miners in the gold fields.

Some of these economic opportunities for women lay in the thriving entertainment industry. Here, the activities of "fancy" girls from the dance halls—who "would not be noticed in Gods Country but here they are very handsome indeed"—often drew expressions of outrage. Prostitutes were traditional targets of middle-class scorn, and the hostility spread out to include women who performed in other occupations. The 49ers routinely encountered the "Shocking Sight" of women tending bar in San Francisco or women running the gaming tables.[17] One Argonaut described women's roles in these operations in a San Francisco public house as follows:

> Add to this, the "Bankers" who are generally women chosen for their *attractive* powers—and you will not wonder that the poor Devil who has been so long away from Civilization becomes reckless, and forgits in the excitement, every thing but the Present—and if he escapes this, the next building, whose doors are always open contains allurements still harder to resist. The front room contains a "Bar" which is tended by girls, who will mix your "Toddy"—chat and laugh, and Drink too, with every one who invited them and then invite you into the Parlor whose doors are always open—here you will find girls dressed in the most magnificent apparel, dancing, walzing, Playing the Piano, or guitar In lounging on the sofa, and sipping, her wine (which costs 15 dollars per Botle) at the expense of the poor Devel, on whose shoulder she leans, until he, half Drunk, or crazy, follows her to chambers and awakes the next morning, to find himself worse off, perhaps, than the one who got "fleeced" at the other house.[18]

Within the camps and the gold fields themselves, women appeared in a variety of roles within an almost exclusively male setting, roles that seem to have defied traditional categories. Among these were women who mined (generally although not exclusively alongside their husbands); women who lived alone in mining camps and pursued their own independent businesses, especially boardinghouses, laundries, restaurants, or bake shops; and women who lived and worked on the surrounding farms and ranches. Of the occupations in demand, the two most lucrative were washing and cooking. These were two areas where 49ers would pay high prices on a continuing basis for services. Dame Shirley wrote with high admiration of the washerwoman in Rich Bar. This woman cleared one hundred dollars a week washing clothes, the fabled one ounce of gold dust a day, and she did so in 1851, when returns in the diggings were only half that sum. According to Dame Shirley, Mrs. R. (for so she called her) drew the unbounded admiration of the men in Rich Bar for the skill with which she performed her services and for the profit she made. "Such women ain't common, I tell you," sighed one man. "If they were, a man might marry, and make money by the operation."[19]

Women who mined in the diggings reflected the presence of families as mining units. Just as 49ers joined together in small companies to live and wash, so family groups could realize the same advantages in labor and living. Reports of women in the gold fields appeared almost as soon as news of gold itself, and their presence seemed worthy of comment in the first great migration to California. "Thousands of men (and even women) are digging and washing out from the earth, pure Virgin Gold in vast amounts," reported a "Correspondent in the Gold Diggings."[20] Whole families—husbands, wives, and children—dug and washed. And finally, within a year, rumors surfaced of a woman who disguised herself as a man to join her husband in the mines.[21] This traditional story, retold in contemporary terms, had accompanied men into battle, on crusades, and even on hunting expeditions for a thousand years. That women mined openly alongside their husbands could not prevent its appearance.

At the same time that they might profit from economic advantages created by the Gold Rush, some women also suffered loneliness and isolation. The scarcity of women that created opportunities for their employment also reduced contact with other women. Far from their families, they found fewer women for friends and confidants. Social constraints made women less mobile than men, and they found it more difficult to travel. Men spent much time and emotional energy in search of male companions in whom they could repose trust; to the extent that women searched for female companions with whom they could do the same—there is no reason to suppose they were less interested in such contacts—they had a much smaller group on which to draw. Accordingly, ties with family often increased in importance.

Lydia Burns scrawled her feelings from the mining town of Placerville to Polly, her distant married sister. Polly's recent letter "was like a drop of water to a thirsty soul when all hope is gone it gives new life to the drooping spirits and cheer me here in a strange land not friendless but far from home." Lydia worked in a "publick house" where she earned fifty dollars a month. The immediate occasion for contact was the recent death there in California of "Brother Thomas," and she wrote with intense feeling of the loss. "He died Christmas night I am very lounely much to dishearten me but I have warm friends." Long ill, she had at last recovered her health, but in her financial circumstances, it was impossible for her to make a trip.[22]

Within a year, she wrote again to record her life and occasional low spirits. "I think of you daily," she recorded. She had "meny very kind friends here but know kind Sister or Brother." As a single woman in a mining camp, even in 1854, she had many admirers. She continued:

> I have had meny chances to change my name but dide not except I dont
> know but I mite been better off and then I mite been worse some times I

think I will Merry the first chance and then I am afraide they may not be kind to me and then I shall wish I hade remained Single.... This is A very pleasant Country but I find meny Sade and loanly hours but I truy to drive them away by thinking Their is better dayes acoming you wrote for me to write if I was ever Coming home I doant know I want to see you all once more but dont knoe as I shall ever get means ever to come it coast a greateale for clothes here.[23]

Lydia Burns's ambivalence about marriage suggests that the larger number of choices in California for women did not guarantee happiness.

LUCY STODDARD WAKEFIELD

No more than Lydia Burns was Lucy Stoddard Wakefield a representative woman in the California gold fields. So varied were the places and duties that each was simply one among several. But this woman was surely more independent and probably more successful than most. The context of the Gold Rush provided a series of new opportunities for her talents.

Lucy Stoddard Wakefield and her husband left New Haven, Connecticut, for California in the spring of 1849. She had long been unhappy in her marriage. As one of her relatives put it, her life was "wretched & miserable pride forbade her to complain of her own choice & stir the stink among her Friends, although he was in the constant habit of tentelizing and insulting her feelings with abusive epithets & jealous aspersions of all her connections."[24] On the way west across the plains, the two agreed to end their marriage. The image of the couple from New Haven discussing such arrangements as the wagon train moved ever farther from the structure and institutions of the East raises the question of whether the dry air of the plains and the thin air of the mountains lent itself to plain speaking and an ease in managing those issues so burdened with baggage in their university town in New England.

Once arrived in California, Lucy Stoddard Wakefield divorced her husband and made her way directly to the mining town of Placerville, where she went into the business of baking pies. It was a product always in demand. "I have been toiling hard for the last two and a half years and am still doing an almost incredible amount of work averaging about 20 dozen pies weekly with my own hands without any one to fetch so much as a bucket of water," she wrote friends. Her life contrasted in almost every way with that of her acquaintances in the East, "people who have so little to do that they do not know how to dispose of either themselves or their time." She knew full well how to use her time on a daily basis in toil so prolonged and severe that she could not "stand up another minute." She rose early, before light, and brought a first batch of pies from the ovens at daylight; a second group she baked in the afternoon to cater to miners leaving the town after errands. Two hundred and forty pies at a dollar each produced a substantial weekly income, which she dispersed in expenses and rent. She worked fourteen hours a day. On the other side of this endless drudgery lay a degree of independence she had never known. Freed from the demands of her husband, she worked for herself, set her own hours, made her own business decisions, and kept what she earned.

When her friends in New Haven inquired whether a friend should come West, she wrote of women's lot in California: "There is no way for a woman to make money except by hard work of some sort." If a woman were willing to come to California and work hard, she might profit from the opportunities associated with the Gold Rush. "I have no doubt she might take home over and above her expenses coming, while here, and going home, $3000, in three years, but they would be three years of toil, hardship, and in some respects severe privations, though if she came over the plains she would be prepared to consider California comforts, luxurious, especially at this late stage of our improved and improving comforts." As for herself, she would soon stop her exhausting cycle of work. "I do not intend to work more than two or three months longer only enough to earn my living," she confided. "I am tired of work and though I have not a big pile, yes I am not ambitious of wealth." She would be satisfied with "a competency...for myself, and a little to give away when I wish in addition to this would make me quite satisfied."

Wakefield may have gone on to do things she never could have done in New England, but she still carried with her New England views of other groups. Placerville had "few women and those generally of the most ordinary class of Dutch, Irish or western women. I know of no women from the Eastern States not any one recently from N York State, and fortunately for the lazy south*rons* very few of them." Her prolonged stay in Placerville only seemed to confirm such ideas. Scorned and ignored by her friends in New Haven after her divorce, she continued to exhibit New England values.

In late 1851, her relative, Leslie Bryson, visited her in Placerville. His account of their meeting and her life offers an additional perspective on a woman making a living independently in a mining town. Bryson thought Wakefield markedly superior to her former husband "in every point of view and uncongeniality of feeling, taste, and everything else seems to me to have been the difficulty between them." In Placerville, she worked "alone but actively in making pies." Within the town, she "commands the respect and admiration of all good people in the country she dwells."

What struck Bryson most forcibly about Wakefield's nature was what he interpreted as its masculine character. Her hard work had "imparted to her additional strength of mind her knowledge of human nature far exceeds that of any woman I have ever met, her talents appear to me of A higher order than I supposed them to be at Home Her head is Masculine rather than Feminine." He concluded from these forceful qualities that she was ill equipped to be a good wife, a view reinforced by her determination: "she vaunts her disregard for the opinion of others." In her comments about the family, she spoke "with no measured freedom." Bryson concluded that "from all I have seen and heard of her in California I respect her more than I ever did at home." His respect arose from a range of accomplishments that she never had a chance to do "at home." In a California Gold Rush town, she had the opportunity to strike out on her own, indifferent to the views of her friends in New Haven and unaffected by the other women in Placerville, with whom she felt a degree of common cause. Lucy Stoddard Wakefield well could have penned the words written by Dame Shirley, "I *like* this wild and barbarous life."[25]

12

HARSH REALITIES:

Hard Luck and Hard Labor in the Gold Fields

In the course of two years a few of the "boys" came straggling back. The first
of these arrivals, I remember, walked up our main street, wearing on his
shoulders a brilliant-hued Mexican serape. It created a sensation. All the
small boys of the village "tagged on behind him," a sort of impromptu
guard of honor. The serape was about all he did bring home. He talked a
great deal of gold and brought specimens, but not in sufficient quantities to
pay all outstanding bills. . . . Relatives of the not returned beset them
with inquiries which they found it difficult to answer, because there was
an idea prevalent in the village that a man in California
ought to make money, and why didn't he?

PRENTICE MULFORD

IN THE EUPHORIA THAT characterized their long-anticipated arrival in
California and thereafter in the gold fields, the Argonauts of 1849 had celebrated the blending of adventure and wealth that would in a few short
months or years change their ordinary lives in the most direct and dramatic
ways. The families and communities who sent the 49ers forth had expected,
if anything, even more. Surrounded by newspaper accounts of the most extravagant claims and subjected to the determined entreaties of future Argonauts, they had every right to anticipate extraordinary returns in proportion to the rhetoric used on all sides.

The early reports had seemed to justify the Argonauts' decisions to join
the stampede to California, for thousands enjoyed a surprising degree of
success in the summer and fall of 1849 and even into the mining season of
1850. After this initial period of optimism, however, just as fortune lay

within reach, it seemed to shimmer in the distance, became indistinct, and gradually began to recede. The expectations of wealth from the gold fields had begun to confront the harsh realities of the placers. Those who made money in the first years of success often invested their gains and saw their fortunes turn to losses. California and the Gold Rush seemed filled with an infinite number of ways to lose, as well as to make, money.

As we have seen, the expectations of those who flocked to the gold fields varied enormously. For all, though, at no time were the returns larger and the plans more grandiose than before the first pan of dirt had been washed in the placers. Together with shovels, boots, and flour, high expectations were part of the universal baggage carried to the mines. For working people like Levi Eckley, who came from a subsistence farm where the wage for a hard day's work was one dollar, California more than lived up to those expectations. Returns of eight to ten dollars a day were possible in the mines. A. P. Josselyn wrote to his sister that he had worked long and hard in the mines, but no longer and no harder than he had worked in Ohio for that customary dollar a day.[1] For those with grander expectations, whether as miners, speculators, merchants, or professional men, advantage from the California gold fields was measured by a different set of numbers. However, all 49ers soon discovered that the Gold Rush had generated a complex and highly competitive economy that conferred advantages on those with capital and luck and that ignored men who possessed neither, no matter how grand their dreams.

One of the astonishing features of the high expectations that the 49ers brought to the gold fields was that they lasted for so long a time, reappearing virtually unchanged in the same words and same numbers in annual migrations in 1850, 1851, 1852, 1853, and even later. In the spring of 1850, William Campbell wrote from Tennessee that "the gold mania for California is the all absorbing subject of this country." He believed that fortunes of from fifty to one hundred thousand dollars could be "realized in two years."[2] Others did not think in such high numbers, but they supported Campbell's views that the dream of instant wealth was still real. That they continued to do so was a tribute not just to the powerful appeal of sudden wealth through gold, but to the lack of alternatives for those who wished to change their economic and social condition, to wipe out the burdensome debts of the past. As late as the summer of 1852, Rufus Brown left for California expecting to return with at least five thousand dollars, a sum that "will make us comfortable with what we have already, and then I can get some easy agency business to attend to, like the Belting Company, and we can live contentedly and respectably, and be together," he told his wife Nellie.[3]

"Mining is not what it was when it was first discovered, men could make something handsome then," wrote Richard Cowley in the fall of 1850, "but it is in my opinion that mining is like an old man—it has seen its best days." Cowley had celebrated his best week's work ever in February 1850; now, in September, he was lamenting the declining opportunities for ordinary miners. The substantial returns of the first gold seasons had been succeeded by the competition of tens of thousands of new arrivals and old hands in search of the same commodity in increasingly confined spaces. By the summer and fall of 1850, Argonauts sensed the changing nature of mining, and they often indicated a sense of uneasiness at their future prospects. The rising numbers of miners added to the growing sense that the nature of mining had changed, and with that sense of change, the California Gold Rush had passed into yet another phase. Surveying the heavy immigration of the previous fall, John Fitch wrote in early January of 1851 that "the prospects...of the great bulk of newcomers...is rather poor."[4]

Certainly, by the end of 1850 good claims were scarce and had to be purchased rather than simply staked out. Thus, a new company might work for weeks or even months to pay off the purchase price before beginning work for themselves. The Argonauts were on the move, searching for new places, canvassing old ones, some flocking to the cities and towns. Wages in the urban places had begun to fall. Concerns about these changes appeared in letters to their families and friends, and in entries in their diaries and journals. In addition to the many successes of the first two seasons, mining had always exhibited troubling qualities. To begin with, veteran miners and beginners alike quickly recognized the random nature of mining for gold. It rewarded one man and ignored the same labors of another a scant fifty feet away. It required periods of intense activity alternated with times of enforced idleness. Good claims might give out without warning, and even the best claims would eventually be exhausted. From its beginnings, the exercise of mining demanded that miners plan for the next claim even as they labored so intensely on their present claim. One 49er observed that more gold would be harvested in 1850 than in 1849, but the increased number of miners had lengthened the odds against any single miner to make a good "raise," which he now reckoned as one chance in ten. And the pressure of numbers meant that "mines will be worked much higher in the mountains and lower down in the hills than last season." Another agreed that "the aggregate is great [but] apportion the amt already received among the assumed population and it will not be $100 a person and some have been here two years—this amt would not provide maintenance for over 100 days."[5]

In response to the heavy immigration in the summer and fall in 1849 and 1850, claims had shrunk in size. In the fall of 1850, not only had individual claims in the vicinity of Placerville been reduced to an area fifteen feet square, as we have seen, but gold was now found only at a depth of at least five feet.[6] Thus, a company had to acquire a claim and then dig down five feet before they could be sure of what they had, and then they might or might not find dirt worth washing. More and more preliminary labor had to be done before the 49ers could test the value of their claims.

In addition to the pressure of numbers, mining itself had become more complex, more expensive, and more collective. When the first waves of 49ers washed gravel in streambeds, they thought of nothing but the limits of their claims and their productivity. When they began to tinker with water levels through damming and ditching, they initiated changes that affected their neighbors up and down the streams. Dams raised water levels upstream; ditches lowered water levels upstream. Thus, one company's successful dam was a disaster for the claims of others. Israel Lord described one such sequence in the summer of 1850. As miners threw a "variety of dams across the streams—sacks of sand, and stone walls filled between with earth and brush are most common"—the effect spread outward: "one dam has thrown the water back over three entire claims, and destroyed the prospects for this season of 40 or 50 men." The case came before the local Miners' Association, and the dam builders prevailed on the grounds that theirs was the older claim. Seniority had arrived in a business that twelve months earlier had been open to any and all, almost without rules.[7]

The perceived erosion of opportunity led to changes in the gold fields. Many went home at the end of the 1850 season—whether proportionately more is not clear; among those who remained, several sought other occupations to protect themselves against the changes brought by the new mining techniques. Of course, miners had left the gold fields—for home and for other kinds of economic opportunity—ever since the discovery of gold in early 1848. What was different was the sense on the part of many that they were leaving in response to reduced opportunity, rather than in response to homesickness, sufficient success to satisfy them and their families, guilt at their absence, or simply in order to avoid the hard physical labor of mining in favor of something less arduous.

Joseph Wood's experiences exemplify the changing fortunes that confronted even the most veteran miners. Wood arrived in the mines in late August 1849 and worked steadily thereafter. His company mined during the rainy season in late autumn, an exercise that produced physical hardship without results: "To sum up the whole matter of our winter's labor so far, we have made nothing." As he contemplated several months of idleness, he wrote in an outburst of candor, "*How green I have been. It is too bad to speak of.* I wrote home great stories about money making in California. Poor Goose! How little I knew of the true state of things." Wood labored through the spring and summer of 1850, periods of optimism ("The weather is beautiful. I feel ambitious and as though my chance in California was good yet") alternating with depression and physical exhaustion ("I have not felt well & have had a great many Ideas in my head all day"). By the close of the mining season of 1850, he was thoroughly discouraged. At the end of two seasons of the hardest kind of physical labor, Wood was "about square with the world." Along with his empty purse went a lack of comfort: "I am lonesome this cold dark rainy night. I have wet blankets to sleep in. I would give an ounce to crawl into my old bed at home & remain there until morning. It would feel good to feel dry and safe. My feet are wet, my back is wet & I am not well."[8]

The increasing sense of failure or flat returns has to be seen not only against the brighter prospects of earlier years, but also against the continuing expectations of those at home. There, families retained faith in their 49ers to seize a share of the golden riches about which they had heard and read so much. Even as the 49ers reassessed their prospects, they had to make a decision about how to convey this news to the families, and the families had to consider how to deal with such news in the context of the community. It is not surprising that many of the earlier hints of changing conditions in the mines came through diaries and journals, where 49ers could speak their inner thoughts and delay making them public, even to their families.

The sense that prospects in the West no longer matched expectations in the states sometimes gave rise to prolonged periods of introspection and homesickness on the part of 49ers. Perhaps these feelings were associated with the passage of time and the lengthening absence from home. When the 49ers did well, the returns from the claims compensated for their hard labors in primitive conditions and their prolonged absence from home. As the amount of gold at the bottom of the cradle declined, the Argonauts began to measure their returns against a variety of intangibles. They wrote of their regret at the prospect of returning with so little, of fading outlooks in the face of a new mining season.[9] That these periods of self-examination alternated with months of intense physical labor under the harshest conditions gave them an added dimension. And, of course, their thoughts must have been affected by what they heard from home, or, in the case of some 49ers, what they did not hear from home, for some Argonauts heard little or nothing, a circumstance that must have added to their sense of uneasiness.

When miners rested in the face of winter rains or in response to the playing out of claims, they fretted over idleness and their prospects for the future, and their nostalgia for home and family grew. Confided Joseph Wood to his diary, "Yesterday I wrote my Father's name in the sand of the Sacramento with my finger agreeable to his request. I wrote it where the tide would wash it out I also wrote other names which are dear to it."[10] They fondly remembered the physical texture of their earlier lives: the smell of hot, home-cooked meals and their favorite dishes, the warmth of the house when returning from church on Sundays. And they missed the old social interactions, the intimate conversations, not to mention the sleigh rides, dances, courting, and parties—what one 49er referred to as "jollification." The 49ers used to imagine themselves at the center of conversations with a rapt audience about their experiences in California. Some men passed the time in playing cards or reading, others in discussion ("I have spent the day in conversation with some very intelligent gentlemen and in walking about"), and some in exploring the watercourses for future claims—"prospecting," as it was already known. Some Argonauts even took time from their intense pursuit of gold to comment on the beauties of the California spring, with its hillsides in bloom, soft air, and bright sunlight. "This has been as beautiful a day as I have ever seen in all my life," wrote C. C. Mobley of a spring day in 1850.[11]

Stung by the severe labor of the mines and the continuing expectations of their families and friends, the 49ers sometimes lashed out at the newspapers, whose extravagant accounts had turned so many faces toward the West. "It is a wicked shame that such Glowing accounts of the miners success should be pictured out in the newspapers & could cause people to leave their happy homes & family & friends and be thus disappointed & brake up so many happy families," wrote one Argonaut in high outrage. "When will people in the states learn to believe the truth when it is told to them?"[12] Perhaps the response to his question was the continuing will to believe by those at home. They had planned, sacrificed, and done without companionship, and perhaps without luxuries or even necessities, and they did not want to be told that the prospects of gold had turned to dust.

THE PHYSICAL COSTS OF MINING

"I would not stay & work in the mines for one year for as much money as Billey Gray ever had; it would kill me, it is the hardest work that ever a man tryed to do," wrote Milton Hall to his father. Presumably Gray was a wealthy neighbor of Hall's, whose financial standing served as a benchmark for the community. In any case, most of the 49ers who spent one or more seasons in the diggings would have agreed with his description of the severity of mining.[13] Even in a world where men and women were accustomed to hard physical labor, the ongoing, intense labor required by mining eventually wore down even the most optimistic and the physically and mentally tough. Wealth was the dream; grinding toil was the reality that for many made it into a nightmare.

The mining costume that served all miners and the heavy beards that they immediately started on their arrival in the placers helped to disguise the physical hardships and physical changes that accompanied the work, but the miners knew full well the cost. They wrote in their diaries and to their families about the toll on their bodies and their health. John Fitch admitted to his brother that "The wear and tear of the mines is very great even on the hardiest, and they all say I am the toughest man they ever saw, but the truth is I take better care of myself than most others."[14] The letters home had a certain defensive quality about them, intended in part to establish the hardships involved in the mines and the level of labor involved in mining. The Argonauts were determined to disabuse friends and families of the ease with which gold might be obtained and fortunes realized. They also wanted to establish how hard they worked in the interest of their families.

One significant aspect of labor in the mines was the constant injury associated with digging, washing, and by the beginning of 1850, damming. From the beginning of work, 49ers suffered from blistered hands, and in the course of their prolonged labors, other injuries, such as crushed fingers from rocks and tools, sprained ankles or knees from walking on uncertain ground and wading in rocky streambeds, and the almost universal back ache from lifting endless heavy burdens. The physical labor for five men involved in digging, carrying, and washing eight hundred buckets of dirt a day may well be imagined. And, of course, mining groups would repeat the operation for weeks and even months, accepting the hard labor in preference to the anxiety that the claim would give out, and fearful that it would give out and leave them to find another claim in the competitive world that surrounded them.[15]

Added to these threats to a miner's safety was the introduction of new techniques that presumably increased opportunities for the miner while also increasing his risk. Among these should be noted the "coyote diggings," short shafts sunk into the side of a hill toward pay dirt, named for coyote burrows and very dangerous to dig and mine. These produced numerous cave-ins. It was also in connection with "coyoting," as it was called, that blasting powder made its appearance, and its introduction into the mines added a whole new element of danger. As early as 1852, miners wrote home that they had suffered powder-related injuries.[16]

In addition to the dangers and injuries associated with their chosen trade were the hazards of communal living with poor sanitation. Men did not have enough clothes to change regularly. Nor could they systematically bathe, except for the constant involuntary baths associated with working in the streams.[17] Miners lived in close proximity to one another, and the open-air conditions of their housing—generally in the form of tents—happily cut down on the odor. Epidemics of smallpox and dysentery stalked the mines each season. What is more, as the prospects in the mines diminished, a monotonous diet of cheap, basic foods was all the miners could afford. This diet, with repetitive meals lacking in fruits and vegetables, made miners susceptible to scurvy. [18]

In the face of such demanding physical conditions, men aged rapidly in the mines. Their hair turned gray, their teeth rotted, their aching backs cried out for relief from the daily labor of digging and carrying. The faces of miners were lined by hard labor, hot sun, and continuing exposure to weather of all kinds. Like John Eagle, many saw their hair turn gray as they labored in the diggings. After two years in the mines, Albert Francisco wrote to his mother, "I am getting very old, mother; you would hardly know me. My hair is quite gray. This country wears a man out very fast." Whether from exhausting labor during the week or hard recreation on Sunday, miners paid a heavy physical price for their golden dreams. After a decade of mining, a California editor commented in 1858, "Nowhere do young men look so old as in California."[19]

THE FAILURE OF HARD WORK AND RIGHT VALUES

A major casualty of the intruding realities in the California Gold Rush was the accepted faith shared by much of the nation that hard work and right values would be rewarded with success. These principles had been a staple of an agricultural society, with its long years of struggle dictated by annual growing cycles, in which faithful application to duty would result in ownership of a tract of land that would assure independence. The same assumptions traveled to the gold fields with the 49ers. Declarations of intentions, farewells, and letters en route to the gold fields all emphasized the determination of the Argonauts to work hard, honor established codes of behavior, and return with the expected wealth to the family. A 49er's declaration in 1851, "If industry and economy will succeed then I stand a chance at least," summarized the views of thousands of others two years after the first wave of Argonauts went to California.[20]

This continuing recognition of the rewards for hard work played a central role in the reports of correspondents and editors. It confirmed that willingness to work hard and to avoid the moral temptations of California would give a handsome return to the Argonauts. Enoch Jacobs, a member of the company on the *Edward Everett,* wrote on his arrival in San Francisco, "The news is highly encouraging. Plenty of Gold can be found by hard work."[21] In the spring of 1850, the California correspondent of an Illinois paper reported, "No one should think of coming here to pick up a fortune without work; but, whoever is willing to live on flap-jacks, and pickled pork, and can carry dirt in a bag half of a day and 'rock the cradle' the other half, the chances are 99 to 1, that he will make from 5 to 10 thousand dollars every year he stays in California."[22]

A corollary to the work ethic quickly developed: those who had failed in the mines—and some had from the beginning of mining enterprise—must have done so because of character flaws and skewed values. That is to say, either they must not have worked hard, or if they had been successful, thanks to the widespread availability of gold, they must have dissipated their good fortune through high living, drinking, gambling, and consorting with loose women. As late as the spring of 1853, after two years in the gold fields, Levi Hillman was convinced that he had achieved a degree of success because of "patience, perseverance, industry, and economy," while he castigated those who failed from "reckless habits, want of ability to act for themselves, or lack of energy."[23]

But 49ers who lived up to both the letter and the spirit of the ethic that held that hard work would mean a "pocketful of rocks" also failed.[24] The gradual disillusionment that followed fundamentally altered the values held by the Argonauts. Observers of the mining scene began to note that even hard-working miners without vices were mining in reduced circumstances, sometimes in want of food and shelter. A cynical attitude that provided a justification for failure and a hedge against the expectations of families looking on so intently from thousands of miles away now slowly replaced the belief in the inevitability of a substantial fortune.

William Brown expressed the mixture of faith and uncertainty in a letter to his parents on arriving in the placers. "There is a great deal of luck in washing Gold, but still all say that a hard fisted laboring man can always get from one to 3 oz. pr day." His own experiences with pick and pan illustrated the unevenness of return. "I was digging about 8 feet from 3 men yesterday who took out 20 oz. while I got $1.00." Over his first three days in the diggings, Brown averaged a dollar and a quarter a day.[25]

The new and dominant ingredient was luck. It turned out that mining was a lottery in which success turned on luck as much as any card game turned on a single card, as haphazard as the throw of the dice. In that respect, it was just like the gambling that right-thinking people so deplored. "Gold mining is Nature's great lottery scheme," wrote Dame Shirley from Rich Bar. "A man may work in a claim for many months, and be poorer at the end of the time than when he commenced; or he may 'take out' thousands in a few hours." And Charles Tuttle wrote to his wife, "You are right in saying the mines are a lottery. Some have made their fortunes but by far the greater portion of the miners are poor." He could have included himself in this latter group. And another 49er carried the new analysis of the gold fields a step further by noting that luck was still connected to hard work, but that hard work didn't guarantee luck. "Gold digging is a perfect lottery—if you are lucky you will draw a prize," he wrote, "but you will have to work in water and mud from morning til night. it is no boys play."[26]

The image of mining as a lottery spread widely, filtering from the camps back to the communities in the East. Joseph Pownall wrote of conditions in California from Stockton in the early months of 1850. He began by noting the "abundance" of gold and then continued,

> To get it must needs require not only very hard work but a fair proportion of good luck also, the latter I consider quite essential, for one man may sink a hole in a portion of the diggings and without much trouble take out 1-2-3-4 more ounces of dust daily, while his nearest neighbor, off only a few feet, equally well accoutered with the necessary implements and withal quite as well raised, educated, and good looking must content himself as well as he can with little or next to nothing.[27]

This inconsistency might appear on a single claim in the same place. A claim might pay well, give out, then pay again, and all—at least to the 49ers who worked it—for no explicable reason. Ben Ross arrived in California in 1850, and he had substantial success. Still, the vagaries of mining caused him to comment: "The most I have made in one day since I have been here is $150.00 and we worked the same place three months after and did not make one dime."[28]

Partly a reflection of actual conditions and partly a justification, the image of California as a giant lottery with a few lucky miners holding winning numbers in some measure displaced the image of California as the land where gold lay strewn upon the ground. What is astonishing is the determination of tens of thousands of 49ers to hold on to their lottery tickets as long as possible, whatever the odds, and to play them out to the end. Orrin Bell's fiancée wrote in 1854 that she was anxious to know whether "your ticket (as you call mining a lottery) proved to be a prize or a blank."[29]

Perhaps the most sobering aspect of the change in values of the miners and in the image of California was realization by thousands of hard-working miners that they would have little or nothing for their labor. The first major recognition of this condition was at the onset of winter in late 1849, when an abrupt change in the weather caught almost all miners un-prepared. William Prince watched hard-handed miners straggle into Sacra-mento, "some with moderate means, others with little or none—some well but unlucky, others sick, & others starved out, or unable to support the severities of the climate in the tents & log houses they have erected."[30] These were men who had labored continuously under the most difficult condi-tions and now found themselves destitute at the onset of winter.

Similar observations appeared with increasing frequency in the next year. "I am perfectly astounded to see so few doing well," wrote Seldon Goff after a visit to Placerville. "I had always said these fellows who did not make out much was lazy drinking fellows but it is not so I have seen many a one, who worked as hard as he could not a dry thread on him come night he would look into his rocker to see the result of his days labor and would find about $1.00 when his board would cost him at least $3.00 there is thousands of such cases."[31]

Robert La Mott had a slightly different impression, namely, that the dis-tinction between self-sufficiency and dependency lay in the difference be-tween working for others and working independently. He passed this obser-vation on to his father as part of a continuing attempt to educate his severest critic about conditions in California. "It would astonish you to see, in this golden country the number of poor men that there are—men who when working for wages do well both for themselves & employers, but can never make their expenses when working for themselves," he wrote. "There are hundreds here now, who if they could raise their passage money would put off home & give the country a bad name."[32]

Stephen Jackson's career in the gold fields covered most of the work pat-terns in the first cycle of the Gold Rush. He worked almost everywhere and did almost everything over two years. The first season, he made between five and seven dollars a day with a cradle. Then, he worked for the Ohio Com-pany for six dollars a day until water carried away the company dam. At the end of two years, he saw his prospect of "a pile" receding. He remained convinced that he could "Do Better here than at home.... But California is a Lottery Ticket."[33]

The continuing hardships and growing uncertainty of returns in the gold fields had a different dimension than these qualities did in the farms or shops of the East. Gold mining, unlike other forms of economic activity in the states, produced an immediate return in a negotiable currency. Thus, all miners—even those in the most marginal circumstances—had money in varying sums at some time or another. But they spent their money continuously to meet heavy expenses. And the claims on which they depended might give out at any time. The uncertainty of the mining business, the high costs in the diggings and the heavy expectations at home left almost all 49ers in a state of perpetual anxiety. Income had to be immediately measured against necessary supplies over the months ahead.

Finally came the unsettling news that the 49ers of highest local reputation for honesty and hard work were not always those making substantial sums. The gold dust that made its way to the farms, villages, and cities of the East "was not always dug by the moral Argonauts, from whom the most was expected," observed Prentice Mulford in his account of Sag Harbor. "It was often the gathering of some of the obscurer members of our community," he continued. "Fortune was democratic in her favors." That so much money might be made in the gold fields by selling liquor and gambling offered credible evidence that the most immoral and dishonest might be among the most successful. As opportunities in the gold fields gradually constricted, 49ers took refuge in their honesty and integrity, rather than their ounces of gold. In reflecting on the news of neighbors in the gold fields, more than one Argonaut could write with feeling that he was moral and broke, while others with dissolute habits and immoral economic ventures had become rich.[34] Whether such accounts satisfied their expectant families and friends was an open question.

13

"CAPITALISTS WILL TAKE HOLD":

High-Stakes Investments and Deferred Returns

BY THE CLOSE OF THE mining season in 1850, mining activity ran north and south for one hundred and fifty miles along the Sierra Nevada. It was a frantic scene of work, movement, confusion, and growing numbers. At the same time, mining had begun to take increasingly diverse forms, with a greater emphasis on more complex mining techniques and with a rising sense of competition. These changes marked a second phase of mining activity that began with the season of 1851 and extended for the rest of the decade.

One 49er noted these changes as early as December 1850. "Mining will pay here for some time to come but it will have to be conducted differently than what it now is," he wrote. "I think all of the old mining ground that is now called worked out will yet pay millions of dollars by working them Systematically it will be attended with much hard labor but Capitalists will take hold of it and make money out of it." Capital always had been significant in the gold fields—in purchasing claims, in establishing a store or boarding-house, in lending money at high interest rates, in speculation in real estate in the towns and cities. Now it had become a dominant feature of mining that affected both veteran 49ers and new Argonauts.[1]

The first mining technique that involved a higher investment of capital, the damming of watercourses, had been in use as early as the summer of 1849. The construction of a dam with an alternate watercourse to extract gold from the exposed riverbed was simply an extension of washing the dirt found on the banks and in the shallows. Of course, it was a more complex enterprise, involving larger groups and more capital.

By contrast with wielding the pick and shovel, or agitating the cradle and long tom, building a dam was a complicated, time-consuming, and expensive business. It involved constructing or at least scratching out the alternative watercourse and purchasing building materials, generally lumber, and by the earlier standards of the diggings it was an elaborate construction project. To execute these demands called for larger companies of men and a greater investment of capital, the organization of a large work force, months of labor to prepare for the diversion, and then a frantic period of intense work to dig up the riverbed and wash gravel before the showers in the mountains produced a torrent that washed out the dam.

One Argonaut described such a damming operation, beginning in March 1850, when he joined a company of fourteen "for the purpose of turning the water from the channel of the river" for a distance of two or three hundred yards. If the exercise succeeded—it would occupy the company for several months—"we will make respectable raises this summer." Work would begin immediately, he wrote, and it would be finished about August 1, giving the company four months to mine the two or three hundred yards of riverbed before the winter rains began. The company would have expenses of more than ten thousand dollars before the members of the company harvested a single ounce of gold. He believed that the only chance for success in California lay in mining riverbeds, but the risks were great, "for in order to turn a river men must expend a great amount of labor, the principal part of the year without any income. So all the capital they may have collected last year is exhausted by the time they are ready for digging." The deferred returns of the exercise raised the stakes, for the whole mining season was now telescoped in a single venture whose success or failure defined an entire year.[2]

Of dams themselves, one 49er wrote, "The main dams are made of double walls of rock & filled in with dirt carried from the bank. The smaller dams are made around small sections when the men are at work with sacks filled with sand to keep out the leakage." The building of a double wall of rock is a vivid reminder of the enormous work involved in these projects. After detailed planning and the assembling of materials, men had to carry heavy loads in cold, rushing water for several months—"it requires constant bailing to keep water out so as to allow working the bed"—all in anticipation of a merely prospective return.[3]

This new technique of river mining did not guarantee success; it only ensured that the stakes were higher. "Daming Rivers does not pay," Richard Cowley concluded after working on a scheme to turn the Mokelumne River. "I have had a hand in making three dams on the river," he declared, and "I am certain I never will be one of the party to build the fourth one."[4]

Dams were hostages to weather patterns, for they were vulnerable to flash floods. Few first-person accounts of experiences in the diggings were as dramatic as those that told of a company turned out in the dark of night to save a dam or to save themselves from a rising river. John Eagle wrote his wife of such an occasion in the spring of 1853. His company—"quite a large company"—had invested five thousand dollars and two months' work on a dam. It began to rain just after midnight, and "the miners turned out about 3 o'clock in the morning, and worked hard from that time till night, the water pouring down all the time in torrents, and the men up to their middles in water part of the time." Some members of the company worked "with all their might" to preserve the dam, which was about five hundred yards long; others labored to protect the side ditch, "about the size of the canal, whose banks were giving way every now and again, and the water bursting into our middle ditch, which we were endeavoring to keep dry (this ditch is nearly 1/2 mile in length)." A third "portion of the men" hurriedly cut a canal down the other bank of the ravine to carry off the rising waters. In the end, the company "saved about $1000 of the work."[5] John Fitch wrote that the early rains in the fall of 1850 had torn out his company's dam. "I shall send this by Mr. Carpenter who will give you the particulars of the severe loss we have met with by having our race swept away in a few minutes by a flood," he wrote to his brother. "He can tell you how in fifteen minutes one hundred thousand dollars worth of property was swept away better than I can describe it to you—So I have got to stay here a while longer than I intended to get my pile."[6] Many others, along with Fitch, delayed their returns to their families in the East in order to recapture their initial investments.

The damming of rivers produced a high degree of both mutual dependence and competition among claim holders. Any dams or diversions that changed the level of water in a watercourse had the potential to alter the value of other nearby claims, as we've seen. William Parker and his friends bought a share of what was supposed to be a very rich claim on the Oregon Ripple. Unfortunately, the claim could not be worked "on account of the company below backing the water on them." Parker's company had to wait for the company to finish their business or for the water to fall. This interdependence produced numerous quarrels and elaborate negotiations. The conflicts ultimately needed a judicial mechanism to mediate between the conflicting parties, and where mediation was impossible, to hand down a decision that would be recognized as the force of law.[7]

Damming projects produced a new kind of claim jumping—or dam jumping—in which the aggressors simply took possession of a dam site long enough to destroy the work. The many conflicts and threats over dams led to continuous alliances with other dam-construction companies for purposes of mutual defense. In the spring of 1850, Isaac Barker joined the Beal's Bar Company to turn a portion of the American River. The company's plans turned out to be completely dependent on the Texas Company, which was turning the river just upstream. The Beal's Bar Company voted to help the Texans mend their race and dam and to take action against the Adventurers' wing dam, a competing enterprise. After four weeks of successful mining, their own dam came under assault by representatives of the Fancy Dam Company, who delivered an ultimatum that they would destroy the Beal's Bar dam at eight the following morning. All members of the company turned out "to resist depredations"; the Fancy Dam aggressors failed to appear, and work resumed, soon to be interrupted by the start of the rainy season.[8] The high stakes, the large numbers of miners involved, and the movement of large volumes of water to the advantage of some and the disadvantage of others continued to produce increased tensions and growing conflicts among neighboring companies.

In order to raise capital for their projects, organizers sometimes sold shares to absentee partners, providing an outlet for investment by merchants and other successful miners. This created an elaborate interlocking economic network that might produce high returns for a mining season, or alternately, bankrupt the participants and the merchants who had given them credit. In order to finance the new, more capital-intensive mining techniques, the Argonauts also increasingly took the profits of one year's work in the placers and invested them in next year's dams, risking their hard-earned capital from one year on the vagaries of weather, cooperation, and luck in the next year. John Fitch fell into just such a cycle. In his first two years in the placers, Fitch did well. Emboldened by his early successes, he invested his earnings in damming operations for the following year. As they failed, washed out by sudden quirks in the weather patterns, Fitch confessed to his wife that he had lost in the third year what he had made in the first two.[9]

The factors of increased labor and capitalization associated with river damming had a parallel in quartz mining. The antecedents of quartz mining—the extraction of quartz rock from underground and its processing to washable gravel—dated from the summer months of 1849. In a time ordinarily associated with the pick, shovel, pan, and cradle, quartz veins near Mariposa had attracted the attention of several groups. The opportunities associated with quartz mining—the potential for profits was enormous—generated great interest and demanded substantial investment. Part of the money for investment came from other successful mining ventures. One Argonaut poured part of the profits from a successful damming project of 1851 into quartz claims. For a single share in a quartz mining company at Forbes Town he paid one hundred dollars, plus another hundred and seventy dollars in assessments. Shares in other companies cost as much as eight hundred dollars each. "There is a perfect quartz mania all over the country," he wrote in December 1851. "And it is reasonable to suppose there will be many failures." So there were.[10]

Quartz claims had the financial characteristics of a giant poker game with many players. The initial cost to join the game—the price per share—was often minimal. But the company could levy endless "assessments" against shareholders as a way of continuing to raise capital for exploration, construction, and especially for purchasing the necessary heavy machinery. So the stakes might increase on a regular basis. At some point, the modest investor, even one who had made a substantial "raise" in the placers, might be forced to drop out. Parker did so when the Forbes Town company levied another two-hundred-dollar assessment on his one share.

Yet, the great profits realized by successful operations drew investors into quartz mining with the obsession of a siren's song. Like the promoters of other seeming advances in technology, its practitioners talked in superlatives and wished to be the first to join new ventures, however risky. Jonas Winchester wrote enthusiastically to his wife of the possibilities associated with quartz mining. In the summer of 1851, he spent two weeks in the young town of Grass Valley examining the prospects of the quartz miners. "We have now some good quartz veins but not the capital to put up a mill. Could I effect the latter, I could scarcely fail to make from $100,000 to $500,000 next year," he wrote. "One mill that I saw started last week at Grass Valley took out as result of ten hours work on Tuesday the 22nd of this month *eight pounds of gold*, or over $1700. The profit of that mill will be $2500 for each 24 hours work—or $750,000 in a year! This is no fiction. . . . From the vein at Carson's Creek, famous for its richness, from $700,000 to $1,000,000 have been taken out since December last, less than eight months *this I know to be so*." That Grass Valley and Nevada City, two young towns, had more than twenty quartz mills in operation by the summer of 1851 testified to the widespread development of this form of mining.[11]

Quartz mining and its heavy capitalization through the issuing of shares now opened up mining enterprise to absentee investors on a large scale. Since the first expeditions to the gold fields, local entrepreneurs had invested in neighbors going to look for gold, and those with more capital had sent sons or shipments of goods to California to benefit from the extraordinary returns available there in the first seasons of gold. But investment in the Gold Rush now moved to another level.

The widespread appeal of quartz mining and the heavy capital investment necessary for such enterprise offered people in distant New York or Boston an opportunity to invest in California mining properties. Hastily organized investment companies soon were touting investment opportunities in quartz mines to people in the East. One such entrepreneur wrote of his "good fortune to become deeply involved in the Quartz mines—& you must be aware that this is the only thing now whereby a fortune can be realized in a short time." He had become a partner with two others in the Hansonville Gold and Quartz Mining Company of California. The lengthy title of the company and the enthusiasm of one of its founders disguised the risks associated with quartz mining, which depended on much costly trial and error. One of the partners in the Hansonville Gold and Quartz Company wrote that the company's mill, soon to go into operation, "will pay better than any other investment possibly can." Unfortunately, the company was unable to realize enough returns in its first several months of operation to pay its workingmen, much less to offer dividends to its shareholders. The prospect of repeated assessments to pay debts and recapitalize the company discouraged the present and future shareholders. But quartz mining was the wave of the future, and its promoters were energetically soliciting investors by the fall of 1851.[12]

The spread of quartz mining helped to reshape the opportunities and obstacles that mining presented to ordinary 49ers, those with little or no capital to invest in such operations. The Argonauts who arrived in the 1851 season and thereafter had a different impression of mining than those from the first generation, for they saw the presence of "several large companies" that seemed to dominate the attractive sites in many places. These quartz companies hired "hands" for one hundred dollars a month and found all the labor they needed. The mining experiences of many 49ers of the second generation of immigrants, those who followed in the footsteps of the original Argonauts of the first two years, included both independent work on a claim and wage labor in quartz mines.[13]

In 1853, hydraulic mining spread through the gold camps and bars, developed in response to the dangers of a cave-in from overhanging banks. Miners directed a stream of water under intense pressure against the side of a hill to loosen gravel that was then directed into a series of sluices for washing. Hydraulic mining, like the other new forms, demanded considerable initial investment to dam a stream and bring its water by flume to a site overlooking the hill. Once the investment was made, however, the cost of operation was low, for a single operator could direct a stream of water that would wash out tons of gravel every hour. These could then be washed in customary ways. Hydraulic mining brought about a violent reconfiguration of the California landscape, and it left in its wake vast quantities of waste tailings, scars that remain today.[14]

All these new forms of mining shared a common need: water. The early mining techniques, which began with swiftly flowing water washing gravel in a pan, expanded to include the washing of vast quantities of dirt measured in tons, and the requirement for water grew in like proportion. Mining and water became synonymous. That the 49ers and later observers divided the mining country into "wet" and "dry" diggings—the latter associated with the southern mines, which lacked natural water supplies for most of the year—confirmed this distinction.[15] With the development of river diversion schemes, quartz mining, and hydraulic mining, access to water had become as necessary as gold-rich gravel.

The search for a reliable, continuous, and cheap source of water generated a variety of economic enterprises associated with the second phase of mining. Providing water to miners on a large and small scale in the bars and camps became an auxiliary economic enterprise almost as significant as mining itself. Water companies organized to finance fluming operations that by 1852 and 1853 were of a size comparable to the large mining operations. Enterprising Argonauts built flumes from the high mountain streams to the mining camps. One of these, three thousand feet long and up to thirty-five feet high, produced a handsome return for the three men who built it. Charges for water ranged from one dollar a day for each member of the company up to as much as four or even five dollars a day. One company planned a ditch to carry water from the North Fork of the American River in a parallel line to accommodate two thousand miners. Some of the recently arrived Argonauts found their first employment in California with flume and ditch companies. Ditching and fluming involved many of the same risks as mining: increasingly heavy capitalization, hazards posed by heavy rains and rising waters, and the need to sell on credit to customers. Many miners could afford to pay for their water only at the end of the season, or at the end of a run of luck. On the other side of the ledger, flume and ditch owners sometimes promised water they could not deliver.[16] These companies rapidly became another in a series of new ways to make and to lose money in the second generation of the California Gold Rush.

As mining expanded, both geographically and technologically, the choices available to individual 49ers became more complex. And as opportunities and risks expanded, the miners had to deal with another problem: explaining their options and choices to families and friends who still thought of the American mining experience as a single miner or small group of friends armed with pick, pan, and shovel, depending on strength and character to work a single claim on a watercourse. The California Gold Rush had changed much since its first two years. As it did so, it complicated the lives and relationships of the miners, who wanted a simple and direct way to make money, preferably in a short time, and then return to their homes and families. Like so much else in California, mining proved to be filled with choices and confusions, and the more so beginning in 1851. The impact of new mining patterns was not simply economic; it spread out to include living and working arrangements, expectations of returns, which were sometimes based on promises given and received under the assumption of different conditions, and eventually, changes in plans to return to families in the East.

The continuing annual waves of immigrants into California produced an increasing number of stores, restaurants, boardinghouses, and saloons. One result of this enlarged competition for business was that retail merchants in the camps and bars (though generally not suppliers in San Francisco or Sacramento) increasingly found themselves forced to offer credit to miners. What had started out as a cash business in the flush seasons of 1849 and 1850 became more and more a credit business. Part of the reason was that river mining and quartz mining deferred income to the end of the season. Another was that large numbers of miners did not do well, or to put it another way, did not do well enough to pay cash for their supplies. Mining on credit became increasingly common, and as credit expanded, so did unsettled accounts. The 49er whose claim did not produce a "raise" simply left camp and went to another bar, where he bought "grub on tick until his cr[edit] runs out when he will make tracks again for some other camp."[17] And so 49ers who had undertaken a voyage to California with borrowed money continued this economic cycle of dependence by mining on credit.

Those who found a profitable claim and worked it hard for a season generally paid their debts and often invested the profits in a more elaborate mining scheme for the following season. After all, if good judgment and hard work could generate two thousand dollars in a season, why not bring the same skills to bear in pursuit of greater profits? William Parker made seventeen hundred dollars on a river claim in 1851, and he immediately invested it in quartz claims.[18] Increasingly, large numbers of miners made only subsistence wages or less, and went into debt, while a select group did well but placed their earnings at risk for the following year.

Confronted by changed circumstances across the mining landscape, some 49ers sought relief in rumors of new strikes in distant places, rich claims where hardworking mining men could recapture the euphoria of 1849. Across California, they met other groups pursuing the same fruitless goals. "When we arrived at the diggings, it was all a humbug," read one account in 1852. "I then returned and went to Caliveras County formed a company of 30 for Quartz mining worked all summer and struck nothing (a complete failure) and spent nearly all I had."[19]

Within the mining community, the changed conditions occasioned much comment. One 49er who arrived in California late in 1850 lamented that he was one year too late: "had I got here one year sooner I could have maid some thing but as it is I do not expect to make any thing worth while."[20] It became increasingly common for Argonauts to bemoan that they had not come earlier. All of the best opportunities apparently had accrued to those who had arrived just the previous season.

In 1854, John Kinkade summarized the changes in mining since 1850. In the intervening four years, he wrote,

> All I have managed to make is a comfortable liveing. And that is as much as the mining population can average if not a little more. Mining is now Reduced to a system. What is commonly termed placer diggings being principly exhausted. The miners are seeking in the bowels of the mountains for primitive leads. This is the most uncertain system of mining yet followed. But the miner who is fortunate enough to strike it reeps this immense fortune. If he is not succcessful in finding a leed his only reward is an empty pocket and compleet disgust. Besides a very large amount of personal experience.[21]

Personal experience did not pay debts at the local store, and it did not satisfy the expectations of families and friends in the East.

The changes in mining associated with the second generation of immigrants did not appreciably slow immigration to the gold fields, and knowledgeable observers thought the number of active miners exceeded one hundred thousand by the 1852 season. With growing numbers of miners, new forms of mining that placed an emphasis on credit, and wages declining in response to larger numbers of laborers, working miners worked harder for less. The decline in wages was steep, from twenty dollars a day in 1848, to sixteen dollars a day in 1849, ten dollars a day in 1850, and down by predictable increments to about three dollars a day by 1856. In the summer of 1854, one 49er described most miners as "destitute creatures," and another estimated that wages across the diggings that year were probably in the range of seventy-five dollars per month. Given the cost of supplies and basic necessities, the miners were doing little more than breaking even.[22] At the same time, gold production in California continued to rise, from ten million dollars in 1849, to forty-one million dollars in 1850 and seventy-five million dollars in 1851, peaking at eighty-one million dollars in 1852, after which it gradually declined until 1857, when it leveled off at about forty-five million dollars a year.

ALONZO HUBBARD

In the late winter of 1852, a new wave of gold mania swept across western Massachusetts. Why it should strike this particular rural area three years after the initial surge of emigration to California was not clear, but in its vision of riches and the surge of response in young people, it was a reincarnation of the early winter months of 1849. Among those who succumbed to its renewed blandishments was Alonzo Hubbard of Lee, Massachusetts. At the time he caught the gold fever, Hubbard had worked for two years as a rodman on the Hudson River Valley Railroad Company, a job he recently had lost, and he already had begun his serious courtship of Anna Marie Bassett, who lived with her parents in neighboring Stockbridge.

In response to the continuing allure of California gold and the lack of attractive economic prospects at home, Hubbard and a half-dozen friends began serious planning for an expedition to California. Once there, Hubbard's cohort had many of the same experiences as earlier 49ers: backbreaking repetitive labor, a sense that mining was a lottery beyond rational planning, dangers from disease and accident, and continuing dependence on and support from each other.[23] At the same time, their experiences differed from those of the first generation a scant three years earlier. Whether they traveled by land or by sea, the first 49ers had a long journey, followed by an extended trek into the diggings, then a period of apprenticeship by observation, and finally a period of serious mining with a company, broken by seasonal changes or other occupations. Hubbard's generation was propelled into the mines within six weeks of departing from East Coast ports, found mining possible only through the purchase of expensive claims, often worked for wages by the day or week, and sometimes pursued mining as a sideline, always hoping for a substantial "lead" (as they called it) that would assure the "raise" with which they wished to return home.

By this second generation, the mysteries of travel, preparation, and "outfit" (as the prospective 49ers called it) were common knowledge. The task of raising funds remained. Hubbard and his prospective companions here pursued separate strategies, depending on relatives and potential investors. His closest friend, Downs, was offered the loan of five hundred dollars for the trip with the understanding that he would repay twice that sum on return. After various unsuccessful enquiries, Hubbard went to the bank and borrowed the money. Bank loans for 49ers had become routine, and the future Argonaut could borrow more than enough "by getting good endorsers." Although the task of raising money had, in a sense, become institutionalized, other members of the family and community remained intimately involved through their signatures on the loan application.

The "Californians," as Hubbard and his companions called themselves, held regular meetings to discuss plans and prospects. As he wrote, "Nothing of importance going on save the California enterprise." Hubbard and another "Californian" went to New York City, where they bought eight tickets on the Vanderbilt Line from New York to San Francisco via Panama. The price was one hundred and eighty dollars each for the accommodation of a second-class cabin without berth. Hubbard's return to Lee was a signal for last-minute preparations: purchasing the "outfit" and negotiating with families about the time of departure and the duration of the expedition. As a final act of separation from his family, Hubbard went to a photographer and had his daguerreotype likeness taken.

Hubbard was not entirely candid about the lack of other important things in his life. With his loan from the bank in place and his travel plans complete, he used this four-week interlude to reach an understanding with Anna Marie Bassett that was "highly credible to her and favorable to my wishes." Hubbard and Bassett followed in the tradition of some earlier 49ers and their romantic interests in making quiet arrangements and private commitments. To his journal, Hubbard confided fantasies about the future with his "beloved companion." He also continued to call on her regularly, with the evident approval of her parents. On February 29, he made a last call on Bassett—"a parting scene" he called it—from which he emerged with the declaration that "the hearts united there are bound by the strongest ties of affection. May they never be sundered." For Hubbard, this was a declaration of love, although made only to his journal.

On March 3, 1852, he and his Argonaut companions—they had christened themselves the Berkshire Company—"parted with all at home to leave for California." Although the sentiments on departing were the same as those affecting the original 49ers three years earlier, Hubbard and his 49er friends immediately embarked on a different travel experience. The Argonauts of '52 traveled by railroad from Lee—"took cars at Lee the company in good spirits"—to New York City. The train stopped in Stockbridge, where Hubbard met Bassett on the platform for what was, presumably, a less austere parting. "If words can tell the depths of feeling I cannot write," he confided. "'Tis deeper in the heart."

After passing the night in New York City and visiting the Barnum Museum, the Berkshire Company departed by steamship for California. The trip took thirty-six days and was so routine as to call forth no comment. By 1852, travel to and from California had become commonplace, and the sea voyage by the steamer had become not only the preferred, but also almost the sole route of returning 49ers, with fares ranging as low as one hundred and twenty dollars, and a passage of five to six weeks.

Hubbard's first comment on the gold mania in western Massachusetts was dated January 1, 1852. On April 10, he and his companions reached San Francisco—"the Empire City of the Gold region"—and within three days they had arrived at Bidwell's Bar. Like the first generation of three years earlier, the members of the Berkshire Company now confronted the reality of the diggings: hard work at a wide range of enterprises. Hubbard and his friends immediately discovered that "claims are all too high for us." Offered four claims for one thousand dollars, they tried to buy for two hundred dollars down, but without success. For a week Hubbard hired out for five dollars a day and board. Then, "the boys" bought a claim for five hundred dollars, borrowing two hundred from a friend at 5 percent a month. The company worked hard, and within a week, Hubbard could write, "Hands are very sore cracked with the sun & water." The claim averaged about two dollars a day each, a "very discouraging" return: "Boys getting really disheartened. This is not what we want." From this initial disappointment, prospects improved, and after four weeks of steady work, the company paid off the two-hundred-dollar note.

Four weeks later, Hubbard began work for the Michigan Fluming Company as a carpenter for six dollars a day, and he continued to work for wages through the summer, using his Sundays to wander up and down the river and examine its bars to spy out claims. He sold his interest in the original company claim to his best friend Downs, having "agreed to take $400 by paying $200 if he takes out $500, $300 if $700, $400 if $1000 is taken out." By midfall he had received several letters from home, one of the original Berkshire Company was dead, and "our Piles are not yet made." The Michigan Fluming Company abandoned its river claim, and Hubbard was out his wages, three hundred dollars, and unemployed. Back at mining, he found better claims and more consistent returns at the cost of hard work. His company worked eight hours on Christmas day, taking "out about 5 ounces."

In his reflections at the end of the year, Hubbard called it "the most eventful to me of any that has passed over head." Over the last six months, Hubbard had been "in several places at work but have made nothing. All my enterprises have terminated unproffitable some of the time having to borrow money to purchase my provisions with." The Berkshire Boys had a cabin, and the survivors were still together. Hubbard's end-of-the-year observations did not include a commentary on his relationship with Anna Marie Bassett. He was too focused on the precarious margin of survival in a difficult economic situation.

Hubbard began the new year mining in partnership with the Phillips brothers. He attended a miners' meeting at Indian Bar, where the issue of water rights and, in this case, the transfer of water from one water company to another had replaced the ownership of claims as a central question of miners. The meeting decided against the water company, much to Hubbard's satisfaction. Over several months, Hubbard and others had dug into the side of a hill, timbering the drift as they went. In late April, he abandoned work on the drift "because it was too dangerous." The weekly division of the company continued to average a little more than sixty dollars for each miner, half the return of 1849, but more than satisfactory by the mining standards of 1853.

In June, Hubbard explored the area around Horse Shoe Bend, which he pronounced "the best looking Gold country I have seen." The company bought three claims on North Fork near Horse Shoe Bend and moved there in late June. Hubbard was now in debt again, and in August, he borrowed fifty dollars from his friend Jared Phillips to purchase provisions for the fall. His personal finances were further depleted by illness. In addition to a doctor's bill, he also paid his friend Downs eighty-two dollars to nurse him for three weeks.

Hubbard and Downs purchased a claim in partnership for eight ounces of gold each. After working the claim for four weeks, Hubbard quarreled with his partner, left the claim, took twenty dollars, "went over to the Store and got drunk." He called it "a go ahead spree." He never identified the cause of the breach, but he and other members of the Berkshire Company moved out of the mountains to the vicinity of Marysville, where Hubbard hired out to "two Dutchmen for $3 a day and board."

In midfall, he wrote a long letter to Anna Marie Bassett, summarizing his expectations for the future. Now in California for some eighteen months and apparently approaching the time he had promised to return, he laid out "full and sufficient reasons for remaining this winter." He characterized the letter as written "with much feeling." Awaiting her reply, he settled down to work, hiring water from a company by the day. He also gave twenty dollars to his friend Sweet, "who has been ill and has trouble finding enough to live on." On Christmas Eve, the Berkshire Boys, now down to three, "bought figs, pies, cakes and went to cabin for Christmas Lunch."

At the close of the year, the "boys" went to the district of Minesold, where they found employment in a company's claim that "consists of a heavy lead of gold running in a hill some 500 feet in depth." Hubbard and his friends went to work underground at a depth of eight hundred feet, with timbers every three feet and cars to take out the dirt. He worked the night shift, rising at midnight, and the difficulty of the labor at this depth and the odd hours pressed his physical strength to its limits. Downs went home, but Hubbard continued to work underground, moving to the day shift in March. His tunnel was periodically "closed down by bad air." The high point of his time as an underground miner was the receipt of a valentine from Anna Marie Bassett in late March. By mid-May, he was "lame all over." The prospects of the North Fork Tunnel Company had begun to decline, his own claims had produced little, and Hubbard decided to go home. The "boys" met at Nevada City to say good-bye, and Hubbard took the stage for Sacramento. At Benicia he inquired about employment on railroad construction but received no encouragement. He and Downs bought steerage passage on the *Yankee Blade* for the cheapest rate, one hundred and twenty dollars each.

The day following his arrival in New York harbor, Hubbard stepped down from the "cars" at Lee and walked home, where he was embraced by his whole family. He had been gone two years and three months. He was shocked to note that his father "had grown old and apparently somewhat enfeebled" and pleased that his sister Josephine "had grown out of all expectations and all had changed in some respects." The next day, he went to church: "How Changed! All hastened to greet me but my companions of other days are gone! The younger ones are grown out of memory." He spent the next week enjoying the quiet of his home—"home is still home and its comforts and blessings are rendered doubly dear by absence"—and reestablishing the familiar ties to his family. He was dazed by the speed of the voyage and the many changes at home; he was at a loss how to explain the range of his experiences over almost two years to his family and friends.

Within two weeks, Hubbard received a note from Anna Marie Bassett, asking him to call and to enter into a "conversation on religion matters, ere we assumed a conspicuous position before the public." Hubbard went with a mixture of trepidation and irritation. His concerns turned out to be groundless, for Bassett had simply responded to her parents' wishes. They pronounced Hubbard's religious views, whatever they were, satisfactory. On November 19, Hubbard escorted Bassett to church in Stockbridge, a public declaration of their ties that "excited much curiosity as this is my first public appearance as a suitor of Anna Marie." The whole affair went off well, and Hubbard stayed the evening satisfied that his future happiness was assured. His adjustment now seemed complete, and he rejoiced on his happy return from the uncertainties of the gold fields.

Hubbard's experiences clearly differed from those of the first generation of Argonauts, but they were not the only experiences that typified this difference. People continued to flock to California from all over the country, from the slaveholding South as well as from the Yankee North. As they did in the East before the Civil War, sectional allegiances made a difference in the experience of the second generation of Argonauts as sectional tensions heightened. But there also were similarities.

MASTERS AND SLAVES IN THE GOLD FIELDS

Robert Dickson left his close-knit family in Burke County, North Carolina, to join the California Gold Rush in the fall of 1852. Dickson was joined in the gold fields by at least four slaves and by his cousin, S. M. McDowell, who also took slaves to California. In 1850, California had entered the Union as a free state; however, neither Dickson nor McDowell apparently felt the slightest uneasiness about taking slaves to California. The written accounts they left, together with those of the slaves themselves, testify to the sectional differences that divided the experiences of the second-generation Argonauts as surely as they divided the nation.[24]

The Dickson family was an extensive one. Robert's father, William Dickson, the patriarch of the clan, remained on the plantation, along with the eldest son, William Dickson, Jr. In addition to his mother, Margaret, the correspondence of Robert Dickson identifies at least five daughters and another son. Robert apparently had incurred debts in North Carolina, and he had undertaken the voyage to California to make money to pay these obligations and, equally important, to establish his credibility as a responsible member of the family. Whenever possible, he sent drafts to his father to pay his obligations. His letters to his sister, his principal correspondent, were affectionate and filled with family pride and longing to be reunited with them in North Carolina. As mining prospects diminished over the four years from 1852 through 1855, he remained optimistic, sanguine that he would retrieve his financial standing and continue to hold his family's respect and love.

Robert Dickson was in close touch with other "gentlemen" from his North Carolina neighborhood in the mines around Woods Diggings. When he recited the health of friends "from home," he was careful to make distinctions important to him and presumably to his audience. In addition to S. M. McDowell, he wrote of J. C. Tate ("he is verry Mutch of a gentleman") and W. A. Collett ("he is one of my particular friends. I consider him a perfect gentleman"). When "Mr. Marquis" became ill, Dickson sat with him at night for two weeks before he died. The weather was cold and rainy, but Dickson did not shirk what he regarded as his duty, and he never considered presenting a bill for his services. Presumably "gentlemen" had a code among themselves that provided for such mutual care. When S. M. McDowell wrote, he was careful to send his "respects" to a wide array of "friends in the old North State," including Colonel Davenport, General Patterson, Colonel Lenoir, and their wives, along with a range of cousins. Military titles were clearly something to be treated with respect in North Carolina.[25]

Robert Dickson took a certain male (and perhaps Southern) pride in his ability to adapt to life in the outdoors and to accept primitive living conditions and diet. "People in North Carolina think they live very hard when they have nothing to eat but Corn bread and Bacon Milk Butter Chickens Eggs and Vegetables of all kinds and someone to cook them for them," he wrote. "What would they think if they had nothing to eat but barley and potatoes and none to cook for them but themself." Like 49ers accustomed to cooks and house servants, Dickson thought himself and others like him distinctly deprived, and he wanted everyone to understand that he accepted such conditions in a good spirit. Presumably "gentlemen" adjusted themselves to life in the gold camps with casual good humor.[26]

In late fall 1852, Robert and his slaves began work in Woods Diggings. He reported that his claim paid from between four and seven dollars a day per hand, but he had to pay one dollar a day for each worker to the water company. Dickson had an interest in five other claims about four miles away on Montezuma Flat. When the claim in Woods proved less productive than he had hoped, he hired out his slaves for seventy-five dollars a month each, or three hundred dollars a month for the four.[27]

S. M. McDowell wrote a series of letters to Robert's family ("My Dear Uncle, Aunt, & Cousins Isabella, Elizabeth, Mary, Anne & Caroline") in which he described the nature of the mining enterprise and the society around them. McDowell pronounced himself disappointed with mining prospects in California. "I cannot clear more than one fifth as much as I expected when I left home," he wrote, "Still there is much more money here than there is in North Carolina, and notwithstanding all the high expenses in this country much more money can be made here, I think, than at home." And, he added, "much more will be spent." Although mining was the "principal employment in this section of the country," many 49ers worked elsewhere. "Merchandising" continued to be a good business, but the severity of the winter and the size of inventories led to substantial variations in profit.

As for society, McDowell thought the Gold Rush brought together "a 'heterogeneous comminglement' of living souls" the like of which he had never seen before or even imagined. He continued:

> We have the English, Irish, Germans, Frenchmen, Welchmen, Italians, Portugese, P. Islanders, Spaniards, Chinese, Chileans, East Indianmen West Indianmen. The Greaser Mexican negroes & Indians and in short from persons from almost all civilized part of earth, judging from their acts, some from the uncivilized portions. But among such a population I am proud to know that there are some noble spirits.

McDowell judged that the "morals of the country are bad." "Piety is almost unknown," he continued. "Gambling and various kinds of dissipation are going on constantly. but Sunday is the principal day for it." Some excellent young men of "judgement, health, and enterprise" had done well and might continue to do well, but most of the miners "work long and hard for moderate wages." The opportunities for wealth in California, he concluded, were "fluctuating and uncertain." It was a guarded assessment, emphasizing equally the moral character of 49ers and the mixed economic opportunities that awaited them—and him.[28]

In spite of his mixed feelings about opportunity in California, McDowell had a run of very good luck. His slaves ("his boys") made a "raise" and "made him some fifteen hundred or eighteen hundred Dollars" over three weeks. Lagan and Lawson were the most productive of the slaves, and he singled them out by name for praise in a letter, although there is no evidence they were further rewarded. The assumption among most Southerners was simply that the master owned the slaves and so owned the product of the slaves' labor, whether cotton, rice, corn, or gold.[29]

McDowell took his money and returned to North Carolina, where, Dickson wrote, he could "describe Cal. just as it is and will do so." Dickson stayed on with his slave John. From the opening of the family correspondence, John had occupied a prominent place in every letter from Robert

Dickson to his family. John's health, varied occupations, earnings, and good wishes to the family were all noted. John often sent his love to his mother, and he asked for the plantation slaves to write letters to him, for "all the Negros gets letters from home but him." Robert Dickson also closed his letters by sending "howdys" to the "Black ones."

Beginning in the spring of 1853, times became hard for Robert Dickson and John. Sometimes Dickson thought he was unlucky; at other times, he continued to have hopes for the future. By the spring of 1854, he was prospecting more than mining, testing from eight to ten claims a week, making wages or less on all of them. Dickson finally concluded he must try something other than mining, a transition that would offer more security but less chance of making a substantial sum. His luck did not improve and instead took a turn for the worse in April 1855, when he was found murdered in his cabin. In the style of so many 49ers, close friends—in this case a cousin—took care of the estate, which was encumbered by debts and scarcely large enough to pay the expenses of a burial.[30]

When S. M. McDowell returned to North Carolina, he left slaves in California to continue mining operations. A group of letters passed between masters and mistresses on the plantation and slaves on the watercourses of the Sierra regarding instructions for their disposition of money. Should the slaves send the gold dust by the usual bank draft, or should they exchange the dust for paper money and bring the money east when they returned? The author of the letter also instructed his wife to bring the children up with proper manners to be "Smart and obedient and alow them to Sauce no person." In addition to greetings, slaves, like their free counterparts, always closed their letters with a request for more mail.[31]

Albert McDowell, apparently S. M. McDowell's servant, mined near Jamestown for two years after his master returned to North Carolina. In May 1855, he wrote to ask permission to remain in the gold fields for another year. He thought he could make four or five hundred dollars in that time "if God Gives me Health," money that he would then remit to his master. Albert McDowell had sent four hundred dollars to his master the previous year, making a total of nine hundred and fifty dollars "since Master Samuel left for home." Albert also forwarded two hundred dollars to his wife, apparently part of an arrangement under which he would remit the largest portion of his earnings to his master but retain a portion of them. With earnings for the year (presumably after expenses) calculated at six hundred dollars, Albert McDowell kept one-third for his wife. This was a substantial sum, but so was the larger amount that he forwarded to Samuel McDowell. Albert McDowell surely enjoyed the degree of independence he found in the mines. The presence of various members of the Dickson/McDowell families in the neighborhood probably offered him some amount of protection, and the continued presence of his wife on the plantation in North Carolina ensured his return.[32]

The Dickson and McDowell families and their activities in California thus had a distinct sectional tinge. Their modes of address were different, and the impression persists of a powerful family force in the presence of an absent but influential patriarch and matriarch who exercised great and unquestioned authority over decisions relative to the family. Furthermore, the sense of their own separate identity in California anticipated by a decade the creation of a Southern nation. But in mining itself and in their approaches to opportunities to make money, Robert Dickson and S. M. McDowell were simply two more 49ers intent on seizing the golden prospects offered by California.

Where their money-making activities differed from those of most 49ers was in their use of African-American slave labor. However, their slaves had a degree of independence in their work unusual for the institution of slavery, but appropriate to the gold fields. Mining involved a repetitive work routine in search of incremental bits of wealth, and only the most rigid supervision could ensure absolute honesty, suggesting that what seems to have been the arrangements these slaveholders pursued, trust and an agreement to share a portion of the returns, were probably the best for effective use of slave labor. Or perhaps the white Southerners had great confidence in the fidelity of their black property. The financial arrangements also suggested a strong degree of incentive for the slave labor of this particular extended family.

14

THREATS FROM WITHIN,
THREATS FROM WITHOUT:

Fear, Hostility, and Violence in the Gold Rush

THE CHANGES IN MINING had immediate effects on the lives of the 49ers. The decreased return on their labor in the mines was often merely sufficient to keep them at work, as we have seen. Throughout California, the daily wage was down and competition was on the increase in all forms of enterprise. The first generation of 49ers had suffered from the disparity between the hopes and dreams that had brought them to California and the realities of the gold fields. With the arrival of the second generation, opportunity seemed to have been reduced even further. Yet every community had its stories about the returned 49er laden with gold dust or bank notes. Sometimes, the Argonauts actually knew men who had found the fortunate "raise" that produced thousands of dollars in dust instead of hundreds. Perhaps it had even happened to them for a brief period. Nevertheless, large-scale success in gold mining for most remained elusive. Good claims gave out; new claims were hard to find, expensive to purchase, and increasingly difficult to hold. Now, as before, costs were high, physical conditions harsh, and the work arduous. But the new mining techniques seemed to diminish the importance of the individual or the small group. With large numbers of miners now everywhere in the gold fields, there was a growing sense that time was running out to make something important of this venture.

The 49ers once again had to respond to the dashing of their hopes and the closing off of their prospects. How might their diminished prospects be explained? How could the rapidly changing realities of the gold fields be squared with their visions of wealth for themselves and for their families?

With these queries came a series of parallel questions about values. Had the 49er become a slave to the goddess of gold? Had he turned his back on the Christian values so widely supported by mid-nineteenth-century American Protestantism? Had he betrayed the support, trust, and confidence of his family by going to California? Had he turned his back on his responsibilities at home, after having asked his family to make considerable sacrifice, financial and emotional, to support this search for a golden future? Not even the endless declarations that 49ers worked not for themselves, but for their families could support the weight of the changing reality of their mining experiences.

These questions went to the heart of the 49ers' sense of personal and group identity. Who were they, anyway? What did they stand for? What kind of people had they become in their months and years of toil in California? Initially, many Argonauts had celebrated their identification with other hard-handed men of similar dress and habits. Although under the mining uniform they all wore lay great variations in class and origin, the division between working miners and others in service occupations, especially those who profited from the hard labor of miners, had been a powerful one in the minds of many 49ers. In the first years, in 1849 and 1850, the distinction between the working miner and a storekeeper, boardinghouse owner, or gambler was a clear one, especially in the eyes of the miners, who spoke with universal disdain of those in the entertainment business and even the professions, since the services of doctors and lawyers had cost the miners many a hard-earned ounce.

In these later years, this distinction became blurred as the mining experience changed. As the placer diggings on the streams gave out and men turned to more capital-intensive exercises in damming and quartz mining, the purity of the contrast between working miners and capitalists gave way to degrees of difference. Miners—or some of them, at least—had become capitalists, investing their money in dams or quartz mines. Others had drifted into the service industries, opening stores or boardinghouses or restaurants. Many had become part of the entertainment industry they professed to disdain, investing or working in saloons, bowling alleys, and worse. As too often happens when groups feel threatened with respect to their identities, many of the 49ers responded not with introspection and philosophy, but with fear and hostility directed against both others like them and those they saw as different. And often, fear and hostility turned to violence.

With the rising anxieties over economic prospects and over personal and group identities in the middle years of the decade came a change in the relationships of individuals to one another and in the temperament of the camps and the several mining societies. What took place was a gradual unraveling of the consensus of rules of behavior that characterized the first mining seasons, when 49ers could hold claims by leaving a set of tools in a hole in the ground, when they could leave their tents unattended, and when strangers returned missing wallets and horses to their owners. Now, men perceived a widespread rise in crime and in violence, and they lamented the absence of institutions of government that would impose order on the mining societies of California. Jacob Engle described a series of robberies and murders to his brother from Rough & Ready in 1852 and noted that "these things is quite common in this Country."[1] Whether crime was on the rise or not, the 49ers increasingly felt threatened by it.

Nothing symbolized the threats felt by the individual 49er more vividly than claim jumping. Alexander Barrington described with considerable satisfaction how he faced down "an Irishman" who tried to "jump" his claim. Later, with his company, he himself "jumped" a claim, after "fuss with owners and another *jumper* We were *victorious* at last!" His notations suggest no special sense of shame at taking another claim by force. The days of a claim securely held by a shovel had passed. For miners to work together as a group now had another rationale beyond simply efficiency; it was a form of mutual protection and solidarity against a world perceived as increasingly hostile.[2] "It is difficult to get claims and there is considerable dispute in consequence," noted Lafayette Fish in his journal.[3] James Rice wrote to his brother, "There is some gold diggings in this Neighborhood but they are badly crowded." He went on to note that the "Sheriff" had called out a local "force" in order to "put a man in possession of his gold diggings."[4]

Robberies and assault also seemed to be on the rise. Many thought the increase in criminal activity was directly related to what they perceived as the decline in opportunity. "These depredations & murders appear to be increasing," wrote William Parker in his diary. "It must be so where the facilities for obtaining money are so uncertain. Many are out of money having spent their time & money all summer on worthless river claims."[5]

Robberies from tents became increasingly common. Furnishings (such as they were) and clothes had marginal value, although their theft could occasion some inconvenience. What was more important was the individual miner's cache of gold. Its vulnerability brought home the vulnerability of every individual miner. Each had to make arrangements for his own gold dust. He might carry the gold on his person and risk losing it even while at work, often in the rushing water that had deposited it in the first place. He also could try to hide it in the tent or cabin, or bury it. To lose his hard-earned gold by robbery was a devastating blow to a miner. Isaac Barker had his purse stolen from the tent. "My hopes are all destroyed," he wrote. Days later, he wrote, he was "still brooding on my loss."[6] This sense of loss in a life of grueling work, thwarted hopes, and the ever-present possibility that one's claim, one's residence, one's possessions might be transgressed and appropriated by others helps to explain the anger toward thieves and the harsh punishments meted out to them in the gold fields.

The 49ers generally approved of vigilante justice, or "lynch law," as they referred to it. As a form of law enforcement, it was quick in execution, democratic in form, and, above all, inexpensive. Argonauts had come to California and the gold fields to acquire wealth, not to build institutions or participate in democratic exercises. They accepted their participation as necessary to the preservation of civil order, of course, but most of them did no more than was necessary to meet minimal requirements of order and safety for persons and property.

Most disputes over claim jumping were settled without recourse to public officials. The parties simply faced off in personal confrontation until one gave up. In case a thief was caught, the camp held a brief trial before a jury of miners. If the defendant was found guilty, the camp tribunal immediately carried out the sentence, which was always physical punishment. This continued a long-established frontier tradition that sought quick justice and punishment without incarceration in order to keep the tax rate low. Alexander Barrington witnessed the execution of such a sentence within a month of his arrival in the mines. "*Horrible* scene, 25 lashes on man's back for stealing a horse," he wrote. "How the poor fellow begged!"[7]

Israel Lord, the Methodist missionary who tried without much success, by his own admission, to turn miners from the gold of this world to the spiritual concerns of the next, wrote often of the informal meetings that dispensed justice in the camps. In January 1850, he noted "an assault committed on a man of the name of Nichols in his own 'diggings.'" He continued, "After dark went down and found that a number of persons had convened, elected a magistrate and constable, and adjourned to Colonel Hamilton's house." Lord went to the house, which he found "jammed" with miners from the diggings. While the jury deliberated the fate of the man charged, the body as a whole considered a resolution "on the subject of claims" to be presented to the next meeting on Saturday evening. As for the trial itself, it "was conducted with the best kind of feeling, the only aim being to establish the truth, and do justice to all. There were no lawyers to delay—no petty technicalities to obstruct the course of justice."[8]

That some kind of collective organization was necessary to protect individuals and their property from theft and violence was understood, but it should be simple and quick. At the same time, it should also be democratic. Consequently, miners organized themselves around bars or camps, and the mining population, called together, enacted local ordinances to preserve order, to resolve disputes over claims, and to establish a kind of rough and inexpensive justice.

A few leaders, perhaps those with experience in other bars or camps, would call for an organizational meeting. Notices would go up on trees and on stakes, men would pass the message from campsite to campsite. The organizational meeting would adopt ordinances for the preservation of claims and social order. It was a kind of pure democracy. All those who chose to be present could speak and vote. The ordinances enacted were similar in dealing with theft, assault, bodily injury, arson, and so forth. This exercise was at once a serious and a temporary one. It was serious in the sense that miners needed—indeed even demanded—the structure it provided. But it was also temporary because this was a transient population. Those who voted in the evening could have departed by next morning. And if the gold-bearing gravel gave out, the whole bar might be deserted in a week. Still, most miners were aware of the arrangements and probably welcomed them. They recorded the meetings and their own attendance with a sense of satisfaction.[9] In their private statements to journals and diaries and in their letters to their families and friends, the Argonauts took a degree of pride in standing up for universal standards of behavior amid the threatening chaos of the gold fields.

XENOPHOBIA

In this new framework for living and working, the Argonauts increasingly directed their collective hostility against outsiders, that is to say, those of foreign extraction. Whatever their fundamental differences, whatever forces were working to put their individual sense of identity and self-worth into question, and however they saw each other as threats to their individual well-being, Americans could unite in the interest of preserving the best mining areas for themselves. However unsure of themselves the Argonauts had become, they still could define themselves against others different from them and take out their frustrations on these victims.

California and its Gold Rush brought together the most diverse societies in the nation, and probably in the world. The summer of 1848 found the mining camps on the gold-bearing streams of the Sierra peopled by Californios digging side by side with their former servants. Slightly further downstream or upstream were groups of Indian peoples—some employed by large-scale entrepreneurs and others mining independently for themselves. These were soon joined by American deserters from the United States Army of occupation and Hawaiian Islanders (called "Kanakas" by the Americans) recently arrived by sea from their islands. In what would soon become known as the southern mines, a growing number of Mexican families had come from Sonora in response to the rumors of gold. These varied peoples already were in place by the time the first ships filled with Americans arrived in San Francisco Bay, and they were the veteran miners of the placers when the first of the overland wagon trains rolled into Placerville in the early autumn of 1849.

These groups, now supplemented by a flood of Americans throughout the first nine months of 1849, were soon joined by peoples from all over the world. The universal language of gold spoke in loud and appealing tones in European and Asian languages. Most of these distant Argonauts came by ship. Even by the autumn of 1849, the Americans arriving in San Francisco marveled at the wide range of peoples from all over the world to be met on the streets of that port.

The immigrants from the eastern United States brought Manifest Destiny to the gold fields, and with it all the term implied for the superiority of white, Anglo-Saxon, Protestant peoples. As we have seen, one of the things that made gold mining a unique economic enterprise was that location was crucial. Someone mining in a particular spot might be rewarded with extraordinary wealth, while miners of equal character and work habits, who labored only a few feet away, might realize little or nothing for their efforts. Americans, already schooled in their superiority, found that the doctrine of their predestined success had practical applications in the gold fields. Although they were not, initially at least, the best miners, they learned from Mexicans, added the experience of a few Georgians and North Carolinians, and soon proclaimed themselves "lords and masters" of the best mining sites.

The instincts fostered through this ideology received added impetus from the rumors that plagued the gold fields, stories of new rich strikes mixed with outrageous conduct of "outsiders," and the more so if such outrages were economic in nature and directed against Americans. These threads were brought together in the pronouncements of General Persifor Smith, bound for California to take command of the American Army. Bombarded by rumors of the large numbers of Latin Americans already arrived in the gold fields by January 1849, Smith, while waiting in Panama, thought these rumors confirmed in the news that the long-awaited steamer *California* had on board numbers of Latin Americans, and that these "greasers" were taking up places that should rightfully go to waiting Americans. Confronted by this presumed outrage and threats of violence, General Smith wrote a letter that seemed to give official sanction to barring foreigners from the gold fields. His letter read, in part: "As nothing can be more unjust and immeasurable than for persons not citizens of the United States... to dig the gold found in California, on lands belonging to the American Government, and as such conduct is in direct violation of the laws, it will be my duty immediately upon arrival there, to put these laws in force to prevent any infraction there."[10] Prospective gold seekers in Peru, Chile, and Mexico found these principles in violation of the earlier pronouncements of Governor Mason that gold might be dug freely by all on the sites. To those Americans in contact with foreign peoples and in any way inconvenienced or economically threatened by them, however, General Smith's statement seemed to stamp with official approval the idea that mining on American soil was reserved for Americans only. It was a doctrine that appeared early in the Gold Rush and eventually expanded to be used against foreign miners from around the world. Those who lived in California in 1848 and foreign peoples who came to California in response to the gold discoveries found themselves under siege from the Americans who were to come in such overwhelming numbers.

This included the original inhabitants of the landscape that became the sites of the California Gold Rush—the California Indians. These Indian peoples already had suffered through a century of European intrusion into their lives. Many of them had been channeled into missions under the Spanish colonial empire. With the independence of Mexico, the subsequent breakup of the mission system, and the confusion attending the war between the United States and Mexico, the California Indians tried to preserve their own worlds by retreating to the remote mountains and the still sparsely settled coastline and interior valleys. This separateness largely vanished with the intrusion of a hundred thousand Americans, Mexicans, Europeans, and South Americans in 1849 in pursuit of gold. The gold seekers invaded the remote fastnesses of the Sierra in search of the yellow metal, bursting into the most distant sanctuaries and hiding places of the Indian peoples. With the recognition of its sovereignty under the Treaty of Guadalupe Hidalgo, the American government made no effort to expel these trespassing Argonauts from this land or even to control them. They had come in numbers too large to be dissuaded by official proclamations. As the Indians responded to trespass and coercion with violence of their own, they became the universal target of all groups in the California gold fields. Rumors of Indian depredations drew together varied miners into groups for reprisals. As the economic conditions of the native peoples worsened, so did the level of animosity against them.[11]

Whatever the fears of miners about their hostility, native peoples were in fact an increasingly distant threat. By the close of the mining season in the late fall of 1849, they largely had disappeared from the gold camps, and the influx of gold seekers (many of them also hunters) had devastated their fragile economic base. In the winter of 1849–50, an especially severe and early winter, many native groups were hungry and on the edge of starvation. Their isolated raids in search of subsistence aroused the fury of the Americans, intent on seeking gold and now spending the winter in remote regions. In response to the perceived threat and occasional attacks over the winter, the American miners organized a series of raids against Indian groups in the mountains. The most vigorous operations took place in the late fall and winter, coinciding with severe Indian needs on the one side and idleness of the miners on the other. One 49er observed of the deliberations that led to these raids that the drunken miners always voted for war, while the sober ones wanted peace. Although the Sacramento *Transcript* and other Sacramento newspapers vigorously supported such expeditions, other newspapers and miners thought such activities were promoted by Sacramento merchants to profit by outfitting the paramilitary expeditions.[12]

The arriving waves of Americans soon found new objects of hostility in foreign miners competing for the best claims. By the fall of 1849 and the arrival of the first large-scale immigrations by land and sea into California, the placers were filling up with thousands of miners, many from distant countries, and the San Francisco *Alta California* already had noted the appearance of a sentiment that the mines were destined for Americans only.[13]

The Mexicans—often called "Sonorans" by Americans because of the province of origin—were the first targets. As early as August 1849, one Argonaut wrote from the Mokelumne River, "We found ourselves surrounded by all nations and Mexicans as far up and down the river as the eye could reach."[14] Like the Anglo-Americans, the Mexicans treated mining as a seasonal exercise, returning to their homes at the close of the season in the late fall. They were concentrated in the southern mines, and their urban center was Stockton. One 49er noted that in Stockton as much Spanish as English could be heard on the streets.[15]

By 1850, Americans in the southern mines had begun systematic attempts to remove the Mexican miners. One Argonaut wrote in July 1850, "A strong feeling of hostility now exists between the American and Mexican populations." This hostility was probably an inevitable outgrowth of American cultural xenophobia, which flourished in the dual contexts of increasing competition for the best claims and the perceived threats to the 49ers' self-identities and self-interests. To these considerable economic and psychological influences should be added the powerful emotions generated by the recent war, a conflict with carefully orchestrated accounts of barbarous conduct, Catholic conspiracies, and cultural inferiority. Accounts continued to circulate widely of the unjust seizure of rich American claims by Mexican nationals, for which the only appropriate response was to take them back.[16]

Within the first year, these early Mexican arrivals had been joined by substantial numbers of Chileans, Peruvians, French, British (especially Scotch and Welsh), and Hawaiian Islanders. By 1851, the Chinese and Australians had arrived in noticeable numbers. Animosity against foreign miners rose in proportion to the number of both Americans and foreigners and the pressure on the streams for good claims.

The Chileans and Peruvians had arrived early in California, in February 1849. The Chileans were especially attracted to the commercial possibilities of the Gold Rush, and leading Chilean merchants immediately established commission houses in San Francisco. Many of the Peruvians were experienced miners, for Peru had been the site of silver mining for two hundred years around the great city of Potosí. Their skill in mining proved no safeguard against the growing hostility of American miners. As General Smith's proclamation against foreign miners circulated, feelings rose against Chileans, already present in numbers in the gold fields. The sparks that inflamed the Americans into action were Fourth of July orations, extolling the patriots of the Revolution and their triumphs over the invaders from Europe. Armed bands attacked several Chilean camps and drove Chilean miners out of the placers toward San Francisco. The furious Chilean miners arrived in the City on the Bay in a tense atmosphere. Anti-Chilean riots broke out in San Francisco in mid-July, fueled by arriving miners of both nationalities, a criminal element that used the cloak of law enforcement in a town without legal mechanisms, and jealousy of Chilean commercial successes. The principal victims were the many well-to-do Chilean merchants, already doing a thriving business, and others who had established profitable service industries, especially in unloading arriving ships. It was a violent outbreak, with death, destruction, looting, and public auctions by the criminals of the goods of the victims. Although a public meeting the next day deplored the events of the previous night and tried many of the perpetrators, it was a troubling example of the appeal of xenophobia. The first outbreaks against foreigners thus already had taken place when the vanguard of the overland 49ers poured into the diggings in autumn. Another noteworthy feature of this violence was that it did not noticeably dim the excitement in Chile over California gold or slow the rush of Chileans toward the placers or the shipment of portable houses and agricultural staples from Chile to San Francisco.[17]

Another clash in December 1849 pitted Chilean miners against arriving North Americans in the diggings outside Stockton. There, the Yankees sought to expel Chileans from their claims in the "dry diggings" by the traditional expedient of organizing a mining district and establishing a code of laws that prohibited Chileans from holding claims. In a conflict further confused by various judges, a night fight led to deaths on both sides, and the Chileans were eventually overwhelmed, arrested, tried, and some of them summarily executed.[18] The pressure of growing numbers, confined by the changing season to a smaller place, had produced a rapidly organized assault on and removal of Chilean miners as foreigners who held claims believed to belong to Americans. This appropriation of others' property—with foreign miners given notice to vacate their claims and those who resisted removed by force—would become something of a model for assaults against foreign miners. It differed markedly from the San Francisco riot. In San Francisco, an absence of law-enforcement institutions produced a riot against foreigners from which there was little or no appeal. In the placers outside Stockton, the two sides each appealed to different legal traditions, the one to the established mechanisms of local government left over from Mexican authority, the other to an honored American frontier tradition in which those present organized themselves into a sovereign body and made and enforced their own laws.[19]

John Hovey of Newburyport, Massachusetts, participated in a number of the organized activities against foreign miners. As early as the middle of November 1849, Hovey noted the presence of large numbers of Mexican miners along the Calaveras River. In mid-December, Hovey wrote, "We had orders from the Alcalde to turn out armed and equipped as the law directs for military duty." The "duty" was to round up some one hundred Mexicans. The members of the vigilante group did their duty and marched the prisoners to the Iowa Bar log cabins, where a local "judge" fined the Mexican miners one ounce of gold each. Hovey and others received a share of the fine for their work.

Two days later, Hovey reported trouble with Chileans, and within a week, the threat of armed conflict with the Chileans led the alcalde to call the local miners into action once again. This time the charge against a group of Chilean miners was murder. Sixteen Chileans were arrested, confined, and quickly tried under rules established by a miners' court. A jury of Americans found them guilty, and they were summarily executed. As a precaution, the alcalde swore in another fifty Americans to take the remainder of the Chileans into custody. The American miners now seized the personal belongings and claims of the dead men; they then auctioned the confiscated items. As a final note, the court appointed a guardian for the surviving six-year-old son of one of the men executed. The next morning, the American miners were back at work on the watercourses, although not without reflections on what had taken place in the previous week: "no one feels like doing any thing." Hovey wrote that the mining district required a "code of just laws," although he did not make a judgment about the relationship of such a code to the events that recently had taken place.[20]

Each of these foreign groups shared common characteristics: they did not speak English, they tended to remain together, and their cultural and ethnic differences were highly visible. As these groups became islands surrounded by an American sea, they increasingly came under attack. Among the most determinedly different and committed to remaining so were the French. The news of the discovery of gold in California, originally greeted with skepticism in France as it was along the East Coast of America, was soon accepted as genuine and aroused wild enthusiasm. To a France divided over the failure of the Revolution of 1848 and mired in an economic depression, the news of gold available to everyone who would go to California was a call to renewal and adventure. More than eighty societies and companies organized within the year to carry passengers to the mines, engage in trade, or in other ways exploit the gold discoveries. Entrepreneurial schemes ranged from prefabricated houses to plans for construction of hotels on the West Coast. In response to this enthusiasm, perhaps as many as thirty thousand French people went to California between 1849 and 1852. There, they lived in self-contained communities, kept to themselves, and vigorously maintained their own language and culture. American miners commented on the loud singing and celebrating of the French on holiday occasions.[21]

The 49ers reported conflicts with the French in early 1850, sparked by the rumor that the French had driven Americans from especially choice mining claims. The French seem to have been singled out among the Europeans, perhaps because of their rich claims, their numbers, their clannish nature, their vigorous defense of their rights, and their complaints over ill treatment. In response to the customary American assertion of sovereignty by a mass meeting, the French resisted loss of their claims and appealed to their consul in San Francisco for support. The arrival of the *Garde Mobile,* a paramilitary force of volunteers used to repress street riots in 1848 and now sent into involuntary exile, further inflamed relations between the two groups. The Americans ultimately prevailed against the French, as they vanquished every group in the diggings.[22]

The upheavals that plagued Ireland, notably the great famine of the late 1840s, propelled tens of thousands of Irish to North America, and some of these families responded to the opportunities associated with gold in California. Michael and Mary McGuire arrived in Philadelphia, Pennsylvania, in early 1848 and bought a farm outside of the city. When President James K. Polk confirmed the gold discoveries in California in early December, Michael took passage with a cargo of pick heads and shovel blades, leaving Mary to manage the farm. In California, he disposed of his cargo and joined the rush to the placers. There, he prospered, and after eight months in the mines, he returned to Philadelphia for his wife and new son, born during his absence in California. In the spring of 1850, the united McGuire family returned to the West Coast.[23]

A substantial number of Irish came from Australia. The Australian contingent included Irish nationalists, convicted and transported, who escaped to California. The Australian rush for California gold also numbered many merchants, whose favorite cargoes were rum, biscuits, and kegs of beef. These were joined by a strong contingent of the sons of prosperous sheep grazers, a few with black or Chinese servants. Arrived in the booming cosmopolitan town of San Francisco in the summer and fall of 1849, the Australians fanned out into the diggings. There, they found the Americans—arriving in waves from the first of the overland migrations—numerically dominant and already beginning to make noises about their rights. Although the Australians were pleased by the American habits of informality and helpfulness, and amused by the American custom of constantly shaking hands and chewing tobacco on all occasions and in all settings, they were less pleased by the American miners' habit of organizing themselves into a sovereign body and making whatever rules they liked. Perhaps the Australians already instinctively sensed that these regulations might be used against all noncitizens, including Australians. Already in the winter of 1849–50, the Americans had begun their assaults on Latin Americans' claims. Within a year, Australians had been tarred with a reputation as convicts sent to California from English jails, and they had become favorite targets of American vigilante movements, especially within San Francisco itself. The charge that Sydney criminals had set a major fire in San Francisco created a charged atmosphere in which Australians often were immediate suspects.[24]

The most culturally distinctive of those who came to California were the Chinese, who became the final target of hostility toward foreigners. Some 49ers reported the Chinese presence as early as March 1851, but the large groups came in 1852. Initially, at least, the Americans found the Chinese curious and nonthreatening. American miners often visited a Chinese camp on Sundays as a form of recreation. Their sharp contrasts in physical appearance, language, and customs made them immediate objects of interest and comment. William Parker first encountered Chinese in numbers on a Sunday in June of 1852 in the vicinity of Orphir. "Saw a large number of Chinese at work on both sides of the river," he wrote. "I suppose they knew nothing about the observance of Sunday. Indeed, it would be strange if the worshipper of Budda should recognize a Christian custom. I told them of the impropriety of their course but they looked at me a moment with a grin, then at one another and finally resumed their work, leaving me to preach at my leisure."[25]

Perhaps as many as twenty-five thousand Chinese arrived in San Francisco in 1852, by which time the golden era of an ounce a day in the mines was long past, and mining was simply hard work with small returns for most miners. The Chinese initially took over the exhausted claims of the Americans and French and worked them for meager yields. Their distinctive appearance, cultural separateness, and cohesion gradually made them targets for outbursts of antiforeign sentiment, which turned into anti-Chinese sentiment as other foreign groups disappeared and left the Chinese as the sole targets of American xenophobia. One 49er, who observed Chinese in the mines in May 1852, predicted that they would soon be "driven out" by the American miners. He was right.[26]

The rise of antiforeign sentiment and the admission of California into the union led to state laws against foreign miners. In April 1850, the new state legislature imposed a tax of twenty dollars a month on all non-American miners. Although tax collectors appeared in the most remote mining camps, the new law was difficult to enforce, the more so because the new levy had to be collected every month. The Chinese were among the most prominent victims of the law because of their inability to respond. The tax collectors simply moved into the Chinese camps, seized their possessions, and sold them at auction to satisfy the tax.[27]

The first tax law aroused opposition on the part of many foreign nationals, especially the French. It was repealed in March 1851 and reimposed a year later at the lower figure of three dollars per month. Despite the lower figure, the message conveyed by the tax remained that foreign miners were different from American miners, that they had fewer rights, and that their behavior was suspect.[28]

American hostility toward foreign miners ran counter to earlier experiences on the agricultural frontier. From the first European settlements, the object of interest was land, and here, the early Euro-Americans and, after the Revolution, the Americans themselves seem to have been not only generous in sharing land, but also anxious to promote foreign immigration. In a vast continent only slowly occupied by the Euro-Americans—at least up to 1815—foreigners were viewed as an asset. To the extent that they occupied, improved, and cultivated lands, they were welcomed. This pattern of hospitality failed in the gold fields, at least with regard to the immigrant groups that did not speak English. Israel Lord noted the contradiction. "It is strange that Americans are not willing to give foreigners an equal chance, when there is so much labor required to secure the uncertain gains which fall to the lot of the laborer here," he observed. "One would be led to think, by the talk of some, that gold can be picked up any where without any trouble, and belong to themselves exclusively; that they had dropped or deposited it to be reclaimed when they deemed most convenient. I, for one, contend that they have the same right to dig for gold here, as in the older States for iron, or wheat, or potatoes."[29] Lord was in a minority. The idea that other peoples might have equal access to gold, however long the odds, was unacceptable to the majority of American miners. In this respect, they expanded their treatment of Native Americans to include non-Americans (or at least all non-English speakers) who occupied attractive claims. To the extent that these groups defended themselves or complained of such treatment, hostility toward them increased in like proportion.

15

WAITING:

A Permanent Condition

THAT THE SECOND GENERATION of the California Gold Rush produced responses in the Golden State that were simultaneously more businesslike and more violent did not change the nature of the burdens imposed on those left behind. Perhaps the longer cycles of economic enterprise associated with the new kinds of mining extended absences from home and made remittances of financial support even more haphazard. It is difficult to identify with certainty any greater reluctance to return or a decline in family fortunes beginning in 1851. Part of the problem lies in the continuity between the two generations. Many of those who came in 1849 and 1850 continued to pursue their fortunes into the season of 1851. The lives of those who remained on the farm or in the shop continued to revolve around children and parents within the extended family.

The customary obligations to children and parents were continuous, and where illness was involved, sometimes overwhelming. In families with financial independence and leisure, the spouses and children, assisted by servants, continued with their usual routines. If the substantial houses were sometimes lonely and cheerless, they were houses nonetheless, with sufficient heat and light and food on the table. These people traveled, visited relatives, managed households, and sometimes assisted with their absent husbands' business affairs. Families with limited financial resources and even straitened circumstances, however, waited for tangible assistance in the form of remittances from the gold fields, as well as news. They often waited in vain.

As the 49ers of the second generation exchanged confidences and views with their families and friends, the Gold Rush lost its exotic air and became another kind of employment. That the economic conditions in California seemed less hopeful was a message that did not always get heard back home, however. And there were things going on back home that the 49ers found difficult to understand as well. Just as the values and even the morals of the 49ers were changing, similar changes were occurring in the beliefs and values of those they left behind. Not the least of these changes was in attitudes toward the place of women in society. Out of necessity occupying roles traditionally reserved for men, some women began to ask why they did not have the right to occupy them by choice.

Just as 49ers did not know how to discuss forthrightly the sexual temptations they experienced in the gold camps and gambling halls and their responses to them, they were perplexed in their turn by the new interest on the part of some spouses and fiancées in women's rights. William Carpenter's fiancée Lucetta Spencer taught school and actively pursued an interest in women's suffrage. From his store in Sacramento—he had established himself in trade after a year in the placers at Rosa's Bar on the Yuba—Carpenter tried to deal with the questions about women's roles that she raised in their correspondence. Their exchanges show her intensity and serious involvement in women's suffrage and education and his evasions of these issues. Instead of responding to them, he wrote about mutual friends and his activities in the gold fields. As a way of diminishing her new roles, he called her "my little politician," a title that was both humorous and condescending. While he paid tribute to her interest in women's rights, he also lamented the absence of women to play traditional roles in California: "Woman with her sunny smiles, cheering tones, and helping hands, is wanting." Throughout a correspondence of two years and a frank exchange of views for a midcentury couple, Carpenter and Spencer sparred and parried without reaching any common ground.[1]

As they had from the beginning of the Gold Rush, however, the majority of the women left behind simply carried on, doing the best they could, struggling to hold together families, businesses, and farms. As the months of absence stretched into years, with both news and money from the Argonauts arriving sporadically at best, their lives began to settle into established patterns. However these patterns may have differed, for both the well-off and those in want, they continued to revolve around correspondence. They spent their time waiting for letters from the other side of the continent, writing for advice, and as time went by, marking the events that grow from the passing days—births, deaths, the surprising growth of children, the subsiding of parents into old age.

Life on Nantucket Island off the coast of Massachusetts long had been regulated by the rhythms of the sea and the departures and returns of the whaling vessels. Beginning in 1849, with the mass migration to California, daily life on Nantucket began to revolve around the arrival and departure of the mail. The return of 49ers and the continuing departures of other gold seekers also fueled speculation about the fortunes and health of those so long absent.

The activities of Susan Folger Gardner of Nantucket reflected the work patterns and leisure routines of the wives who remained behind in these modest households. Related through her parents and her husband to two of Nantucket's prominent families—the Folgers and the Gardners—Susan Folger Gardner watched her forty-seven-year-old husband Charles depart for California in 1852. Although she could not know so at the time, this was the beginning of a series of upheavals in her life. Within a month of his departure, their only child (a son, Willy) died. Her son taken from her and her husband absent, she began a period of quiet mourning from which she gradually emerged through her employment in a dry-goods store and through socializing with her friends and relatives.

In the quiet pattern of her daily life, Gardner tried to think of Charles and his next letter and to keep at arm's length memories of little Willy. A stormy day and high seas no longer represented a change in the weather; it signified that "'twill be impossible for the [mail] Boat to come today, and I shall have to pass the time in anticipation." From the window of her store, she welcomed a heavy snowfall because with its "Merry Sleigh bells . . . it breaks the dull Monotony of each day, there is so little of anything here, except social gatherings & dancing once a fortnight, lectures & debates at the Lyceum." The social functions at home were staples of diversion and pleasantry—"sewing, singing, and chatting"—and "the time has passed off so pleasantly." The daily routine of home and store made the evenings and their social interactions the focal point of the day. Invited friends played whist and "chequers," organized musicales, or conversed about books and the issues of the day. Gardner tried "as much as is in my power to be cheerful," she wrote, rejoicing that "this eve I have had a little Music company" to enliven the gathering.

Memories of the last year, beginning with little Willy's death, continued to intrude. Charles had left them both well "to go and try his fortune in the golden land, and in one short month, I was left, as it were alone in the world, at least I felt so, almost heart broken." She had not attended a large social gathering since Willy's death. Her only consolation was the hand of a Divine Providence acting "for my good, altho' I could not view it so, he was too good, too pure, to live in this cold world, and seeing him suffer made me feel willing to say, I will give him up." She now felt ready to visit with some of her friends, but only in small groups.

Throughout the spring of 1853, men and women from the Nantucket community constantly arrived from and departed for California. A large number of women, perhaps twenty, left during this four-month period from January through April 1853. Gardner wrote of the exodus, "There seems to be quite an emigration from our little Isle, it seems so lonesome to have so many of our good citizens leaving us. they all go with great hope of prosperity and success. I hope it may be realized, it certainly is a great undertaking particularly those with little families." The daily mail packet from the mainland brought a continuous flow of men and sometimes families returning from California. Gardner reported their arrival with rejoicing for their families and envy that she was not one of those blessed. The same vessel carried one or two and sometimes as many as five or six—she referred to them as "Californians"—to the mainland, whence they went to New York to catch the steamers for California. She reported with regret the departure of her friends to meet their husbands in the gold country, although she showed no interest in going there herself. Noting the difficult passage of her friend Mrs. Alley, she reflected that no woman should make that voyage, especially a woman alone. Every family in Nantucket seemed to have someone in the gold country. In addition to her husband, Gardner also had a nephew in business in San Francisco.

Her thoughts returned, several times a day and at night, to the postal service. The mail arrived from the mainland daily, and as soon as it was "opened" at the post office, a friend immediately delivered her letters to her home. It was one of the gestures of mutual assistance available in such a community. Charles, who had labored for several months on a farm in California, had left for the mines. He was now out of contact, with no address, and, she wrote, "I fear I shall not hear from my dear Husband...still, I have the organ of hope large, and cannot but think I shall get one." Saddened about life after the death of her young son, she remained eternally optimistic—"Ah I live in hope" she confided to her diary—"about the next mail." She continued about her prospects for a letter, "I will try to be patient as I may not get one then, but it is an anxious life to live, between hope and fear." Husband Charles tried the mines, found the life too hard—"too much exposed to the wet, having to stand in the water all the time"—and unremunerative, and returned to farming near San Jose.

The Gardners wrote often to one another, although his letters arrived in Nantucket at irregular intervals, often three or four at a time, followed by several mails without any. The California mail went out on Friday, an important day in her calendar. On a usual Friday, she sent him a letter of eight pages, nine newspapers, and a *Gleason's Pictorial*. When she received letters from California, members of two families came to her house to read them. She, in turn, hurried down the street to read them to her eighty-eight-year-old mother. On some of these occasions, she freely embellished—"my imagination was quite fertile"—telling her mother what she wished to hear and invariably making the letters longer and with more human interest. She once commented that she "was glad I do not have to read it twice over, I doubt whether each time would tell exactly the same story."

Gardner found her work at the store sometimes tiring, but always diverting. It gave her a schedule; it provided a routine of work. She had worked at the store for three years, and she found the duties often pleasant (visiting among the employees and customers) and occasionally boring and onerous (inventories and marking new goods). Sometimes it also offered recreation. One day, when trade was "dull," she and her friends invented an exercise— "we tried to see who could leap on to the counter the easiest without placing the hands upon the counter." Suddenly, "I almost fancied myself a Miss instead of an old lady." She was, in truth, forty-two years old, certainly not a "Miss" by Nantucket standards.

Gardner had continuing trouble with her teeth. Her dentist, who came to the island regularly from New Bedford, had extracted all her teeth, and he prepared a set of false teeth that never fitted properly. She had agreed to pay fifty dollars for the set and finally had to make arrangements to go to New Bedford for fittings. She was anxious to have them well in place before her husband returned. She worried constantly that she was aging faster than her absent husband.

Gardner organized social affairs of several kinds to fill her quiet hours, often with the Bunker family in the house where she lived. She also carried on an extensive correspondence with eight people, including her husband. Nantucketers exchanged calls, especially on Sunday. Gardner always had at least four callers on Sunday, for example—her niece's sisters (sometimes with husbands, sometimes without) and other friends in town. She also visited regularly her aging mother. Although she frequently referred to her friends "on the continent"—as she called the mainland—she did not make casual visits. She had planned a four-week vacation from the store in May (she preferred to make the ocean crossing to the mainland in good weather) to visit her sister and her sister's husband in Springfield. Her employer at the store grudgingly gave her the four weeks.

When the weather was good, Gardner attended the local lyceum, where she reported on a paper delivered by a man but written by a woman. She speculated on the author, settling on Mrs. George Starbuck, who was known to have written other such works. She also had her first meeting with Miss Stone, a lady who had come to deliver two public lectures on "female rights." Openly skeptical, Gardner went to the lecture and was enormously impressed. The woman, dressed in bloomers, spoke for two hours to an attentive audience. "I really had thought we had all the rights that belonged to us," she wrote, "but upon listening this evening, I find, we are wronged and hope for a change in some respects." Miss Stone not only lectured persuasively, she was also a powerful debater who was "more than a match" for those who raised questions and objections. Gardner much regretted Miss Stone's departure from Nantucket Island and thought the local cultural and intellectual scene the poorer for her leaving.

When the weather turned warmer with the coming of spring, Gardner began to make regular visits to her son's grave. She constantly searched for reasons for his death—"nor could I be comforted, my husband away, and our only darling child taken from me, I almost felt that I had nothing to live for"—especially immediately after the departure of Charles for California. Even with the consolation of religion and the boy's new heavenly home, she found it difficult to accept the loss of her only child, whatever the attractions of the next world.

Gardner belonged to a class with a degree of assured physical comfort. She also worked long hours, for income and also for distraction. Her trials while awaiting her husband's return record the common occurrences of death and illness, especially among children, that made up the lives of such spouses. After her own son had been lost to a fever, she made a list of the deaths of several other small children, reporting formal calls on the bereaved parents, especially mothers, and funeral arrangements. Gardner also noted the anxieties associated with the long whaling voyages of two to three years, and she expressed concern for the safety of her brother, who was a captain in a packet service up and down the coast. Perhaps these traditions of seafaring made the continuing absences of husbands in California easier to bear, but Gardner's own case involved other memories.[2]

CHILDREN GROW UP

As months stretched into years along the watercourses and in the camps in California and plans to return home were postponed in a series of decisions that seemed natural, children grew up in the families and communities where the missing husbands and fathers long had been absent. As we've seen, for example, when Alonzo Hubbard returned to Lee, Massachusetts, after two years in the gold fields, he was forcibly struck by the changes that had taken place in his absence. The growth of children meant a series of decisions and changes in parents' lives: whether or not to send children to school and at what sacrifice; how to deal with adolescents who wished to leave school and lead independent lives; the issue of marriage for young men and young women; the choice of careers for those who had left school.

The 49ers left home with instructions for their children to serve as obedient supports for spouses in a family often left to its own devices by the hurried departure of a father. Relationships with children turned out to be fragile, dependent as they were on a wide range of variables, including the age, finances, and expectations of the parents. In part, the issue of how to guide children growing up was an extension of relations between the Argonauts and their wives. The absent Argonaut was the father figure responsible for instilling precepts of behavior and fashioning the family unit into a self-contained social and economic mechanism. He was also two thousand miles away.

The 49ers insisted on their presence as continuing figures in the family. Absent fathers asked their spouses to speak frequently of them, share news of them with their children, and make sure that the children able to do so wrote regularly to California. The receipt of periodic notes from children—generally appended to the wife's letter—was taken as a sign that both mother and children were doing their duty. Failure to write or to do so regularly became the grounds for complaint. The unwritten assumption was that the wife was responsible for the children's behavior in this regard.

In response to letters from their children, which they regarded in the same light as letters from spouses, as marks of deserved affection and concern, the 49ers often wrote separate letters to their children, asking their support and obedience and promising in return gifts from California. Solomon Gorgas wrote his children separate letters with little homilies. "If you have seen the many poor little children, who came across the plains, many of them almost naked & without anything to eat, walking and riding through the hot day, under the burning sun, & through the clouds of dust," he lectured them, they would have a proper appreciation for their good fortune and the work necessary to maintain their comforts. He asked that they pray regularly, especially for his success and safe return, attend school faithfully, apply themselves in their lessons, obey their mother unquestioningly, and assist her in all things. He concluded by reminding them of their good fortune and by encouraging them to be thankful for it.[3] Probably his children, and those of other 49ers for that matter, would have opted for the excitement of a journey across the plains instead of the boredom associated with attending school and doing household chores.

In response to directions, and perhaps spontaneously in some cases, children also wrote letters to their fathers. These seem to have had many purposes: mandatory declarations of love and affection, dictated by the mother to remind their fathers to come home; exercises in writing and self-discipline; demonstrations to their fathers of attainment in school; and not least, expressions of their love for the absent parent, to provide fathers with welcome letters. Most of this correspondence, however, had the content and format of letters dictated or carefully superintended by mothers. They were designed as ritual statements of fidelity and obedience, mixed with references to the father's responsibility to return soon. John Fitch's son wrote to him a letter that covered all the basic issues between 49ers and their children: "I am afraid you will get killed by the Indians, and I am sorry you have to work so hard. I hope you will be successful in turning the river, and I hope you will get enough gold to come home soon." He concluded with reference to his own responsibilities: "I am going to try to be a better boy than I have been and try to improve my mind, and get along with studies and mind what you tell me and try to help Grandmother and Mother all I can."[4] The young Fitch's letter was something of a model for what young children (and by implication, their mothers standing at their shoulders) thought a father would wish to hear, items that he had very likely inquired after in his letters to them.

That they were ritualistic did not lessen the chore of writing them, or if we are to believe the responses, the pleasure in receiving them. One 49er expressed this unreserved enthusiasm in his journal on receiving a letter from his eldest daughter when he wrote, "More than a year had expired since I received a letter from my family. I truly rejoiced And when I persued it & found that all were alive & I hope that I was thankfull I was Gratified Surely. I immediately bought a Pair of Spectacles & soon Devoured the contents."[5]

These were the letters of young children, generally enclosed in a letter from their mother. Not all children of 49ers and their spouses were young, however; some were young adults. These wrote letters of quite a different nature. They wrote as equals, with their own interests and opinions. When tension and friction developed between husband and wife, these young adults might be the third party through which they offered their views to one another. The 49ers would then spend more time in writing their teenaged sons and daughters than their wives, from whom they were becoming estranged. As the tone of his letters to his wife grew more quarrelsome, and hers to him the same, Ephriam Delano wrote more and more to his son George, whom he addressed as an equal. Delano liked to fantasize about the two of them mining together in remote and exotic California, far from the continuing demands of home, spouse, and younger children.[6]

These struggles to maintain ties were not universal. The exchanges between farms and shops on the one hand and mining camps on the other show that some 49ers ignored their children, just as they ignored their families. Others probably wanted to do much for both, but found themselves disappointed in their labors in the gold fields and reacted by distancing themselves from family expectations. That their families expected much because of the 49ers' own grandiose schemes did not comfort the miners as they contemplated another season in the placers with little or nothing to show for it. The attitudes toward children that emerged seemed to reflect the attitudes toward their families generally.

The continuing interactions between home and the gold fields over children were punctuated by moments of heady triumph and stark tragedy. Given the hazards of childhood at the time, with its range of diseases and fevers, 49er children of all ages died while their fathers were in California. The devastation wrought by the news of this tragedy in a remote gold camp may be imagined. The power of the loss was increased by its final nature. By the time the Argonaut received news that the child had become ill or injured, he or she had died, in spite of the best efforts of spouse and doctor, and likely already had been buried. The death of the young son of William and Susan Folger Gardner during his sojourn in California was only one example among many.

The finality of a child's death robbed the 49er of the absolutions that were part of the rituals that surrounded death in midcentury America. He had no chance to offer advice, to pray for the child's recovery, to console his wife and surviving children, and to participate in the collective act of grieving at the burial. Instead, after the death came mutual recriminations about responsibility, the fatalistic consolation of religion, and the uplifting declaration that the family would be reunited again in heaven. For the wives, it brought the collective support of family, neighbors, and community; for the 49ers, apart from the bustle of the tent and murmured words of support from close friends, there was nothing but the vast spaces of the California mountains and foothills stretching out on every side. The death of a child once again brought to consciousness the distances that separated the Argonauts from their families, distances that had set the two groups on different paths.

As their children grew toward adulthood, the separated parents confronted a new series of questions: What about future work for the young men? What about marriage for the young women? Both parents seem to have assumed that these distinct divisions were appropriate. Should a young man just in his teens be permitted to go to sea? Should a student at a university be allowed to leave school in order to seek his fortune? And what about those young men who wished to follow their fathers to California, into the mines or into the stores? What should be the position of the parents? And what advice might the father offer that would address the diminished prospects in California, while at the same time give a legitimacy to his own decision to labor there unrewarded for a period of years? Parallel to these questions lay a separate set for daughters maturing into young women. Who was to establish guidelines for behavior? Who should meet prospective suitors and pass judgment on them? What sorts of training should a young woman have to prepare her for marriage? Who was responsible for the training and futures of children? And when fathers, to a degree, vacated their duties, what kinds of rights did they have to direct the lives of children from thousands of miles distant? When James Wilson, a widowed congressman and lawyer from New Hampshire, went to California in 1850 to seek his fortune, what most outraged Mary Elizabeth, his eldest daughter, was not the lack of financial support, although that was serious. Rather, she was angered that her father had left her alone to advise and counsel two younger daughters and a young son. These were supposed to be his responsibilities. Mary Elizabeth Wilson Sherwood—she married during the first year of his absence—now found herself accountable for two households. In addition to her husband and new son, she had to guide her sisters and brother.[7]

PARENTS GROW OLD

Not all 49ers were married, and of those who were married, only a portion had children. A larger group had surviving parents. Among these parents, some continued to love and support the missing Argonaut, and others threw up their hands and denounced the journey west as a waste of family resources. The attitudes of mothers and fathers often were different. Fathers tended to be stern and businesslike. They acted out what they thought of as their roles as models to prepare their young sons to earn a living and to discharge the responsibilities due to parents and family. Even those who gave permission for their sons to go to California often did so on a carefully structured schedule that called for the 49ers to return promptly with their earnings in hand. They pointed out, sometimes in the most direct way, that they themselves had worked hard to acquire the farm or store, had provided for their families, had worked to train their sons in similar values, and that they expected the expedition to California would reflect these lessons of life, rather than depart from them.

Mothers played a different role, offering affection and support amid the difficulties and disappointments of the mines. In the face of increased competition and small returns, fathers characteristically advised more hard work and greater economy, while mothers pleaded for sons to take care of themselves and return without risking illness. John Slatford's mother wrote him constantly to urge that he leave the gold fields and come home before he ruined his health.[8] The two separate voices produced a kind of parental counterpoint. This is not to say that these two points of view were exclusive. Sometimes women headed families and offered both kinds of advice. Other parents did not write, whether from anger or indifference.

In a world in which children traditionally took over responsibility for aging parents, the removal of part of this support network was a serious issue. Samuel Brown, the eldest son of the Brown family of Toledo, wrote to his younger brother, William, in the gold fields of the latter's responsibility to his parents. William replied, "In your letter you say that I am the main stay of my parents & by returning home I can comfort them more than by staying here. Which is true but I must get enough to get home & back with, without geting *flat broke*. Then I can think of returning & not before."[9] The younger Brown conducted three separate correspondences with his family. To his father, he wrote of his economic prospects in the most optimistic terms; to his mother, he confided his fears about his business prospects and the details of his personal life; finally, to his brother, he inquired about the economic situation of his parents (the father's ice company was in serious straits) and exchanged views about the responsibility of each family member for economic support in case of the business's failure.

William Brown even treated his parents as separate economic entities. He sent a substantial quantity of gold to his mother, giving as a reason that his father's business might fail, and he wanted to keep this gold separate from his father's affairs. His father found out about the transactions and was furious. Brown tried to calm him by explaining that the gold he had sent to his mother was inferior in quality to the gold sent to the father. But he also noted the shaky condition of his father's business affairs. And throughout, his brother continued to insist on the younger son's ongoing responsibility to the parents, an obligation that could not be discharged from California.[10]

Over a period of years, some parents became bedridden and took sick; others died. The rush of grief, like that associated with the death of a child, was all the greater for the great distances that separated Argonauts from their families, the lapse of time before the news could be communicated, and the sense of helplessness these produced. Even as he engaged in lighthearted correspondence about his father's gold fever ("at any rate I trust he will not get so far gone as to be obliged to have it *shaken* out of him by other fevers, as I did"), Rinaldo Taylor received word of his mother's death. He expressed shock that he had been so long in hearing, that his mother had been in the grave for several months before he knew of her passing. He delivered the eulogy of a distant son: "to think that when I return from this long tedious voyage, that her kind greeting will be wanting. The image of her pale face as she looked when I parted with her at the dawn is still fresh in my memory—little did I think it would be the last look."[11] Others shared similar experiences of shock and delayed grief. Over the eight years that he was in California, William Farnsworth's father died and his brother-in-law committed suicide.[12] George Wheeler learned of the death of his wife's father and her sister, to which tragedies he offered the observation, "It is of no use for me to attempt to pen my feelings on this occasion. Language can not express it I had looked long and anxious for this letter but little did I expect to have such sad tidings."[13]

With illness and death came the status of widow or widower for the survivor. The change in the status of parents that 49ers found almost as violent and startling as death was remarriage. Stunned by the death of his beloved mother, Jacob Engle was further distressed by the news of his father's quick remarriage to a woman he did not know and never had heard of.[14]

As the length of time that they were separated from each other grew, the relations between an Argonaut and his family deteriorated, even if death or age did not intervene. Sometimes the response to the decision to go west was alienation from the 49er's family, a condition that some began by actively seeking and that many lived to regret. California and the Gold Rush could be seen as a way to escape the ongoing pressure of parents, especially fathers, to "be responsible." So young Argonauts sought to distance themselves from their parents and to conduct their lives as adults. The Gold Rush certainly accelerated this inevitable coming of age and sometimes led children to repent their hasty flight. In March 1853, after two years in California, Charles Plummer addressed a letter to his father. He wrote of the usual topics of interest—mining, morality, religion in California, and the arrival of the peculiar Chinese. Then, at the close of his letter, he broached the issue that seemed to have been the subject of the letter from the beginning and the force behind his impulse to write. What emerged was an account of his last days in Boston, when the busy 49er, fired with self-confidence over his decision to go to California and with self-importance over participation in a company of like-minded young men, parted with his father under circumstances that seemed to reflect an unintended indifference. "Do you remember the last time we met?" he began.

I often think of it, and how abruptly I left. It was in Elm Street, Boston. You had Frank by the hand and called out to me as I was crossing the street in company with several others who with myself constituted a "provision committee" of the great & glorious New England Company. We were then on an inspection mission—they could not tell me where to come and find them, and therefore I was forced to cut you short, or lose them and my business for the day, which then seemed very important.

Plummer had carried the impression of that parting with him in the mines for two years, and it grew more significant with silence. He now wrote in the most direct way, "I want much to see you, and have no cause to doubt you would like to see me, and feel inclined to ask when I am coming your way." The answer from Boston was a long silence. In Plummer's four years in California, his father never wrote a line to him.[15]

Others who maintained faithful contact with their parents exercised great caution in their correspondence, taking care to say nothing that would alienate or anger. William Brown wrote circumspectly to his father and more openly to his mother. He feared to admit that he had gone into the express business, apparently because of the inferior status associated with such an occupation in Ohio. Only with his descriptions of his new and extravagant lifestyle did Brown declare his independence from the values of Toledo, and here he was defensive about his expenditures for billiards and the theater, as we have seen. When he was shot to death on a San Francisco street in 1856, his father displayed a sudden interest in his business and estate. The younger Brown might have been gratified or chagrined to know of this level of concern in death after the indifference in life.[16]

One 49er appended a special note to a letter, complaining about recent correspondence and his relations with the family: "not one word is sayd about any member of the family—what does it mean? keep nothing from me—Since last august not one word have I had from either father or mother—what can it mean? Are they displeased with their wild boy? or is it an oversight in you to mention their names." In his next letter, he noted that he had heard from no one in the family except Hannah and James, saving only a single line from his father. "If it is not cool comfort for a man to be living in these wild, mountains thousands of miles from his once was friends and his home, and feel that he is deserted by them he left behind, I do not know what is."[17] The 49ers of the first and second generation left behind thousands of families thus damaged by their prolonged absences.

16

LOST LOVE, LOST FAMILIES

"How many a happy family has been broken up since the Gold of California has been heard of God only knows," wrote John Slatford's mother to her son in early 1852.[1] From the moment of departure, relationships among 49ers and their families had experienced strains and uncertainties; as these absences lengthened, the anxieties over family relationships increased in like proportion, and these patterns repeated themselves with continuing annual migrations to the gold fields.

Both the men who went to California and the women who stayed behind entered into a new range of experiences, as we have seen. Spousal and family relationships underwent a change unlike any other heretofore seen on such a large scale, as distinct in its numbers and its widespread effect as the mobilization of armies on the opening of the Civil War. As we have seen, as well, the results of these prolonged absences could range from the ideal to the disastrous. As time went on, the effect on families tended toward the disastrous.

LOST LOVE

Wives increasingly complained to their 49er husbands about what they regarded as negligent treatment. Jane Delano had objected to her husband's voyage to the gold mines in the spring of 1852 from the start, and her anger followed him into the placers. After a long silence, he received a letter from her, and he responded to it with the comment, "Jane I can tell you I dreaded to open it and kept it with me over one hour before I could muster courage to open it but still Jane I thought you wrote." Delano constantly reassured her of his intense devotion to his family. "As for my forsaken family I never shall for I think daily of my wife and children and the thoughts about my family is never one day out of my mind and I can tell you Jane the thoughts of you and the children is ever near and pleasing to me," he wrote. Of course, his spirited defensiveness did not address the central issue of his absence, whether his venture compensated in whatever way for the loss of his presence and affection over a period of years.[2]

Harriet Goff, wife of an absent 49er, laid her husband's departure to a lack of love. To her charges, Goff replied from Hangtown, "I was very Sorry to hear of your feeling so disheartened it made me feel bad to think you had entertained the opinion that you was not cared for, &c I think if I know my own feelings, that there is no one cares more or thinks more of their family than I do." He continued, "I hope by the time this Letter reaches you, that you will cast off all those gloomy feelings and Sorrows that you seem to entertain." The evidence of his affection, he argued, was that he missed all the womanly services that she performed for him. His "widower" status was proof that he cared for his family.[3]

Quarrels between husbands and wives sometimes started over a perceived lack of concern for the family and the failure on the part of one or both parties to write regularly. Letters were a symbol of interest and support. Eben Chapman of Danvers, Massachusetts, vented his dissatisfaction with family and friends in a single letter in which he spoke of a long-standing hostility that probably lay behind his voyage to California in the first place. Yet he took particular offense at the indifference to his hard work and sacrifices. "The last letter I receive was written 2 years ago this month from My Wife I sent a draft to her more than one year ago for 2 hundred dollars and it was returned to me," Chapman wrote to Eben Hunt.[4] In a world in which spouses and parents constantly importuned absent 49ers to remit money from the gold fields, Chapman's rejection was highly unusual.

Those women left behind in the rush to California became known as "49er widows." The designation "widow" nicely captured the emotional, financial, and legal void into which some wives had descended in the absence of their husbands. Yet unlike real widows, they had no independent legal status. They could not dispose of their husbands' estates as they wished; they could not seek other romantic attachments; they did not have sole legal responsibility for the surviving children. The term long had been in use, but its applicability was especially poignant in the second generation of the Gold Rush because of the lengthening absences. It was already conceivable that some husbands from whom nothing had been heard for months or years might not be intending to return. Their wives lived on in a perpetual condition of emotional and legal uncertainty.

Sometimes under the influence of distance, time, and sense of desertion, spouses sought other relationships. The 49er "widows" and fiancées and the sizable number of people on both sides of the continent who remained less formally committed to each other often lived solitary emotional lives. Aside from the economic difficulties they may have confronted, their letters often testify in endless detail to their loneliness and deprivation. It is not surprising that some sought companionship and even emotional attachment elsewhere. And from the far end of the continent, some 49ers were quick to accuse their wives of degrees of infidelity.

Perhaps the voyage to California was a final separation in a marriage that had been on the verge of collapse for some time. In mid-nineteenth-century America, divorce was a serious step, one that marked a man and a woman as outside the bounds of traditional and perhaps respectable society. Albert Francisco, who departed New Orleans for the gold fields in the summer of 1849, left his wife Minerva already long separated from him. "I can get no letter from Minerva, though I have written fifty," he confided to his mother. "I am sure she could not treat me so unless she had ceased to love me." Francisco left two hundred dollars for his wife so that he could not be accused of deserting her. He told his mother to burn the letter that detailed his suspicions of Minerva. Even after he had been in California for eighteen months, he still longed to hear news of her, although she never wrote to him. Francisco deliberately lived surrounded by strangers, for he feared "the sympathy of friends or the scorn of enemies. I prefer being among those who know nothing of my troubles, for then I am not reminded of them, and will soon forget them." After his divorce, Francisco spent much time worrying about whether he could remarry. He asked his mother to find out whether he could do so. Because of his uncertain marital status, he felt uncomfortable in the presence of women. "I cannot enter female society feeling as I do. My conscience tells me I am an intruder and it certainly is so."[5]

Francisco met a woman in California to whom he wished to pay court. His description of her defined one man's image of a desirable woman at midcentury. "She is the perfect pattern of a woman," he wrote. "Entirely domestic in her nature not given to the fashionable foibles of the day—modest to a fault—as innocent as a child, and withal so candid and so good natured, that a man must have a heart of stone not to entertain for her the most exalted opinion." Caught between the loss of his first wife and endless frustration in the prospect of pursuing another, Francisco spent his five years in the gold fields in a continuing search for emotional riches. That he was not successful at mining and only marginally so at storekeeping seemed a sideline. He invested his emotional energy in a correspondence with his mother and brother.[6]

Sometimes the new relationships were with old friends, perhaps those who had come to offer support and companionship in lonely times. The return of the 49er from the watercourses to the drawing rooms of formal houses might sometimes unleash an emotional storm over endangered affection. When he went to the gold fields in the spring of 1849, Gustavus Swasey left his wife Jane and children in Boston. After mining with success for some months, he lost his money belt, containing fifty-four ounces of gold, to a thief ("I feel like lying face downward and never again attempting to struggle with my sad fate"). At the same time, his creditors could not pay him ("I am so wretched I am determined to go home as soon as I can get enough to pay my passage"). After a brief, unsatisfactory return home, Swasey parted from his wife and set out for California a second time. In Panama, he changed his mind and returned unannounced to his family. There, he made a series of unpleasant discoveries about his wife. Jane used snuff: "I must confess it was a disagreeable discovery. I express'd my aberrance of the practice. She says Alice Wiley taught her but that it is a filthy practice and she will abandon it, and I believe she will for my sake." But far more disturbing was the disclosure that his wife had been engaged in private correspondence with a mutual friend, William Litton, using her sister Sarah "as a cover for their proceedings." After several unpleasant scenes, Gustavus and Jane Swasey, plus the children, and William Litton went to San Francisco together, where relations between husband and wife further deteriorated. Gustavus Swasey found himself without a wife, family, or business. His search for wealth in the gold fields had become secondary to a series of personal crises.[7]

It was no easier to maintain an enduring relationship for those who were engaged. Even for those with the most firm commitments to one another, the march of the months into years meant plans perpetually deferred. The man thought that he must display a record of success for his intended and her family, yet California had become an uncertain place to achieve such a status. And if California turned out actually to be the land of gold, he was often reluctant to give up the opportunities of a lifetime to hasten home, when in one year he could make as much money as he could in five in New York or Illinois. His betrothed supported his ambitions and honored his determination to do these things for her, but eventually she preferred that he come home, fulfill his commitments to her, and then the two of them would make plans for the future. Even the most devoted fiancée might become restless after a period of years.[8]

Then, too, each party was aware of the shadowy temptations that surrounded the intended. She heard endless tales of the temptations of California, and he remembered the parties and many eligible men, some of them his friends, who lived in the neighborhood. The relationships of more than one couple showed the strain of male friends in the village or city block who seemed overly solicitous in their attentions to long-suffering fiancées. Suspicions sometimes led to recriminations, explanations, apologies, and reaffirmations. Or they might lead to the end of a long engagement. A final side effect of these connections over such a great distance and so much time was to sour life-long friendships between male friends over what were perceived as unwarranted attentions to fiancées, official and unofficial. That old friends might exchange angry letters over such contact by eligible young bachelors was one indicator of the strains imposed by prolonged separations.[9]

Sometimes the search for California gold ended fond hopes and permanently blighted bright prospects. Sarah Trask, of Beverly, Massachusetts, was twenty-two years old in 1850 when the man she hoped to marry, Luther Woodbury, sailed for California. Trask lived with her widowed mother (her father had died of consumption two years earlier) and her unmarried brother in a small house. Throughout the days, she worked by hand-stitching the upper part of shoes for large shoe shops in Lynn and Beverly. It was piecework of the most arduous and repetitive kind, for which she was paid the sum of four cents per pair. Her ambition was to earn one dollar a week. She passed her time waiting for Luther in company with her friends, all sewing away and helping one another. Luther Woodbury's death at sea in January 1851 on the return voyage to Beverly ended her hopes. In a spasm of pain she wrote, "Why care I for life, since I have seen my brightest hopes die. Would that California had never been heard."[10]

LOST FAMILIES

The stresses and tensions that accompanied the mass migrations to California from families and communities across the eastern half of the nation finally destroyed many families. The failure of 49ers to live up to their promises of support for those back home, let alone to realize their dreams of great wealth, took a toll, but even success could bring division and contention in its wake. So could the division of authority between absent husbands and the wives and other family members left with the responsibilities of raising children, caring for the elderly, and keeping the family businesses and farms running. The hardships of the Gold Rush imposed strains and worsened existing tensions within the Argonauts' families, often causing ruptures. And finally, the changes wrought in both the 49ers and those they left behind by the long separation made strangers of them all, those in the East and those in the West each having adapted to ways of life that those on the other side of the country finally could not comprehend.

Problems caused by money began early. Through the wide range of support arrangements the 49ers made for those they left behind ran two common threads. First, from the moment of their initial departure, the Argonauts emphasized that their spouses and immediate families would want for nothing. Everything would be taken care of, they assured them. The 49ers promised to send money as soon as they had begun to claim their share of the fabled riches of the California placers. John Fitch not only sent drafts from the gold fields to his wife with instructions that if troubled by money matters, she would have recourse to his brother, he also remitted funds to his brother George, more than one hundred ounces of gold dust in 1850 alone, with the charge, "I wish you not to fail to see that my wife has money to meet her wants."[11]

This basic assumption of success in the expedition ran parallel to another understanding, that 49ers would share their successes with members of their extended families. When Solomon Gorgas wrote about family sacrifices and dividing up the wealth from his expedition to the gold fields, he mentioned his wife's sister, Mary, and wrote of her and her contributions to the family in his absence, "Sister Mary too, shall not suffer from any debt due her from our dear departed mother, if I am successful—she too shall be remembered."[12] Many Argonauts wrote in grandiose terms, magnanimously dividing up wealth that lay in the future, a fortune so vivid in their minds that they almost considered the Solomon-like judgments they anticipated in its distribution more taxing and awkward than amassing the gold itself.

In good faith, spurred by the public testimonies to wealth in newspapers and letters, they had set forth in full confidence that their earnings soon would support their families. Some of the arrangements for financial assistance seem to have worked well, supported by the goodwill of family members and the success of the 49ers in remitting funds. Others clearly proved inadequate. The gap between promises and the reality of the returns often grew, sometimes to large proportions. When this happened, it both alienated the unfortunate adventurer from his immediate family, which he had failed to support, and caused tensions and problems between them and the extended family to whom they otherwise might hope to turn. The disappointment of great expectations had social as well as psychological effects: it led to the breaking of promises that are among the ties that bind husband to wife and family to family.

Of course, some Argonauts simply left their families in perilous financial straits when they departed for the gold fields. That they did so—and admitted it at the time and later—reflected a degree of irresponsibility tempered with the knowledge that given their impoverished financial condition, they could justify seizing the opportunity to acquire wealth without the usual prerequisites of name, education, and social standing. That they should wish to participate in order to change the impoverished condition of their families, they reasoned to themselves, was understandable, even if it meant abandoning those same families to that condition.

That some of the well-intentioned Argonauts would surely fail, whether from incompetence or bad luck or both, was inevitable, and these failures left destitute or dependent their spouses and families. After two years in the gold fields, John Kerr wrote his mother of the condition of his wife. "I have received per last steamer a letter from Elmira. I pity her from the bottom of my heart. She must have a hard time of it. I have not been able to send her any assistance since I have been out here. She represents herself and Children as being almost naked. God help them." Kerr wrote constantly of his intentions to bring his wife and family to California, or to return to them in the East. He never made the move, frustrated by indecision and by his uncertain financial prospects. Finally, in 1857, after eight years in California, he asked a friend to prepay postage on a letter to his wife, "for I presume she has no money to pay for anything."[13]

Success, however, called forth its own range of problems. Once the returns began to flood in, who was entitled to what? What were the legitimate expectations of different individuals within the immediate and extended family about the distribution of rewards? The continued flow of profits from the gold fields generated an atmosphere like that associated with reading a will. And in many cases, the will might be read every two or three months. Rising expectations and jealousies generated their own stresses as surely as failure.

These divisions might be intensified by varied results within the same family groups, in cases where one member had achieved great material success and another brought home nothing but stories. That one part of the family should be favored over another seemed a most awkward end result. And what was to be done with the estates of those 49ers who died in California? Squabbling over the estates of dead Argonauts assumed unfortunate bitterness in some cases, surely enhanced by the grief over death at such a distance from his family. In some cases, this condition might be further complicated by the responsibility of someone to care for him, and the sense that this individual had failed in his responsibility. When Gustavus Swasey's brother Joseph died, Mother Swasey expected that the estate would come to the entire family. From California, Gustavus did send on the funds from Joseph's estate, but not until he had deducted a substantial part of the estate to cover four hundred dollars that Gustavus had loaned his brother. The mother asked that the entire estate be paid over to the family. Gustavus replied that "to expect money from me under such circumstances was certainly absurd, not to say unjust." He offered to pay what she thought was fair. The conclusion of their negotiations, he wrote, "left me evidently dissatisfied—but I cannot help it. I am poor and must take care."[14] The family remained dissatisfied as well and demanded the full amount.

As we've already seen, debts incurred by 49ers to launch the California enterprise also put often unbearable financial pressures on the ties that held families together. These pressures extended into the larger community, as well. With few exceptions, everyone who started for the gold fields began the trip in debt, whether the obligations were unofficial, within the family, or formal, to a neighbor or a bank. Of course, the debt was tiny by comparison with the anticipated profits, but debts they were. When profits on the grand scale envisioned by the departing Argonauts failed to materialize, those left behind to pay off the debts found themselves embarrassed and alienated from their communities. Whether within the family or in the neighborhood, the effects of debt increased the strains on the families of the 49ers.

A third source of contention had to do with investment of returns from the gold fields. The issue began with a discussion over where to put returns from the diggings. Many 49ers initially, at least, preferred to keep their hard-earned money in California, mesmerized as they were by interest rates of up to 5 percent per month and dogged by continuing heavy personal expenses. As investment opportunities spread out to include shares in river mining, fluming projects, hydraulic operations, and quartz mines, they had additional opportunities that, in some cases at least, had returned enormous profits to the lucky shareholders.

At first, 49ers could make an argument that no safe way existed to transfer funds from west to east, except by trusted friends returning from the gold fields. Rapid changes were occurring in transportation routes and costs, however. By 1850, although some 49ers still continued to carry their money around with them and a few still insisted on using friends to carry gold dust to their families, transmission by bank draft made possible the transfer of funds to any family in the East with access to a bank. With the steady flow of funds from those successful in the placers, decisions had to be made about what to do with hundreds and, in some cases, thousands of dollars.

George Lawson gave detailed instructions to his parents about the distribution of his draft for four hundred dollars:

> I want you to give Robert the use of thirty dollars of it, Alex twenty & Isabella twenty, which will leave thirty dollars out of the hundred, which I gave to you & Mother $15.00 apiece (as a present) I want you to act as agent for me & let the other three hundred out at interest in the way you can. And the interest will be yours untill I return principle & all if I never do, but I hope I shall.[15]

What is arresting about his instruction was his decision to share his good fortune with his siblings and his trust that his parents would make the best investment of the additional funds. It was a triumphant moment for the 49er, which displayed his sense of generosity to members of his family.

For 49ers from the farm, land and cattle were the favored investments. Allen Varner gave his parents specific directions to put his returns from the gold fields into cattle.[16] For those from small towns, town lots and small businesses were attractive. And Argonauts from everywhere liked money put out at interest, but with substantial security. William Farnsworth had careful instructions for the twelve hundred dollars that he was sending home: "When you receive it I think if you have a chance you had better put it at interest if you cen git it out on a Mortgage for one year or two." As for the options, "You in your last letter spoke favorably of bying a Grist Mill but I think I shouldnt want to go in with out seeing it myself for I am afraid of San [?] River, it rises so quick and high but you now best how safe it would be, if you receive enny money from me I had rather you would keep it to yourselves."[17] Thus, anxiety and stress over money in connection with the Gold Rush proved unavoidable. It came to those who made money in California, as well as to those who did not.

Another dimension of the interaction of money and family lay in the investments in the West made by family and friends in the East that somehow went awry in the great maze of California economic opportunities during the Gold Rush. Several friends from Salem, Massachusetts, invested in Isaac Perkins's store in Sacramento. Perkins felt torn. He had become a kind of investment center for the family and the community, but with this universal acclaim came responsibility for all sorts of odd bits of money and goods. To his brother, he wrote, "I have taken the responsibility of investing five Thousand Dollars of the money that did not belong to me." These arrangements and others produced strains within the family. "Brother Joseph" did not feel that he had made sufficient profit on his investment. Isaac wrote in reply,

> Now I think this is quite unreasonable & ungenerous in him for if the
> store did not make money it was not my falt God know I done all I could
> I worked hard all summer when It was hot anough to melt you. he often
> ust to tell me he would not stay in our store for any money & why did
> I stick to it at the risk of my health & perhaps my Life it was because he
> & others had there money investid there & I was put there to do the
> best I could.

Isaac was indignant at these misplaced expectations. "Now I dont blame him for doing the best he can with his money but when he invests & it dont hapin to do as well as he expected, I dont like to here falt found & this grumbling I dont like it, but You knew his disposition." Within two months, Isaac Perkins sold out his interest in the store with the comment, "the risk was too [?] great as regards your friends."[18]

Next spring, Perkins was back in the retailing business. Now his relatives shipped him goods on consignment. Perkins was unhappy about these arrangements and the expectations they generated. "I hope none of my Friends will ship me any more Goods for I can not make anything on consigned Goods," he wrote. And later, he told his brother that consigned shipments from the East, while they may have flattered the other members of the family, were a losing business proposition. As for sending money home, Isaac Perkins refused. "I can do much better here with my money than I could with You, what loan at 6 pr cent pr annum I rather let it at 5 pr cent a month." By the end of the year, Isaac Perkins had begun to speculate in Sacramento properties that he bought for delinquent taxes. Later, he invested in a judgment against a man who had a large tract of land. For eighteen hundred dollars, he wrote, he stood to make "something handsome out of it." And soon thereafter, he went into the lumber business. Finally, he invested in a toll bridge and bought half a sawmill. Of all his economic activities in California, Perkins was most enthusiastic about the mill. "If I dont have any bad luck I think I can make my pile out of this in One Year." The array of investment opportunities in California matched that of any developing American frontier, driven forward by the continuing annual increases in population from the states,[19] but as Perkins's relatives repeatedly let him know, these schemes swallowed up money that might have been returned to the family and invested in local neighborhood enterprises.

Friction over money was not the only cause of dissension within families, however. Other, stronger resentments seemed even more significant: status within the family, questions of power and authority, and issues of special privilege. This range of considerations often had a long history that antedated the emigration of family members to California. Their departure and the changes in relationships brought about by their migration simply brought long-standing tensions to the surface in a heightened form. Several examples suggest the way the Gold Rush heightened such tensions within relationships.

The arrangements made by John Fitch for his spouse when he went to the gold fields produced continuous conflict. Fitch asked his mother to visit wife Theodosia ("Dotie" in family correspondence) and the children "often and comfort and cheer her up all you can." Fitch gave financial responsibility for the family to his brother George. Fitch sent most of the California dividends to his brother for various investments; to his wife, he conveyed some small sums for her personal use. Instructions indicated that George remained the depository for the largest portion of the money. But it was not money itself that caused the conflict between George and Dotie. Although the reasons for the disagreement were never spelled out in specific terms, Fitch's letters convey the distinct impression that his wife and brother had clashed over authority in making decisions and the tone of address involved in their ongoing relationship. In the summer of 1851, when he had been gone two years, mounting resentment culminated in an open quarrel and Fitch wrote from California to his brother about the report of their conflict presented to him: "I have also received one from my wife complaining of your treatment and I must say it surprised and pained me and I hope you have both ere this allowed kindly feelings to resume their sway in your breasts toward each other." Fitch tried to play the role of the neutral peacemaker, with the comment, "I have no heart to write or say anything more on the subject." The disagreements persisted, and he was obliged to return to it once more. "I deeply regret there should have been any cause of complaint and cannot but think there must have been some misunderstanding somewhere."[20] Burdened by conflict at home but constrained by the need for the goodwill of both parties, Fitch's response to the quarrel was to ignore it. Instead, he continued to write copiously on his promising prospects in the placers.

Some families already were so riven by the problems and contentions brought on by their precarious financial situation that the additional strains caused by an Argonaut's decision to seek a solution in the wealth of the gold fields simply made them crumble in clouds of insult and recrimination. Solomon Gorgas went to California to pay debts and improve his family's financial standing. He immediately heard that the financial embarrassment of the family had been compounded when his brother, Charles, signed a note as security for a friend and became responsible for the debt. Charles increased the awkward situation by his bravado and threats when he visited Gorgas's wife, Mary Frances. From his camp near Placerville, Solomon Gorgas attempted to smooth over these financial and personal disagreements. Gorgas explained to his wife that Charles was upset over his financial situation. "He was scared," wrote Gorgas, "& as is his custom, talked about what he was going to do—without really designing it—merely for the purpose of distressing you & Sister." He asked her to be understanding of the situation and concluded, "I am sorry my dear that there are those circumstances to trouble you; but if the Lord grant us our health & strength we may yet return with enough to satisfy some of our creditors."[21]

Gorgas's efforts didn't work. The divisions within the Gorgas family continually erupt across the pages of their correspondence. Jacob was an "ungrateful brother," and "Sister Mary" seemed to have lost out in the division of the estate of "our dear departed mother." Solomon Gorgas already had made promises he couldn't keep to include "Sister Mary" among those who would receive shares of his California fortune, as we've already seen. Perhaps he had borrowed money to make the trip to California; perhaps the expedition arose from a joint family venture in which all contributed and all expected to be enriched. He did not say. But what he did say about the dispute within the family confirmed the sense of unhappiness and disarray that had them at each other's throats.

Not the least cause of contention within families, however, was the fact that the 49ers and their families had grown to be strangers to one another. From the mining camps to the towns, cities, and agricultural valleys, the 49ers saw the Gold Rush as unique in ways other than simply the opportunities for wealth it presented. It was also an experience that by its distance from familiar sources of support and comfort, its exposure to different peoples, customs, and values, and its competitive, all-male character encouraged independence. And as we already have seen, many 49ers found themselves routinely doing and accepting things that they never would have entertained or countenanced at home, from professionals working at hard labor in the mines to men of humble origins operating as bankers, and from Sabbath breaking to gambling and prostitution. Thus, the Argonauts came to regard themselves as different from the men who had boarded the ships and wagons to head west. They had been tempered by their experiences and hardships.

Because of this growing sense of estrangement, many 49ers felt equivocal about returning home. One offered a common observation: "I shudder when I think of the many trials and temptations to which I have been subjected," he wrote. "How hard it is for the wanderer to turn his steps homeward, those who have never been severed from friends, from the associations of their childhood, imagine that an absence of a few months would fill their minds with an unconquerable desire to revisit scenes that were familiar."[22] Indeed, so powerful was this sense of difference that, as we will see, it constantly informed one of the central topics of the 49ers' correspondence with their families: would the absent one ever return home?

17

THE PERMANENT LURE OF SUCCESS, THE ENDURING SHAME OF FAILURE:

"When a Person Gits to California It Is Hard to Say or Tell When He Gets Away"

THE ADVENTURE IN CALIFORNIA, so simple and straightforward when described to the family in the parlor, turned out to be involved and elaborate. The issue of when to return and under what circumstances stretched out indefinitely. The large number of 49ers who talked confidently of going to California and returning within a year soon had to admit that they would be gone at least two years and very likely more. They couldn't say for certain when they would return. Then, too, there was the question of how to return with little or nothing. How was the 49er to justify his prolonged absence when he returned with no more than he departed with? As we have seen, before the 49ers had departed, those they were leaving behind had wished to have an exact date for their prospective return. From that point until the question was settled, it called forth almost every human emotion that could be conveyed by letter or personal message. To pose and respond to these endless queries about a date became a standard part of the correspondence formula of the Gold Rush. It was a subject eventually addressed by even the most evasive of the Argonauts who maintained contact with home.

PROMISES RECONSIDERED

In the debate over whether or not to go to California the issue of returning was central. Because the trip to California imposed emotional and financial hardships on families, a decision to go to the gold mines had to be made in conjunction with a declaration to return home at a specific date. The two were inseparable in the minds of those who wrestled with the question. The answer to the question of when and under what circumstance to return helped to define the wide range of arrangements, accommodations, and plans that accompanied the decision to go and the prelude to departure. In the end, the impression persists that future 49ers who wished to "see the elephant" and pick up nuggets promised whatever was asked of them.

With the arrival of the Argonauts in California, the issue of the time and circumstances of returning to their families and communities took on a dual perspective: the view of the individual, family, and community back home versus the view of the 49ers from the mining camps. For spouses, family, friends, and the community, the salient issues were responsibility, commitment, the sharing of burdens, and all the ongoing duties associated with families, as we have seen.

From their side, some 49ers honored the commitment to return after a specified period, or, alternatively, sought dispensation to stay longer, but a substantial number treated earlier negotiations and agreements as superseded by the reality of California and the gold fields. When to return was something that only they could judge, they declared, because they were the only party sufficiently well informed of the many variables involved to make the decision. John Craven wrote to his wife, "You can rest assured that I will not remain in this country one moment longer than I am forc'd from a duty to *you* and our little ones," but "the time is now approaching when there will be a chance to make something in the mines and I consider it my duty to make this trial."[1] Soon after arrival, what had begun some months earlier as a collective agreement became an issue over which the 49ers had almost complete control. They might, where they chose, evade the issue, make plans to return on a specific date and then change their minds, or simply refuse to discuss the question.

Ephriam Delano conveyed this new perspective in a letter to his wife Jane. "You wanted me to say when I was Coming home," he wrote. "That I cannot say for when a person gits to California it is hard to say or tell when he gets away." He went on to confirm his loyalty to her and the children and his desire to return "as much as any other one," but he concluded that he "Cannot Come this summer. I think I shall start in the fall if nothing happens it is now very pleasant here."[2] Whether the two closing sentiments of determination to return in the fall and the pleasant conditions were linked was not clear, but this Argonaut seemed to find an infinite range of things that changed his plans. So did numerous others. John Fitch used the appeal to responsibility for those back home that ran through so many of the letters from the gold fields to explain that the chance nature of the hunt for gold was itself a compelling incentive to remain in California. "Sorry that I did not go home last fall as you seem to feel so bad about my staying, and the prospects of accomplishing much I find so poor," he told his wife. Yet it was precisely his poor year and disappointing prospects that led him to stay. In retrospect, he should have gone home, but at the time, his sense of mission demanded that he pursue every opportunity. "If I had gone home then without looking in other places, I should not have been satisfied or thought I had done my duty to you or to my children." And he concluded, "Had I only consulted my own feelings & inclinations I should have been home long ago, and I thought I was acting for the best, by staying—but whether so or not time must determine."[3]

The strategy that Ephriam Delano and others employed simply changed the contract from a promise to return on a specific date to a general promise to return. One 49er wrote after two years in California and innumerable enquiries about his return: "You want to know in almost every letter when i am a coming home it would be an impossibility for me to set any time when I expect my return it may be in one year and it may be in 5 the last words that I promised you when i took the last farewell parting when i last shook you all by the hand and when our last tears were mingled together that i would return and if my life and health is spared i shall meet you all again in this world."[4]

That their families had a right to offer an opinion on when they should return, they accepted; that their families could dictate their futures, they increasingly denied. The Argonauts had become new men in California, as we have seen. The observations of the 49ers often took on the quality of a returned crusader, tempered by a religious experience of such overwhelming intensity that it was impossible to explain to mere mortals—especially those clamoring relatives who had remained untouched in familiar surroundings. Mixed in with their new-found sense of their independence—their transformation from second and third sons and husbands and fathers to tough, seasoned veterans of the Gold Rush—also was a firm commitment to success. They had come a long distance and worked for months up to their waists in freezing water in the streams of the Sierra, or perhaps they had tried their hand at several enterprises, ending up running a business in one of the new camps, or perhaps they had risked and won and lost fortunes in investments. They did not intend to return without finishing what they had set out to do. A spell of adversity, whether a claim played out, a dam carried away by a spring freshet, an exodus of customers to newly discovered diggings, or the collapse of a carefully planned development project, only fixed their individual resolve to make another attempt. They were always conscious of others who had made "a raise" after many failures; many intended to join this select group.

This quality of persistence turned out to be one of the ironies of the California mining experience. Gambling was one of the universally deplored vices in the gold camps, yet even those 49ers who shrank from risking hard-earned gold dust on the turn of a card could not rid themselves of the temptations to keep playing the "lottery" they all knew mining to be. So the most upstanding of the Argonauts, such as John Fitch, accepted and even welcomed the risks associated with another season in the placers, a second or third damming enterprise, another search for the Mother Lode or for its equally wealthy cousin, another trade to try their hand at, another chance at a fortune. It was as if the force of their desire combined with their knowledge of other dramatic successes to generate the presumption of an astonishing success, whatever the odds. Thus, the decision to return could be made only after the 49er faced the reality that although all lotteries have winners, few players win.

There also was another component to this sense of independence and self-assertion on the part of some. As we have noted before, America at mid-century may have been a land of opportunity, but among those faced with the prospect of working hard jobs for long hours and low pay, as well as for those confronting debt and failure amid the prosperity of others, it also generated much dissatisfaction. The impulse not to return that many 49ers shared was sometimes the product of contempt for what could seem the oppressive and arbitrary conditions of life back in the states. Something of the sort was the reason Allen Varner rejected his parents' appeal to return home in the winter of 1850–51. Varner recollected his solemn promise to return within three years of his arrival in California. He intended to abide by it, he said, "But you must recollect that I set out with a good constitution health and a brilliant future if fortunate if I remained I might be a Hewer of Wood or drawer of water or what was worse to my feelings A Laborer for the stupid ignorant tow-headed Hoosier Because He happened through the luck of Father to be lord of the soil But depend upon it if I meet with not misfortune I'll show you a trick worth two of that, And not be miser neither."[5] In California, nobody was going to tell him what to do, not even his parents. Men like Varner clearly had long memories of what they had left behind, and were not disposed to welcome a return to it.

Returning home also was made difficult for some by the accumulation of small, subtle adaptations they gradually made to life in the West. The 49ers began confused and homesick in an alien land that was different physically and culturally from what they knew, with a mining society that was chaotic, competitive, and impersonal. Over a period of months, they adjusted. They found friends; they accepted the values of the gold fields. And they came to find the land had its own appeal, mountains and valleys of great beauty in a temperate climate that let them live and work outdoors at almost all seasons of the year.

As the Argonauts adjusted to California, many of them came to like it. They liked the climate and the physical appeal of the new state. They liked the economic opportunities. Many also found the openness of a new society attractive. They found no native aristocracy in California, for they were little aware of and less affected by the presence of the original families of the Californios who had owned elaborate ranches and had wielded so much local influence, and they felt that new arrivals could work at any occupation without fear of being looked down on and could advance to any level in society to which their talents entitled them. Coming from a world structured by social and economic distinctions, they saw themselves as having been catapulted into a stimulating, creative chaos where opportunities for economic advancement were beyond number and where talent would be the sole arbiter. And even as they wrote of the great stresses of the mines, and the competitive nature of mining, with its larger numbers and its necessity for greater investment in capital-intensive enterprises, they continued to hold on to their view of California as an open society.

Thus, with the passage of months and the arrival of a new mining season, hesitant and homesick pilgrims had been transformed into veterans of the diggings, mining camps, and towns. As they grew in confidence (and also in frustration), their homes and families seemed increasingly distant. They were fading images that came to them on creased sheets of paper, occasional daguerreotypes and locks of hair, each of these mementos conveyed through the postal and express mail services at irregular intervals. Sometimes these voices from an earlier life had a querulous quality about them, as they addressed the 49ers as the dependent children they remembered or the young and indecisive men of only scant months and later years before, little aware of how they saw themselves changed with self-confidence and assurance. As these changes took place, and as their homes took on a distant glow of nostalgia, they also found that their sense of independence, achievement, and self-confidence seemed sometimes incompatible with returning to this old way of living.

It is not that they did not dream of going back. The common denominator of every 49er's vision of success in the gold fields was a triumphant return home. They wanted to achieve something notable. They wished to be known in the family annals as someone who had set forth on a voyage of adventure to distant and dangerous California, triumphed over all obstacles, and returned with wealth that far exceeded a herd of livestock, a section of land, or half a dozen town lots.

A new message in a new tone therefore emerged in the 49ers' correspondence: that to come home was the easy way out. The opportunities and demands of California offered challenges that would separate those who could pay the price in time and arduous labor from those who would turn tail and run to the comforts of warm feather beds and savory home-cooked meals, they told the wives who slept in those beds and the mothers who cooked those meals. The real Argonauts of '49 were made of stern stuff, they said, and they were up to meeting the challenge. The challenge demanded that they stay in the diggings or in the shop and persevere in the name of their families. The other side of the ledger was an open contempt for those who had given up the chance to do something for their families and returned too soon. One 49er described both this confidence and contempt in these terms:

> We know you would cheerfully assist us at home, if we were there, but we now have an opportunity to which if we improve aright will be of great advantage to us. . . . But with anything like luck we *cant fail,* & Lord only knows what sends so many Georgians home, except the reflection of how "comfortably I may live at home at my Father's hard earnings." I know many who refuse large wages here & go home. If necessary I would give names.[6]

The intimation that the names of such returned 49ers already were publicly tarnished with shame as failures and shirkers suggested that families themselves should embrace the sacrifices of the 49er and his determination to soldier on in the face of continuing hardships. Better a casualty in the battle for a golden future than to be branded a coward for desertion.

The new world of California in general and the mines in particular produced an unceasing series of new situations and confronted the 49ers with an infinite number of decisions. That these should be collected into a code of conduct was inevitable, and that these principles should be called the "Miner's Ten Commandments" was probably equally inevitable in this openly Protestant nation at midcentury. Designed to instruct the miner in the standards of the camps, they dealt with claims (concentrate on your own and do not covet your neighbor's), gambling (it cost many a miner a hard-earned "raise"), Sabbath observance (to be honored), and conduct within the company (unquestioned loyalty to this group). The idea of the Ten Commandments was probably also reassuring to those in the East who worried about their family members in California confronted by new and exotic people and surroundings. Among the commandments, the seventh dealt with the urge to return:

> Thou shall not grow discouraged, and think of going home before thou hast made thy "pile," because thou hast not "struck a lead," nor found "a rich crevice," nor sunk a hole upon a "pocket," lest, in going home, thou shalt leave four dollars per day, and go to work, ashamed, at fifty cents, and serve thee right; for here, by staying, thou mightest strike a lead and fifty dollars a day.[7]

It concluded by commanding the miner tempted to return home to "keep thy manly self-respect, and then go home with enough to make thyself and others happy."[8] Thus, the Argonaut, however beleaguered and homesick, had a greater duty to his family. And his decisions in such circumstances would reflect on his masculinity. It was a powerful image and a compelling one for 49ers surrounded by the masculine culture of the California gold fields.

COMING TO TERMS WITH FAILURE

For individual 49ers, the decision to return or not to return touched on another range of questions as great as that of duty and responsibility at home: the reasons for the expedition to California in the first place. The answer was simultaneously simple and not so simple. That is to say, almost everyone had gone to California to mine for gold. But what constituted a satisfactory resolution of the trip? What was enough gold or a sufficient attempt to find gold? What represented success, an acceptable return from so many years in the placers? And alternatively, who was prepared to admit failure in this enterprise and at this stage in life? So a central question for many a 49er involved creating a set of circumstances and reasons that would justify returning home without having met his own minimum expectations or those held by his family and friends. And under these circumstances, how should the 49er prepare to meet the happy but questioning glances that wondered how such minimal returns justified so much collective sacrifice and deprivation over so many years?

In a way, returning home was the ultimate form of coming to terms with failure. The idea of failure was not easy to assimilate in the nation at midcentury, and the more so in an enterprise filled with popular stories of dazzling successes of incredible magnitude. It was not something that had been much a part of the lexicon of young America because even those who struggled on the land for years ended up with something, if only an eighty-acre tract. Those who did not had failed in private, and they simply left and moved somewhere else and started the cycle over again. Now the failures were of the most public kind, and perhaps many of those who vanished into the golden hills of California did so because they could not return to their families, friends, and communities empty-handed. Even those who intended finally to come home would not face doing so in adverse circumstances. One Argonaut wrote that he refused to consider coming home because of "mortification" over his failure. Even though he had worked at a variety of occupations in addition to mining, as a carpenter and in a post office, he had made nothing. He was unable to support his wife, anguished about it, and determined not to return until he could bring something with him. And another 49er expressed the same hesitation to return to his mother with the explanation, "I dislike the idea very much of returning without making any thing...besides I know that a good deal would be said about me as every person in the states think that no person that is industrious can come out here without making a fortune." To his sister and brother, he simply explained that his plans to return always had been "thwarted by some unavoidable circumstances."[9]

Many did not wish to measure their battered trunks and thin pouches against the cheers of that departure morning two or three or even four years before or the achievements of those from the community and perhaps from even within the family who had done more. "I cannot think of returning home from the *Land of Gold* with *Nothing*, notwithstanding the chords of Fraternal, Conjugal and Paternal Love are drawing me towards home," commented Levi Hillman. "Would you want me to return without making every exertion to better our condition even though I might be obliged to remain here longer, than I intended to stay." Of course, his wife would accede to his request. Later, he offered another dimension of his hesitation to return when he wrote, "but you know what I said to my friends when I came away—that when I came back they might know that I had more money than when I went away." To satisfy both his promises to his family and his boasts to his friends, he now worried, "I must make something."[10]

Thus, the issue of coming home called forth an array of fundamental questions for the 49er. It led him to review his past; it confronted him with prospects for the future. It invited him to see his investment of time and energy against the successes or failures of others, in the camps and at home. It cast his expedition to California in relation to his sense of himself and of his family and community. It asked him to separate out the several parts of his sojourn in relation to one another. In light of the new technology available within a few years of the initial rush to California, actually to make the trip home was a simple matter. To make the decision to do so was much more difficult.

For their families, coming to terms with failure was an emotional as well as a financial issue. Even those who had failed in the search for riches could reward their spouses and children and parents by going home. Yet this aspect, too, highlighted the complexity of the decision. It meant different things to different people. William Swain, after months in the diggings, returned to his wife Sabrina and his daughter satisfied that five hundred dollars—not much, by most accountings—was all that he would make in the gold fields, with the comment, "I have made up my mind that I have got enough of California and am coming home as fast as I can."[11] The Swain family emerged more unified and cohesive than ever on William Swain's return.[12] Other families found the coming to terms with failure far more difficult. The prospects of great economic advantage were powerful stimulants not easily forgotten or glossed over.

One response to the possibility of failure was the insistence by the 49er's wife on more effort. When Solomon Gorgas confided to his wife, Mary Frances, that his store was not doing well, she replied by urging him to leave the soft life of storekeeper for the harder and presumably more remunerative work of the mines. Gorgas hastened to do so. When he had mined without notable success for a year and suffered great physical hardship for his effort, he wrote of his determination to come home. He informed his wife of his decision with some hesitation and added the comment, "Perhaps, you will be dissatisfied too" at his decision to return with little.[13]

What represented the minimum standard for success? Ten thousand dollars was frequently mentioned as the standard in newspaper articles. Returning veteran miners sometimes actually lived up to it. After a few months in the mines, however, most 49ers' standards for success tended to change. At the onset of his first winter in the mines, Albert Leonard wrote that he would not return home without two or three thousand dollars. Some simply wanted to "square accounts with the world."[14]

The decision whether to stay on in California or to go home presented itself seasonally, beginning with the miner's first winter, with its rain and snow at the higher elevations and rapidly rising watercourses that ended the mining season. If a 49er was going to go home, the onset of winter was the best time. Profits, if any, were in the pouch; expenses, always high, could be ended. But it wasn't long, especially at lower elevations, until the California spring set in, with its profusion of wildflowers covering the hillsides and valleys, warm and sunny days, and a return of optimistic prospects for another season in the gold fields. As it did, schemes for making money proliferated, and the trip homeward might be postponed for another year.

With the changing character of mining techniques, the timing for returning home also changed. With capital tied up in more and more elaborate projects that involved many others, and with the returns on such enterprises deferred until the end of the season, the 49ers found it more difficult simply to pack up their trunks and leave. Sometimes they wished to remain to collect debts due them. Responding to requests for his return, a 49er from North Carolina noted that "it is hard to give up a good business after Labouring hard two years to build it up." Morris Sleight's wife wrote from Chicago every year on his birthday, pleading for him to come home, and Sleight always replied that the quartz business was difficult to leave, and he would need at least a year to wind up his affairs.[15]

To the continuing concern on the part of wives, children, and parents that the Argonauts would become destitute and find themselves stranded in California, the 49ers scoffed. It was a natural concern for families when they viewed their kin thrown into a society of strangers where one could not depend on relatives for assistance. The miners hastened to reassure them that even those who had lost everything in the mines could pick up enough work as day laborers in San Francisco or Sacramento or Stockton to pay their passage after a month's labor. They might have added that the returning 49ers, who almost all went home by the new and cheaper seagoing routes, first had to emerge with ticket and pouch intact from the temptations of San Francisco. Almost every returned or returning miner had tales of companions seduced by the bright gaming tables that clouded his judgment and, in the end, cleaned out his stake.

A number of 49ers who did go home returned to California, as we have seen. We have no way of knowing the size of this group or a distinct pattern to their activities. Some stayed in the East for a few weeks, others for some years. Others once again went alone in a continuing search for wealth over a short time, repeating their intention to return. Some Argonauts found the worlds that they remembered drastically changed; others found farms and villages boring and the euphoria of emotional reunions rapidly replaced by the drudgery of repetitive labor. Perhaps they also resented their continuing treatment as young people to be guided in their decisions by parents and older siblings. Whatever the reasons, supported by more rapid and cheaper means of transportation, the waves of those going to California in the decade of the 1850s included substantial numbers of those making second and sometimes third journeys.

Some Argonauts ultimately returned to the West Coast with their families, clearly intent on making a permanent home in California. Others wanted to do so but discovered that their wives, who had solidified their allegiances to their families and communities during the 49ers' prolonged absences, did not wish to leave. They feared the overland expedition or sea voyage, both raised to a high level of danger by popular account. They shrank from the barbarous nature of California society portrayed in many accounts of the Golden State. They did not wish to leave the networks of friends and neighbors that had supported them for so long.

Amos Stearns had gone to California in 1852, where he found a substantial degree of prosperity as superintendent of the "Argus" mine. His wife had refused to accompany him overland or by sea, saying that she would go only when she could make the complete journey by railroad. Stearns commuted to Ohio to visit her at irregular intervals over the next twenty years. During his lonely nights at the mine, he read the Bible, baked bread, sang songs, and greased his boots. He also occasionally "mourned my absence from home, So Much and at so little profit," he wrote. On a late fall day in 1871, he left Oroville for San Francisco, where he finally was reunited with his wife at the Russ House. He had not seen her for three and one-half years. He confided to his journal that he gave her twenty dollars to spend as she liked, and they returned to Oroville, where he toured her around his mining properties "in a Slay." With his wife settled with him in California at long last, his success seemingly complete, and his life consolidated, he immediately ceased to keep a journal.[16]

As the Golden State grew in population and its population thus grew in permanence, economic opportunities proliferated in like proportion. Those who found mining unrewarding and frustrating shifted over to occupations more familiar and in line with their own skills and experiences: working in the construction businesses, in agriculture in the interior valleys, or as skilled artisans and tradesmen. But as before, there were those who dreamed of golden fortunes to be found in the mines. However much the promise of California expanded to include the more common economic pursuits, until the outbreak of the Civil War shifted the nation's attention and resources elsewhere, Argonauts still departed for the West looking for gold.

18

THE RIPPLES SUBSIDE:

The End of the Gold Rush

*Sometimes on visiting my native village I stand before one of those old-
fashioned houses, from whose front door thirty-four years ago there went
forth for the last time the young Argonaut on his way to the ship.
But within all are strangers. The father and mother are past anxious
inquiry about their son. The sisters are married and live or have died
elsewhere. A new generation is all about. They never heard of him.
The great event of that period, the sailing of that ship for California,
is sometimes recalled by a few—a few rapidly diminishing.
His name is all but forgotten.*

PRENTICE MULFORD

HIGH TECHNOLOGY AND HARDSCRABBLE

THE SEARCH FOR GOLD and its harvest continued undiminished during
the 1850s, and annual gold production in California stabilized in 1857 at
about forty-five million dollars. The shape and scope of mining continued
to change in the direction of the increased use of technology and the increasing demand for capital to finance it. Entrepreneurs of several kinds
came to exercise a powerful influence in the mining business. Some of them
had begun to call themselves "engineers," but whatever the title, they had
access to capital and mastered the new technology for the deep mining and
exploitation of quartz veins, large-scale hydraulic enterprises, and major
damming projects. Many such enterprises initially failed, but eventually a
professional knowledge emerged that transformed mining into an industry
with a high degree of corporate structure and technological sophistication.[1]

One 49er who arrived in the diggings in 1857 (the term "diggings" was still
in use) described one of the new mining operations, running "a bedrock

tunnel to get into their claims." The tunnel was already 530 feet under ground, with another 30 feet to go, and cost from eighty to one hundred dollars a foot. He concluded: "So you can judge what it costs in money to get into these hill claims to say nothing about the number of lives that are lost, by premature explosions and other accidents."[2] More and more, Argonauts worked for someone else, all or part of the time they were in the gold fields.

Over this decade, many individuals and small companies were reduced to a hardscrabble existence, working for marginal returns today and the hope of a "raise" tomorrow. Accounts emphasized the familiar themes of hard work and widely varying returns on the watercourses of California. At the other end of the continent likewise lay monotonous arduous work on the farm for marginal returns and little hope of anything better in the future. Whatever their working conditions in the diggings and elsewhere in California—and they were often of the harshest kind—they continued to express the commitment to hard work and hope for the future that characterized their predecessors in an earlier generation.

For those who had the capital to benefit from the new mining patterns, the profits could be substantial. Amos Stearns reported that his personal net profit for the year August 1, 1858, to July 31, 1859, was $5,269.74 and 1/2. Aside from the precision of the number, the size of the return for a single individual is what attracts our attention. At one hundred dollars per week for an entire year, Stearns had averaged one ounce a day, the accepted return for the golden year of 1849. Almost ten years later, his returns would have been the envy of most miners pursuing their fortunes in California.[3]

Mining operations for many 49ers had undergone a remarkable change, yet the values and patterns echoed with those of the first generation. How much return at what rate? What were the expenses? How did prospects in the gold fields or elsewhere in California compare to those in the farm or shop that awaited them at home? Sullivan Osborn arrived in California in 1854 full of hopes for a better future. He also came armed with a complete roster of virtuous beliefs and disciplines, from temperance to a constant search for self-improvement, calculated to safeguard him against every temptation and ensure his success. Throughout his stay, he kept a list of his good and bad habits, with a constant emphasis on enlarging the first and diminishing the second. He criticized himself for reading romances instead of "better food for the mind," and he reported with much moralizing a case of adultery on the other side of the ravine involving a young doctor from Virginia and the wife of one of the miners. At the end of four years of hard labor, he was even financially. He had lost his hopes, but he had not lost his capacity to offer judgments on human behavior around him.[4]

Although he understood full well the odds against success in mining in 1855, Osborn also could write of the continuing ambition that drove him and so many others, an influence that "by its promptings thousands pursue shadows for years at last to have them vanish and find twas all a dream." To pursue his dream, he had left a home, "kind parents and all the enjoyments of life." With the passage of years gradually came an end to "the hopes and prospects" that had been "most ardently cherished." "Six years ago," he wrote, "I was young full of high hopes and bright anticipations of the future but they have long since perished and with them every fond ambition all I've thought or wished to be." Yet he did not go home but instead went into ranching. Osborn farmed in solitary introspection, as befitted his constant self-examination. He lamented in his diary the isolation associated with the pursuit of wealth that had robbed him of any social interaction with women.[5] For him, the Gold Rush was over.

For those who, like Sullivan Osborn, determined to stay, the end of the Gold Rush was played out in many places—not just the diggings. The "shadows" of success lay in the range of opportunities still available in California. Accompanying the rising influence of capital in the mining enterprises was the continuing growth of urban centers and the emergence of agriculture as a major commercial force.[6]

There were new kinds of fortunes to be made in the expanding cities. Within San Francisco, the shrewdest members of the legal profession presided over a merger between law and real estate. Through suits over land titles in San Francisco, the construction of business blocks, and later the adjudication of Spanish land grants that gave title to some of the best lands in the state, lawyers and their favored clients laid the foundation for some of the largest and most lasting fortunes to come out of the first decade of the Gold Rush.[7] Although cities had problems—especially developing class tensions and growth that threatened to submerge basic services such as streets, water, and sewage—whatever the immediate difficulties that confronted them, they continued to grow, despite economic booms and panics, natural disasters of fire and flood, and cycles of political corruption and reform. Indeed, the latter only added to the rising influence of lawyers.

By the middle of the 1850s, the influx of Argonauts had created a large and stable market for agricultural products. From beef for miners to hay for animals, this burgeoning market drove prices of foodstuffs up and offered profits that if not equal to those of the gold fields were certainly more reliable. As 49ers returned to farming, initially, they were apologetic. After all, had they crossed the continent or sailed around the Horn to till the soil and manage stock? These were all-too-familiar callings, far from the more exotic challenges of searching for gold nuggets in the swift streams. Forty-niners across the California landscape sent samples of their gold harvest to families across the eastern half of the nation; not a single one recorded sending samples of the soil. Yet the soil would prove enormously profitable—or at least would provide a steady income. With stories of fortunes in potatoes or beef and the steady market for hay and draft animals came the growing recognition that agriculture provided an attractive option for those who sought genuine economic advantage, rather than simply the excitement of the mines and mining. [8]

Like mining, agriculture was seasonal and needed water, but from this common ground, the two economic exercises diverged in their capital requirements. The 49ers could mine—in the first generation at least—with a set of tools, a primitive shelter, a few provisions, and a single set of clothes. Even at "Gold Rush prices," most Argonauts could wash gravel in the streambeds. The venture into agriculture demanded a more elaborate investment. It also meant making a longer-term commitment to staying and working in California. The investment gap narrowed in the second generation of mining, when the 49ers had to purchase claims at escalating prices or invest in dams to join the mining exercise. Agriculture continued to require a commitment to remain for a period of years but in return afforded a more stable living. As the Gold Rush unfolded over the years, many observers commented that a modestly successful 49er who had invested in a farm instead of shares in a dam or quartz company would have laid the basis of economic independence.[9]

As the settlement of California continued, as transportation to and from the East became easier, and as the West became in many ways more and more like the East, those who pursued enterprise in California in the years before the Civil War tended increasingly to measure their lives and economic prospects against economic opportunities back home—on the farm, in the shop, in the factory, in the professional offices and salons. Frequently, they found them to measure up well. What is really significant, however, is that 49ers now had begun to see life in California and life in the states in the same terms. The accounts of life and labor in the gold fields, farms, and cities of California in the years before the Civil War confirm the extent to which, thanks to the Gold Rush, the West had become part of the fabric of the nation.

SETH AND ASA SMITH

Asa Smith was an Argonaut who became a Californian and a Californian who saw himself as part of a transcontinental enterprise. Asa's brother Seth left his father, mother, and Asa himself on a farm outside Baltimore to join the annual emigration to California in the spring of 1850. He went immediately to the diggings on the Feather River and, by his own account, found astonishing success. Through the spring of 1851, he wrote confidently that "a man can average 25$ [a day] all the year round I think he works half as hard as he would on a farm." He continually measured his work and returns against the daily drudgery required on the farm, expressing the view that miners who come home "can not be content to stay there nor any body else they will never be satisfied to dig all day for their old wages after having been out here." He speculated that he would have five hundred dollars on hand clear by his twenty-third birthday, for him an astonishing sum. At the end of the 1851 mining season, Seth Smith returned to the farm.[10]

The hard work and meager returns associated with farming in rural Maryland did not satisfy him. In the summer of 1853, Seth Smith took the steamer back to California, accompanied this time by his brother Asa. Seth had put his California earnings into the farm to support his parents and sister Mary and had borrowed the money to return from Uncle Ezra, who also went to California with the Smith brothers. Uncle Ezra went to work in a hotel in Auburn; Seth and Asa mined on Morris Bar. The Smiths were disappointed with the results and their prospects. By late 1853, with claims expensive and the work as arduous as ever, Seth Smith called his decision to return to California "the greatest piece of folly ever heard of." He went on, "I had enough to pay Uncle Ezra & build a barn too.... It was like an early marriage done in a hurry and repented of at leisure."[11]

Seth and Asa worked in the heat of the summer and fall mining season; in the evenings, they wrote of how much they wished to return home. Seth continually lamented the returns of two to three dollars a day, but he admitted that work on the farm would be as laborious and the profits no greater. During the fall, by carrying "dirt" fifty yards to a cradle, the two men made about one dollar a day each, or just about expenses. Seth became openly discouraged. Asa continued to view the enterprise with some optimism, but he recognized the intense competition for good mining sites. Asa called California "pretty well turned over I can tell you every place where it will pay—anything at all is worked if not by Americans—by Chinese—with their long tails and umbrella heads—they will work for 2 and 1/2$ pr day." Yet this sum was often more than the Smiths averaged.[12]

The next year, 1854, was a hard one for miners and their merchant suppliers throughout the gold camps, and the Smiths had their share of the problems. A series of sudden rainstorms washed out the dam of the company that provided their water, further setting them back. As the brothers soldiered on into 1855, they began to buy water from a water company at a cost of two dollars for each man. They had now to wash four dollars of gold each day to start even.[13]

Throughout his stay in California, Asa saw his family as a small company engaged in two economic enterprises, one on the East Coast the other on the West. Asa Smith treated his sister as a full partner in this company. That she, like his father, labored in only one of these businesses did not make her contributions less significant to him or less worthy of his respect. He always treated her as an equal, and when the opportunity arose, he took care to reward her in small ways that let her know that her labors were appreciated. He also helped pay off notes of indebtedness that were coming due on the farm back home, although he complained that times in California "are *hard* let me tell you." As for expectations of their immediate return to the East, he thought it unlikely. Instead, he advised his father to "hire a hand" and to rest as much as possible.

Family and neighbors wrote to Seth and Asa Smith to inquire about prospects in California. Asa painted a sober picture of hard work and meager return: "Tell Sydney he needn't want to come to this country—hard labor—harder living—and still harder company—to pay a man for his rashness." Whatever the hardships of work and hard times that afflicted so many miners in California, however, Asa believed "we can make a little more here than there."[14]

Asa continued to take a lively interest in the farm in Maryland. He always inquired about crops for the coming growing season, livestock prospects, and changes in the neighborhood. In early 1856, in response to news a railroad would soon pass near the farm, he advised his parents to permit the railroad to build as close as possible to the farm and then to sue for damages. He continued to describe conditions in California as rugged for miners. "This is a hard country on the constitution of man—hard work—wet through every day & then have to go home & do your own cooking & then a hard bed to rest on—no feathers not one," he wrote.[15] These complaints had been heard in precisely these same words since the first 49ers arrived six years earlier. Yet Asa Smith showed no interest in returning to the farm in Maryland.

In the spring of 1856, Asa and Seth Smith suffered another financial reverse. They had lent out part of their hard-earned mining money at high interest; the debtor defaulted, and the Smiths lost the three hundred and fifty dollars due them. Despite improved mining prospects, Asa and Seth fortunately had begun to make improvements on "a ranch" as a hedge against risks.[16]

In summer 1858, Seth left for home, broken in health and no longer able to "perform the physical labor connected with mining." Henceforth, Asa and Seth corresponded, two veteran Argonauts who knew both the mining camp and ranch at one end of the continent and the Maryland farm at the other. As he settled into the routine of the farm, Seth began to complain about the monotonous work and the scanty returns, and he talked of returning to California. From the site of their claims, Asa advised him to stay in Maryland, reminding him of the hard labor and uncertain returns he had left in California. In the last six months, Asa reported, he had cleared about one hundred and fifty dollars. If necessary, he would send some money to help with debts on the Maryland farm, but he reminded Seth, "if your health is not sufficiently recovered to stand another siege of five years as hard labor as this time you had better stay where you are—money or no money."[17] Asa's mother died in 1859, and he received news of her passing with resignation. "I am glad one of us was home at least to comfort & console the rest in their affliction," he wrote with reference to the presence of his brother Seth. He continued his close contact with the family, sending one hundred and fifty dollars to help with expenses, including "a little for Sister if she should have need of it which I am quite certain."[18]

At the end of six full seasons of mining, Asa's physical condition showed the years of long, hard work, under harsh physical conditions, and he began to cast around for another occupation. Of his health in July 1860, he commented, "I could do a great deal better at our business if my nerves were more steady as the long siege of mining has taxed my system so that I find it almost impossible to regular them—though I have made every effort by strict attention to the laws of regimen—but it availed not much & maybe I will have to relinquish eventually this business on that account."[19]

The fact that Asa still refused to return to the farm in Maryland despite hard times in California after 1854 indicates that he had made a conscious choice based on opportunity. In the final analysis, Asa Smith saw life in the diggings and on the ranches in California as part of a continuum of labor with life and work on the Maryland farm. Asa remained devoted to his family in the East and to the farm, and he saw clearly the kind of hard work demanded by both. But in California there remained the elusive possibility that one of these sunny afternoons, he would stumble onto a rich claim. Then, within a few months or even weeks, such a "raise" would wipe out the memories of sore backs and frustrating mining seasons. It was this vision that kept the 49ers in pursuit of the elusive shadows.

NOAH GEBHART

One consequence of the growing similarity between the East and the West was that in the West in the later years of the Gold Rush, as in the East when the migration began, the opportunities for those not possessing the advantages of money, education, and social position had grown scant. The dark side of the efforts at self-assertion and independence made by the likes of Allen Varner appear in the struggles endured by Noah Gebhart, who left Ottumwa, Iowa, for California in 1852, a member of a company that bought thirty claims near Grass Valley. After a brief trip home in 1854, Gebhart returned to the gold fields to renew his search for a "rase," as he always wrote the word. Unlike Asa Smith, who saw his hard work in his mining ventures in California as simply an extension of the hard work on the farm back home in Maryland, Noah Gebhart was driven by an almost frantic desire to escape the conditions of the life he had led. But in the new social and economic conditions characteristic of California at this late stage of the Gold Rush, doing so proved no more possible than it had been in Iowa. Noah Gebhart's command of grammar and spelling were marginal, and his wife Martha could neither read nor write. As someone who saw only the edge of the world of letters and numbers, Gebhart came to the gold fields as a marginal figure, driven by considerable bitterness about his lot in life, and a marginal, embittered figure he remained.

Gebhart pursued mining on the larger scale associated with so much of the second generation. When he returned to California in 1855, he launched a great mining venture, which he described in these terms: "I went to work & Have gotten up a company for the purposes of Cutting the great falls out of the Middle Fork of the American river." It was an elaborate project, typical of those in the second generation of mining, with a capital of fifty thousand dollars divided into 200 shares of two hundred and fifty dollars each.[20] Gebhart held ten percent of the stock. Through the summer months of 1855, he supervised a crew cutting through the rock formations of the American River. The company failed. At the decisive moment, the sides of the cut so laboriously blasted out of the landscape collapsed. After this failure, Gebhart found himself constantly at work to make up his losses. As he wrote to his friend Dibble, "You must understand that I only want to make up the losses I have sustained which I think I can make by fall."[21] His declarations to his family a year later represented the determination and sacrifice that echoed through a thousand letters home: "I got in debt and had to turn out to work by the Day to get money to live while I am prospecting I never lived harder and worked harder than I have this last year."[22] Each new season brought new hopes of enough success to let him break free of the cycle of losses, sell out, and return to Iowa. He never succeeded.

He also grew increasingly distant from his family. Gebhart left eight children behind in Ottumwa, ranging in age from one to twenty. The youngest son, Manfred, born in 1855, was presumably conceived during Gebhart's brief return home in 1854. In the intervening years, his family underwent continuing change. With children spread across almost a generation, Gebhart struggled to keep track of them all, asking about the new baby's growth and the names and ages of his grandchildren, a series of awkward and embarrassing inquiries. When one of his sons complained about being apprenticed to a pharmacist, Gebhart urged him to make the most of this fine chance. He indicated that by studying hard and mastering new skills, his children would not end up like him, lonely in mind, broken in body, and in debt in a remote mining camp in California. When his daughter Sarah announced her engagement to a Mr. Majors, she did not ask her father's permission. He was apparently too distant and uninformed. Gebhart never had met Majors, and he wrote his sons, "I would be glad to know more of him than I know now he rote me a verry good sensable letter in regard to his Marage with Sarah."[23]

Noah Gebhart had a touching faith in the power of education to lift his children to a higher station in life. Ease in reading and fluency in writing, he believed, would smooth the way of his sons and daughters to a better life than he could achieve. Underlying his continuing determination to battle through a series of losses was the overriding belief that his efforts were making more and better education possible for his children. He wrote, "All I want to give the Chldren is as good an Education as I can it is all my Desire I want to make Men of the Boys." He sent a message to his wife—because she could not write, the couple communicated through the letters of the children—to "get some friend who is willing to assist you to keep the children at a good school & at such a one as they should be kept at till I can come & see to it myself."[24]

However, the Gebhart family was in constant need of funds, and Gebhart had none to send. In the face of failed mining projects, persistent debts, and a stream of appeals from his children, Noah Gebhart's letters became irate and bitter. He criticized their correspondence habits, their spelling and grammar, although his was primitive in the extreme, and their failure to send him complete news about the old neighborhood. Gebhart's sense of frustration was sharpened by rumors that had begun to circulate about him in Ottumwa. According to reports relayed by his children, he led a life of dissipation and had married again in California. Gebhart was furious at being forced to defend himself against such accusations and against his family's fears that he would never come back to Iowa, yet, at the same time, he repeatedly postponed his return, giving additional credibility to the stories.[25]

Like so many others, despite his setbacks, and despite his growing distance from his loved ones, Gebhart found reasons to stay. His setbacks had not diminished his spirit, and he could write, "I am Determined to be found among them trying to make a rase before I think of coming home. this may seem hard to you but it is my Determination to do so as I am sure that if I can ever make anything I can do it much easyer hear than I can in Iowa."[26] What is affecting about this faith is that in the later years of the Gold Rush it was less and less likely to bear fruit. He worked in a series of jobs to raise funds to pursue opportunities in quartz mines. He was eager to become a part of the new quartz "excitement," and his own quartz claims were "all my hopes of making a rase." As he had in his first big venture on the American River, Gebhart was prepared to risk everything on a single throw of the dice. When a man offered him one thousand dollars for one of the quartz claims, he refused, holding out for more. To his chagrin, the man took his capital to the Fraser River.[27]

Gebhart struggled on for another four years, resigned to the failure of his current prospects, but optimistic about the future. Like his friend Dibble and their companions, who "have not made very well yet but live in hopes," Gebhart also lived "in hopes."[28] He worked at a series of occupations, eventually in construction. Noah Gebhart was murdered in 1862. By then, his family in Iowa had long since turned its collective attention from his distant struggles to the Civil War and the opportunities and sacrifices associated with this new, national adventure. His alleged murderer escaped from a jail that had been built by his victim. This unhappy act was, in a sense, a recapitulation of Gebhart's experiences in California. Although both pluck and luck always had been assets in the Gold Rush, pluck by itself no longer was enough, and Gebhart had more than his share of bad fortune. California's golden promise had called forth Noah Gebhart's best efforts in a way Iowa could not, but they proved as fruitless in the Golden State as they would have among the more circumscribed opportunities he thought he had left behind. For some 49ers, the assimilation of California into the broader social and economic life of the nation meant that a door that had seemed to open on a better life was being closed.

FROM SEA TO SHINING SEA

Even some of those who had not done well in the search for gold or other economic advantage determined to make California a permanent residence. Of these, some determined to stay in California and never return; others returned to their families and, dissatisfied with small wages, hard labor, and unhappy family situations, were soon bent on returning to California. "But few came home to remain," remembered Prentice Mulford, "they 'staid around' home for a few weeks, turned up their noses at small prices asked for drinks, cigars, and stews, treated everybody, grew restless and were off again."[29]

The decision to put down permanent roots in California had powerful implications for families in the East. Families now had to acknowledge that the Gold Rush had brought about a kind of cell division. What had been seen as a family with an absent member or members came to be seen as a family divided, dispersed, and grown into two separate entities. Whatever arrangements had been made in response to a temporary absence, even calculated in years, now had to be refigured to take into consideration a permanent separation. As with all separations, even the most fecund, this was not always an easy process. One of the continuing dimensions of this move to the West was the struggle over the issue of other members of the family joining the 49er in California. Several elements emerged in these discussions. Some wives refused to move to California, or set difficult conditions for doing so, like Amos Stearns's spouse, as we have seen. Others went with great reluctance. Winslow Pierce, of Rock Island, Illinois, had joined the rush to California in the summer of 1849. A medical doctor who had risen above an impoverished childhood, Pierce had married Georgiana ("Georgy") Moore, a daughter of one of Rock Island's most prominent families. Pierce's practice in Marysville prospered in ways that he never could have expected in Rock Island, and in 1851 he ran successfully as the Democratic Party candidate for Comptroller of California, a post that paid five thousand dollars a year.

While Pierce was waging his statewide campaign, another struggle was taking shape in the parlors of his in-laws in Illinois and Indiana. There, Georgy's sisters and mother were campaigning vigorously to keep her from going to California to join her husband. Her presence and that of her son Harry were necessary to make sure that the family would remain united in the eastern half of the continent, they believed. The news of Winslow Pierce's successes in California had spread through the family branches, and the departure of the wife and son might well indicate a permanent move to the Golden State.[30] For his part, Pierce cited the large numbers of respectable "ladies" who recently had arrived to make their homes in the Golden State. He coaxed her to bring her sister Kitty so that they might both enjoy the wonderful climate and improving society of California. If she would not come ("Do be courageous"), he said, he would resign the office and return to her, but he would much prefer to remain in California: "here I will take a stand among men free from those petty little envys or jealousies that are in Rock Island."[31]

Two months after Pierce's election, Georgy decided to join him. The price that he paid for this victory over his in-laws, however, was high. The Moore family heard such news with "deep regret that any California associations have affected the movement of any part of our family."[32] Then, in the spring of 1852, with his wife about to depart for California, Pierce received an anonymous letter, accusing his wife of infidelity. Pierce rallied to his wife's defense, wrote her enclosing a copy of the letter, and affirmed his belief in her innocence—"You could never have Suffered any man to have presumed for a moment on your virtue or your chastity or even your thoughts." He asked that she share the letter with Kitty, but as for others, "the enclosed must not be exposed or left where it can be Seen." Nor did Pierce propose to impart the letter to the other Moore family members in Illinois and Indiana. He chose to treat it as a private matter.[33]

Whatever the source of this letter, Pierce discovered that despite his successes in the Golden State, as a result of his decision to establish his family permanently in California, his hopes of being accepted into the Moore family had been dashed—besides Kitty, only one other sister, Jane Moore Pomeroy, supported his venture to California. Pierce never forgot the opposition of "some of those silly & mistaken brothers & sisters." And he concluded with great feeling, "But I do say before God this night to you dear Kitty that I was *right* in the matters for which I was *blamed*." Between the family and himself there had settled "that *eternal* silence." All his attempts at reconciliation were rebuffed. Pierce suggested that a driving influence in his ambition and the decision to hazard a voyage to California was grounded in his determination to put distance and independence between himself and his wife's family.[34]

When Georgiana Pierce (with son Harry, the apple of Winslow's eye) arrived in San Francisco in early 1853, the Pierce family was reunited after a separation of more than three years. During the session of the legislature, they lived in Benicia, close to the capital in Sacramento, where Pierce had an office. When the legislature was not in session, they lived in San Francisco. It was an idyllic interlude for the Pierce family, and Winslow Pierce basked in the smiles of his wife and son, weighing a post at a bank in San Francisco or becoming a candidate for United States Senate.[35] But the separation from Georgy's family and the creation of a new, happy family in the West had come at a cost that still exacted payments, as subsequent events proved.

Georgiana Pierce's health, always fragile, declined through the summer and fall of 1853. In early February 1854, the whole family returned to Indianapolis, the new seat of the Moore family. Winslow Pierce immediately left for Washington, D.C., to check on his political prospects. He then went back to California, leaving Georgy in the care of her family. As her condition worsened, she wrote him plaintive letters, urging his return. He postponed leaving San Francisco, eventually arriving in Indianapolis in mid-December. There, by his own account, he stayed at a hotel because of his reluctance to face her, separated from his dying wife by the divisions of their families. A pitiable exchange of letters detailed their longing for one another across this final distance of a few miles. He finally visited her four days before her death. In spite of their intense love for one another, they had spent four of their last five years apart.[36]

Winslow Pierce was fortunate. Early in his residence in the mines, Lemuel Hopkins determined to make California his future home. To that end, he undertook steps to bring his wife and family to join him. In this he was frustrated by her views and those of her mother.

> In reference to my wife coming to California, I have only this to say, that it would be the most desirable thing that I can think of, but she has expressed her preference, in favor of staying with *her friends* there, consequently I shall never ask her again to come, as I would not have her come against her wish, in favor, to have her here dissatisfied and discontented, would be worse than her absence.[37]

To persuade her to come, Hopkins wrote, he had "used all the persuasions I thought proper," but to no effect. He continued his determined campaign to persuade her to come to California over the next five years, however. Finally, he wrote his brother in the summer of 1859, "I sent home seven hundred dollars for my wife and children to come out here and before you get this, they will have started if they come at all, which I presume they will do. unless old Mother Phelps prevails on Carrie to stay, which she has succeeded in doing for a long time." He was right. She still refused to make the trip.[38]

Some 49ers married in California. Those who did attempted to maintain contact with their families in the East, sending daguerreotypes and locks of hair, long descriptions of the new wife, the new house, and the new children. Both sides sometimes wrote at length about the eroding effect of distance and to maintain the sense of family identity.[39]

Whether they married there or moved their families west, those who remained in California long enough saw large changes in their families. Younger siblings married, new births enlarged the family circle, elderly parents died, and sometimes family members moved. In 1871, after twenty years in California, John Kinkade sat at the kitchen table and peered at the recently arrived photographs of his relatives. He finally had to admit that he did not recognize the likeness of any of his eastern family. Too much time had passed; too many changes had taken place in families.[40]

Some families deliberately broke off contact with their departed 49er. Albert Tucker left Rhode Island for California in 1849. He heard from home for the last time in 1850. He spent the next ten years wandering across the mining landscape of the West, and in the winter of 1861, settled in a cabin on the Fraser River in British Columbia, he attempted once again to establish contact with letters to his father and sister. He had recovered from a lengthy illness "with a longing desire to hear from home once more though I never hear again." He concluded with the plea, "I hope sir you will do me the favor to answer this letter." Both his father and his sister did so.

Tucker was overjoyed at the reunion by mail and saddened at how much had changed. The letters, however welcome after eleven years, were "freighted with tidings of heavy import—deaths plentiful and foremost among them stands the name of my mother." Tucker's mother had been dead for several years; his brother had been arrested and tried for an unnamed crime, an event he described as "awful circumstances happened to the family in 1855 that I learned of through the newspapers." He feared his father's continued poor opinion of him, although he had worked for years to succeed. As for his own affairs, he confessed that "matters have gone very poorly with me ever since I left home—I have gone through everything in the shape of hardships and privations, first in California and now in this country; and the good that has come of it is little enough."[41]

Aside from his mother's passing, the other great shock for Tucker was the change in his sister. He had left her a schoolgirl, "running up and down the hill with a satchel on her arm or standing at the open window fronting the cherry tree of a spring morning with a minstrel book on her hand singing melodies." Now, she was a married woman with children. The words "baby boy" and "husband" leaped at him from the page. "The little school sister disappears as by magic and there stands another in her stead; yet she is the same and I ask myself what is she like." Tucker wrote a long description of his sister as he now imagined her, a grown woman with her own family. Also in his portrait was "her aged and afflicted father, her wandering ne'er do well brother and an outcast wretch." Such was the account that he composed "in a log cabin, stretched on my bunk, pen in hand I work away with a howling storm driving round me." In addition to continued contact, Tucker had a final "petition" for his family. He wished to have a picture of them, and he described what he wanted in detail: "I want to see five figures daguerreo-typed—those figures to be my father and sister, my sister's two children and her husband. I wish these figures grouped as follows. Let my father sit in front on the right, my sister at his side, her babe in her lap, little Fanny holding on to her left hand, and my sister's husband standing behind the two chairs."[42] In return, Tucker promised his own likeness, "a picture of the old gold hunter, so you may compare the doctor (as miniatured and sent to mother in '49) with the gold hunter of the present." He closed with several quotations from scripture that asked forgiveness for everyone. Throughout this heartfelt contact, he never suggested that he would return.[43]

THE VANISHED 49ERS

Some 49ers simply disappeared. This was the ultimate form of separation. They vanished into the vast spaces, the new landscape, and the innumerable economic opportunities of California at midcentury. This group not only never returned home, it lost contact with home. These lost connections were probably both accidental and deliberate. Miners often moved from camp to camp; mail service was uncertain. Many 49ers did not write much; some did not write at all. Family correspondents were likely to be more persistent, but even these faithful scribes could fall by the wayside. Others certainly seized the numerous opportunities of distance and anonymity to sever connections with friends and relatives in the East.

As hopes began to fade for letters from these fathers, brothers, and sons, their families reconstructed their lives and moved forward with the duties associated with day-to-day living. The names of those departed for the gold fields continued to be heard around the dinner table, in conversations after church, and among young people for many months, sometimes years. Gradually, however, in their communities, memories of them dimmed, crowded out by the arrival of the latest news from those in California who corresponded regularly and those recently returned. Only in their families did the memories live on, and there with only occasional reference, and after a long while, not at all.

Prentice Mulford understood these changes in his own village. They were like a pool, with the water parted by a dramatic event, waves spreading out in response to the interruption, and a gradual calming, with the water eventually joining to make a smooth surface once again. After a generation in Mulford's village, the waters had become still again, and only the parents—"past anxious inquiry of their son"—and an occasional sibling remembered the departed Argonaut. "The sisters are married and live or have died elsewhere." The girl that the Argonaut had courted—"she with whom he sat up that last Sunday night in the old-fashioned front parlor on the old-fashioned sofa"—she married someone else.[44] The families and the villages adjusted to their prolonged absences and eventually accepted that they would never return.

Up to the end of the decade, the occasional Argonaut continued to trickle back to the village, as Mulford noted, "an object of curiosity and of some importance if he brought any money with him, or rather as long as the money he brought with him lasted." But people's attention was turning elsewhere. Compelling national events had overtaken the drama of the Gold Rush. The sectional conflict that turned into a great civil war offered another splendid opportunity to leave home, to join together in "companies," and to march off to music, prayers, and shouts. Just as some of this new generation of volunteers found great deeds and others suffered pain and death, so a third group made fortunes. "The California fortune of that time was a mere pimple compared with the fortunes made by the war," remembered Mulford.[45] The Civil War wrote a dramatic conclusion to the faded people and memories of the California Gold Rush. Those who did not make fortunes settled for martial glory and monuments. The Gold Rush left no monuments—only memories.

Even after the years of war and then a long period of national reconciliation, some continued to search for their relatives and friends vanished into California. Sometimes they sought out those who had known them; sometimes, they posted public announcements in newspapers. From Kalamazoo, Michigan, in the autumn of 1899, on the occasion of the fiftieth anniversary of departure for the gold fields, Rufus Dickinson sought his brother. "Mr. Editor. a Brother of mine by the name of William Rufus Dickinson went to california in the spring of 1849," he wrote. Later, he was joined by another brother, "Horace Brown Dickinson who owned a good Property there on the Pacific Coast." Rufus Dickinson had lived in Halsey, in Legon County, Oregon, and later in the "Rougue River Valley but I have not been able to learn what town or county he lived in. I have not heard from either of them in most 30 years. I was about ten years old when they left home. After father & mother died they seemed to forget to write. Rufus worked in the mines part of the time. He was a violinist also. I would be glad to learn what became of them."[46] He spoke for many others.

19

"THE DAYS OF OLD, THE DAYS OF GOLD, THE DAYS OF FORTY-NINE":
The Gold Rush and Memory

THE CALIFORNIA GOLD RUSH was about wealth. The powerful surge of gold fever that afflicted so many families and communities over a decade rested on the expectation of economic advantage. The Argonauts of '49 and subsequent years, on the voyages to California and later in the diggings, talked and wrote about wealth and what they would do with it, measured against their absences from their families over a period of years. Yet almost before they were out of sight of the harbor or the tree line on the plains, these self-selected Argonauts began to think of their voyages as part of a larger and less selfish exercise. Instead of an enterprise in self-aggrandizement, they claimed, the rush of tens of thousands to California was about building an empire, the expansion of the continental nation, and so the representatives of the Republic went west, among other things, to reclaim the new territories acquired from Mexico, from Catholicism and despotism (represented by Santa Anna), and to establish the national presence in the eyes of the Indians of the plains. J. R. Boyle, a young 49er from Tennessee, asked his mother and family to write to him in the "golden Land," and he reflected the sense of national purpose when he wrote that she and other members of his family could read about him in the history books.[1]

Whatever their differences of economic status and sectional orientation, the 49ers of all generations found themselves united by participation in the great national adventure at midcentury. This sense of participating in a unique experience took hold in California and conferred on them a powerful sense of their own different identity, especially those who returned to their families and communities. There, they tried to explain these experiences to a wide-eyed but uncomprehending audience of family and neighbors who insisted on asking how much gold the Argonauts had brought with them. That so many returned with so little surely reinforced the growing sense that the Gold Rush was about much more than money, that participation in this extraordinary event conferred membership in one of the country's exclusive clubs, reserved for pioneers and the vanguard of American civilization and democracy. What was gold by comparison with such participation and the memories that came from it? So even as those who returned home celebrated their return with their families and in their communities, the events of these past years assumed great importance, and as young and energetic men grew older in humdrum routine lives, their participation in this great national adventure took on a golden glow.

THE FIRST MEMORIES

Many 49ers had developed close friends and joined tight-knit communities in California. Even as their families and communities in the states called on them to return, the Argonauts found themselves with a powerful allegiance to these friends in the gold camps. These were the individuals with whom they had worked, lived, and shared their dreams and schemes in the placers and other places in California. They were also the people to whom they gave their trust and allegiance in work and leisure, in good times and hard times. Only with great reluctance did some 49ers leave their companions in the diggings, to part from the truest friends of their adulthood. So California came to symbolize more than gold nuggets; its mines were the place of lasting friendships, loyalties forged in explosions of physical energy and labor and in the leisure of long evenings around the fire and longer winter days, bonds that exceeded anything that 49ers had known within their families. When they returned home, they came back to old relationships often changed and sometimes unhappy. Whatever their pleasure at good food and a warm bed, they had left something unique behind. Not surprisingly, they often missed it.

The nostalgia for the days of the Gold Rush also included memories of the landscape, work routines, and a kaleidoscope of events and places. One

49er wrote of his first year away from home, "I have seen sights in the last twelve months that will long be remembered."[2] R. G. Moore wrote how much he missed a companion who had left the gold fields: "I would like very much to See you—my old Friend—and talk with you of old times." That these "old times" dated from only a year and a half earlier did not make them, in his mind, any less memorable and affecting.[3]

REMEMBERING IN SONG

From the beginning, the 49ers sang. They sang as they marched to the wharves, on shipboard, and around the campfires on the way to California. They sang in the diggings and in the towns. They sang to themselves; they sang in groups; they were sung to by entertainers. Later, they sang on the way home and after their return. Only what they sang changed. When the days of the Gold Rush ended, the songs remained to remind the 49ers and the nation of the days gone by.

The first songs had appeared with the first companies and the first chartered ships. Indeed, so rapidly did they appear that it was almost as if songsters had known ahead of time about this vast movement of people to a strange and distant place. The first songs expressed an optimism and enthusiasm about the venture west consistent with the extravagant reports in the press, as well as a sadness at parting from family and friends. The original songs used well-known popular airs. "Oh, California," to the tune of "Oh! Susanna," was one of the most popular of the early songs. Among its verses was the declaration:

> I soon shall be in Frisco.
> And there I'll look around,
> And when I see the Gold lumps there
> I'll pick them off the ground.
> I'll scrape the mountains clean, my boys,
> I'll drain the rivers dry,
> A pocketful of rocks bring home—
> So brothers don't you cry.[4]

This account expressed the incipient power of the American migration in its capacity to change the landscape and seize every opportunity for wealth.

Along with the sense of preparation ("We've formed our band and are well mann'd") went the expression of sorrow at parting. Yet even here, the focus was on the distress of those left behind, not on those setting forth on the great adventure:

> O! don't you cry, nor heave a sigh,
> For we'll all come back again, bye and bye,
> Don't breathe a fear, nor shed a tear,
> But patiently wait for about two year.[5]

The basic tune and verses could be expanded to include any place of origin and adventure on the way to the gold fields. The song "Oh, California" mentioned "Salem City," but any four-syllable place would do as well. A variation—also to the tune of "Oh! Susanna"—included "We started from Old Beverly, / Mid cheers from great and small" and continued "The fair sex wept, the boys hurrahed / And we'd no time to cry."[6] Not that it was appropriate for men to cry in popular verse. Such displays of sentiment were reserved for journals and letters.

Another group of songs celebrated the arrival of the seagoing Argonauts in California. They recounted the difficulties of the voyage to San Francisco and the problems of keeping the company together once arrived ("We'd forty men of forty minds, instead of one alone"). The verses explored the various kinds of employment open to the 49ers and those who did not wish to work, who "can loaf and take their ease." The songs spoke to the 49er fantasy of a world in which those with right values who worked hard would prosper ("And may a fortune be in store for every honest man"), and those who wished simply to get by could do so in California's golden landscape. Perhaps it also spoke to a fear of idleness and the uneasiness of a society in which citizens of the Republic could live lives of leisure.[7]

Most of the Argonauts came by land in '49, and they needed several songs—with titles such as "Crossing the Plains"—to pass the long evenings around the campfires. Of these, the best known was probably "Sweet Betsy from Pike," which recounted the voyage of Betsy and "her lover Ike" from Pike County across the plains to "old Placerville." On the way, they stopped over in Salt Lake City, where Betsy fought off the advances of Brigham Young. The songs of the 49ers sometimes contained these strong anti-Mormon sentiments, which were associated with the personal experiences of so many Argonauts in coming by way of Salt Lake City.[8] This group of songs included "Seeing the Elephant," whose fourteen verses carry the 49er across the plains, through the peculiar Mormon society of the Great Salt Lake, and into the mining country, where he encounters Chinese ("And robbed the Chinese of their rice") and African-Americans ("I robbed a nigger of a dollar") and is expelled from a camp for an affair with another miner's wife.[9] It was not a recitation of virtues, but its presentation before a group of 49ers in a dusty canvas-topped saloon must have been greeted with appreciative shouts and laughter.

In the diggings or pursuing opportunities in the camps and towns, the 49ers continued to express their joys and sorrows in songs, but here the singing often involved both popular and professional performances. Among the professional entertainers were many who toured the camps and bars with variety shows. The verses they sang spoke to the adventures and misadventures of the 49ers in the diggings. They noted the contrast between the popular accounts ("At home they think we ought to have gold on our cabin shelves") and the realities of gold mining ("You may work till you're tired and wet, / The claim you just bought is good for nought"). The villains in this world were the "big ditch companies" that controlled the water, the "business man" who constantly "whined" about his bills, and the omnipresent gamblers who lifted many a hard-earned ounce from the working miner. The subject matter of songs also covered miners' meetings, with their endless discussions of the finer points of claim rights by miners who were progressively more intoxicated as the evening wore on.[10]

One group of songs about the 49ers in California sung around the campfires and in the saloons had a strong element of nostalgia and pathos. These songs described the hard working conditions ("With woolen shirt and rubber boots, in mud up to my knees, / And lice as large as chili beans fighting with the fleas"), the chancy returns, and the gouging of merchants, water ditch owners, and lawyers. They catalogued the migration of miners from placering to damming and then to quartz ventures, all with the same result. They noted the arrival of other groups and hostility toward them ("He told the Greasers they were out, / And Jonathan was in, sir"). They also spoke of miners in the distant reaches of the Sierra jilted by their wives and sweethearts. Such sentiments must have reflected hidden fears rarely expressed openly, except perhaps privately to one another. Finally, they also spoke to memories of home, the tearful partings, the last images of the family on the porch or road. Along with the "dreams of home" in the "cold and dreary" camp went the hope that the absent 49er would still be remembered by family and friends: "When at home his name is spoken, / Does some loved one weep or sigh?"[11]

Miners fashioned an array of songs to celebrate their hard lives, but these accounts were often humorous. The titles—"The Unhappy Miner," "The Lousy Miner"—indicate the subject matter. The words often contrasted the harsh and unpleasant condition of the camps with the clean and comfortable world of home, with waiting wife, children, and parents. Another group of songs dealt with the return home. The optimism of these verses gave a sharp contrast with the difficult conditions in camp. "I'll leave this world of rags and dirt" ran a favorite line. An undercurrent of these songs was the vision of the successful miner returning in triumph with gold in his pouch. "I shall have a better prospect now, for I have ample means," they sang. The idea of returning with little or nothing was so sensitive that songsters did not attempt to deal with it.[12]

Over the dozen years of the Gold Rush, the song was a perfect vehicle for expressing the common world of the miners and for the kinds of entertainment they enjoyed. As part of an oral tradition, it did not demand reading skills. The song also was flexible. After a half-dozen standard verses that covered the mining world generally, 49ers could create additional stanzas that spoke to their special place or circumstances. The adaptability of the songs made them popular entertainment features in the variety shows of the tent saloons of the diggings and the richly decorated dance halls of the cities. Audiences would sing and shout their approval as tune followed tune, old familiar favorites and new additions to the repertoire. The song also fitted into the entertainment formula of the mining country, with its many drinking places and itinerant professional entertainers. For the traveling troupe, the core of mining songs offered a universal entrée into every mining camp or bar.[13]

A final group of songs dated from twenty years later, songs of reminiscence and nostalgia. "I remember, I remember, when once I used to mine," ran one opening line. The living and working conditions were still described as hard, but they now were treated as barriers that the true 49ers had surmounted. They could look back on them with the perspective of veterans who wished to celebrate this part of their past. The verses had lost the edge of humor. Instead, a rosy hue suffused those youthful days of home-baked bread, hard labor, and comradeship.

> And I often grieve and pine,
> For the days of gold, the days of old,
> The days of forty-nine.

Then, comrades were "staunch and brave, and true as steel," but now they have begun to drop by the wayside. Stories of "Kentucky Bill," "New York Jake," "North Carolina Jess," and "Hackensack Jim" gave a protean quality to the experience. Certain things had changed for the worse in "this land of liberty," according to these songs. Back then, "the country was right and the boys all white / In the days of '49." In their praise for the past, some Argonauts expressed a nostalgia for the racial and cultural world of antebellum America.[14]

One of this last group of songs, "The Song of the Argonauts," composed in 1876, seems to have been designed to be sung at gatherings of old 49ers:

> We are assembled here today
> A band of Pioneers,
> To celebrate with grateful hearts,
> Events of by-gone years.

With voices raised to "Dear friends of long ago" the Argonauts had come full circle. The sad refrains once voiced by those left at the doorstep as the young 49ers went to California had become the words of the aging Argonauts as they looked back and celebrated their achievements and the passing of their comrades. In this world, the 49ers were "Pioneers" who had "unlocked the golden ore, in gulch and cañon dark." Themes of hard work and triumph ("But perseverance won") were echoed by the rich voices of middle-aged men who recalled what they now remembered as the heroic achievements of their youth. That this youth seemed to be fading gave it an additional golden glow.[15]

THE GOLDEN YEARS

For thousands of 49ers who made the trek to California and then returned to the humdrum existence of farm and trade and store, the memory of the months on the swift streams of the Sierra seemed to separate out different stages of their lives. On the one side, in their years as Argonauts lay not only risk and hardship, but also exuberance, youth, friendship, and independence. On the other lay the warmth and love of families, the reassurance of the familiar and the comfortable, and the years of repetitive labor and growing responsibilities as their status changed from young men into adults.

One of the expressions of this memorable interlude in their lives appeared with the publication of county histories. A blending of commercial opportunity and the desire to remember the achievement of the early pioneers, county histories were commissioned reminiscences, catalogues of achievement by first families of counties, blended with accounts of county history and occasional documents. Into these stories of family achievement by hard work and appropriate values came special events of note: marching off to volunteer in wars and the rush to find gold in California.

This list of local 49ers sometimes exposed an awkward, unfinished part of the county's past, for many of the Argonauts from nearby villages and farms were not successful, others only modestly so, and some never returned. Yet this listing suggests the pride of many in their participation in the Gold Rush. Among the events that intruded into the routine of the county's seasonal cycles, the mobilizing of some of its young men for a trek across the continent in search of gold was one of the most notable.

The accounts in the county histories—like the histories themselves—tended to be repetitive. They noted that the gold fever carried off many residents, including those of wealth and standing; that the emigration to California provoked a flurry of economic activity within the county through sale of farms and stock to finance the trip to the land of gold; that many returned with wealth, although the degree of wealth varied, and 49ers were generally closemouthed about the exact sum; that the activities of the returned Argonauts provoked another cycle of economic enterprise, as they spent and invested their returns from the gold fields. Sometimes, the accounts listed the membership rolls of local companies, with rosters and officers.[16]

Individuals preserved their own sense of identification as 49ers in different ways. Some of them did it privately with their families. William Swain from upstate New York, whose letters and diary survive as one of the most complete accounts of the rush to California in 1849, celebrated each year with his wife Sabrina. On the date of his return from the gold fields, she would put on the dress he brought her, and the two would mark the occasion with a formal family dinner. At the close of the evening, she would toast "Her Forty-Niner," and he would raise his glass in tribute to her strength and courage in managing the farm and their small daughter during the years of his absence. This small-scale family celebration included William's brother George, who had been so faithful in assisting Sabrina, and later (after his marriage) George's wife and family. Eventually, when William and Sabrina Swain's children grew up and married, their extended families became part of the annual dinner.[17]

Others sought to celebrate their participation in this great national adventure in a public and formal way. On June 29, 1888, a group of veteran Argonauts organized the Society of California Pioneers of New England. They chose a board of officers from among themselves and also acted favorably on seventy-four applications for membership. Thereafter, the society met monthly at the Crawford House, a hotel in Boston.

Early in September 1888, the society held its first annual "reunion and banquet," in which 150 members and distinguished guests "participated in good cheer and social festivities." The membership roster at the time totaled 223. Annual celebrations followed on the same date, featuring a dinner, speeches, and music from an orchestra. After speeches and other public pronouncements that went on for five hours, the members sang "Auld Lang Syne" and adjourned. The New England society exchanged greetings and professions of friendship with the San Francisco Pioneers, New York society, and Sacramento Pioneer Society, as each group sought to identify and to hold some portion of the strange and shimmering past they all shared.[18]

The business of recapturing the past and shaping memories for the present assumed an immediate seriousness. One of the speakers read a letter from a former resident of the Boston area now living in San Francisco "denying certain published slanderous statements relative to the character of those who were among the first of the Pioneers to California." The nature of the charges were never specified, but presumably they covered the standard indictments of the period: evading honorable debts, fleeing family responsibilities, companies composed of the ne'er-do-wells and undesirables of the community. From the perspective of nearly forty years, earnest speakers rose to defend the New Englanders who joined the Argonauts of '49. In presentations both serious and humorous, speakers recalled the seriousness of purpose and the special New England qualities. A "Comrade" from Rhode Island—the veteran 49ers referred to one another as "comrade"—celebrated the "life and genius of the typical Yankee, ready for any adventure, rich in expedients, a jack-of-all-trades and professions, as miner, merchant, justice, writing and dancing master, hydraulic engineer, photographer—anything to turn an 'honest penny or nimble sixpence.' "[19]

Immediately upon their formal organization, some of the New England Pioneers began to consider the prospect of recapturing the sense of the place and the time of the Gold Rush in a direct way. Eventually, the veteran 49ers agreed that the most appropriate means was "an excursion to California." The object was "a trip across the continent, and a visit to the old mining-camps of '49." After a year of planning to coordinate the eastern participants with the western places, the party of original Argonauts and friends came together at the Fitchburg railroad station on April 10, 1890. The group included 84 "Pioneers," with their wives, sons and daughters, and 64 additional friends, making in all a party of 149. Sixty-nine of these were "ladies." Others joined the overland adventure at several stations along the route.

The veteran 49ers and their families and friends traveled west on "a vestibule train, the heaviest and longest that ever crossed the continent." It included two dining cars, seven sleeping cars, and a "composite car" with a library, barber's chair, bathroom, and smoking compartment. Boston papers called it "the most thoroughly equipped train that ever left that city."[20]

A crowd estimated at two thousand came to say good-bye in a ceremony marked by speeches and garlands of flowers. "Just at four o'clock the final signal was given, the hand-shake and the kiss; then, as the magnificent train rolled away, bearing our pilgrim Argonauts toward the golden shores of the Pacific, there rose from the crowd of comrades...and the well wishers...a ringing send-off." Once again, crowds of well-wishers and onlookers came to the station as they had come forty years earlier to the wharves or village squares, and with laughter and tears they sent the old Argonauts westward to a new adventure. A chronicler summed up the blending of the departures: "How the memories came trooping through our minds, and how we looked forward to one more glimpse of the old localities! We were Pioneers again, and how we all joined in the chorus as a lady of our party sang THE SONG OF THE FORTY-NINERS."[21]

Once the travelers arrived in California, two ceremonies stood out from the score of others. The city of Pasadena had arranged a large reception in the Arroyo Seco, where more than one thousand people waited to greet the veteran 49ers. The returned Argonauts and their families dined on "ice cream, lemonade, and strawberries from an apparently inexhaustible supply." As the climax to the afternoon's festivities, a group of 49ers reenacted the Gold Rush when, on a signal, "a party of miners, with pack train and all accoutrements, came trudging down the gulch, headed by a grizzly old veteran on horseback." The parade of men and animals proceeded to recreate the search for gold so familiar forty years before:

> They were all characteristically dressed, with big revolvers and knives at their sides. Having unpacked the weary, sleepy, forlorn, shaggy-eared burros, they commenced washing for gold.
> The cradle and pan were taken to the stream, and a half hour devoted to the search. Gravel was soon running through the rocker, and the color was shown, when a yell greeted the rich strike.[22]

Later, the entire party headed to the "Gold Rush country," where the veteran 49ers proudly showed their wives, children, and grandchildren their original claims. More than one returned Argonaut came with an original journal and delighted in comparing its descriptions with the landscape some forty years later. Sometimes new mining techniques such as the hydraulic hose and its streams of water had obliterated the hills in which they used to work.[23]

Thus, a group of veteran 49ers acted out in one forty-day period the recurring cycle that had taken so many men from their doorsteps over so many years. They determined to go, made arrangements for transportation, departed from their loved ones (or took them along), crossed the continent, and disembarked in California. There, this select band of men dressed as miners during the day and as gentlemen at night. Surrounded by their families, they ate and drank well. What propelled them on this cross-continental journey, however, was not the luxury accommodations that they enjoyed on the train and in California. Rather, it was the memories of the greatest adventure of their lives. As they stood by the side of the streams of their youth, shovel and pan in hand and rocker at the ready, the years fell away. Once again, they were the Argonauts of '49.

HISTORIANS AND SOURCES

HISTORIES AND HISTORIANS

THE DRAMATIC EVENTS of the California Gold Rush seem to call for a
Homer, a Cervantes, or a Tolstoy to chronicle the ambitions, experiences,
successes, and failures of the hundreds of thousands of Argonauts who
crossed oceans and a continent to the rushing streams of the Sierra and the
wide streets of the growing cities of California. It was the adventure of a lifetime and the journey of the century. Such a chronicler would sing an epic of
extraordinary activities by ordinary people, would give them a permanent
place in the annals of America's pioneers, a vanguard of men and later
women who carried the nation's flag and ideals to the far-western reaches of
the nation at great personal risk and sacrifice.

The many chroniclers that we do have, from all parts of the nation and
abroad, range from the eloquent to the banal. The California Gold Rush
was the ultimate expression of democracy in its literary as well as its economic dimensions. Anyone—regardless of economic or social condition
and without regard to education—could keep a journal. Many did. The
largest group began their journals in the ports of the East Coast and in the

villages of Independence and St. Joseph at the edge of the overland trail, from which points they described their emigrations by sea and land to California. While a few began as correspondents of local newspapers or with a view to publishing their accounts, the overwhelming numbers simply set out to describe a new series of worlds to their families in the East, to share the wonder of discovery and the achievement of dreams along with the sense of difference from what they had left behind—whether in the streets of Panama or in the approaches to Fort Laramie. Once arrived in California and at work in the diggings, most of the diarists and amateur correspondents had other things to do than write, and professional journalists, travel writers, and a few determined diarists are the ones who give us descriptions of the morning light in the canyons of the Sierra, the sounds of rushing water, the clang of mining tools on stone and gravel, and the silence and peace of the tents and cabins at night. All of these paid tribute to the physical setting, intensity, and energy of that world, from the isolated camps to the frantic activity of the bars to the bustle of the cities.[1]

As the immediacy and impact of the Gold Rush faded in the rise of sectional controversy in the East and the discovery of new mineral wealth at other sites in the West, the accounts from the California placers diminished and eventually dropped from view. Replacing these first-hand accounts over the next generation were a series of reminiscences of the tumultuous days of '49. Less immediate and dramatic and more thoughtful and analytical, these accounts relate the wider experiences associated with the Gold Rush, beginning from the eastern seaboard, through the gold camps, to the emergence of a stable and almost sedate California, beyond the powerful initial influence of the Gold Rush impulses. Their authors ranged from professional men of letters like Prentice Mulford to participants like Sarah Royce, who wrote of her experiences crossing the plains and in the gold camps from the perspective of twenty years.[2]

In addition to this new generation of storytellers, who enlarged our understanding of these powerful events, three major figures appeared almost simultaneously who placed the California Gold Rush in the context of the nation's history. The first was a chronicler and collector who gathered and preserved the records of the vanishing 49ers who had been part of this experience. Hubert Howe Bancroft was not so much a historian as an industrialist in the line of other important industrial figures in the late nineteenth century. He brought to the writing of the history of the American West the same elements of organization, capitalization, and scale that Andrew Carnegie brought to the making of steel, John D. Rockefeller to the production and marketing of oil, and J. P. Morgan to finance. For a generation, from 1870 to 1900, Bancroft collected documents about the American West, and he and his many anonymous scribes wrote multivolume histories of the western states and territories. The one for California is seven volumes long, covers almost six thousand pages, and is based on his own source materials. It is a tribute to Bancroft's energy, resources, and ruthlessness as collector that modern historians still begin their studies of mid-nineteenth-century California by reading him, for his documents are still central to our work.[3]

Almost at the same time as the publication of Bancroft's seven volumes, which began in 1884, appeared two other interpreters of the California Gold Rush experience. Among the first Americans to have professional training in the new historical seminars, Charles Shinn wrote the outlines of his *Mining Camps: A Study in American Frontier Government* in a seminar at Johns Hopkins University.[4] In the mining camps of California, Shinn found the genius of the American spirit mixed in appropriate parts with the American sense of democracy. According to Shinn's work, when confronted with a lack of institutions, Americans in the camps adopted their own, wrote and proclaimed a code of laws, established a judicial mechanism to enforce the code, and held trials to punish the guilty and release the innocent. Shinn applauded and defended California popular sovereignty as part of the distinctively American genius in institution building. It was, in his view, the spirit and the achievements that celebrated American democracy, inventiveness, and independence.

That Shinn's miners' courts continued to function after statehood and the establishment of an official court system did not bother him. He agreed with frontier editors that "ermined judges" with high regard for the niceties of law invariably released criminals for lack of evidence to inflict themselves upon society again. Nor did he seem especially concerned that sovereign bodies of miners seemed unusually harsh in dealing with foreigners in the gold fields, and that many of their extralegal actions were taken against noncitizens and those who did not speak English, especially the native Spanish-speaking Californians, the original European inhabitants of California, whose rights presumably were protected by the treaty of cession of 1848 and whose forcible removal from the placers opened their attractive mining sites to occupation by more newly arrived Euro-Americans.

All these things deeply disturbed Josiah Royce. Royce was an academic by training, later a professor of philosophy at Harvard, who knew the Gold Rush years through the stories of his mother. Royce was attracted to the challenge of a history of early California in part because he was born in the Gold Rush camp of Grass Valley, and he often wondered how the experience of growing up there had shaped his world and that of his parents. At the age of thirty, he wrote a history of California subtitled *A Study of American Character,* covering the years from 1846 to 1856.

For Royce, the Gold Rush was a mixed experience. It burst on the scene not only with the golden light of wealth, but also with the darker hues of moral and economic temptations to dazzle a moral and upright people, an experience that would show "both the true nobility and true weakness of our national character." Royce summarized these views in his introduction to John Marshall's discoveries that triggered the Gold Rush:

> All our brutal passions were here to have full sweep, and all our moral strength, all our courage, our patience, our docility, and our social skills were to contend with these our passions. Whoever wants merely a eulogistic story of the pioneer life in California must not look for it in history, and whoever too tender souled to see any moral beauty or significance in events that involve much foolishness, drunkenness, brutality, and lust must find his innocent interests satisfied elsewhere.[5]

Royce cared deeply that American miners expelled Mexicans from claims they held by right of discovery, hung Chileans who did not understand English, and discriminated against the Chinese at every turn. He lectured the young state of California about its moral shortcomings in the tone of an understanding but disappointed father. The lecture over, Royce returned once more to the study of philosophy.

The next sixty years saw historians celebrate the Gold Rush as part of America's triumphant march westward, the conquest of the continent and the spread of American values and institutions across the vast expanse of the trans-Mississippi West. In the twenty-five-volume *Chronicles of America,* published in the 1920s, for example, the volume on the California Gold Rush focused on the mass movement of the 49ers west in the context of the transformation of California from Spanish and Mexican to American.[6]

What we might call the modern study of California and the Gold Rush began in 1947 with the publication of Rodman Paul's *California Gold: The Beginning of Mining in the Far West.* Paul's book represented a marked departure in tone from the previous reverential treatments of the Gold Rush as laying the foundation for America's continental empire. It was also noticeably different in content. Paul identified and analyzed the main themes that would become the standard interpretations of the Gold Rush for the next generation. Paul's emphasis was on mining as a business, and more specifically on the increasing complexity of mining techniques and mining organizations in the years from 1848 to 1870. By exploring techniques, machinery, and corporate organization, Paul concluded, first, that mining rapidly became highly technical, with substantial investment and corporate organization, and with a parallel disappearance of the single prospector and even the small mining party; and second, that the California placers became the mining laboratory of the world, where techniques were perfected for export to the subsequent mining frontiers of the American West and throughout western Europe. He also analyzed the influence of gold on the development of the state of California, the significance of law for miners and mining, and the contributions of popular songs and fiction in spreading the story of California gold. Paul's book changed the way that historians look at the Gold Rush experience, and his volume, reprinted several times and still in print, became the standard interpretation of the Gold Rush for the next thirty years.[7]

Within the last fifteen years, new historians and new kinds of histories have appeared to examine the California Gold Rush. From these varied studies have emerged new themes and variations on old ones. Among the new subjects are the emergence of the Gold Rush as an example of a new community, the identity of groups of 49ers who lived and worked together, and the transition of some mining camps from placer to quartz mining and the changes that accompanied this transition.[8]

A second group of themes that have emerged includes the continuing interaction between the East and the West. The California Gold Rush is no longer narrated as a story set entirely in the rushing waters of camps and bars; rather, it includes connections between the 49ers and the families they left behind. These connections have prompted continuing discussions over issues of authority and preferment, sometimes seen in the context of monetary advantage, but not always so. The great emigration of 1849 and subsequent years rearranged the order of decision making and authority within families, and an analysis of these new arrangements tells us much about family life and gender roles in America at midcentury, as well as about the variations produced by the California Gold Rush.[9]

Historians of California also have begun to reconsider the influence of the Gold Rush on the state's history. New studies have noted the significance of traditional influences like religion in the evolution of California society in the 1850s and the importance of the railroad as a force in the development of the state in the last half of the century. The Gold Rush now is treated as one of many factors in the emergence of modern California, along with the rise of agriculture and the emergence of the colossus of urban southern California. In short, historians now believe, the Gold Rush made California different, but the state also shared many characteristics of growth and maturity with other states.[10]

Finally, other historians have treated the California Gold Rush as the opening act in the extension of mining across the range of the West in the last half of the century. Here, the Gold Rush becomes a significant formative series of events in establishing patterns of economic exploitation and social adjustment, but it is only an introduction (albeit a large and dramatic one) to the spread of mining for gold and silver into the most remote parts of that section.[11]

SOURCES

The California Gold Rush ranks with the American Civil War as the most written-about, remembered, and recorded series of events in nineteenth-century America. And like the records of the Civil War, the records of the Gold Rush tend to focus on certain events. The distance and duration of the expeditions to California and the particular characteristics of mining and other occupations also meant that the accounts assumed particular forms.

Diaries

The trip to California, whether overland or by sea, generated an outpouring of diaries unequalled in the history of the nation to that point. The more than four hundred surviving accounts for the overland travelers and half again that number by sea travelers were the product of a variety of conditions.[12] These include the leisure time associated with both kinds of expeditions, but especially the sea voyage, wherein the able-bodied participants had little or nothing to do for a period of months. The absence of a systematic mail service in the course of voyages by land or sea also meant a substantial gap of six months or more in the contact between 49ers and their families, and many Argonauts kept journals with the idea of sending them to their families on arrival in California or of preserving them to present on their return. The 49ers also were well aware that they were participating in a great national adventure, the march of American civilization across the continent with a view to making California a part of the nation. So these participants saw themselves as a part of a heroic enterprise in which their participation should be recorded. The many organized companies that formed the basis of travel by land and by sea also meant that systematic reports had to be made to both investors and local community newspapers. Several companies included local editors as members and many others identified a member responsible for conveying news and accounts to the local newspaper. Finally, many participants had read the travel guides of the day and systematically recorded their own reactions to the great landmarks of transcontinental migration, such as Fort Laramie, Chimney Rock, Salt Lake City, or the ports of call on the sea voyages.

The hundreds of records that survived—presumably only a portion of those originally penned—focus on the voyage to California itself. As we've seen, the writing patterns of the Gold Rush chroniclers changed upon arrival in California. This is not to say that several good diaries have not survived of 49ers in the mines, including some by women. Many have. Yet it is also reasonable to comment on the changed tone of the accounts. For most diarists, the reality of the mines replaced the fantasies of the voyage by sea or overland and the dreams of the future. In the face of the work demanded by the placers, few diarists could discipline themselves to write extensively of their experiences; they contented themselves instead with accounts of the weather, of meals, and especially of gain and loss. Still, some of them are revealing about the interaction of the small groups of miners living and working together, reflecting as they do the expectations and dissatisfactions of 49ers with their new associates and communities.

Letters

The writing patterns of correspondence between the placers and the towns on one side and the states on the other assumed many shapes. Some letter collections are large and complete, running to a hundred letters or more. A few even contain correspondence in both directions, a boon to the observer who would like to describe and analyze the interaction between both groups.

Another kind of letter collection of special usefulness contains letters exchanged between family members who discussed the internal affairs of the extended family, often with reference to how the absence of the 49er changed affairs within the family. Several of these collections have survived, some of them covering a long period of time, extending through the Civil War. The search for such manuscripts is complicated by the indexing procedures of individual archives, under which the collection may not be indexed by reference to the California Gold Rush. This is common in cases in which the letters of the 49ers themselves have not survived and so are not a part of the collection.

The correspondence patterns of the Argonauts themselves cover a wide range. Some wrote regularly, others only rarely. We have a small number of letters written by amanuenses. We have letters by 49ers who were semiliterate. Others demonstrated a professional fluency and a total command of the English language. The diverse sources of participation in the Gold Rush, ensuring as it did representatives from every sector of America's societies, are well represented in the letter collections. Finally, letters have survived from slaves to their masters and to their families in the South. Not surprisingly, these accounts have their own voices and concerns.

The 49ers who wrote with some regularity and took their duties as husbands, fiancés, sons, brothers, and friends seriously had diverse correspondence responsibilities.[13] Several members of the family had to be written to, and the Argonauts often did so with different voices. That is to say, they had one tone and content for their wives, another for their sisters, a third for their parents, and perhaps even others. From such accounts can emerge three or four different views of the Gold Rush and individual participation in it.

Memoirs and Reminiscences

As the California Gold Rush faded in its immediacy and became increasingly suffused with the light of adventure and visions of glory—of empire building, the taming of the continent, and the emergence of a great continental nation—the original participants began to turn out memoirs and reminiscences. These are of various sorts: records left for family members; celebratory contributions to county histories; collections of the writing of "old pioneers"; the result of requests by local newspaper editors for venerable local figures to pen accounts of their participation in the great national events, including the Gold Rush, that could be published serially; and a few more complete and detailed accounts written deliberately for publication in book form. Whatever their origins, these memoirs began to make their way into print by the middle of the 1850s and appeared in a continuing stream up to the turn of the century.

In their tone and content, they lack the immediacy of contemporaneous accounts. Instead of the difficulties of work in the placers and the awkwardness of family relationships, they emphasize the heroic aspects of the Gold Rush experience in which they participated: the challenge of the plains, the Americanization of California, the creation of a continental nation.

Newspapers

Newspapers were the public record of the Gold Rush. As such, they give several insights into the popular perception of what happened in California over the dozen years from 1848 to 1860. The intensity of coverage and the nature of the news changed quickly. The dramatic announcement of the discovery and its confirmation by officials of the government spread across the eastern seaboard in December 1848. The first papers to describe the Gold Rush in detail, especially its most dramatic aspects in terms of the quantities of gold available and the ease with which it might be acquired, were those in the eastern ports. The dailies of New York, Boston, New Orleans, and Charleston gave the news prominence for the first months of 1849, complete with details on the several companies departing from these ports. The search for gold and the rush of Americans to California faded from these papers with the departure of the companies in the winter and spring of 1849. Space devoted to the Gold Rush then declined and the tone fell several octaves to the level of the rest of the news. After all, the 49ers were in transit, so there was little to report. With their arrival in California in the fall of 1849, a new spate of accounts appeared, describing the Gold Rush towns, the diggings, the varied collection of peoples. Subsequent annual migrations generated their own local interest, but the Gold Rush gradually faded as national news, replaced by politics and the growing sectional crisis that accompanied the close of the Mexican War.

By December 1848 and January 1849, local newspapers, which borrowed heavily from the major dailies and weeklies, had begun to print the accounts of the discovery of gold in California. These reports had moved beyond the official statements to the first-person accounts of supposedly reliable sources in the gold fields themselves, accounts that actually often bordered on fantasy.

By the spring of 1849, the real focus of coverage of the Gold Rush had shifted to the many papers published in small cities and towns, with special emphasis on those communities that had organized and dispatched companies to California. Local journalists, sometimes professionals associated with local papers and sometimes simply amateurs elected to the position of scribe by their companies, wrote regularly to the local paper.[14] Their accounts represented a running commentary on the details of the expedition to California, with special attention to dangers overcome and the mention of individual names on a regular basis. Added to these reporters of a semi-official nature were those individuals whose letters to their families found their way into print. This publicizing of the Gold Rush experience through the publication of private letters had become so common by the winter of 1849–50 that many 49ers made specific note in their letters home that these were for the family only and not for publication. Given the candor with which individual 49ers sometimes described members of other families within the community, such discretion was understandable and wise.

Through the succeeding years of the Gold Rush, the newspapers of small cities and county-seat towns, often places with many representatives in the gold fields, became the leading sources of public information on the continuing Gold Rush. Editors continued to publish letters from their fellow citizens or culled from the correspondence of families. They became a source of steady information on the ongoing event that had changed the lives of so many. They continued to note the departure and return of friends and neighbors long after news from the gold fields had faded from the newspapers of the large cities and major ports.

The California newspapers played a special role. They first trumpeted the news of gold discoveries to Californians and others within hearing and reading. They were the first carriers of the gold fever that would later infect so many editors and correspondents, and through them, people from the coastal ports to the interior villages and farms everywhere.[15]

MANUSCRIPTS

The manuscripts listed here are mostly letter collections, although a few memoirs and reminiscences are among them. The manuscript collections are characterized, among other ways, by their varied geographic locations. Almost every historical society and depository with manuscript collections in the East and Middle West has Gold Rush materials, a fact that reflects the universal nature of the response to gold. In addition, listed here are contractual agreements and the constitutions of Gold Rush companies.

Alabama

Alabama Department of Archives and History
Chapman, Harvey; Clayton, J. E.; Milner, John Turner.

California

Bancroft Library, University of California, Berkeley
Alexander, James; Anderson, Thomas; Bailey, J. Milton; Ballew, Horace M.; Barnes, James S.; Barnes, Otis; Beaman, Alfred; Beck, Morris; Berry, G. E.;

Bradford, Sandy; Brainard-Forbes; Brown, David; Brown, Rufus; Bush, Charles W.; California Gold Rush Letters; Canfield, John; Collbreath, John C.; Cowell, Benjamin; Day, Emeline; the Delong Family; DeWitt, Alfred; DeWitt, Margaret; Dressler, William; the Dulany Family; Dunnell, John Henry; the Edwards Family; Elder, William; Ferris, Hiram G.; Goss, Milo J.; Hall, Milton; Hanson, William; Harlan, Charles T.; Harris, Ira; Hewes, David; Hills, Thomas; Jackson, Stephen; Jewett, William S.; the La Mott Family; Locke, Jonathan; Mann, Henry Rice; McDermiad, Finley; McGrath, Hugh; Meder, B.; Miller, Christian; Miller, Newton C.; Nagy, John; Odall, Rodney P.; Packer, Henry B.; Prince, William; Randall, Charles Henry; Raymond, George A.; the Ross Family; Sherwood, William; Smith, Seth; Spiegel, Henry V.; Stevens, A.; Sumner, Sherman P.; Thompson, Asa; Tuttle, Charles A.; Wayman, John Hudson; Wells, Epaphroditus; Wiley, James L.; Willey, Lucas; Wing, Stephen; Wright's Company.

California State Library, Sacramento

Godard, H. B.; Goff, Selden; Jackson, Charles P.; Josselyn, Amos Piatt; Kerr, John M.; Kessler, Frederick; Leonard, Albert; Martin, John L.; Perkins, Isaac; Townsend, Beeson; Tracy, Frederick; Wells, William; Winchester, Jonas.

California State University, Chico

Stearns, Amos Keyes.

Coloma History Center

"Friend Martha"; Kays, Nathan W.; Moddy, Joseph L.; Parvin, O. R.; Smith, Martha Grover.

Henry E. Huntington Library and Art Gallery

Abbe, Edward P.; Ames, Peramus G.; Anable, Henry Sheldon; Anonymous, Letter to Wife; Anonymous to Lizzie; Ashley, Algeline J.; Averett, George W.; Bailey, Mary Stuart; Baker, H. C. D.; Barker, Isaac; Barrington, Alexander; Baxter, Benjamin; Bean, Hiram; Beeching, Robert; Blanchard, Nathaniel; Brooks, Mary Jane; Brown, William A.; Bryson, Leslie; Buckingham, Charles E.; Burns, Lydia H.; Butterfield, Robert W.; Carpenter, William O.; Chapman, Eben; Christman, Enos L.; Clapp, John T.; Clarke, James A.; Coates, G. C.; Comstock, L.; Cool, Peter Y.; Craven, John J.; Crawford, John D.; Crawford, Ronald; DeCosta, William H.; Delano, Ephriam; Denniston, William F.; DeWolf, David; Dimmick,

Kimball; Eagle, John H.; Eckley, Levi; Ellis, Charles; Engle, Jacob; Farnsworth, William; Fish, L. I.; Fitch, John R.; Fitch, Luther; Foster, Isaac; Francisco, Albert N.; Gorgas, Solomon; Gould, Edward; Gray, Charles G.; Herbert, William A.; Heywood, Jonathan; Hopkins, Lemuel B.; Hovey, John; Huan, Catherine M.; Hubbard, Alonzo; Hyde, Aaron H.; Jackson, Thomas H.; Jacobs, Enoch; Johnson, Charles D.; Kent, Henry; Kinkade, John T.; Lasselle, Stanislaus; Lawson, George; Lord, Israel S. P.; Magruder, J. H.; McFarlan, John R.; Miller, E. H.; Mobley, C. C.; Morse, Ephriam W.; Muzzy, Horace; Osborn, Sullivan; Owen, Isaac; Parker, William T.; Pearce, W. E.; Perkins, E. D.; Plummer, Charles G.; Pond, Ananias R.; Pownall, Joseph; the Prince Collection; Rice, James F.; Riggin, James C.; Ritenour, Milton; Rowe, Charles; Saxon, William A.; Schufelt, S.; Snowden, Samuel; Speak, Alexander; Stone, John H., Story, Charles H.; Swasey, Gustavus; Sweetser, A. C.; Townsen, D.; Townsend, Jacob; Varner, Allen; Wakefield, Lucy Stoddard; Ward, Harriet Sherrill; Wheeler, George N.; Wilkins, James F.; Wolcott, Lucien; Wood, Joseph Warren; Woodlin, Stephen; Woods, James W.; Wooster, John B.; Yale, Gregory.

Holt-Atherton Special Collections, University of the Pacific, Stockton
Baker, John D.; Fletcher, John D.; Fouts, D. Lambert.

Connecticut

Beinecke Library, Yale University
Applegate, George; Cowden, John; Gish, John; Kendrick, Benjamin F.; Lyne, James; Moxley, Charles G.; Rothwell, William R.

District of Columbia

Library of Congress
Craven, John J.; Ewing, Thomas; Williamson, Robert S.

Illinois

Chicago Historical Society
Hayes, Owen; Hearn, Thomas; Kimberly, Edmund Stoughton; McKee, Amos S.; Prickett, George W.; the Sherman Family; Sleight, Morris.

Indiana

Indiana Historical Society
The Pierce-Krull Families.

Iowa

State Historical Society
Keen, Richard A.; Kuhlwein, Hugo F.; Swan, Chauncey; Thrailkill, Jacob.

Kentucky

Margaret I. King Library, University of Kentucky, Lexington
The Trabue Family.

Massachusetts

Massachusetts Historical Society
Bailey, Alfred; Baxter, George H.; Johnson, Joseph; Pierce, John B.; Snow, Caleb H.; Taylor, Rinaldo.

Nantucket Historical Association
Bunker, Asa; Ewer, Peter Folger; Pease, William C.; Worth, Henry C.

Michigan

Bentley Library, University of Michigan
Bell, Orrin G.; Birney, McClear; the Hanicard Papers; Martin, Julia Bird; Sutton, Richard; Woodruff, David O.

Clarke Library, Central Michigan University
Blackwood, Thomas and Jane; Dickinson, William Rufus; Latimer, David.

John Cumming Collections, Mount Pleasant
The Dibble Family; the Wisner Family.

Minnesota

Minnesota Historical Society
Hillman, Levi C.

North Carolina

Department of Archives and History, Raleigh
Brown, W. Vance; McBridge, J.C.; Norcom, James; Parks, Thomas; Rogers, Mary Jeffreys.

Perkins Library, Duke University
Barton, Jesse; Boyles, Eliza; the Campbell Family; Childress, Nannie; Comer, Nathaniel; Gardner, Susan Folger; Gault, William and Sylvanus; Gebhart, Noah L.; Goodrich, Isaac; Graham, James; Green, Adeline E.; Hearns, Thomas; the Hemphill Family; Hundley, Alonzo; Long, John W.; Pelouze, Henry.

Southern Historical Collections, University of North Carolina, Chapel Hill
Andrews, B. W.; Dickson, William; Gardiner, William M; Gundry, John; Hayden, Jacob S.; the Holliday-Pendleton Families; Horn, Daniel A.; King, Thomas B; the McClellan, Stonebreaker, and McCartney Families; the Milligan Family; Milner, Joseph; the Perkins Family; Woodfin, Nicholas W.; the Wright and Green Families.

Oregon

Oregon Historical Society
Church, Charles A.; Fletcher, John Eliot; Mossman, Eli; Motley, Obadiah; Scott, William J.; Smith, John M.; Sullivan, Joshua; Thompson, Arthur H.; Wood, Joseph W.

Rhode Island

Rhode Island Historical Society
Dean, Larned; Gardiner, William; the Pearson Family; Pierce, William A.; Potter, Arthur R.; Tucker, Albert G.

NOTES

ABBREVIATIONS OF MANUSCRIPT DEPOSITORIES

BAN   Bancroft Library, University of California, Berkeley.

BENT   Bentley Library, University of Michigan, Ann Arbor.

CHI   Chicago Historical Society, Chicago, Illinois.

CLAR   Clarke Historical Library, Central Michigan University, Mount Pleasant, Michigan.

CSL   California State Library, Sacramento.

DLC   The Library of Congress, Washington, D.C.

DUKE   Perkins Library, Duke University, Durham, North Carolina.

HEH   Henry E. Huntington Library, San Marino, California.

IND   Indiana Historical Society, Indianapolis.

KING   Margaret I. King Library, University of Kentucky, Lexington.

MASS   Massachusetts Historical Society, Boston.

MINN   Minnesota Historical Society, St. Paul.

NAN   Nantucket Historical Association, Nantucket, Massachusetts.

NCDAH North Carolina Department of Archives and History, Raleigh.

ORE   Oregon Historical Society, Portland.

RIHS Rhode Island Historical Society, Providence.

UNC Southern Historical Collections, University of North Carolina, Chapel Hill.

UOP Holt-Atherton Special Collections, University of the Pacific, Stockton, California.

YALE Beinecke Library, Yale University, New Haven, Connecticut.

INTRODUCTION

1. For trustworthy numbers on the California Gold Rush, I have relied here and elsewhere on Rodman W. Paul, *California Gold: The Beginning of Mining in the Far West* (Cambridge, Mass.: Harvard University Press, 1947), esp. appendix A, 345–48.

2. John Mack Faragher, *Sugar Creek: Life on the Illinois Prairie* (New Haven: Yale University Press, 1987), 201.

3. C. C. Mobley, diary, October 12, October 21, 1850, HEH.

4. Throughout this study, I use the terms "49er" and "Argonaut" interchangeably to identify individuals or groups who went to California between 1849 and 1860 for economic advantage associated with the Gold Rush. Economic advantage means simply that at least some of the group that we identify as 49ers did not go to wash for gold but to work in other satellite occupations that drew business from the Gold Rush. Thus, the terms include those who went to work at their trades in San Francisco or other urban centers.

I: CALIFORNIA'S GOLDEN REVOLUTION

1. On the controversies that arose over the gold discoveries, I have followed Rodman W. Paul, *The California Gold Discovery: Sources, Documents, Accounts, and Memoirs Relating to the Discovery of Gold at Sutter's Mill* (Georgetown, Calif.: The Talisman Press, 1966), especially the introduction. Paul notes, "In the particular case of the California gold discovery, the difficulty is that no one anticipated, few witnessed, and fewer still immediately recorded the event. The scene was a small and isolated lumber camp, located over forty miles from even the frontier outpost that was Sutter's Fort. Sutter's Fort, in turn, was on the edge of a thinly settled, remote province recently captured from Mexico. The participants in the gold discovery were simple people who had had little education and felt little incentive to keep written records" (18).

2. Hubert Howe Bancroft, *History of California,* 7 vols. (San Francisco, 1884–90), 6:1–14. For a generation, from 1858 to 1889, Bancroft collected manuscripts on the history of the American West, and armed with these materials, he and his stable of writers created multivolume histories of the western states and territories. The history of California was seven volumes and more than six thousand pages long. Bancroft's history of California is still a starting point for a study of the Gold Rush.

3. Albert L. Hurtado, *Indian Survival on the California Frontier* (New Haven: Yale University Press, 1988). Chapter 6 is an excellent account of the Indian population on the eve of the Gold Rush and its response to it.

4. Walter Colton, *Three Years in California* (New York, 1851), 246.

5. Thomas Larkin to James Buchanan, June 28, 1848, *The Larkin Papers: Personal, Business, and Official Correspondence of Thomas Oliver Larkin, Merchant and United States Consul in California,* 10 vols., ed. George P. Hammond (Berkeley: University of California Press, 1951–64), 7:304.

6. In this sequence of immigration to the gold fields, I have followed Bancroft, *History of California,* 6: chapter 7.

7. On Mason as governor, see David Alan Johnson, *Founding the Far West: California, Oregon, and Nevada, 1840–1890* (Berkeley: University of California Press, 1992), 23–26. Johnson observes that "the gold rush altered the terms of politics fundamentally" (26).

8. Colton, *Three Years in California,* 19.

9. Mason's report is printed in full in *House Executive Documents,* 31st Cong., 1st sess., no. 17.

10. These gold deposits and the techniques used to harvest them were known by the Spanish term "placer," and Americans quickly brought into common use "placers" to identify the sites on gold-bearing streams where mining was taking place. See Paul, *California Gold: The Beginning of Mining,* 140–41. A more complete analysis is Otis E. Young, Jr., *Western Mining: An Informal Account of Precious-Metals Prospecting, Placering, Lode Mining, and Milling on the American Frontier from Spanish Times to 1893* (Norman: University of Oklahoma Press, 1970), chapter 4.

11. Larkin to Charles Oliver Sterling and John S. Williams, July 28, 1848; Larkin to Stephen Reynolds, June 3, 1848, *The Larkin Papers,* 7:324, 292. The term "Kanakas" referred to Hawaiian Islanders.

12. Sterling to Larkin, July 9, 1848, ibid., 7:312–13, 7:313, 7:321.

13. Quoted in Paul, *The California Gold Discovery,* 91–92. A clear description of the operation of the cradle is in Paul, *California Gold: The Beginning of Mining,* 52–53. I have used the term "cradle" throughout.

14. William R. Ryan, *Personal Adventures in Upper and Lower California,* 2 vols. (London, 1850), 2:17.

15. Larkin to Buchanan, June 28, 1848, *The Larkin Papers,* 7:304.

16. Quoted in Paul, *The California Gold Discovery,* 91. The Mormons were among the first to arrive in the gold fields in numbers. See J. Kenneth Davies, *Mormon Gold: The Story of California's Mormon Argonauts* (Salt Lake City: Olympus Publishing Company, 1984). The term "diggings" (the 49ers always used "diggins") refers to the site of actual mining operations on the watercourses of the Sierra. Or to put it another way, "diggings" are the places where people dig. As mining for gold turned out to be an earthmoving exercise compared by many to construction of the most arduous kind, the reference to digging was appropriate.

17. Peter H. Burnett, *Recollections and Opinions of an Old Pioneer* (New York, 1880), 272.

18. Ryan, *Personal Adventures,* 2:21, 2:39–40.

19. E. Gould Buffum, *Six Months in the Gold Mines: From a Journal of Three Years' Residence in Upper and Lower California, 1847–8–9* (Philadelphia, 1850), 105; Burnett, *Recollections and Opinions,* 273. Buffum went on to add that the portion of the river claimed over three miles would, in fewer than six months, be expanded "for forty miles above where we were, and that thousands, would find their fortunes upon it."

20. Larkin to Buchanan, June 28, 1848, *The Larkin Papers,* 7:304; Mason quoted in Paul, *The California Gold Discovery,* 96.

21. In response to the departure of its staff, the San Francisco *California Star* ceased publication on June 14, 1848.

22. Quoted in Paul, *The California Gold Discovery,* 98. Larkin noted that the injection of large quantities of gold into the California economy in the summer of 1848 had caused government drafts (heretofore highly sought) to fall rapidly in value. Larkin to James Young Mason, July 1, 1848, *The Larkin Papers,* 7:308.

23. Buffum, *Six Months in the Gold Mines,* 105.

24. Colton, *Three Years in California,* 255. Colton had missed the advantage associated with hired hands, but his comments capture the wonder of wealth for a few individuals. He is referring to Chestnut Street in Philadelphia.

25. Ibid., 251–52.

26. Ibid., 247–48, 253.

27. Ryan, *Personal Adventures,* 2:85–86.

2 : GOLD FEVER

1. All epigraphs attributed to Prentice Mulford are from *Prentice Mulford's Story: Life by Land and Sea* (New York, 1889).

2. In this account of the spread of news about the discovery of gold, I have followed the outlines of Ralph P. Bieber, "California Gold Mania," *Mississippi Valley Historical Review* 35 (1948–49): 3–28.

3. Bieber lists the newspapers that published Larkin's letters, from Boston to St. Louis, from New Orleans to New York, over the month from mid-September to mid-October. Ibid., 16, n. 82.

4. Quoted in ibid., 16.

5. The New Orleans *Daily Crescent,* November 25, 1848, is one example. Ralph Bieber left his extensive collection of newspaper clippings—from 150 newspapers from every state and the District of Columbia—to the Henry E. Huntington Library, where they form the starting point for any historian who wishes to examine the spread of news about the gold discoveries and the reactions of communities large and small. Cited hereafter as Bieber Collection, HEH.

6. *House Executive Documents,* 30th Cong., 2d sess., 1:56–69. Based on his July trip to the mines, Mason estimated that four thousand people were harvesting from thirty to fifty thousand dollars a day, or an average of ten dollars for every man, woman, and child.

7. Washington *Daily Union,* November 30, 1848, Bieber Coll., HEH. Anticipating a great transcontinental migration, the *Daily Union* "presumed" that when the news became generally known "among our go-ahead countrymen, there will be a road of human bodies from St. Louis to the Pacific." Ibid., November 23, 1848.

8. President Polk's address to the Congress, December 5, 1848, is in House Executive Documents, 30th Cong., 2d Sess., 1: 1–44. The reference to gold in California is on page 10.

9. Washington *Daily Union,* December 14, 1848, Bieber Coll., HEH.

10. Bieber has collected these references and many others. "California Gold Mania," 21.

11. *Boston Daily Journal,* February 5, 1849, contains an excellent representative selection of ads. Newspapers could act as community organizers, as the Michigan *Marshall Statesman* did in the organization and departure of the Michigan Wolverines (January 17, March 7, April 11, 1849). Among the sermons published, see the Reverend E. N. Kirk, the *Boston Daily Times,* January 9, 1849; Reverend Beecher, ibid., January 29, 1849. All citations from Bieber Coll., HEH.

12. Bieber, "California Gold Mania," 16–25, provides a detailed account of the spread of news, with many quotations.

13. *Raleigh Star & N. Carolina Gazette,* March 28, 1849.

14. The *Jackson Mississippian,* October 26, 1849, provides one example. The Helena, Arkansas, *Southern Shield* answered in detail the query "will it be safe to take negroes" to California. February 24, 1849. The Kentucky *Louisville Daily Journal,* May 9, 1849, lays out the Georgia plan to force slavery on California. Bieber Coll., HEH.

15. Dudley T. Ross, *The Golden Gazette: News from the Newspapers of 1848–1854* (Fresno, Calif.: Valley Publishers, 1978), is a collection of clippings on the Gold Rush from a wide range of newspapers across the nation.

16. Mulford, *Prentice Mulford's Story,* 2.

17. Charles Harlan to Julia LeGrand, December 8, 1848, Papers, BAN; Joel and Christina Thomas to Nathaniel and Katharine Comer, July 15, 1849, the Comer Papers, DUKE. The Mulligan Family Correspondence, January–June 1849, UNC, illustrates the outbreak of the "gold fever" in South Carolina and Georgia. One correspondent commented that the emigration from Virginia would be especially great because "she possesses a greater number than any other state of men too lazy to labor and too proud to remain contented in poverty." William Cook to John Rutherford, March 28, 1849, Rutherford Papers, DUKE.

18. Texas *Corpus Christi Star,* January 13, 1849. That the gold fever stretched as far west as the Hawaiian Islands is shown by the Honolulu *Sandwich Island News,* July 13, August 3, September 21, 1848, Bieber Coll., HEH.

19. New Orleans *Daily Picayune,* March 4, 1849, Bieber Coll., HEH.

20. Examples from one city appear in the *Boston Courier,* August 16, 1849; *Boston Daily Journal,* February 5, 1849; *Boston Daily Evening Traveller,* March 22, 1849, Bieber Coll., HEH.

21. Rhode Island *Woonsocket Patriot,* February 16, 1849. Other arguments in favor of not going to California are in the Bangor, Maine, *Daily Whig & Courant,* January 29, 1849, and the *Concord New Hampshire Statesman,* February 2, 1849, all in the Bieber Coll., HEH.

22. John Kelsey to parents, brothers, and sisters, Cedar Rapids, Iowa, February 16, 1849, *Palimpsest* 72 (1991): 116. Such examples could be found in every territory and state in the Union, and in almost every town.

23. A. P. Josselyn to his sister, May 19, 1850, Letters, CSL.

3: "THIS IS A HARD THING, THIS BREAKING UP OF FAMILIES"

1. David Allan Comstock, *Gold Diggers and Camp Followers, 1845–1851* (Grass Valley, Calif.: Comstock Bonanza Press, 1982), 169–72, is a compelling recreation of such a debate.

2. David M. Potter's introduction in *Trail to California: The Overland Journal of Vincent Geiger and Wakeman Bryarly* (New Haven: Yale University Press, 1945) is a good account of the limitations imposed by seasons.

3. John Cumming, ed., *The Gold Rush: Letters from the Wolverine Rangers to the Marshall, Michigan, "Statesman," 1849–1851* (Mount Pleasant, Mich.: The Cumming Press, 1974), 2–3; Ephriam Morse, journal, July 5, 1849, HEH. Morse's company retired the uniforms before going to the diggings.

4. Charles Harlan to Julia LeGrand, August 18, 1848, Letters, BAN.

5. Daingerfield to his mother, October 21, 1850, Letters, BAN. Another example is Rufus to Nellie Brown, March 26, 1852, Letters, BAN. Susan Gray, *The Yankee West: Community Life on the Michigan Frontier, 1830–1860* (Chapel Hill: University of North Carolina Press, forthcoming 1996), provides an excellent context in her analysis of debts as a part of the web of economic life in a rural community at midcentury.

6. The preface to Sidney W. Hardy's journal (1849–51) sums up the reasons that propelled men to California in search of gold. MS copy on loan from Professor Donald R. Kelley, Rutgers University.

7. Chapman to his wife Caroline, December 31, 1849, Letters, ALA; Taylor to his wife, May 30, 1849, Letters, MASS.

8. One example of a marriage that put an end to California plans appears in Rebecca Camfield to Octavia Milligan, February 18, May 13, 1849, Milligan Family Papers, UNC. A father and son talking constantly of going to California for reasons that seem related to family posturing can be found in the Charles Anthony Hundley Papers, DUKE.

9. David Campbell to his nephew, April 22, 1850, Campbell Family Papers, DUKE.

10. Sarah E. Trask, diary, July 22, 1849, Beverly Historical Society, Beverly, Mass. Luther Woodbury did go to California and died on the return voyage, confirming Sarah's views of the irreparable damage done by the lure of gold.

11. See, for example, Allen to David Varner, December 12, 1850, Letters, HEH; C. Cassil to Hannah, his sister, and James Kinkade. Silence reflects continuing displeasure with "their wild boy" for going to California, May 5, 1850, Kinkade Correspondence, HEH. Of course, parents were not invariably hostile, but one 49er wrote that his family all but "drove me away." William A. Brown to his mother, November 21, 1851, Letters, HEH.

12. James Barnes to Jeremiah Barnes, October 21, 1849, Letters, BAN. Other examples are Alexander Barrington to his mother: she should not grieve "on account of your children," undated, 1855, Letters, HEH; also Hiram Bean, diary, September 23, 1849, HEH.

13. William Cosby to Lucy D. Trabue, May 12, 1852; February 23, 1853, Trabue Letters, KING.

14. Katherine A. White, comp., *A Yankee Trader in the Gold Rush: The Letters of Franklin A. Buck* (Boston: Houghton Mifflin Company, 1930), 31.

15. *Woonsocket Patriot,* February 16, 1849, Bieber Coll., HEH.

16. Robert Samuel Fletcher, *Eureka: From Cleveland by Ship to California, 1849–1850* (Durham: Duke University Press, 1959), 41–42.

17. William to Sarah Farnsworth Blake, March 26, 1854, Letters, HEH; John to Margaret Eagle, September 26, 1852, Letters, HEH; James Barnes to Jeremiah Barnes, October 21, 1849, Letters, BAN; James S. Holliday, *And the World Rushed In: The California Gold Rush Experience* (New York: Simon & Schuster, 1981), 57.

18. William Dixon to Mary Pendleton, undated, April 19 and May 21, 1849, Papers, UNC.

19. Rufus to Nellie Brown, March 26, 1852, Letters, BAN.

20. Potter, ed., *Trail to California,* includes a brief analysis of the several routes and their costs. John Unruh, *The Plains Across: The Overland Emigrants and the Trans-Mississippi West, 1840–1860* (Urbana: University of Illinois Press, 1976), is a detailed account of migration overland.

21. James Barnes to Jeremiah Barnes, October 21, 1849, Letters, BAN. Later correspondence shows that Barnes's father advanced one hundred and fifty dollars to his son for the trip. Andrew Cairns's family pooled resources to send him to California. *California Historical Society Quarterly* 46 (1967): 207–18.

22. Seth Smith, letter of April 24, 1851, Letters, BAN.

23. Ormsby to his sister, January 12, 1849, California Gold Rush Letters, BAN.

24. Constitution of Wright's Company of Gold Diggers and Hill's letters, October 3, November 7, 1849, BAN. Thirty-three men signed up; the company disbanded after three months in California.

25. Ballew contract, June 6, 1850, BAN. Ballew put up a two-thousand-dollar bond in the form of real estate, and he left behind a wife and two children; Edward Family Papers, March 20, 1850, BAN; David Campbell to his nephew, April 22, 1850, Campbell Family Papers, DUKE. John Cumming has described the Monroe, Michigan, company in *The Gold Rush: Letters from the Wolverine Rangers,* v.

26. Thomas D. Clark, ed., *Gold Rush Diary: Being the Journal of Elisha Douglas Perkins on the Overland Trail in the Spring and Summer of 1849* (Lexington: University of Kentucky Press, 1967), xiv–xv, 158–60. Harmar was a small town close to Marietta.

27. Among the collections that show such affluence and options are the Blackwood Papers, CLAR; the Gregory Yale Papers, HEH; the La Mott Family Correspondence, BAN; the Thomas Ewing Papers, DLC.

28. Taylor to his wife, August, 22, 1849, Letters, MASS. James Alexander asked his wife to borrow money from "Cousin Jo," September 21, 1851, Letters, BAN.

29. Charles to Maria Tuttle, May 12, November 7, 1850, Letters, BAN; John O. Holzhueter, ed., "From Waupan to Sacramento in 1849: The Gold Rush Journal of Edwin Hillyer," *Wisconsin Magazine of History* 49 (1966): 213.

30. Hall to his father, April 25, 1852, BAN. This suggests that the arrangements for subsequent waves of Argonauts were similar to the earliest arrangements.

31. Thompson to Robinson, April 1, 1849, the Thompson Letters, ORE.

32. The Trabue letters, KING, and the Eagle letters, HEH.

33. Milo to Catherine Goss, April 11, 1850, Letters, BAN; William to Nancy Prince, May 19, 1849, Letters, BAN.

34. William to Nancy Prince, May 19, June 1, 1849, Letters, BAN; Wilson to Nancy Day, March 31, 1853, Correspondence, BAN.

35. Fitch asked his mother "to visit Theodosia often and comfort and cheer her up all you can," March 6, 1850, Letters, HEH; Schufelt asked that Cousin John visit his wife Margaret, March 15, 1850, Letters, HEH.

36. Rufus to Nellie Brown, February 15, February 12, 1852, Letters, BAN. Brown's letter in early 1852 suggests that little had changed over three years in the cycle of preparation to go to the gold fields.

37. Gregory Yale to his wife, December 8, 1849, Letters, HEH. Yale gave his wife permission to go to Florida over the winter.

38. Charles to Maria Tuttle, April 17, 1849, Letters, BAN. Charles pointed out a potential danger in one of their male friends.

39. See, for example, Ames to his wife, December 12, 1852, in which he tells her to seek consolation in prayer. The Ames Letters, HEH.

40. Epaphroditus Wells to his wife, May 17, June 16, October 18, 1849, Letters, BAN; Rufus Brown to his wife, March 22, 1852, Letters, BAN.

41. Benjamin Cowell to his wife, November 11, 1849, Correspondence, BAN. Joshua Sullivan to his wife, May 8, 1849, Letters, ORE. Sullivan left her with four children in Peru, Illinois. Obadiah Motley to his wife, April 11, 1849, Letters, ORE. Motley also left four children.

42. William Dressler to "My Dear Boyes," undated, 1850, Letters, BAN; William Elder to his wife, June 17, 1850, Letters, BAN. Elder made the promise as he traveled through Panama.

43. Aberdeen, Mississippi, *Monroe Democrat,* February 7, 1849, Bieber Coll., HEH.

44. *Boston Daily Times,* January 9, 1849, Bieber Coll., HEH.

45. *Boston Daily Times,* January 29, 1849, Bieber Coll., HEH. Edward Abbe noted that his company would give the library of the ship *Edward Everett* to the city of San Francisco to "return learning & literature in exchange for the gold we expect to receive." Diary, June 27, 1849, HEH.

46. *Boston Evening Transcript,* December 18, 1849. Other sermons in opposition appeared in the Bangor, Maine, *Daily Whig,* October 6, 1849, and Rhode Island *Woonsocket Patriot,* February 16, 1849. The New Hampshire *Concord Statesman,* February 2, 1849, ran an editorial castigating men for deserting their families. All are in the Bieber Coll., HEH.

47. Several sermons urged success: the Arkansas *Washington Telegraph,* April 4, 1849; the Bangor, Maine, *Daily Whig and Courier,* October 6, 1849, Bieber Coll., HEH.

48. On the efforts of men to master emotions from a young age, see E. Anthony Rotundo, *American Manhood: Transformations in Masculinity from the Revolution to the Modern Era* (New York: Basic Books, 1993), 44–46. A fictional account by a celebrated California author of an emotional departure for the gold fields is Joaquin Miller, *'49: The Gold-Seekers of the Sierras* (reprint, Upper Saddle River, N.J.: The Gregg Press, 1970), 12–13.

49. Robert to Harriett Beeching, journal, September 10, 1849, HEH; William T. Parker, diary, March 25, 26, 1850, HEH; Margaret DeWitt to her mother, May 29,

1850, Letters, BAN. See also Charles Buckingham, diary, September 15, 1849, HEH.

50. William Rothwell, journal, April 8, 13, 1850, YALE.

51. Joshua Sullivan to "Dear wife and friends," May 8, 1849, Letters, ORE; James Lyne to his aunt, May 9, 1849, Letters, YALE.

52. William to Georgiana Pierce, September 28, 1849, the Pierce-Krull Letters, IND; Harvey Chapman to his mother, July 7, 1850, Letters, ALA; James Alexander to his wife, August 24, 1851, March 22, 1852, Letters, BAN; Henry Spiegel, letters of March 28, April 7, 1850, Letters, BAN.

53. White, comp., *A Yankee Trader in the Gold Rush,* 31.

54. John Cowden to Theodore Garretson, March 4–9, 1849, Letters, YALE.

55. Bloomington *Indiana Tribune & Monroe Farmer,* February 24, 1849, Bieber Coll., HEH.

56. The term "seeing the elephant" characterized the Gold Rush as simultaneously exciting, elusive, and potentially dangerous. It also represented the common experience of the hundreds of thousands who eventually would call themselves the Argonauts of '49. These gold seekers thought of themselves at some point (it varied according to the introspective natures of the participants) as engaged in a singular venture that was both serving themselves and their families and serving the nation as a whole. The best account of the term and its wide and varied use is John Phillip Reid, *Law for the Elephant: Property and Social Behavior on the Overland Trail* (San Marino, Calif.: The Huntington Library, 1980), ix–x.

4: JOURNEY AND ARRIVAL

1. William H. DeCosta observed that the most popular amusement on the sea voyage was "Keeping a Journal." Journal, February 16, 1849, HEH.

2. Lafayette Fish, journal, October 6, 1849, HEH; Rinaldo Taylor to his wife, May 28, 1849, Taylor Letters, MASS.

3. William Elder to his wife, August 28, 1850, Letters, BAN; William Daingerfield, undated, 1850, Letters, BAN.

4. William Saxon, journal, May 26, 1849, HEH; Enoch Jacobs, journal, March 11, May 14, June 16, 1849, HEH. George F. Kent, journal, August 18, 1849, HEH, wrote of the "numerous petty quarrels and misunderstanding which have occured on board."

5. Edward Abbe, journal, January 30, 1849. Abbe's unreconstructed aristocratic view of the world, including his regret that the California Gold Rush attracted so many ordinary people, appears in February 4, June 17, 1849, HEH. Benjamin Baxter, a recent Yale graduate, celebrated his superior learning and physical conditioning in Baxter, journal, April 4, 1850, HEH. One 49er's declaration that so many members of the Yale University classes of 1848 and 1849 were in California (including Abbe) that it made the Gold Rush sound like a college reunion. See the Connecticut *Hartford Daily Courant,* March 3, 1850, Bieber Coll., HEH.

6. William Saxon, journal, May 26, HEH; John Craven to his wife, May 6, 1849, Letters, HEH. John Fitch's advice from his brother was probably representative: "I

hope you will not forget to be careful of your health, and avoid associating with those who are dissolute or gamble or behave disreputably." Brother to Fitch, April 18, 1849, Letters, HEH.

7. Rinaldo Taylor to his wife, May 30, June 13, 1849, Letters, MASS. That not all Northerners responded negatively to the institution of slavery was shown by Milo Goss, who admired the Southern climate and style of life, including the institution of slavery. He believed "from what I have seen, that slaves as a mass are better cared for and happier than the free blacks in the North." Goss to his wife, the Goss Letters, April 18, 1850, Letters, BAN.

8. Taylor to his wife, July 8, 1849, Letters, MASS. The most detailed account of a 49er's reaction to Panama is James P. Jones and William Warren Rogers, eds., "Across the Isthmus in 1850: The Journey of Daniel A. Horn," *Hispanic American Historical Review* 41 (1961): 533–54. John Haskell Kemble, *The Panama Route, 1848–1869* (reprint, Columbia: University of South Carolina Press, 1990), is a complete study.

9. J. E. Clayton, diary, January 20, 1850, ALA; James Barnes to his parents, December 9, 23, 1849, Letters, BAN; Milo Goss to his wife, June 18, 1850, Letters, BAN.

10. J. E. Clayton, diary, January 27, 1850, ALA; William Elder, June 4, 1850, Letters, BAN; Christian Miller to his family, April 27, 1849, Letters, BAN.

11. Rinaldo Taylor to his wife, July 8, 1849, Letters, MASS; J. E. Clayton, diary, January 21, 1850; S. Schufelt, letter, March 3, 1850, HEH.

12. Jacob Townsend, journal, April 12, 1849, HEH; William A. Brown, March 28, 1849, Letters, HEH.

13. William Denniston, journal, April 1849, HEH; John Stone, brief notes, April 14, June 28, 1849, HEH; journal, Enoch Jacobs, April 29, 1849, HEH.

14. William DeCosta, journal, February 15, [1849?], HEH.

15. Elder to his wife, June 17, 1850, Letters, BAN.

16. Although by far the largest number of overland 49ers went by way of the California Trail, a sizable minority went by way of the southern route. The standard account of this alternate route and its people is Ralph P. Bieber, *Southern Trails to California in 1849* (Glendale, Calif.: Arthur H. Clark, 1937).

17. Comstock, *Gold Diggers and Camp Followers,* 179–88, is an account of two men who took the "Pioneer Line."

18. John Milner to his sister, May 18, 1849, Correspondence, ALA.

19. Henry Packer to Mary Elizabeth Judkins, April 30, 1850, Letters, BAN.

20. Charles Harlan on Northerners, October 20, 1849, February 24, May 25, 1850, Letters, BAN; John R. Fitch described New Englanders and eastern men as a guarantee of a good society, in July 17, 1849, Letters, HEH; Richard Cowley hated people from Massachusetts, and his quote is from his diary, September 13, 1851, HEH. James F. Wilkins, journal, May 15, 1849, HEH.

21. Benjamin Baxter, journal, August 17, 1850, HEH; Henry Kent wrote of Missourians' indifference to losing half a family, "they think no more of it than you would to see a toad humped up in a garden in the thunderstorm." Henry to Joshua Kent, December 19, 1852, Letters, HEH.

22. William R. Rothwell to his father, April 16, 1850, Letters, YALE.

23. This anonymity continued in California. Peter Cool noted that when the sheriff appeared in the diggings to "summon us" to serve on a grand jury, the miners refused to give their names. The sheriff left without names or jurymen. Cool, journal, November 3, 1851, HEH.

24. Robert Beeching, journal, September 18, 1849, HEH; Horace M. Ballew, letter of September 8, 1850, Letters, BAN.

25. John Gish, letter, December 29, 1850, YALE; Joshua Sullivan, letter, May 8, 1849, ORE. Dale L. Morgan noted that the 49er surge through Utah produced a burst of favorable publicity for the Mormons, transforming a despised sect of fanatics into a solicitous people anxious to help exhausted and stranded travelers (at a price). Morgan, ed., "Letters by Forty-Niners, Written from the Great Salt Lake in 1849," *Western Humanities Review* 3 (1949): 98–99.

26. John Unruh, *The Plains Across,* is the best account of violence and bloodshed on the overland migration.

27. Charles Buckingham, diary, October 31, 1849, HEH.

28. Rinaldo Taylor to his wife, December 30, 1849, Letters, MASS.

29. John Collbreath to parents, brother, and sister, June 30, 1849, Letters, BAN.

30. William Daingerfield to his mother, August 10, 1850, Letters, BAN. The *Nantucket Enquirer* quoted a correspondent, "money never looked of so little consequence as it does here." April 8, 1849. See also the Newburyport *Daily Herald,* December 19, 1848.

31. Edward Abbe, diary, July 9, 1849, HEH; Albert G. Osbun, diary, June 16, 1849, HEH.

32. John J. Craven to his wife, September 18, 1849, Letters, HEH.

33. Lafayette Fish, journal, January 11, 1849, HEH; Taylor to his wife, December 30, 1849, Letters, MASS; Goss to his wife, June 29, 1851, Letters, BAN.

34. John C. Collbreath to his parents, June 30, 1849, Letters, BAN; Taylor to his wife, August 22, 1849, Letters, MASS. Alexander Spear, journal, April 9, 1850, HEH, is an observation by a man of limited education.

35. Lafayette Fish, journal, January 11, 1849, HEH.

36. Isaac Owen, journal, November 16, 1850, HEH.

37. Delaware *Wilmington Weekly Commercial,* August 10, 1849, Bieber Coll., HEH.

38. Allen to Elias Varner, December 16, 1849, Letters, HEH.

39. James Wilkins, journal, June 26, 1849, HEH.

40. Richard Cowley, journal, October 8, 1849, HEH; Daingerfield, letter of November 14, 1850, Letters, BAN.

41. William to Charlotte Prince, December 15, 1849, Letters, BAN.

5 : OLD BONDS AND NEW ALLEGIANCES

1. Goss to his wife, June 29, 1851, Letters, BAN; William to Charlotte Prince, September 24, 1849, Letters, BAN; Thomas Forbes to Hezekiah Brainard, March 15, 1850, Letters, BAN. See also William Daingerfield to his mother on the transition: "This is a truly wonderful country—everything seems to have a go ahead motion and I pity the poor devil who is sick here without money. All come here to make

money and the kindly sympathies are left behind them but California shows man as he is and not acting a part." October 21, 1850, Letters, BAN.

2. William Rothwell, journal, April 10, 1850, YALE; George to Lewis Applegate, December 9, 1849, Letters, YALE.

3. Nantucket *Enquirer,* December 24, 1849. Edward Byers, *The Nation of Nantucket: Society and Politics in an Early American Commercial Center, 1660–1820* (Boston: Northeastern University Press, 1987), is an excellent introduction to Nantucket on the eve of the California Gold Rush.

4. Benjamin Baxter, journal, March 25, 1850, HEH.

5. John Gish, articles of agreement, February 14, 1850, YALE.

6. James Lyne to his brother, June 2, 1849, Letters, YALE. Lyne noted that several others had considered returning home.

7. For example, William Swain from upstate New York joined the Wolverine Rangers from Marshall, Michigan. See James S. Holliday, *And the World Rushed In,* 90–93. On the overland experience generally, once again see David Potter, ed., *Trail to California: The Overland Journal of Vincent Geiger and Wakeman Bryarly* (New Haven: Yale University Press, 1945), and John Unruh, *The Plains Across.*

8. George Applegate to his brother Lewis, December 9, 1849, Letters, YALE.

9. James Lyne to his brother, June 30, 1849, Letters, YALE.

10. J. E. Clayton, diary, February 20, March 9, 1850, ALA.

11. J. E. Clayton, diary, April 4, 1850, ALA; Thomas Forbes to Hezekiah Brainard, March 15, 1850, the Brainard-Forbes Letters, BAN.

12. Rinaldo Taylor to his wife, August 22, 1849, Letters, MASS.

13. Ibid.; Rodney Odall to his parents, August 8, 1850, Letters, BAN; Milo to Catherine Goss, March 30, 1851, Letters, BAN. Enoch Jacobs reflected on partnerships, journal, August 20, 1849, HEH; John Hovey reflected on joining a company of four for the mines, journal, July 31, 1849, HEH; Ephriam Morse, journal, August 16, 1849, HEH, writes that three messes make "quite a little village." Ralph Mann, *After the Gold Rush: Society in Grass Valley and Nevada City, California, 1849–1870* (Stanford, Calif.: Stanford University Press, 1982), 17–20, is an excellent analysis of living arrangements in two camps.

14. Thomas O. Larkin observed men working in groups of four or five as early as June 1848. *The Larkin Papers,* 7:304. William R. Ryan noted the influence of the cradle in promoting social and work divisions, *Personal Adventures in Upper and Lower California,* 2 vols. (London, 1850), 2:17.

15. Among the many examples is Allen to Elias Varner, December 16, 1849, Letters, HEH, to the effect that someone from his company would write home in case he became ill.

16. Harvey Chapman to his wife Caroline, April 19, 1850, Letters, ALA.

17. Ryan noted that under the arrangements for forming companies, no sick man should be abandoned in the mines. *Personal Adventures,* 1:211–13. See also Isaac Foster, journal, January 29, 1850, HEH, on sickness.

18. James Barnes to his father, February 26, 1851, Letters, BAN. Ryan described the general provisions for forming a company in *Personal Adventures,* 1:211–13.

19. Joshua Sullivan to his wife, July 27, 1850, Letters, ORE; John Gish wanted to be paid for nursing his friends, John to Mary Gish, February 4, 1851, Letters, YALE.

20. The Kimberly Letters, CHI; Joshua Sullivan to his wife, March 17, 1850, Letters, ORE.

21. C. C. Mobley, diary, June 25, 26, 1850, HEH. This is one of the rare comments made by 49ers using gendered language.

22. Obadiah Motley, April 15, 1849, Letters, ORE; C. C. Mobley, diary, September 16, 1850, HEH; Rinaldo Taylor to his wife, October 22, 1849, Letters, MASS.

23. William A. Brown to his sister Josie, April 5, 1852, Letters, HEH.

24. Henry Spiegel, July 14, 1850; November 25, 1851; February 14, 1852, Letters, BAN. Henry Spiegel was a complete correspondent. In addition to his mother and brother, he also wrote to his nieces and nephews and on one occasion (April 12, 1850), he sent greetings to twenty people in Bennington by name.

25. David Hewes to his mother, August 31, September 14, October 7, December 8, 1850, Letters, BAN.

26. John Collbreath, March 14, June 30, August 18, 1849; December 12, 1850, Letters, BAN.

27. James to Jeremiah Barnes, May 30, 1851, Letters, BAN.

28. Wilson Day, September 8, 22, November 9, 1853, Family Correspondence, BAN.

29. Charles Randall to father and mother, September 24, 1850, Letters, BAN.

30. Cumming, *The Gold Rush: Letters from the Wolverine Rangers,* iv–v, notes both local and absentee capitalists who backed the Michigan companies.

31. Henry Spiegel to John Spiegel, June 7, 1850, Letters, BAN.

32. George Applegate to Lewis Applegate, January 2, 1852, Letters, YALE.

33. Jane to Thomas Blackwood, undated 1850, Letters, CLAR.

34. G. K. Hill to John Gish, August 13, 1850, Letters, YALE.

35. Henry to Ann Worth, July 7, August 1, October 24, 1849, Letters, NAN.

36. James Lyne to Henry Lyne, November 29, 1849, Letters, YALE.

37. James Lyne to Henry Lyne, April 17, 1850, ibid. James Lyne died in California in early 1850. Another letter of neighborhood news from William R. Rothwell of Fulton, Callaway County, Missouri, to his brother Tom, October 27, 1850, Letters, YALE, suggested that news about health and location were both more significant and welcome than details about financial success or failure.

38. See, for example, Reid Mitchell, "The Northern Soldier and His Community," in *Towards a Social History of the American Civil War,* ed. Maris A. Vinovskis (New York: Cambridge University Press, 1990), 78–92. See also Reid Mitchell, *Civil War Soldiers* (New York: Viking Penguin, 1988), esp. 56–89, on the continuing influence of home communities on the lives of Northern soldiers during the Civil War. Mitchell concludes, "The community never entirely relinquished its power to oversee its men at war" (83). Examples of correspondents reporting moral failures in the California Gold Rush are many, including the Harlan Letters, BAN, and the Prince Letters, BAN.

39. Henry Packer to Mary Judkins, February 23, 1851, Letters, BAN.

40. Alexander Barrington described the public whipping of a man for stealing a horse in his journal, July 17, 1850, HEH. Compare the similarity to early judicial proceedings on the trans-Appalachian frontier in Malcolm J. Rohrbough, *The Trans-Appalachian Frontier: People, Societies, and Institutions, 1775–1850* (New York: Oxford University Press, 1978), chapter 2.

41. The standard early work on this subject was Charles Shinn, *Mining Camps; A Study in American Frontier Government* (New York, 1885), which contains a wealth of material but suffers from the author's confidence in Euro-Americans to dispense justice to other cultural groups, of whom there were a large number in California during the Gold Rush.

42. Israel Lord, journal, February 24, 1850, HEH. Two weeks later, Lord attended another "miners' meeting" at Boone's Bar, some three and one-half miles up the river. Journal, March 9, 1850.

43. Israel Lord, journal, November 1, 1849, HEH.

44. Ibid., April 28, 1850.

45. Ibid., May 2, 1850.

46. Henry Packer to Mary Elizabeth Judkins, May 20, 1851, the Packer Letters, BAN. Alexander Barrington described a "nigger dance" in Little Deer in his journal, September 26, 1850, HEH.

6: THE SCARCITY OF WOMEN

1. Rinaldo Taylor to his wife, May 30, 1849, Letters, MASS.

2. William to Charlotte Prince, April 27, May 14, 16, 19, 1849, Letters, BAN. From April 1849 to June 1851, Prince wrote 117 letters to his wife.

3. James Lyne to his sister, May 4, 1849, Letters, YALE.

4. Rinaldo Taylor to his wife, July 8, 1849, Letters, MASS.

5. Rinaldo Taylor to his wife, May 28, 1849, ibid.

6. William Prince to his wife, October 21, 1849, Letters, BAN; William A. Brown to his father, July 25, 1850, Letters, HEH.

7. William Prince to his wife, August 4, 1849, Letters, BAN.

8. Sherman L. Ricards, Jr., "A Demographic History of the West: Butte County, California, 1850," *Papers of the Michigan Academy of Science, Arts, and Letters* 64 (1961): 469–91. Ricards calculates that the 1850 population of Butte County was 3,473 males (97.08 percent) and 104 females (2.92 percent) (489). See also G. Cassil to Hannah and James Kinkade, June 5, 1850, Kinkade Correspondence, HEH.

9. James Lyne to his sister, May 4, 1849, Letters, YALE.

10. Epaphroditus Wells to his wife, July 5, 1850, Letters, BAN.

11. William Daingerfield to his mother, June 6, 1852, Letters, BAN; James to Jeremiah Barnes, June 14, 1851, Letters, BAN; Horace Ballew to his wife, undated but probably early 1851, Letters, BAN.

12. C. C. Mobley, diary, July 16, 1850, HEH.

13. George Raymond to his sister Sarah, June 3, 1850, Letters, BAN. William Daingerfield to his mother, undated 1850, Letters, BAN.

14. Seth Smith to his father, April 24, 1851, Letters, BAN; William A. Brown to his mother, June 13, 1851, Letters, HEH.

15. Laurie F. Maffly-Kipp, *Religion and Society in Frontier California* (New Haven: Yale University Press, 1994), chapter 6, is an insightful analysis of the mixture of class, gender, and religion in early Gold Rush California.

16. Finley McDermiad to his wife, January 11, 1851, Letters, BAN, is an example of women willing, indeed, anxious, to come to California; Charles Tuttle promised that he would bring his wife, January 20, 1850, Letters, BAN, but he later reneged.

17. E. D. Perkins, "Sketches of a Trip: Marietta Ohio to Sacramento, California," October 12, 1849, HEH.

18. Rodney Odall to his parents, August 8, 1850, Letters, BAN.

19. Henry Packer to Mary Judkins, May 28, 1850, Letters, BAN.

20. Louise A. K. S. Clapp, *The Shirley Letters: Being Letters Written in 1851–1852 from the California Mines* (Salt Lake City: Peregrine Smith, 1985), 74–82, which recounts "Dame Shirley's" experience as a "mineress," is an excellent example of the exalted, almost regal, treatment of a "lady" in a mining camp. The quote is from page 74.

21. David O. Woodruff to his sister, August 23, 1851, Letters, BENT.

22. Charles Tuttle to Maria, November 7, 1850, Letters, BAN. Letters in the Trabue (KING) and Mossman (ORE) collections also illustrate this point. The 49ers also had only contempt for women of the indigenous peoples of California, whether Indian or Mexican. They saw these groups as a part of the natural landscape, and as such, they were not considered "ladies." Men at the time did not wish to join in permanent union or even temporary social contact with them.

23. Karen Lystra, *Searching the Heart: Women, Men, and Romantic Love in Nineteenth-Century America* (New York, 1989), is a fine account of the standards of courtship that 49ers carried west with them.

24. Henry Packer to Mary Judkins, October 29, 1850, Letters, BAN.

25. Rotundo, *American Manhood,* chapter 6, describes the attitudes toward women that young men absorbed on growing up and that they brought with them to California.

26. John Cowden to Miss M. B. Donaldson, August 26, 1850, Letters, YALE.

27. Eli Mossman to his brother and sister, October 26, 1850, Correspondence, ORE.

28. William Scott to his brothers and sisters, February 10, 1849, Letters, ORE; John Milner to his sister, January 11, 1850, Letters, ALA; Seth Smith to his brother, May 27, 1851, Letters, BAN. See also James Lyne, who carved the names of girls he admired on Chimney Rock, May 22, June 30, 1849, Letters, YALE.

29. John Collbreath to his family, October 1, 1850, Family Letters, BAN; Charles Dulany to his sister, February 26, 1850, Family Correspondence, BAN. Charley Mulford wrote to his cousin Cornelia: "there is but little hope for me, for I presume you will all be married off and scattered to the four winds before I shall reach the home of my childhood, and there will not be even one old maid left for me." David Allan Comstock, *Gold Diggers and Camp Followers,* 313.

30. George Raymond to his sister Sarah, June 3, 1850; B. L. Rick to Raymond, December 26, 1852, Letters, BAN.

31. Robert La Mott to his sister Annie, September 23, 1850, Robert to his mother, November 20, 1850, Correspondence, BAN; John Nagy to his brother, August 14, 1853, Letters, BAN.

32. Aaron Hyde to his mother, January 26, 1851, Letters, HEH.
33. William Cosby to his sister, September 26, November 22, 1852, the Trabue Papers, KING. William Cosby to his sister, December 26, 1852; November 11, 1853; March 22, 1854, ibid. Other letters, for example, September 26, October 18, November 7, 22, December 16, 1852; November 11, 1853, show Cosby's persistence in pursuing this theme.
34. "Biographical Sketch," Milner Papers, UNC. The Kinkade Correspondence, esp. August 28, November 1850, HEH, shows the determination of one 49er to marry.
35. Henry Packer to Mary Elizabeth Judkins, April 30, September 7, 1850; August 30–September 6, December 5, 1851; May 11, 1852, Letters, BAN. On more than one occasion, Mary expressed concern that Henry's morals had suffered in California.
36. Asa Thompson to Abby Hobbs, September 19, December 24, 1854; February 24, 1855, Letters, BAN. Amid the camaraderie and brotherhood of the small mining company, some 49ers were modest and ever secretive about their contact with eligible women. George Prickett asked Julia McKee to wrap her miniature—a "mark of confidence and affection"—in order to disguise it. May 8, 1849, Letters, CHI.
37. Seth Smith to his father, April 24, 1851, Letters, BAN.

7: "I COULD SELL SOME OF THE FURNITURE"

1. Henry to Ann Worth, August 1, 1849, Papers, NAN.
2. See, for example, the Dressler Letters, BAN.
3. Jonathan to Jane Heywood, March 8, 1851, Letters, HEH. The archivist notes that this and other letters from Jonathan Heywood were probably written by an amanuensis.
4. Paramus Ames to his wife, December 12, 1852, Letters, HEH.
5. Rinaldo Taylor to his wife, January 14, March 29, 1850, Letters, MASS.
6. John Fitch to his brother, July 12, 1851, Letters, HEH.
7. Charles to Maria Tuttle, April 6, May 16, 1849, Letters, BAN.
8. Charles to Maria Tuttle, May 12, 1850, ibid.
9. Maria to Charles Tuttle, February 23, 27, 1850, ibid.
10. Maria to Charles Tuttle, February 23, 1850, ibid.
11. Maria to Charles Tuttle, February 27, March 15, 1850, ibid.
12. John to Margaret Eagle, June 13, 1852, Letters, HEH.
13. Milo to Catherine Goss, July 13, 1850, Letters, BAN.
14. Catherine to Milo Goss, August 25, 1850, Letters, BAN. Emphasis is hers.
15. Jane Blackwood to her cousin Margaret, January 5, 1850. In yet another example of different messages to different correspondents, Jane Blackwood always writes in the most optimistic tones to her husband, rarely mentioning her idle, lonely hours.
16. Jane to Thomas Blackwood, February 11, 1849; Thomas to Jane Blackwood, December 26, 1849, Letters, CLAR. Note that the reply to Jane's query was dated ten months after her letter and probably did not reach her for another six weeks.
17. Thomas to Jane Blackwood, February 13, 1849, Letters, CLAR.

18. Mary Ann Nelson to Jane Blackwood, August 3, 1849, Letters, CLAR. In this letter, Nelson refers to the recent paternity suit trial in which Thomas was found innocent.

19. Jane to Thomas Blackwood, undated 1850, ibid.

20. Cousin Thomas to Cousin Jane, March 12, 1850, ibid.

21. On occasion, a 49er would use the term "a raise" to describe the success of a particular unit of work, as after his company of four took ninety-three dollars from a claim in one day, Israel Lord wrote, "It is not often we make such a *raise*" (emphasis his). Lord, journal, May 15, 1850, HEH.

22. Exchanges between John and Margaret Eagle, June 13, 28, September 26, October 29, 1852; June 10, August 10, 1853, Letters, HEH.

8 : OCCUPATIONS

1. Ephriam W. Morse, "Voyage Boston to California," July 26, 1849, HEH.

2. H. Comstock to Mr. and Mrs. Levi Comstock, June 5, 1849, Letters, HEH.

3. Edward Abbe, journal, July 11, 1849, HEH. Abbe was typical of those seagoing 49ers who brought "gold washing machines" with them. These would be quickly discarded in favor of the cradle.

4. Buffum, *Six Months in the Gold Mines*, 72; William Denniston, journal, November 15, 1849, HEH.

5. Alexander Spear, journal, April 28, 1850, HEH.

6. J. E. Clayton, diary, March 23, 1850, ALA; William Farnsworth to Increase Blake, April 9, 1853, Letters, HEH.

7. S. Schufelt letter, March 3, 1850, HEH, is a description of the area around Placerville.

8. Joseph Warren Wood, journal, October 5, 1849, HEH; John to James Kinkade, June 5, 1850, Correspondence, HEH.

9. Henry Kent, diary, December 19, 1852, HEH; Benjamin Baxter, journal, June 5, 1850, HEH.

10. See, for example, Duane A. Smith's excellent study, *Mining America: The Industry and the Environment, 1800–1980* (Lawrence: University Press of Kansas, 1987).

11. Solomon Gorgas to his wife, diary and letters, December 25, 1850, HEH. Gorgas was describing the mines around Placerville in 1850.

12. See, for example, John Milner to his father, "My experience little as it is is worth a fortune. Any Ga miner can make a fortune here. I do not know one of them who has not made money in the mines." December 23, 1849, Letters, ALA.

13. E. D. Perkins, "Sketches of a Trip: Marietta Ohio to Sacramento, California," September 19, 1849, HEH.

14. S. Schufelt letter, March 3, 1850, HEH.

15. Richard Cowley, journal, January 19, 1851, HEH; Israel Lord, journal, April 28, 30, 1850, HEH.

16. William Pease to his parents, July 1, 1849, Letters, NAN.

17. Robert to Julia Sweetser, May 1850, Letters, HEH.

18. William A. Brown to his parents, September 15, 1849, Letters, HEH.
19. John Milner to his father, August 15, 1849, Letters, ALA.
20. The figures are from Paul, *California Gold: The Beginning of Mining,* 43.
21. Peter H. Burnett, *Recollections and Opinions of an Old Pioneer* (New York, 1880), 273.
22. William T. Parker, diary, July 31, 1850, HEH; Israel Lord, journal, February 22, April 2, 1850, HEH. Lord kept very precise notes about the area and value of claims.
23. John Hovey, journal, September 9, 10, 1849, HEH; William T. Parker, diary, July 31, 1850, HEH.
24. Alexander Barrington, journal, June 26, 1850, HEH.
25. Lafayette Fish, journal, June 30, 1850, HEH; Richard Cowley, journal, February 26, 1851, HEH.
26. Henry Kent, diary, November 13, 1853, HEH.
27. William Daingerfield to his mother, October 21, 1850, Letters, BAN; Gregory Yale to his wife, February 1, April 23, 1850, Letters, HEH. Yale urged her to say nothing about the size of his fees, fearing that such information was "apt to get into the papers—and I would be mortified."
28. William to Charlotte Prince, April 25, November 27, December 13, 1849; May 21, 1851, Letters, BAN. Edward Abbe noted that the *Aurora* had sailed from Nantucket for California in February 1849 with lumber, provisions, and house frames. Diary, February 14, 1849, HEH.
29. Rufus to Nellie Brown, February 22, June 24, June 28, August 30, 1852, Letters, BAN.
30. William Elder to his family, August 28, 1850, Letters, BAN.
31. John Milner to his father, December 23, 1849, Letters, ALA.
32. Edward Abbe, journal, October 12, 15, 16, 19, 1849, HEH.
33. Fitch to his brother, January 6, 1851, Letters, HEH.
34. James S. Barnes to his family, August 30, 1851, Letters, BAN; Wilson to Nancy Day, September 22, November 9, 1853, Correspondence, BAN; William to Sarah Dressler, July 20, 1851; March 14, May 1, 1852, Letters, BAN. As late as the summer of 1852, Amos McKee camped out at the edge of the desert with fresh mules and water at fifty cents a gallon. McKee letter, August 15, 1852, CHI.
35. John Milner to his father, January 10, 1850, Letters, ALA.
36. Henry T. Packer to Mary Elizabeth Judkins, August 24, October 29, 1850, the Packer Letters, BAN. They also "purchased a small tent building and opened a retail liquor and provision concern." Ananias Pond, "Life in the Mines," January 5, 7, 8, 1850, HEH.
37. Epaphroditus to Emma Wells, July 5, October 6, 1850, Letters, BAN. Rodman W. Paul, *California Gold,* documents the declining wages in the gold fields (349–50).
38. Richard Cowley, journal, March 30, April 6, 20, May 17, 1851, HEH.
39. John to Medorem Crawford, May 15, 1851, Letters, HEH; Isaac Perkins to brother, August 30, 1852, Letters, CSL.
40. A. C. Sweetser to Littlefield & Blood, November 27, 1850, Letters, HEH. On a retail and wholesale level, William Carpenter's store in Sacramento made between forty-five hundred and five thousand dollars in 1851. William Carpenter to Lucetta

Spencer, December 22, 1851, Letters, HEH. Carpenter's store was located next to Colis P. Huntington's.

41. Seldon to Harriet Goff, July 20, December 20, 1850, Letters, CSL; Solomon Gorgas to his wife, September 9, 1850, Diary & Letters, HEH. George Kent noted in December 1849 that a tavern keeper was "making money probably as fast as almost any man in the county." Journal, December 1849, HEH.

42. John Milner to his father, November 14, 25, December 23, 1849, Letters, ALA.

43. Lafayette Fish, journal, October 16, 27, 28, November 1, 17, 20, December 6, 9, 11, 14, 15, 1850; February 4, 10, 1851. The quotes are from November 1, 17, December 14, 1850, HEH. Fish returned to his home in the fall of 1851. See also George Raymond to his sister Sarah, June 3, 1850, where he writes that he was doing much better at storekeeping than at digging. Letters, BAN.

44. John to Margaret Eagle, December 25, 1852, Letters, HEH.

45. Alexander Barrington, journal, May 13, 1850, HEH.

46. William A. Brown to his family, April 7, July 25, 1850; February 13, November 21, April 8, August 8, 1851; January 13, February 14, August 11, 1852; February 13, January 25, March 27, 1853, Letters, HEH. For an account of two other 49ers in the express business, see Comstock, *Gold Diggers and Camp Followers,* chapter 26.

9: "THE REAL ARGONAUTS OF '49"

1. E. Gould Buffum, *Six Months in the Gold Mines,* 180.

2. Correspondence between 49ers and their families suggests that throughout the first decade of the Gold Rush, the cost ratio of boarding at a house or restaurant to cooking for oneself remained at about 2:1. That is to say, in 1849, board was sixteen dollars a week and cooking eight dollars; by 1851, these numbers had fallen to eight dollars and four dollars respectively. Seth to Asa Smith, May 27, 1851, Letters, BAN.

3. S. Schufelt to Cousin John, March 3, 1850, Letters, HEH. By 1850, miners were also using quicksilver machines to extract fine gold. William T. Parker, diary, September 3, 1850, HEH.

4. F. T. Sherman to his mother and father, November 18, 1849, Correspondence, CHI.

5. William T. Parker, diary, ca. November 3, 1850, HEH. Seth Smith noted that in August, his company worked only until ten or eleven o'clock each morning. Seth Smith to his father, August 21, 1853, Letters, BAN. Richard Cowley writes that his company also lost track of time. Journal, December 8, 1850, HEH.

6. Joshua to Susan Sullivan, March 17, 1850, Letters, ORE.

7. Christian Miller to his family, March 23, 1851, Letters, BAN; William Rothwell to his father, September 15, 1850, Letters, YALE. Isaac Foster, who celebrated his fifty-ninth birthday in the gold fields, noted the ways that miners exploited their bodies to the point of "prostration and sickness" in the reckless search for gold. Journal, November 16, 1849, HEH. A. P. Josselyn wrote to his sister that he had worked hard in the mines, but no harder than he had worked in Ohio for one dollar a day. Letter, May 12, 1850, Letters, CSL.

8. John to Margaret Eagle, June 13, 1852, Letters, HEH.

9. C. C. Mobley, diary, June 21, August 3, 8, 1850, HEH. I did not find a record of a miner expelled from a company for poor work, but members of companies were expelled for other reasons, e.g., stealing (Luther Fitch to his sister, April 17, 1851, Letters, HEH), drinking and gambling (Israel Lord, journal, March 31, 1850, HEH).

10. William T. Parker, diary, September 16, 1850, HEH; John to Ruth Fletcher, June 24, 1850, Letters, UOP.

11. S. Schufelt noted that his company washed any dirt that returned from six to twelve cents a pan. March 3, 1850, Letters, HEH. Isaac Barker washed 275 panfuls for ten dollars in gold, or four cents a pan. Barker, diary, April 5, 1850, HEH. As the mines became less productive, the miners had to wash more buckets each day to stay even. See Paul, *California Gold: The Beginning of Mining*, 120.

12. John Hovey, journal, October 30, November 4, 1849, HEH.

13. Robert Butterfield to his brother, March 9, 1853, Letters, HEH.

14. Richard Cowley, journal, December 1, 1850, HEH. The quiet interlude of evening sometimes became active. Benjamin Baxter wrote about one miner who threw a grizzly bear cub into his tent in order to see the reaction of his companions. Baxter, journal, May 12, 1850, HEH.

15. Robert to Julia Sweetser, May 1850, Letters, HEH. John Kinkade's company worked a half day on Christmas. John to James Kinkade, December 26, 1852, Correspondence, HEH.

16. John to Margaret Eagle, September 26, 1852, Letters, HEH.

17. Charles Bush to his parents, August 23, 1850, Letters, BAN. Ephriam Delano wrote his wife that he had become so accomplished "at house keeping" that when he returned home he expected to take over these duties. Ephriam to Jane Delano, August 29, 1853, Letters, HEH.

18. Isaac Barker, diary, March 25, 1850, HEH; Lafayette Fish, journal, December 23, 1850, HEH.

19. Isaac Barker, diary, March 28, 1850, HEH. Barker described meals in detail on several occasions in May 1850. James Alexander noted occasional quarrels about cooking and making beds. James to Frances Alexander, January 20, 1852, Letters, BAN. Joseph Conlin, *Bacon, Beans, and Galatines: Food and Foodways on the Western Mining Frontier* (Reno: University of Nevada Press, 1986), chapter 3, is an excellent account of food preparation and consumption in the Gold Rush.

20. David to Matilda DeWolf, December 12, 1849, Letters, HEH; Jacob Engle to his brother, February 7, 1850, Letters, HEH; Richard Cowley, journal, October 19, 1851, HEH. Some miners continued to eat plain food as an economy measure. See C. C. Mobley, diary, August 21, 1850, HEH.

21. James Clarke, journal, May 1, 1852, HEH.

22. Lafayette Fish, journal, December 23, 1850; February 4, 1851, HEH.

23. Joseph Warren Wood, journal, November 30, 1850, HEH.

24. George Kent, journal, December 1849, HEH.

25. Daniel Woods, *Sixteen Months in the Gold Diggings* (New York, 1851), 11 (entry for April 2, 1850). John Hovey lived in an elaborate "cottage," with two rooms, a kitchen, "parlour," and bedrooms. John Hovey, journal, December 1, 1849, HEH.

Joseph Warren Wood and his mess built their "winter quarters" on December 8. The "house," as he called it, was eleven by fifteen feet, with a stone back for a fireplace and a cloth roof. Wood, journal, December 8, 9, 1849, HEH. The *Alta California,* December 31, 1849, contains a long description of that hard winter in the diggings.

26. James E. Davis, ed., *Dreams to Dust: A Diary of the California Gold Rush, 1849–1850* (Lincoln: University of Nebraska Press 1989), 88. Among entertainments were visits from the Indians, with friendly competitions in shooting the rifle against the bow and arrow.

27. Estimates of the mining season vary. John Hovey wrote that under the best conditions, miners worked eight months a year (Hovey, journal, June 30, 1850, HEH), while George Murrell judged that miners worked only three to four months a year "on account of high water." See Jane Apostol, ed., " 'The Fickel Godess Evades Me'—The Gold Rush Letters of a Kentucky Gentleman," *Register of the Kentucky Historical Society* 79 (1981): 108.

28. To the places where young men congregated, E. Anthony Rotundo might have added mining camps. See *American Manhood,* 62–71.

29. Henry Packer to Mary Elizabeth Judkins, May 20, 1851, Letters, BAN.

30. One company required an "anti Swearing, Temperance & Anti-Tobacco Pledge," Charles to Lydia and Sue Church, November 27, 1849, Letters, ORE.

31. Israel Lord, journal, August 4, 1850, HEH.

32. John to Margaret Eagle, December 25, 1852, Letters, HEH.

33. Peter Y. Cool, journal, HEH, is among those who commented extensively on the temperance movement and its relationship to the new values of California.

34. Henry Packer to Mary Elizabeth Judkins, May 20, 1851, Letters, BAN.

35. Susan Lee Johnson, "Bulls, Bears, and Dancing Boys: Race, Gender, and Leisure in the California Gold Rush," *Radical History Review* 60 (1994): 4–37, is an acute analysis of the ways in which leisure is a window on the roles of gender and race in the gold fields. She notes that "leisure . . . proved a site in which oppositions such as male vs. female and white vs. nonwhite were thrown into disarray" (8).

36. William A. Brown to his sister, May 5, 1851, Letters, HEH. Brown's own experience suggests that many men, himself included, spent money in quantities never before imaginable.

37. William T. Parker, diary, November 3, 1850, HEH.

38. Isaac Barker, diary, November 10, 24, 1850, HEH.

39. John to Margaret Eagle, March 12, 1853, in which he recommended Stowe's book to his wife, tells her where to buy it, and says that "if you have not time to read it, mother and Net will read it to you, of nights, after the store is closed." Margaret managed the store alone after John's departure for California. *Uncle Tom's Cabin* was published in 1852, first serialized in a magazine. Eagle found a copy "in book form here" in California by early 1853. Letters, HEH.

40. Davis, *Dreams to Dust,* 92. William T. Parker passed several Sundays wandering through deserted camps and picking up books. Diary, November 1850, HEH.

41. Peter Y. Cool, journal, July 26, 1851, HEH, after washing one shirt; Alexander Spear, journal, June 9, 1850, HEH.

42. "Dame Shirley's" account of the Fourth of July celebration at Rich Bar, including a poem written for the occasion, is in Clapp, *The Shirley Letters,* 137–44.

43. Joseph Warren Wood, journal, December 25, 1849, HEH. John Canfield noted in 1855 that his company would have worked on Christmas Day but it was too cold. John to Henry Canfield, December 26, 1855, the Canfield Letters, BAN.

44. Ephriam W. Morse, journal, November 29, 1849, HEH.

45. E. D. Perkins, "Sketches of a Trip: Marietta Ohio to Sacramento, California," December 25, 1849, HEH. One of his friends had just died, and in a burst of fatalism, Perkins thought his death only a harbinger of "many such scenes."

46. Joseph Warren Wood, journal, January 1, 1850, HEH; Lafayette Fish, journal, December 25, 1849, HEH.

47. William Denniston, journal, July 4, 1850, HEH.

48. San Francisco *Alta California,* December 29, 31, 1849, has extended accounts of the early winter.

49. George W. Groh, *Gold Fever: Being a True Account, Both Horrifying and Hilarious, of the Art of Healing (So-called) During the California Gold Rush* (New York: William Morrow, 1966), considers the state of the medical arts.

50. Allen Varner to Elias Varner, November 12, 1849, Letters, HEH; J. H. to Thomas C. Magruder, October 7, 1851, Letters, HEH. Magruder's brother lived in Washington, D.C., hence the basis for the comparison.

51. William A. Brown to his parents, August 19, 1849, Letters, HEH. Brown himself mined for only a few months before settling in San Francisco.

10: THE URBAN 49ERS

1. John C. Collbreath to his parents, June 30, 1849, Letters, BAN.

2. Albert Gallatin Osbun, "The California and the South Sea," June 16, 1849, HEH.

3. Bayard Taylor, *Eldorado; or, Adventures in the Path to Empire* (1850; reprint, New York, 1949), 57, 226.

4. Roger W. Lotchin, *San Francisco, 1846–1856: From Hamlet to City* (New York: Oxford University Press, 1974), esp. chapters 1–6, is a complete introduction to the emergence of San Francisco as a city.

5. Alfred DeWitt to his father, April 14, September 24, 1848, Letters, BAN.

6. Milo to Catherine Goss, March 14, 30, May 1, 15, 1851, Letters, BAN.

7. Milo to Catherine Goss, June 29, July 15, 1851, ibid. On the Committees of Vigilance, see John Caughey, *Their Majesties, the Mob* (Chicago: University of Chicago Press, 1960).

8. Milo to Catherine Goss, November 14, 1851; January 15, 1852, Letters, BAN.

9. Robert to Daniel La Mott, January 13, 1850, Family Correspondence, BAN. In addition to the business correspondence of Alfred DeWitt—he wrote very little in a personal way—Peter DeWitt, Jr. (1848–53), Peter DeWitt, Sr. (1849–50), and Theodore DeWitt (1849–52) also wrote business letters. BAN.

10. Robin Winks, *Frederick Billings: A Life* (New York: Oxford University Press, 1991). Chapters 8 and 9 provide an excellent account of the rise of San Francisco as a

commercial city and of the Vigilance movement as seen through the eyes of one of its prominent lawyers.

11. John to Lottie McCracken, April 30, November 26, 1849, Letters, BAN. The Mc-Cracken Letters are a wonderful source of information on the urban gentleman, set against a backdrop of the hurly-burly of Gold Rush San Francisco.

12. John to Lottie McCracken, October 8, 1851, ibid.

13. William A. Brown to his mother, March 18, April 8, June 13, November 21, 1851, Letters, HEH.

14. David Hewes to his mother, February 24, June 29, 1850, Letters, BAN.

15. E. D. Perkins, "Sketches of a Trip: Marietta, Ohio to Sacramento, California," October 6, 1849, HEH; Joseph Warren Wood, diary, October 19, November 3, 1849, HEH. E. T. Sherman to his father and mother, November 18, 1849, Family Correspondence, CHI.

16. Joseph Warren Wood, diary, November 3, 1849, HEH; Enoch Jacobs, journal, January 10, 1850, HEH; Seldon Goff to his wife, July 20, 1850, Letters, CSL. A. C. Sweetser to Littlefield & Blood, May 24, 1850, Letters, HEH, discusses attempts to establish benevolent institutions.

17. James Barnes to his brother, May 30, 1851, Letters, BAN.

18. John to Margaret Eagle, June 13, 1852, Letters, HEH.

19. Israel Lord, journal, December 22, 21, 30, 1849, HEH. Lord penned a vivid description of Sacramento under water on December 22.

20. Israel Lord, journal, January 3, 4, 1850, HEH.

21. Israel Lord, ibid., February 20, July 21, 1850.

22. Israel Lord, ibid., August 22, 1850.

23. Israel Lord, ibid., August 11, 1850.

24. Israel Lord, ibid., May 29, 1850.

25. John to Julia Ann Baker, October 10, 1853, the Baker Letters, UOP.

26. John to Julia Ann Baker, September 20, October 10, 1853, ibid.

27. John to Julia Ann Baker, October 10, 21, November 8, 1853, ibid.

28. John to Julia Ann Baker, December 10, 1853; April 13, 1855, ibid.

29. New Hampshire *Exeter Newsletter,* December 17, 1849.

30. Isaac Owen, journal, February 3, 1851, HEH. The *Sacramento Transcript* has a series of accounts of Placerville that make useful comparative reading, especially June 3, August 19, September 9, 1850; March 3, 1851.

31. Robert to Daniel La Mott, January 13, 1850, Family Correspondence, BAN.

32. Harry to Daniel La Mott, January 23, 1850, ibid.

33. Robert La Mott to his father, February 15, 1850; Robert to his mother, June 23, 1850, ibid.

34. Roger W. Lotchin, *San Francisco, 1846–1856,* chapter 2, discusses San Francisco's urban rivals, including Benicia and New York.

35. Robert La Mott to his mother, June 23, 1850, Family Correspondence, BAN.

36. Robert to Daniel La Mott, n.d. 1850, ibid.

37. Harry La Mott to his mother, August 12, 1850, ibid.

38. Robert La Mott to his father, August 13, 1850, ibid.

39. Robert La Mott to his father, September 9, 1850, ibid.

40. Harry La Mott to his mother, September 11, 1850, ibid.

41. Robert La Mott to his brother Will, October 19, 1850; Robert to his mother, December 16, 1850, ibid.

42. Harry La Mott to his father, March 13, 1851; Robert to his father, March 15, 1851; Harry to his mother, June 8, 1851, ibid.

43. Robert to Annie La Mott, September 23, 1850, ibid.

44. Robert La Mott to his father, March 25, August 10, October 29, 1851; Robert to his mother, March 1, October 6, November 29, December 3, 1851, ibid. The La Mott family were prolific correspondents. No one complained of not being written to enough, a rarity in the Gold Rush experience. Letters involved all members of the family and subjects. They discussed business in all its forms with their father, the home and garden with their mother, and mutual friends and social activities with their sister.

45. James Barnes to his brother, May 30, 1851, Letters, BAN.

II: WOMEN IN THE CALIFORNIA GOLD RUSH

1. Rhode Island *Woonsocket Patriot,* February 16, 1849, Bieber Coll., HEH.

2. Maria to Charles Tuttle, February 23, 1850, Letters, BAN. A newspaper account of a woman's experiences in the first months of the Gold Rush, dated April 1848, was reprinted in the *Raleigh Star & N. Carolina Gazette,* March 7, 1849.

3. Emeline Day, journal, April 14, 21, 1853, BAN. Two contrasting journals both dating from 1852 are those of Algeline Ashley (excited about the trip across the plains) and Mary Stuart Bailey (distraught by separation from her friends), both in HEH.

4. *Raleigh Register,* February 3, 1849. A different kind of notice headed "A CHANCE FOR A LADY" described the forthcoming departure of someone who intended "to live as a gentleman should live, and also having great expectations in the Gold Regions" and invited applications to share his golden dream for "a partner, in the shape and form of an interesting and handsome young woman, who has the nerve to undertake the perils of an overland trip &." She must be frugal during the first year or so, "while we are accumulating our fortune. As widows are dangerous things, none need apply. The successful applicant for a hand and heart that pants for wealth and distinction, must be young, handsome, accomplished, agreeable, healthy, even-tempered, resolute, and possessing a share of fortitude, sufficient to bear with severe trials." Reprinted from the *Van Buren Intelligencer* in the Little Rock *Arkansas State Democrat,* February 16, 1849, Bieber Coll., HEH.

5. There is a laudatory editorial in the Mobile *Alabama Planter,* March 5, 1849, Bieber Coll., HEH.

6. Washington, D.C., *Daily Union,* February 27, 1849, Bieber Coll., HEH.

7. Kentucky *Louisville Daily Journal,* May 31, 1849. The San Francisco *Alta California,* May 24, 1849, noted that the scheme was enthusiastically welcomed in California. Both are in Bieber Coll., HEH.

8. Bloomington *Indiana Tribune & Monroe Farmer,* February 24, 1849, Bieber Coll., HEH.

9. Little Rock *Arkansas Banner,* September 25, 1849, Bieber Coll., HEH.

10. Margaret DeWitt to her father and mother, July 30 1849, May 15, 1850, DeWitt Papers, BAN.

11. Margaret DeWitt to her father and mother, August 28, 1849, ibid.

12. Margaret DeWitt to her father and mother, September 28, November 28, 1849, ibid. In a letter to her father: "I will bring my letter to a close, and I dare say you will be glad—for I believe gentlemen do not care much to read what ladies write especially if they have no more to say than I." November 30, 1849.

13. Margaret DeWitt to her father and mother, August 14, 1850, ibid.

14. Henry Packer to Mary Elizabeth Judkins, October 29, 1850, Letters, BAN; Milton Hall to his father, April 25, 1852, Letters, BAN. In John Stickney to his wife, July 13, 1850, the Sweetser Letters, HEH, Stickney wrote that "Lady Cookes are *scarce & expensive*."

15. Emeline Day, journal, October 2, 1853, BAN.

16. Mary B. Ballou to "My Dear Selden," October 30, 1852, quoted in Nancy Woloch, ed., *Early American Women* (Belmont, Calif.: Wadsworth, 1992), 272.

17. Benjamin Baxter, journal, August 10, 1850, HEH; William A. Brown to his father, July 25, 1850, the Brown Letters, HEH; C. C. Mobley, diary, November 1, 1850, HEH.

18. Anon to Lizzie, October 15, 1853, HEH.

19. Clapp, *The Shirley Letters,* 39.

20. Newburyport, Massachusetts, *Herald,* December 14, 1849, Bieber Coll., HEH.

21. North Carolina *Fayetteville Observer,* January 8, 1850, ibid.

22. Lydia Burns to Polly Burns Hall, September 18, 1853, the Burns Letters, HEH.

23. Lydia Burns to Polly Burns Hall, June 1854, ibid.

24. The story of Lucy Stoddard Wakefield lies in two documents: Wakefield to Lucius and Rebecca, September 18, 1851, Letter, HEH; and Leslie Bryson to "Friend Stoddard," December 3, 1851, Letter, HEH. Bryson was a merchant/speculator in San Francisco; he was one of the first to import Chinese labor under contract.

25. Clapp, *The Shirley Letters,* 198.

12 : HARSH REALITIES

1. S. Schufelt, letter, March 3, 1850, HEH; A. P. Josselyn to his sister, May 12, 19, 1850, Letters, CSL.

2. William B. Campbell to his uncle, April 10, 1850, Papers, DUKE. Campbell modestly noted that "I have the right sort of enterprise and energy to succeed in such a business."

3. Rufus to Nellie Brown, July 22, 1852, Letters, BAN.

4. John Fitch to brother, January 6, 1851, Letters, HEH. Rodman W. Paul estimates the numbers of miners and wages as: 1848, five thousand miners, daily wage, twenty dollars; 1849, forty thousand miners, daily wage, sixteen dollars; 1850, fifty thousand miners, daily wage, ten dollars; 1852, one hundred thousand miners, daily wage, six dollars. *California Gold: The Beginning of Mining,* 43, 349–50.

5. John C. Collbreath to his family, June 25, 1850, Letters, BAN; Charles to Nell Harlan, February 24, 1850, Letters, BAN.

6. Solomon Gorgas to his wife, September 9, 1850, Letters, HEH.

7. Israel Lord, journal, July 16, 1850, HEH.

8. Joseph Warren Wood, journal, February 8, March 8, 30, April 15, November 24, 1850, HEH.

9. Charles Harlan to Julia Le Grand, February 24, 1850, Letters, BAN; Henry T. Packer to Mary Elizabeth Judkins, April 27, 1851, Letters, BAN.

10. Joseph Warren Wood, diary, October 14, 18, 1849, HEH.

11. C. C. Mobley, diary, April 12, 17, 27, 1850, HEH.

12. Milton Hall to his father, August 15, 1852, Letters, BAN.

13. Ibid.

14. John R. Fitch to his brother, January 6, 1851, Letters, HEH.

15. John Hovey, journal, September 24, 1849, HEH; Isaac Barker, diary, September 11, November 2, 1849, HEH.

16. G. C. Coates to Jane Coates, August 6, 1852, Letters, HEH. For a technical explanation of "coyoting," see Otis E. Young, Jr., *Western Mining: An Informal Account of Precious-Metals Prospecting, Placering, Lode Mining, and Milling on the American Frontier from Spanish Times to 1893* (Norman: University of Oklahoma Press, 1970), 110–11.

17. Ananias R. Pond, "Life &c.," October 28, 1849, HEH.

18. On the improvement of the diet of miners, even in the face of declining returns, see Conlin, *Bacon, Beans, and Galatines,* chapter 6.

19. John to Margaret Eagle, October 29, 1852, Letters, HEH; Albert N. Francisco to his mother, June 9, 1852, Letters, HEH; North San Juan *Hydraulic Press,* October 30, 1858, quoted in Paul, *California Gold,* 84.

20. Henry T. Packer to Mary Elizabeth Judkins, February 23, 1851, Letters, BAN.

21. Enoch Jacobs, journal, July 6, 1849, HEH.

22. Correspondent in Evergreen Valley, California, for the Illinois *Belleville Advocate,* May 23, 1850. Bieber Coll., HEH.

23. Levi to M. Hillman, March 3, 1853, Letters, MINN.

24. The phrase comes from the correspondence of William A. Brown to his parents, Letters, HEH.

25. William A. Brown to his sister, August 19, 1849; to his parents, September 15, 1849, Letters, HEH.

26. Clapp, *The Shirley Letters,* 123; Charles to Maria Tuttle, May 12, 1850, Letters, BAN; F. T. Sherman to father, November 18, 1849, Correspondence, CHI. Tuttle continually apologized for not sending more money home; he was one of few 49ers to acknowledge an ongoing responsibility to his family. For another woman's observations along the same lines, see Eliza Farnham, *California, Indoors and Out* (New York, 1850), 307–09.

27. Joseph Pownall, journal and letterbook, February 22, 1850, HEH. Pownall went on to say, "Nevertheless, any man with untiring energy can manage to accumulate in the course of 12 mo's what would be considered in any portion of the U.S.A. a very fair sum of money."

28. Ben Ross to his sister Elizabeth, October 1, 1851, Family Correspondence, BAN.

29. Emily D. Brownell to Orrin Bell, December 31, 1854, Papers, BENT.

30. William to Charlotte Prince, December 18, 1849, Letters, BAN.

31. Seldon Goff to his wife, July 20, 1850, Letters, CSL.

32. Robert La Mott to his father, March 25, 1851, Correspondence, BAN.

33. Stephen Jackson to his mother, December 10, 1851, Letters, BAN. The tone of the correspondence from Thomas Anderson to his family changes dramatically over three letters, dated February 17, 1850 (great success), September 10, 1853 (great expectations), and April 16, 1856 (failure), Letters, BAN.

34. Mulford, *Prentice Mulford's Story,* 4; Willis Dixon to Mary Pendleton, March 20, 1852, the Holiday-Pendleton Papers, UNC.

13: "CAPITALISTS WILL TAKE HOLD"

1. Seldon Goff to his wife, December 20, 1850, Letters, CSL. Goff went on to observe that these investors and their schemes would replace the large transient population of miners, "a class of people who live from hand to mouth as the saying are & are compelled to work where they can obtain gold *Easiest.*"

2. John Kinkade to James and Hannah Kinkade, March 21, May 5, September 6, 1850, Correspondence, HEH. Another account of a damming operation in 1850 is Joseph Pownall to "My Dear Thomas," Diary and letterbook, August 5, 1850, HEH. The *Alta California* described a scheme to turn a river as early as June 21, 1849.

3. William Parker, diary, September 9, 1850, HEH.

4. Richard Cowley, journal, October 13, 1850, HEH. Albert Francisco from New Orleans compared such mining operations to speculation in cotton and "fancy stocks." Albert Francisco to his mother, May 16, 1853, Letters, HEH.

5. John to Margaret Eagle, April 26, May 27, 1853, Letters, HEH. Eagle followed a common pattern by concluding his harrowing account on an optimistic note: "we have made another beginning, and I hope we will succeed this time."

6. John Fitch to his brother, September 25, 1852, Letters, HEH. To his wife, Fitch was graphic and apologetic; to his brother, businesslike and detailed. On river mining, see Young, *Western Mining,* 113–18, esp. illustrations on 115 and 116.

7. William Parker, diary, February 2, 1851, HEH. W. P. Robinson to G. P. Didson, May 18, 1852, Parks Coll., NCDAH, discusses lawsuits over dams that changed the water level.

8. Isaac Barker, diary, September 26, October 31, November 4, 1850, HEH.

9. John Fitch to his wife, October 23, 1851; February 16, March 21, April 23, 1852, Letters, HEH.

10. William Parker, diary, November 8, December 14, 1851, HEH.

11. Jonas to Susan Winchester, July 31, 1851, Letters, CSL; Mann, *After the Gold Rush,* 24–28. The quartz-mining business temporarily collapsed in 1852–53.

12. T. H. Jackson to William Prince, October 30, December 13, 1851; October 14, 1852, Letters, HEH. Jackson and Prince also corresponded on investing in county scrip, which rose dramatically with the passage of a state funding bill, and state comptroller's warrants. Such state paper represented an alternative investment opportunity to quartz mines. Jackson to Prince, May 14, 1852. Another early

discussion of quartz mining is John McFarlan's journal, dated mid-1852, 181–92, HEH.

13. Jacob S. Hayden, diary, August 21, 1852, UNC. On quartz mining, see Paul, *California Gold*, 130–37.

14. Otis E. Young, Jr., *Western Mining*, 125–31. Young writes that the water "was ejected from a pivoted nozzle like that of a fireboat" (127). On the environmental impact of the new technologies, see Smith, *Mining America*, esp. chapters 1–3.

15. Paul, *California Gold*, discusses the "dry diggings," 113–15. He also notes the division into northern and southern mines and the changes to include a "central" section after 1851. See Paul, *California Gold*, chapter 7.

16. Henry Kent, diaries, June 20, 28, July 11, September 9, 25, 1853, HEH. Richard Keen is also an example of a man who found employment in "water companies," diary, 1852, Indiana State Library. On water companies, see Paul, *California Gold*, 160–64.

17. William Brown to his father, December 31, 1850, Letters, HEH.

18. William T. Parker, diary, November 8, 1851, HEH.

19. Christian Miller to his family, July 6, 1852, Letters, BAN.

20. John to Mary Gish, July 20, 1851, Letters, YALE.

21. John to James Kinkade, August 8, 1854, Correspondence, HEH.

22. John Wayman, letters of June 12, 1854, and April 25, 1855, Letters, BAN; Milton to David Ritenour, November 8, 1854, Letters, HEH. Young, *Western Mining*, calculates that the total California gold production for the decade of the 1850s was five hundred and sixty million dollars, which works out to an annual return for each miner of two hundred and fifty dollars (124). On numbers of miners, see Paul, *California Gold*, 43.

23. This account of Alonzo Hubbard's life as a 49er is based on his journal, 1852–54, HEH. It parallels the experiences of Nath'l Blanchard, who borrowed two hundred and fifty dollars for one year at an interest rate of 12 percent to make the trip. Once in California, he hired out for eighty-five dollars a month and boarded himself, worked in a meat shop, and used his wages to prospect claims. He paid off his note two years later. Among other expenses, he contributed two dollars to send a blind man back to Ohio. Blanchard journal, HEH.

24. The William Dickson Family Correspondence, UNC, contains a wealth of material about this family, with an emphasis on affairs in North Carolina. The exchanges suggest the degree to which life continued on in very customary ways, even as distant relatives reported exotic experiences in California. The correspondence of two young people, filled with references to the California Gold Rush and its influence on their society, can be found in Elizabeth Roberts Cannon, ed., *My Beloved Zebulon: The Correspondence of Zebulon Baird Vance and Harriet Nowell Espy* (Chapel Hill: University of North Carolina Press, 1971).

25. Robert Dickson to "My Very Dear Sister," December 10, 1852; to "My Very Dear Father and Mother," January 24, 1853, Letters, UNC.

26. Robert Dickson to "My Very Dear Father and Mother," January 24, 1853, ibid. Dickson's comment about the lack of a servant class resonates with the complaints of officials at the opening of the gold rush.

27. Robert Dickson to "My Very Dear Sister," December 10, 1852, ibid.

28. S. M. McDowell to "My Dear Uncle, Aunt, & Cousins," undated but presumably early 1853, ibid.

29. Robert Dickson to "My Very Dear Father and Mother," January 24, 1853, ibid.

30. Junius Gates to William Dickson, April 26, 1855; R. M. Dickson to "My Dear Brother," April 24, 1853; R. M. Dickson to William and Margaret Dickson, May 27, 1854, ibid.

31. To Master James Woodfin, April 25, 1853, Papers, UNC.

32. Albert McDowell to "My affectionate Mistress," July 13, 1854; to "My Dear Master," May 15, 1855, Woodfin Letters, UNC. A case in which a slave owner from Mississippi who took three slaves (later freed) to California for the Gold Rush sued for their return is analyzed in Ray R. Albin, "The Perkins Case: The Ordeal of Three Slaves in Gold Rush California," *California History* 67 (1988): 215–27.

14: THREATS FROM WITHIN, THREATS FROM WITHOUT

1. Jacob Engle to his brother, June 3, 1852, Letters, HEH.

2. Alexander Barrington, journal, September 20, 1850, HEH.

3. Lafayette Fish, journal, June 30, 1850, HEH.

4. James Rice to his brother, July 21, 1850, Letters, HEH.

5. William T. Parker, diary, September 13, 1850, HEH.

6. Isaac Barker, diary, June 25, 26, 1850, HEH.

7. Alexander Barrington, journal, July 17, 1850, HEH.

8. Israel Lord, journal, January 5, 1850, HEH.

9. Ibid.

10. Quoted in Jay Monaghan, *Chile, Peru, and the California Gold Rush of 1849* (Berkeley: University of California Press, 1973), 114.

11. Albert L. Hurtado, *Indian Survival on the California Frontier* (New Haven: Yale University Press, 1988), chapter 6, is an insightful analysis of the California Gold Rush from the Indian perspective.

12. *Sacramento Transcript*, May 23, October 25, 26, November 8, 20, 25, December 5, 1850; Benjamin Baxter, journal, May 19, 1850, HEH.

13. San Francisco *Alta California*, April 19, 1849. An antiforeign resolution by the Mormon Island Mining Association is reported there on August 2, 1849.

14. John Hovey, journal, August 25, 1849, HEH.

15. John Cowden to Theodore Garretson, August 14, 1849, Letters, YALE; Richard Cowley, journal, July 21, 1850, HEH, maintained that miners in Stockton went armed with pistols and knives and the city had a greater sense of violence, all of which reinforced the stereotypes of a Mexican presence. On the diversity of population in the southern mines, see Susan Lee Johnson, "Bulls, Bears, and Dancing Boys: Race, Gender, and Leisure in the California Gold Rush," *Radical History Review* 60 (1994): 7–8.

16. Paul, *California Gold,* 27–28, 48; Enos L. Christman to Peebles Prizer, July 21, 23, 1850, Letters, HEH. Benjamin Kendrick to his father, October 8, 1850, Letters, YALE, writes of the expulsion of Mexican miners.

17. Monaghan, *Chile, Peru, and the California Gold Rush of 1849,* chapters 10–13. The influx of so much gold into Valparaiso and the many commercial opportunities associated with the Gold Rush minimized distress at the news of the anti-Chilean riots. On the powerful influence of the Gold Rush in Chile, see chapter 16. For an American perspective, see Florence Morrow Christman, ed., *One Man's Gold: The Letters & Journal of a Forty-Niner, Enos Christman* (New York: McGraw Hill Book Company, 1930), an account of Christman's visit in Valparaiso in November 1849.

18. Monaghan, *Chile, Peru, and the California Gold Rush of 1849,* chapter 19. Also see Steve Giabocci, "Chile and Her Argonauts in the Gold Rush, 1848–1856," unpublished M.A. thesis, San Jose State University, 1967, esp. chapter 5.

19. See Charles H. Shinn, *Mining Camps; A Study in American Frontier Government* (New York, 1885), and his chapter on "The Difficulties with Foreigners in Various Camps," 212–24.

20. John Hovey, journal, November 9, December 14–16, 28, 30, 31, 1849; January 1–5, 1850, HEH. See also Monaghan, *Chile, Peru, and the California Gold Rush of 1849,* 243–48.

21. Howard R. Lamar, ed., *Gold Seeker: Adventures of a Belgian Argonaut during the Gold Rush Years* (New Haven: Yale University Press, 1985), xviii–xxii. Abraham Nasatir, *The French in the California Gold Rush* (New York, 1934), is a complete study. The best of the many French accounts are Daniel Lévy, *Les Français en Californie* (San Francisco, 1884); Léon Lemonnier, *La Ruée vers l'or en Californie* (Paris: Gallimard, 1944); and Liliane Crété, *La Vie quotidienne en Californie au temps de la ruée vers l'or (1848–1856)* (Paris: Hatchette, 1982).

22. John Hovey, journal, April 5, 1850, HEH; Joseph Warren Wood, journal, December 1, 1850, HEH.

23. F. D. Calhoon, *49er Irish: One Irish Family in the California Mines* (Hicksville, N.Y.: Exposition Press, 1977), chapters 1–5.

24. Jay Monaghan, *Australians and the Gold Rush: California and Down Under, 1849–1854* (Berkeley: University of California Press, 1966), chapters 6–9, 15.

25. Charles Plummer to father, March 14, 1851, Letters, HEH; William T. Parker, diary, June 20, 1852, HEH. James Clarke's account in his journal in 1852 of Chinese doing laundry in a river is one of interest and wonder, not hostility. Journal, May 1, 1852, HEH. Stephen Woodlin to his wife and children, May 15, 1853, Letters, HEH. Henry Kent, diary, May 1, 1853, HEH, writes of a Sunday visit to a Chinese camp.

26. William Carpenter to Lucetta Spencer, May 7, 1852, Letters, HEH. Leslie Bryson to Friend Stoddard, December 31, 1851, HEH, contains an account of his intention to bring in three hundred Chinese laborers under contract. Henry Anable, journal, September 25, 1852, HEH.

27. Henry Kent, diary, May 24, 1853, HEH.

28. On the Foreign Miner's Tax, see John Walton Caughey, *Gold Is the Cornerstone* (Berkeley: University of California Press, 1948), 194–95.

29. Israel Lord, journal, May 11, 1850, HEH. Lord feared that foreigners would en-
danger themselves by aggressive and noisy behavior.

15 : WAITING

1. William Carpenter to Lucetta Spencer, December 22, 1851; March 22, April 18,
1852, Letters, HEH. Carpenter returned home and married Spencer in 1853.
2. This account is based on Susan Folger Gardner, diary, January–April 1853,
DUKE.
3. Solomon Gorgas to his children, September 11, 1850, Letters, HEH.
4. John Frederick to John Fitch, August 14, 1849, Letters, HEH.
5. A. R. Pond, journal, March 13, 1852, HEH.
6. Ephriam to George Delano, December 12, 1852; March 6, May 21, July 4, 1853, and
others, Letters, HEH.
7. Nancy Coffey Heffernan and Ann Page Stecker, *Sisters of Fortune: Being the true
story of how three motherless sisters saved their home in New England and raised their
younger brother while their father went fortune hunting in the California Gold Rush*
(Hanover: University Press of New England, 1993), ix–xiv, 49–50. See especially
Elizabeth to her father, November 5, 1858 (212–15), in which she reproaches him
for his continuing absence from his family.
8. Mother to John Slatford, March 3, 1853, Letters, BENT.
9. Samuel to William A. Brown, August 18, 1851, Letters, HEH.
10. William A. Brown to his mother, November 25, 1850; Brown to his father, December 31, 1850; Brown to his brother Samuel, August 18, 1851, Letters, HEH.
11. Rinaldo Taylor to his wife, January 14, 1850, Letters, MASS.
12. Jesse Tarbell to Susan Farnsworth Blake, January 8, 1856; William Tarbell to Susan
Farnsworth Blake, September 18, 1859, the Farnsworth Letters, HEH. William
Farnsworth died in New York in the spring of 1859 on his way home from the gold
fields.
13. George Wheeler, journal, February 7, 1851, HEH.
14. Jacob Engle to his brother, February 15, 1852, Letters, HEH.
15. Charles Plummer to his father, March 10, 1853, Letters, HEH. Plummer wrote a
similar letter to his father dated January 9, 1855, also without result.
16. William A. to Samuel Brown, August 18, 1851, Letters, HEH.
17. G. Cassil to Hannah and James Kinkade, May 5, June 4, 1850, Kinkade Correspondence, HEH.

16 : LOST LOVE, LOST FAMILIES

1. Mother to John Slatford, March 2, 1852, Letters, BENT.
2. Ephriam to Jane Delano, late summer or early autumn, 1852, Letters, HEH.
3. Seldon to Harriet Goff, December 20, 1850, Letters, CSL.
4. Eben Chapman to Eben Hunt, March 24, 1852, Letters, HEH.

5. Albert Francisco to his mother, February 12, 1852; July 27, 1851; April 24, 1854, Letters, HEH. Although Lucy Stoddard Wakefield dissolved her marriage in California, the sources of the conflict predated their trip across the plains. Wakefield to friends, August 25, 1851, Letters, HEH.

6. Albert Francisco to his mother, April 24, 1854, Letters, HEH.

7. Gustavus Swasey, journal, 1849–55, HEH.

8. David Allen Comstock, *Gold Diggers and Camp Followers*, 379–81, recounts the rising tensions between two couples. In his next volume, *Brides of the Gold Rush, 1851–1859* (Grass Valley, Calif.: Comstock-Bonanza Press, 1987), the 49ers return and claim their brides, and the couples go to California.

9. See, for example, Christman, *One Man's Gold*, 87–95, in which Christman's friend, Peebles Prizer, who had recently broken off his engagement, begins to pay regular calls on Ellen Apple, Christman's fiancée.

10. Sarah Trask, diaries, Beverly Historical Society, Beverly, Mass. With Luther buried at sea, she wrote, "I have seen my Best friend on earth, Depart for a far Country, with bright prospects before him and my hope was, that he would do well, and return safely. . . . But how vain were my hopes, For Death has claimed him [too], for his own."

11. John Fitch to his wife, February 16, 1851; Fitch to his brother, September 25, 1850, Letters, HEH.

12. Solomon to Mary Frances Gorgas, December 25, 1850, Letters, HEH.

13. John Kerr to his mother, March 15, 1851; Kerr to Dick, March 31, 1857, Letters, CSL.

14. Gustavus Swasey, journal, March 3, 1850, HEH.

15. George Lawson to his parents, August 26, 1851, Letters, HEH.

16. Allen Varner to his parents, August 19, 1850, Letters, HEH.

17. William to Increase and Sarah Farnsworth, May 13, 1853, Letters, HEH.

18. Isaac to Daniel Perkins, September 29, October 13, December 14, 1850, Letters, CSL.

19. Isaac to Daniel Perkins, September 14, October 30, 1851; January 13, April 2, August 30, September 26, 1852, ibid.

20. John Fitch to his brother, March 6, 1850; August 9, July 12, 1851, Letters, HEH.

21. Solomon to Mary Frances Gorgas, December 25, 1850, Letters, HEH. He also wrote a letter advocating Christian forbearance and forgiveness in the face of family bitterness, John Fitch to wife, February 16, 1852, Letters, HEH.

22. John M. Kerr to his mother, March 15, 1851, Letters, CSL.

17: THE PERMANENT LURE OF SUCCESS, THE ENDURING SHAME OF FAILURE

1. John J. Craven to his wife, May 20, 1850, Letters, HEH.

2. Ephriam to Jane Delano, April 24, 1853, Letters, HEH.

3. John Fitch to his wife, February 16, 1852, Letters, HEH. Horace to Fidelia Muzzy, March 28, 1857, Letters, BAN, discusses his decision to stay in California another year—he had already been there three—and her disappointment.

4. James to Jeremiah Barnes, April 29, 1851, Letters, BAN.

5. Allen Varner to his parents, January 31, 1851; March 14, 1852; December 12, 1850, Letters, HEH. John Slatford's mother pleaded that he come before he ruined his health, March 3, 1852, Letters, BENT.

6. John Milner to his father, January 7, 1850 [1851?], Letters, ALA. Perhaps it is significant that Milner made such an appeal—a mixture of the work ethic and family honor—to his father.

7. "The Miner's Ten Commandments," published for A. W. Potter, Main Street, Nevada [City], HEH. The tenth "Commandment" directed the 49er to honor his wife and family and return to them, but only after accumulating "enough" to satisfy them.

8. "The Miner's Ten Commandments," copyrighted in 1853 by James M. Hutchings, Placerville, El Dorado County, California, HEH.

9. James M. to Caroline Burr, September 29, 1851; August 25, 1852, the Green Letters, DUKE; Daniel Horn to his mother, November 1, December 14, 1850; Daniel Horn to "Brother & Sister," November 30, 1852, Letters, UNC.

10. Levi Hillman to his family, December 9, 1852; February 6, 1853, Letters, MINN. Hillman went to California in the spring of 1852.

11. Quoted in Holliday, *And The World Rushed In*, 409.

12. Ibid., 445–46.

13. James to Caroline Burr, December 22, 1850, the Green Papers, UNC; Solomon to Mary Frances Gorgas, January 27, 1851, Letters, HEH.

14. Albert Leonard to his family, January 20, 1850, Letters, CSL; John to Margaret Eagle, September 26, 1852, Letters, HEH.

15. B. H. Andrew to his brother, March 16, 1856, Letters, UNC; Rose to Morris Sleight, September 8, 1853; Morris to Rose Sleight, October 20, 1853, Collection, CHI. Sleight was fifty-nine years old in 1853.

16. Amos Keyes Stearns, diaries, February 26, April 2, 1871; November 29, December 2, 14, 15, 1872, Special Collections, California State University, Chico.

18: THE RIPPLES SUBSIDE

1. Young, *Western Mining*, 125–42. Figures for annual production are from Paul, *California Gold: The Beginning of Mining*, appendix A.

2. G. E. Berry to his family, November 16, 1858, Letters, BAN.

3. Amos Keyes Stearns, diaries, August 10, 1859, Special Collection, California State University, Chico.

4. Sullivan Osborn, diary, January 19, 1855, HEH. Of women in California, Osborn wrote, "There can be little doubt that women are good in their proper spheres and when honest and virtuous have a beneficial influence on society. but for a man to bring his wife to this country only prepares the road to her ruin, as well as to make a cukold of himself." In his analysis, Osborn ignored the guilt of the gentleman involved.

5. Sullivan Osborn, diary, August 9, 1857, HEH.

6. On the vigilante movements of 1851 and 1856, see Philip J. Ethington, *The Public City: The Political Construction of Urban Life in San Francisco, 1850–1900* (New York: Cambridge University Press, 1994), chapters 2 and 3.

7. Winks, *Frederick Billings,* chapters 8 and 9, analyzes the influence of lawyers in these crucial areas. Winks is especially insightful in his description of the intersection of law and commercial real estate.

8. Donald J. Pisani, *From Family Farm to Agribusiness: The Irrigation Crusade in California and the West, 1850–1931* (Berkeley: University of California Press, 1984), discusses the significance of water in early California agriculture.

9. Note the case of the arriving Irishman Michael Maguire, who ignored the advice to invest his money in land and headed, instead, to the gold fields. Calhoon, *49er Irish,* 13–14.

10. Seth Smith to his father, July 9, 1850; April 24, 1851; Seth to Asa Smith, May 27, 1851, Letters, BAN.

11. Seth Smith to his father, October 9, 1853, ibid.

12. Asa Smith to his father, July 24, August 19, September 4, September 22, 1853; Asa Smith to his sister Mary Smith, August 19, 1853, ibid.

13. Asa Smith to his sister, January 8, 1854, ibid.

14. Asa Smith to his parents, April 28, August 26, September 30, December 2, 1855, ibid.

15. Asa Smith to his parents, January 15, 1856, ibid.

16. Asa Smith to his parents, May 31, 1856; February 17, 1857, ibid.

17. Asa Smith to his parents, December 14, 1857; August 15, 1858; Asa to Seth Smith, December 13, 1858; May 31, 1859, ibid.

18. Asa to Seth Smith, June 3, July 30, 1859, ibid.

19. Asa to Seth Smith, July 20, 1860, ibid.

20. Noah Gebhart to his wife and family, May 26, 1855, Letters, DUKE.

21. Noah Gebhart to Friend Dibble, April 13, 1855, ibid.

22. Noah Gebhart to "Dear Wife & Family," February 26, 1856; July 26, 1857, ibid. He noted in this letter that a general depression had descended on mining everywhere, with water scarce and debts uncollectable. He did not say whether he was a debtor or creditor.

23. Noah Gebhart to Sarah, September 15, 1857; Gebhart to son, November 1, 1857; January 1858, ibid.

24. Noah Gebhart to his wife and family, June 30, 1853; July 19, 1855, ibid.

25. Noah Gebhart to "Dear Family," June 1, 4, July 26, 1857, ibid.

26. Noah Gebhart to "Dear Wife and Family," July 26, 1857, ibid.

27. Noah Gebhart to his son, November 1, 22, 1857; August 1, 1858, ibid. Gebhart found his failure to sell the claim the more embarrassing because one of his sons had made a recent appeal for money.

28. Noah Gebhart to "Dear Wife & Children," June 30, 1853; February 18, September 15, 1857, ibid.

29. Prentice Mulford, *Prentice Mulford's Story,* 5.

30. Winslow to Georgiana Pierce, June 11, 1851, the Pierce-Krull Letters, IND.

31. Ibid.

32. Winslow Pierce to Christina Moore, October 11, November 11, 1851; Helen Moore Rockwood to her mother, November 13, 1851, ibid. Helen Rockwood saw the de-

parture of Georgy and Christina as Pierce's revenge on the family members for their treatment of him. At the same time, she thought that Christina's voyage to California might "be for the best" and if Christina would do well, "perhaps it may not be best to oppose her? What are your own private views on this matter?" she queried her mother. Helen Moore Rockwood to her mother, January 26, 1852, ibid.

33. Winslow to Georgiana Pierce, June 13, 1852, ibid.

34. Winslow Pierce to Christina Moore, January 25, 1853, ibid. Georgiana's brother in California, O. F. Moore, attempted in his letter of February 1, 1854, to make peace between Pierce and the family.

35. Winslow Pierce to Christina Moore, February 27, March 30, June 5, 1853, ibid.

36. Georgiana to Winslow Pierce, June 22, August 4, December 1854 [the last is dictated]; Winslow to Georgiana Pierce, December 15, 16, 1854. The driven nature of Winslow Pierce emerged in a letter dated April 1854 to George W. Tifft, of Buffalo, enclosing thirty dollars to repay ten dollars that Pierce had borrowed in 1841. Tifft was surprised and impressed, as Pierce intended that he should be. See Tifft to Pierce, April 13, 1854, ibid.

37. Lemuel Hopkins to his brother, May 17, 1854; May 28, 1859, Letters, HEH.

38. Lemuel Hopkins to his wife, February 13, May 15, 1854; May 25, 1859, Letters, HEH.

39. John Kinkade introduced his new wife to his family in the East, in Kinkade to his brother James and family, May 20, 1853, Letters, HEH. Kinkade went to California in 1849.

40. John Kinkade to his family, June 6, 1871, ibid.

41. A. G. Tucker to his father and sister, January 10, November 6, 1861, Letters, RIHS.

42. A. G. Tucker to his father and sister, November 6, 1861, ibid. Tucker himself was the "ner'er do well brother," and the "outcast wretch" to whom he referred was the nameless brother and his crime.

43. Tucker to "Dear Sister," November 6, 1861, ibid. For another example, I am indebted to Alice Hutchens for providing me with manuscript materials.

44. Mulford, *Prentice Mulford's Story,* 5.

45. Ibid.

46. William Rufus Dickinson Papers, Letter to the editor, November 14, 1899, CLAR.

19: "THE DAYS OF OLD, THE DAYS OF GOLD, THE DAYS OF FORTY-NINE"

1. J. R. Boyle to "Dear Mother," March 29, 1849, Letters, DUKE. Boyle's sighting of a Seminole chief reinforced his sense that he had become part of history rather than simply reading about it.

2. James to Rebecca Jane Riggin, May 8, 1851, Letters, HEH.

3. R. G. Moore to "Friend Dantzler," May 30, 1851, Letters, DUKE.

4. Richard A. Dwyer and Richard E. Lingenfelter, eds., *The Gold Songs of the Gold Rush* (Berkeley: University of California Press, 1965), 18.

5. Ibid., 15.

6. Ibid., 19.

7. Ibid., 21.

8. Ibid., 44. On racial and anti-Mormon sentiments, see their introduction, 6.

9. Ibid., 53–54.

10. Ibid., 76–77.

11. Ibid., 87, 114.

12. Ibid., 174–77.

13. George R. MacMinn, *The Theater of The Golden Era in California* (Caldwell, Id.: Caxton Printers, 1941) is a complete account. I am indebted to Richard Butsch for calling my attention to the world of popular entertainment in Gold Rush California.

14. Dwyer and Lingenfelter, eds., *The Songs of the Gold Rush*, 184–95.

15. Ibid. 184–95.

16. For example, *The History of Grundy County, Missouri* (Kansas City, 1881), chapter 4, "The Gold Fever." The history of *Wake: Capital County of North Carolina* (1881), 414–15, notes that the population of the county was to no serious effect "significantly diminished through any general exodus to the west, as was true of some other areas."

17. James S. Holliday, *And The World Rushed In: The California Gold Rush Experience* (New York, Simon & Schuster, 1981), 449–50.

18. Nicholas Ball, *Pioneers of '49* (Boston, 1891), chapter 1.

19. Ibid., 2.

20. Ibid., 4. The Boston press coverage appears in the *Boston Evening Transcript*, April 10, 1890, 6. The California cities scheduled for stops by the train included Redlands, Pasadena, Riverside, Los Angeles, San Diego, Fresno, Sacramento, San Francisco, and San Jose, where there were scheduled "receptions and many other festivities." On a dissenting view of the original voyage to California in 1849 by a woman who told an interviewer "the whole affair was about the most melancholy I ever was a participant in." The *Boston Evening Transcript,* April 19, 1890, 7.

21. Ball, *Pioneers of '49*, 5.

22. Ibid., 63.

23. Ibid., 90–94.

HISTORIANS AND SOURCES

1. For the large number of journal accounts for the plains, see Marlin L. Heckman, comp., *Overland on the California Trail, 1846–1859: A Bibliography of Manuscript and Printed Travel Narratives* (Glendale, Calif.: Arthur H. Clark Company, 1984). Among the many examples of the second kind are J. Goldsborough Bruff, *Gold Rush: The Journals, Drawings, and Other Papers . . .* (1849); J. D. Borthwick, *Three Years in California* (1857), which covers the years 1851 to 1854; and Taylor, *Eldorado.* Of special interest is Clapp, *The Letters of Dame Shirley.* Her letters under the pen name Dame Shirley brought the mining camp alive and delineated the special place of women in it.

2. Mulford, *Prentice Mulford's Story.* Sarah Royce, *Frontier Lady: Recollections of the Gold Rush and Early California* (1932).

3. Bancroft, *History of California*. In addition, Bancroft wrote a one-volume interpretive history of California, *California Inter Pocula* (San Francisco, 1888). See also the noteworthy (if less celebrated) Theodore H. Hittell, *History of California*, 4 vols. (San Francisco, 1885–1897).

4. Shinn, *Mining Camps*. Shinn's book has been reprinted several times. Shinn also published *Land Laws of the Mining Districts* (Baltimore: Johns Hopkins University Studies in Historical and Political Science, 1884), a compilation of mining codes.

5. Josiah Royce, *California, from the Conquest in 1846 to the Second Vigilance Committee in San Francisco: A Study in American Character* (1886; New York: Alfred A. Knopf, 1948), 175. Royce was assisted by almost unrestricted access to Bancroft's collection of California materials. See Robert Glass Cleland's introduction to the 1948 edition, xvi–xvii, and the author's preface to the 1886 edition, xxxii in the 1948 edition. See, as well, Robert V. Hine's biography of Royce, *Josiah Royce: From Grass Valley to Harvard* (Norman: University of Oklahoma Press, 1991).

6. Stewart Edward White, *The Last Frontier, Part I: The Forty-Niners* (New Haven: Yale University Press, 1918).

7. Paul, *California Gold: The Beginning of Mining*, usefully supplemented by his *The California Gold Discovery, Sources, Documents, Accounts and Memoirs* (Georgetown, Calif.: 1967). Another important history of the Gold Rush years is Caughey, *Gold Is the Cornerstone*. A significant essay in recasting historians' assumptions about 49ers on the overland trail is David Potter's introduction to *Trail to California*.

8. The best study is Mann, *After the Gold Rush*.

9. Note especially Holliday, *And The World Rushed In*, the first study to make a strong connection between 49ers and the families they left behind; Heffernan and Stecker, *Sisters of Fortune*, a dramatic account of three daughters managing a household in the absence of their father; Linda Peavy and Ursula Smith, *Women in Waiting in the Westward Movement* (Norman: University of Oklahoma Press, 1994).

10. See, for example, Maffly-Kipp, *Religion and Society*; William Deverall, *Railroad Crossing: Californians and the Railroad, 1850–1910* (Berkeley: University of California Press, 1994); and especially, Kevin Starr, *Americans and the California Dream, 1850–1915* (New York: Oxford University Press, 1973).

11. This group is framed on one side by Paul, *Mining Frontiers of the Far West, 1848–1880* (New York: Holt, Rinehart & Winston, 1963), and William S. Greever, *The Bonanza West: The Story of Western Mining Rushes, 1848–1900* (Norman: University of Oklahoma Press, 1963), and on the other by Paula Mitchell Marks, *Precious Dust: The American Gold Rush Era, 1848–1900* (New York: William Morrow and Company, 1994).

12. Heckman, *Overland on the California Trail*, contains 403 entries.

13. Forty-niners sometimes wrote often and openly to male friends, presumably as correspondents in whom they could confide successes and failures hidden from the family. The best published example is the *'Dear Charlie Letters': Recording the Everyday Life of a Young 1854 Gold Miner . . . As Set Forth by Your Friend, Horace Snow* (Mariposa, Calif.: Mariposa County Historical Society, 1979).

14. Cumming, ed., *The Gold Rush: Letters from the Wolverine Rangers,* notes the case of James Pratt, editor of the *Marshall Statesman,* who became a leading figure in the organization of the Wolverine Rangers.
15. The best collections of newspapers for the California Gold Rush are the Ralph Bieber Collection, HEH; and Dudley T. Ross, *The Golden Gazette: News from the Newspapers of 1848–1854* (Fresno, Calif.: Valley Publishers, 1978).

INDEX

252, 310*n*4; ordinances for, 220; physical demands upon, 133–34; responsibility of, 249, 258, 334*n*26, 341*n*3, 341*n*6; return of, 36, 64, 68, 80, 81, 82, 210, 256–62, 263–65, 272–73, 278, 288, 341*n*5; shame of self, 263; shelter, 145, 328*n*25; slaves as, *See* Slavery; standards for, 264; subsequent journeys to California, 265–66, 271, 274; support for, 73–74, 77, 80, 125; taxing of, 228; temptations of, 49, 147, 148–49, 247; and trade opportunities, 129–30; values of, 195, 217; view of each other, 89–90; wealth of, 83–86; women as, 98–99, 180–81; work ethic of, 192–93, 341*n*6

Miner's Ten Commandments, 261–62, 341*n*7

Mining. *See* Gold mining

Mississippi, gold seekers from, 29, 39

Mississippi Rangers, 49–50

Mississippi Valley, 26

Missouri, gold seekers from, 29, 37, 52, 73, 84

Mokelumne Hill (California), 165

Mokelumne River, 199, 223

Money, 66–67, 70, 124, 319*n*1; anxiety over, 251; distribution of, 251; as a "raise," 117, 325*n*21

Monterey (California), 8, 9, 17–18, 156

Mormans, 14, 286, 311*n*16, 319*n*25, 344*n*8

Mothers. *See* Families

Mulford, Prentice, 21, 28–29, 32–33, 107, 135, 276–77, 281–82, 296

Murder, 214, 226, 276

Music, 67; and song, 285–89

Nantucket, (Massachusetts), 73, 85, 320*n*3

Native Americans, 7, 8–9, 12, 13, 62, 90, 123, 125, 221, 222–23, 229, 311*n*3, 329*n*26, 337*n*11

New England and California Trading and Mining Association, 50, 57

New Hampshire, gold seekers from, 165

Newspapers, 22, 23–24, 25–28, 29–30, 38, 150, 190, 193, 223, 300–301, 303–304, 312*n*3, 312*n*5, 313*n*11, 313*n*15, 346*n*15; and publication of family correspondence, 28, 303–304

New York, gold seekers from, 39, 40–41, 102

New York Herald, 23, 27

New York *Journal of Commerce,* 23

New York Society, 291

New York Volunteers, 14, 17

North Carolina: gold mines in, 13, 15, 123; gold seekers from, 211, 336*n*24

North Fork Tunnel Company, 210

Oberlin College, 38

Obstacles, 93

Occupations: creation of, 128; non-mining, 154, 276

Ohio, gold seekers from, 42

Ohio Valley, 26

Ordinance of 1785, 10–11

Oregon, gold seekers from, 19

Oregon Ripple, 199

Overland migrations, 19, 40, 61–66, 74–75, 93, 98, 120, 121, 130–31, 136, 176, 286, 315*n*20, 318*n*16, 319*n*26, 345*n*7; and domestic chores, 62–63, 93; and value of money on, 70

Panama, 58–59

Parents. *See* Families

Paul, Rodman, 298–99, 310*n*1

Pennsylvania, gold seekers from, 38–39, 53

People: meeting new, 63, 64, 318*n*20, 318*n*21; variety of, 66, 213, 220

Peru, gold seekers from, 222, 224

Philadelphia *North American,* 23

Pierce, Winslow, 52, 277–79, 343*n*32, 343*n*34, 343*n*36

Placers. *See* Gold mining, locations

Placerville (California), 166, 182, 183, 195, 331*n*30

Politics, 277, 278–79, 311*n*7

Polk, President James K., 24, 313*n*8; and State of the Union Address, 24, 26

Poverty, 34–35, 39, 43, 110, 195

Prices, 69; gouging of, 153

Profits, 119, 129, 132, 133, 134, 148, 154, 158, 159, 167, 201, 249, 250, 268, 269

Prospecting, 190, 214

Prostitution, 67, 99, 128, 148–49, 180

Punishment, criminal, 219, 226, 322*n*40

Designer: Barbara Jellow
Compositor: Impressions Book and Journal Services, Inc.
Text: 11/13.5 Adobe Garamond
Display: Mona Lisa, Adobe Garamond
Printer: Edwards Bros.
Binder: Edwards Bros.